CW01024341

Shores of Paradise

Shores of Paradise

The life of Sir John Squire,
the Last Man of Letters

JOHN SMART

Copyright © 2021 John Smart

The moral right of the author has been asserted.

Apart from any fair dealing for the purposes of research or private study,
or criticism or review, as permitted under the Copyright, Designs and Patents
Act 1988, this publication may only be reproduced, stored or transmitted, in
any form or by any means, with the prior permission in writing of the
publishers, or in the case of reprographic reproduction in accordance with
the terms of licences issued by the Copyright Licensing Agency. Enquiries
concerning reproduction outside those terms should be sent to the publishers.

Matador
9 Priory Business Park,
Wistow Road, Kibworth Beauchamp,
Leicestershire. LE8 0RX
Tel: 0116 279 2299
Email: books@troubador.co.uk
Web: www.troubador.co.uk/matador
Twitter: @matadorbooks

ISBN 978 1 8004 6399 8

British Library Cataloguing in Publication Data.
A catalogue record for this book is available from the British Library.

Printed and bound by CPI Group (UK) Ltd, Croydon, CR0 4YY
Typeset in 11pt Minion Pro by Troubador Publishing Ltd, Leicester, UK

Matador is an imprint of Troubador Publishing Ltd

To Sue

Shiftless and shy, gentle and kind and frail,
Poor wanderer, bewildered into vice,
You are freed at last from seas you could not sail,
A wreck upon the shores of Paradise.

(J. C. Squire: 'An Epitaph')

Contents

Prelude

At the beginning of the twentieth century the fat and complacent Jack Squire led a group of reactionary poets who dominated and controlled English poetry and publishing. They were Little Englanders who looked backwards, resisted modernism and shut their eyes to all the artistic developments in Paris, Berlin and London during and after the First World War. They called themselves Georgians, but became known as the Squirearchy, cricket-playing men who wrote watered-down escapist poetry about larks, nightingales and a countryside that had largely ceased to exist.

This is an exaggerated but substantially accurate version of the critical myth that developed in the 1920s and became the orthodoxy of later years. Only recently has it come under scrutiny. The critic John Gross seemed to have Squire in mind when he characterised the Georgians as 'associated with everything that an intellectual of the day was liable to wince at most – cricketing weekends, foaming tankards, Sussex-by-the-Sea, pale green pastorals, thigh-slapping joviality'.[1] Stefan Collini picked up the theme of 'the rather beery backslapping bonhomie and self-satisfied anti-modernism of Sir John Squire and his acolytes'.[2] Hywel Williams put it more melodramatically: 'He is read only to be reviled as a tweedy reactionary'.[3] The chorus continued.[4]

The only problem with this authorised version of J. C. Squire and the Georgians is that it is, in nearly all respects, misleading, a caricature full of half-truths and exaggerations. G. K. Chesterton described 'a certain coarse and at present very common mental process which consists in creating a false classification to swamp a unique thing.' This critical myth is certainly untrue to the way the Georgians were viewed at the time and the way they viewed themselves. The critic Tim Kendall wrote, 'The First World War was, in literary terms, a Georgian War.' D. H. Lawrence hailed the first *Georgian Poetry*. Wilfred Owen wrote to his mother proudly, 'I am held peer by the Georgians. I am a poet's poet.'[5] Ivor Gurney read *Georgian Poetry* in the trenches and told his friend F. W. Harvey, 'the young poets think very much as we.'[6] *Georgian Poetry* contained verse by poets as different as Edmund Blunden, Robert Graves, Siegfried Sassoon, Robert Nichols, Isaac Rosenberg and D. H. Lawrence.

Squire's name and reputation is inextricably linked with Georgian poetry. The slippery label needs careful definition. All the Georgians denied hotly that a group identity covered them. Did that grouping really exist? If so, who were its members and what was its nature? How did Squire fit in with the poets of whom he was often seen as the titular head? 'Georgian' has been used as a word for a group, a period, a type of verse – or as simple abuse. I have used the word in a broad sense to cover both those men and (one) woman who appeared in Edward Marsh's five anthologies, *Georgian Poetry* from 1912 to 1922, and those who sympathised with them.[7] The poetry of an English tradition, Hardy, Housman, Sassoon, Blunden, Gurney, Walter de la Mare and Edward Thomas has not received the critical attention that the imagists, Pound and Eliot, have gained, but for twenty years it was the mainstream and the most widely read English poetry.

'Poetry to him was the alpha and omega of existence,' wrote his friend Alec Pryce-Jones. It was as a poet that Squire wanted to be remembered. Most critics of the time saw him as a questioning, intellectual, *modern* poet. He was not seen as a Georgian or belonging to any other school, but rather as an exceptional and individual writer. What struck them was the variety of Squire's verse and how difficult it was to characterise or to label. He wrote sonnets, odes, alexandrines and free verse. He might write about a rugby match, an airship, the moon, the death of a dog, war, a stockyard. He was not, as 'Georgians' were accused of being, 'a lark lover', and in fact only wrote very rarely about country life. He was the least 'Georgian' of the so-called Georgian poets: 'His poetry is far less escapist and stooky and wainy than we supposed,' wrote John Betjeman.[8] Philip Larkin thought his poetry was based on 'the terrible underlying the normal'. 'It often betrays a tragic sense of life and a private melancholy bordering on despair.' The *Aberdeen Press and Journal* wrote in January 1922: 'He is absolutely distinctive among the writers of the present century; he is uncompromisingly original. He is as modern as they make them and his thought in his poetry is of a sage.' *The Times* had no doubt that he was a genius and 'had earned his place among the most brilliant of our present-day poets and critics.'[9]

In his essay 'It Could only Happen in England', Larkin wrote that 'it is as obvious as it is strenuously denied that in this century English poetry went off on a loop-line that took it away from the general reader. Several factors caused this. One was the aberration of modernism, that blighted all the arts. Another was the emergence of English Literature as an academic subject, and the consequent demand for a kind of poetry that needed elucidation. One, I am afraid, was the culture-mongering activities of the Americans Eliot and Pound.'[10] Squire was at the centre of the losing resistance to that loop-line.

The range of Georgian poetry was never as narrow as its modernist critics suggested. Poets who could produce poems as varied and memorable as 'Snake', 'The Listeners', 'Dulce et Decorum Est', 'Adlestrop', 'The Road not Taken' and 'Everyone Sang' cannot be easily dismissed. As the century progressed Auden, Larkin, Ted Hughes and Heaney all owed much more to Hardy and Owen than to Pound and Eliot.[11]

The dramatic change in Squire's literary fortunes is one theme of the book. Perhaps worse than hostile criticism is to be forgotten – and that has now become his fate too, along with prominent and popular writers of his day such as Hilaire Belloc, Maurice Hewlett and Hugh Walpole, who were all friends.[12] How could Squire have been such a central figure during and after the First World War and now be almost invisible? What social and literary forces lie behind this reversal?

For more than twenty years Squire edited the monthly *London Mercury*. With a circulation of up to 20,000 it held sway over the world of literary magazines, amusing, informing and infuriating its readers. *The Times* called it 'the most enterprising literary monthly of its period in England,'[13] but it has been generally forgotten. 'Few literary journals of the early twentieth century can claim the editorial scope, critical importance, and historical scorn of the *London Mercury* and its exclusion from the canon is a mysterious and gaping hole in the archive of literary modernism.'[14] The importance of the magazine in the twenties and thirties and Squire's role as editor are major themes of this book.

Squire approached political and social issues with the same passion as he lived the rest of his life. In the 1920s and 1930s he was one of the first campaigners for the preservation of rural England. He fought against commercial development of historic buildings and led the campaign to save Stonehenge. He founded the Architecture Club to encourage the best young architects and to stimulate debate between architects and non-architects. His politics puzzled many of his friends. How did a leading socialist, a member of the executive committee of the Fabians before the Great War, editor of the *New Statesman* and Labour candidate for Cambridge in 1918, turn into the Liberal candidate for Brentford and Chiswick in the 1924 election and then an admirer of Mussolini and chairman of a fascist club in the thirties?

'Jack' was immensely clubbable and often surrounded with laughter. The word 'generous' seems almost glued to his name. Siegfried Sassoon thought him the 'most generous of men' and J. B. Morton called him 'the most generous and affectionate man I ever met...' He was everyone's friend, a good companion and 'Jack' to all the world. 'There are hundreds who owe their start in literature to his encouragement,' wrote John Betjeman. He acted as patron to poets such as Edmund Blunden, Ivor Gurney, W. J. Turner and Edward Davison and writers such as Alan Pryce-Jones, Henry Williamson and J. B. Priestley. He was always ready to help the depressed, the down-and-out and the down-at-heel. A man of powerful feelings, his love of his wife and family inspired some of his best poetry. And yet he sometimes behaved badly towards them: his marriage failed; he lost touch with his sister, his son Anthony and daughter Julia.

Writers as different as Virginia Woolf, John Betjeman, Alan Pryce-Jones and Beatrice Webb all knew that Squire was not simply a John Bull or a Jack Falstaff. A complex man, his public persona of wit and humour belied a dark side; far from cheerily bucolic, he was almost morbidly fascinated by death. There was a privacy and inner self he guarded and kept secret from even his closest friends. His poetry was where he could most nearly tell the truth about himself, but inspiration was fitful and dry periods when he could write nothing were frequent.

Squire's life is the story of these conflicts and contradictions: the Victorian who looked forward to a socialist new world; the Fabian who became Chairman of a fascist club; the knighted writer who became a bankrupt alcoholic; the best-known journalist, editor and man of letters of his day who has become completely forgotten.

A Fine Swarm

On 15 December 1932 nearly five hundred people attended a lavish 'complimentary' white-tie dinner held in the art deco banqueting room of the Dorchester Hotel, Park Lane. Decorations were worn. The cover of the menu showed the crest of the *London Mercury* from which streamed coloured banners labelled Literature, Social Life, the Law, Art, Architecture, Cricket, Music and Shooting. Two chubby putti, one in cricket pads, the other with a fishing rod, held up the cauldron of Plenty. The dinner was in honour of John Collings Squire, a celebration of his achievements as poet, critic, essayist and editor of the *London Mercury*, the literary magazine he had founded in 1919. Forty-eight years old, and no longer the elegant, long-haired romantic figure who had been compared with Rupert Brooke, 'Jack' Squire's hair was thinning and his waist thickening. He was wearing tie and tails and sported in his buttonhole an enormous pink carnation.

Squire had planned the party, helped by a group of aristocratic women friends. They felt that he was drinking too much, writing too little and generally slipping. A celebration might cheer him up and put him on the right path again. A committee of the great and the good was formed, led by Viscountess Lee of Fareham, the Hon. Mrs Roland Cubitt, Lady Northcliffe and the Hon. Mrs Christopher Fremantle. Squire himself increasingly took control of the scheme – and transformed it into something much bigger and grander. Nowhere but the Dorchester would do; everyone famous whose names he could remember should be invited. He spent night after night, becoming more and more haggard, doing and undoing elaborate table plans and trying the patience of his friends.

The guests sitting at fifty-four tables faced seven courses. The film director Basil Dean sat with three of the most important publishers of the century: Sir Frederick Macmillan, Geoffrey Faber and the founder of Penguin books, Allen Lane. Squire's very successful literary agent A. D. Peters was there. Journalism was represented by J. L. Garvin, editor of the *Observer*, the communist gossip columnist 'William Hickey' (Tom Driberg of the *Daily Express*), and Squire's drinking companion J. B. Morton ('Beachcomber' in the same paper). The lion-hunting society hostess Lady Sybil Colefax ('Old Coalbox' according to Osbert Sitwell) presided over the world of fashion and celebrity. The women in Squire's life were separated around the room: his wife Eileen sat beside him at the top table; his mistress, Cecily Severne, was at the aristocratic table. Henrie Mayne was discreetly tucked away at the artistic Table 4 along with the popular novelist A. J. Cronin and the drama critic James Agate.

British and foreign aristocrats mixed with military men such as the 'Iron Duchess', Gerald Wellesley, later Duke of Wellington, and civil servants and politicians including Duff Cooper, recently elected as Conservative MP for Westminster and soon to oppose Hitler and Appeasement. The monocled Edward ('Eddie') Marsh, Winston Churchill's Private Secretary and patron of the arts, was surrounded by the poets he had chosen for his Georgian anthologies twenty years before. The professorial Lascelles Abercrombie, one of the original 'Dymock' poets, sat with Walter de la Mare, then at the height of his reputation as poet and storyteller, and Edmund Blunden, 'the mole of Merton', uncomfortable in such grand company. Among other writers at the party were the novelist E. F. Benson, A. P. Herbert, the novelist Rose Macaulay, whose brother Jack Squire had known at Cambridge; the poet Charles Morgan, Vyvyan Holland, the son of Oscar Wilde, and the poet Laurence Binyon, whose elegy 'For the Fallen' encapsulated their feelings about the First World War for millions.

A younger generation was represented by the debonair Alec Waugh, Evelyn's elder brother, stalwart of Squire's cricket side, the Invalids, and author of the once scandalous *Loom of Youth*. John Betjeman, whose first book of poems, *Mount Zion*, had just been published, always grateful for the start Jack had given him, sat with Alan Pryce-Jones. Recently sent down from Oxford, he was now Squire's sub-editor at the *London Mercury*. The minor aristocracy and the military were out in force. Squire's beloved sister Dorothy, whose fare and ticket he had promised to pay for, and perhaps did, sat at a family table, and friends and collaborators at the *Mercury* were at another one. There was a separate table reserved for the press – Squire never missed an opportunity for publicity.

One reporter was surprised to note that purely literary people were in a minority. The guest list was witness to Jack Squire's gift of friendship and to his central position in fashionable London society. The prolific novelist Cecil Roberts wrote that it was a vindication of the power of the pen to bring together so many professions and schools of thought, 'a heartening demonstration of unity in the face of simple merit.'[15] There was a table where Squire had decided to put all the bores together. He was delighted when after the dinner they thanked him for providing such good company.

It was agreed to keep the speeches short. Man of letters and creator of the 'Father Brown' stories, G. K. Chesterton, as Chairman, spoke first. He praised Squire's achievements as poet and prose writer. He was someone who had controlled creative power, 'steering a middle course between stupid and congested conservatism and the sudden outburst of madness which showed that the mind had come to its end'. Duff Cooper, then Financial Secretary to the War Office, was effusive: Squire, remarkably, had Keats in his heart, Shakespeare in his blood and Chaucer in his bones. The Principal of the Royal College of Art, Sir William Rothenstein, who had drawn Squire's portrait ten years earlier, added his praise and congratulations.[16]

The guest of honour, overwhelmed by the occasion, and perhaps also by the wine, for once found speech-making difficult. He replied briefly to the toasts, with a catch in his voice, ending in rhyme, to laughter: 'For me I never cared for fame/Solvency was my only aim.' He added that he had achieved neither, but had got what was far better, a great number of friends. He basked in the stamping of feet and applause of the 'fine swarm', as he called it to his sister, and through thick round spectacles beamed at his guests. It should have been an absolute high point of his life.

Alan Pryce-Jones, however, found the evening too painful to recall. He noted that the committee was entirely composed of aristocrats; there were no writers on it. Writers there were among the guests, but no Eliot, no Auden, no Virginia Woolf, no Sitwells, no Evelyn Waugh. Some of Squire's critics such as the publisher John Murray were disgusted with what they saw as self-promotion and felt that, despite what he said, he was aiming at a knighthood. Squire's speech itself was a lame anticlimax. His professional life had often been dangerously on the edge, but somehow, at the last minute, he had always managed to save the day. But not this time. This was the moment when the editor whom Pryce-Jones admired, and looked on protectively, as almost a younger brother, could not control his words. He did not want to remember the tears running down Squire's face behind the thick-lensed glasses, a face suddenly grown very old. After the dinner, as if embarrassed, guests hurried quickly away into the night and what should have been a triumph was a disaster.

Chapter 1

The Honeysuckle and the Bee:
In My First Flower-time

In my first flower-time, when the lily broke its sheath
Each day brought surprise from the dark lake underneath:
I wandered unknowing when I lay down at night
What image at morning would burn upon my sight.

Vigil by vigil the hours that flushed me passed,
Beyond my controlling each vision dimmed the last;
Forest of dreams was I, as I sauntered or slept:
But of all that wild life how little have I kept.

From their vast coloured worlds of passions, thoughts and dreams
In speech men have gathered only fragments and gleams;
And I too, I leave here, before I pass on,
These petals to show through what glades I have gone.[17]

A family story. Long, long ago, a mysterious figure arrived by night
at a Devon coaching inn. He was a finely dressed Spanish 'grandee',
swarthy of complexion, accompanied by a little boy, also well dressed.

Perhaps he was a pirate who had landed in one of the coves that studded the coast. Perhaps he was a smuggler. Perhaps he looked like one of the 'strangers of the night' Squire wrote about later who had to abandon their boat in a storm and row ashore:

Men curious, natural and wild,
As dark as buccaneers,
Shaggy and dark, with shining eyes
And earrings in their ears.'[18]

After a short stay the stranger disappeared into the darkness, leaving the boy behind. He did not speak any English but the kindly couple who kept the inn took pity on him and brought him up as one of the family. They decided to name him 'Collings', an old English surname sounding as close as possible to the name of the mysterious Spanish gentleman.

Another story. On a cold winter's night a baby was found on Plymouth dock swaddled in a shawl or a Spanish mantilla. The boy grew up and married a Devonshire girl. Their granddaughter was Jack Squire's mother who named her son John Collings Squire and told him these stories about his Spanish origins.

Since the seventeenth century generations of the Squire family had farmed in Devon villages skirting Dartmoor, in Winkleigh, Inwardleigh and Sourton. They were yeomen, living in farmhouses and rich enough to leave substantial wills. Jack's grandfather, Thomas, the son of John and Joanna, was born in the small village of Broadwood Widger[19] in 1805. He later moved to Lamerton, twelve miles from Plymouth, where his family were born. According to the 1871 census he was a farmer of 300 acres, comfortably off, employing three men on the farm and four servants to look after the house. Jonas Squire was born there in 1856, the fifth of six children. His eldest brother Thomas duly inherited the farm and Jonas trained as a veterinary surgeon. In 1881 he was living in the New Market Inn in Tavistock, where his elder brother John was the innkeeper. At the age of twenty-six he was now qualified as a vet. He must have known his fellow vet in nearby Plymouth and, through him, met and got to know his daughter, Elizabeth 'Bessie' Rowe Collings, an attractive woman three years younger than him.

She was also a Devonian, born and bred in Plymouth. Her childhood was very different to her husband's landed background. Her father ran a successful veterinary practice in Princess Street, employing an assistant and an apprentice. Jonas and Bessie married on a summer day, 30 July 1883; she was twenty-five and he was twenty-eight. Mr and Mrs Squire set up home in the centre of Plymouth, very close to the Hoe; the census of 1891 shows them settled in her father's adjoining pair of spacious Victorian buildings at 1 and 2 Princess Street in the parish of Saint Andrew. The busy street was full of tradesmen and the census shows a wide range of trades and occupations – a milliner, a coach proprietor, several dressmakers and lodging-house keepers, a merchant's clerk, a grocer's assistant, a retired builder and a fish salesman. It was a bustling and active lower middle-class community which Jack recalled as a series of bright images: 'Scented coffee grinding in one window, waxen barbers' busts in the next, the beauty of an ironmongers and a corn chandlers, the little sailor-suited figures in a tailor's window, cheese, oranges, the desiccated rings of grocers' apples...'[20]

Jonas joined his father-in-law's practice as a veterinary surgeon and employed an assistant who lived with the family. If the outside of their house was plain, the inside, where Mrs Squire presided, was a contrast; the rooms were fussily decorated in crowded Victorian style with 'woolwork screens, canary cages, plush photograph frames, Bohemian vases hung with lustres, countless little tables, bric-a-brac and water-colours of raging Cornish seas.'

Two weeks before the birth of his son, there was a family crisis. Jonas owned up to his wife that he had not told her the truth about his financial situation. He owed gambling debts and now demanded money from her. A week later she had a fall; her baby was a month premature and given small chance of living by the doctor. John Collings Squire was almost certainly born at Princess Street on 1

April 1884 – but Bessie put 2 April on his birth certificate to avoid any unwelcome jokes. Despite a difficult start he managed to survive several serious illnesses in his first two years. Jack was the eldest child: his sister Annie (or Nan) was two years younger. Unusually, he was not given any of his father's Christian names: perhaps Bessie had little reason to want to remember him. Sister Dorothy (Dolly or Doll or Dot or Dotty) followed within the space of three and a half years and became Jack's closest companion.

His very first memories were of the intensity of colour and form, 'feeling mystery though unacquainted with the word for it'. In his collection of marbles he gazed at the coloured spirals imprisoned within the glass. He was given balls of wool to make reins for human horses and was entranced by the brilliantly coloured strands of wool, 'blazing bright like Blake's tyger'.

> Vermilion on a skein would melt into purest orange and that into a pure yellow and that into a green; or a pale celestial blue would pass into a blue more gorgeous, and that into purple... in those simple ropes of wool the dazzlingly vivid colours were almost disembodied, like the hues of a luminous cloudless sunset. The child did not know what he was doing but he would hold the skeins in his hands, his eyes very still, sighing from the excess of delight. Colour was his divinity, which took him out of himself. ... he strove to plunge into the heart of the colour as the religious mystic into the bosom of God.[21]

Even then he knew, though he could not put his feelings into words, something of what he later called, 'the grief of unattainment, for, with all his straining of heart and eyes, he could never reach the inmost core of those heaving waves of splendour.' That feeling of something ungraspable that lay just beyond reach and could only be hinted at was a thread that would run through his life. Almost his first memory was of fields in the rain looked at from a window: 'I can remember that feeling too deep for tears longer than I can remember anything.'[22] His elders would remark: 'Isn't he a good little boy; he amuses himself so nicely.'

The family employed a cook and a nursemaid, Mary Collier, who used to take the children out for long walks on the moors. Jack remembered how she used to croon to him sentimental rhymes about Jumbo the Elephant being sold to Phineas T. Barnum as an exhibit in 'The Greatest Show on Earth':

> Jumbo said to Alice, 'I love you.'
> Alice said to Jumbo, 'I don't believe you do,'
> For if you really love me, and what you say is true,
> You wouldn't go to Yankee-land and leave me in the Zoo.'

Bessie had a good voice and sang folk songs such as 'Widecombe Fair' and the 'Fox Song' to him in his cradle:

> Old mother Slipper Slopper jumped out of bed
> And out of the window she popped her head,
> Crying 'Oh John, John! The grey goose is gone
> And the fox is over the down, oh!'

Most of all he loved the harlequinade and the pantomime: 'Joey with the sausages, who called the Pantaloon father, the Harlequin in snakeskin and wand and Columbine flitting light as thistle down.' The culmination of the pantomime was the transformation scene where, after each veil of shimmering gauze had lifted to reveal a new vista of silver or golden light filled with ideal beings, there finally appeared at the glowing heart of the scene the Fairy, the Goddess 'erect and immobile, beautiful beyond human hope.'[23]

Jack was a clever, imaginative child, who could read and write at the age of three. From his earliest years he devoured books. First of all came pretty picture books and children's stories, Caldecott's and Kate Greenaway's. On his third birthday he was given 'Poetry for the Young', an anthology where he found Coleridge's 'Ancient Mariner'.

His party piece, recited at his mother's knee, was a poem about 'an antediluvian man of sesquipedalian height who let out the blood of an ichthyosaurus with a polyphloisboisterous shout.'[24]

When he was about six he fell very ill with scarlatina. The vicar was called and asked him what he wanted to be in life. 'I want to be a soldier,' came the reply. 'What kind of soldier?' the vicar asked, expecting to be told Horse, Foot or Artillery. 'A General,' Jack said without hesitation.

Soon afterwards he got to know a little girl of about the same age and they used to spend their time looking over the blue waters of Plymouth Sound. 'We hadn't said very much. We had merely sat occasionally on benches looking at the mighty placid Sound with our nurses, and caught eyes and touched hands. Then one day I heard she had gone to the Ladies' Bathing Place and had been drowned. I could not realise it. In my bed at night I tried to call her back. Now I am uncertain of her name. But she had an eager freckled little face and she went without any sort of fulfilment. And the unconscious tides still ebbed and flowed; and the sun sparkled on the wavelets; and at low water I cut my feet on the sharp rocks and peered into the fathomless pools at anemones, and scuttling crabs and minnows, and pebbles and shells, isolated for some hours from the deep, and slithered on dark rocks slimed over by cabbage-green weed and only sometimes remembered the child who had been drowned.'[25] 'This was the moment when the shadow of death came over me'. It never left him.

At the age of seven he swapped his tin soldiers for a Victorian favourite: Mrs Valentine's illustrated *Sea Fights and Land Battles*. In his nursery he found and pored over an illustrated book of natural history: *The Universe: or the Infinitely Great and the Infinitively Little*. Most important to him were Hans Andersen's fairy stories. 'It was always the romantic, the beautiful, the sad I loved, and never the macabre such as renders terrible the starker folk-tales of Grimm.'[26] The sense of the beautiful and the contrast with the horror of an infernal world was a marker for the future in his poetry. The secret of

Hans Andersen's appeal to the young boy was that he never lost the vision that adulthood obscured. Children, he thought, were naturally all 'little animists' and poets retain something of that vision. Squire thought that 'Under the skin of reason and acquired knowledge there is an I who not only thinks of every leaf as a person (and no two of them, through all eternity have ever been the same), and even of every stone as a person.'[27]

The colour and sound of words struck him most. Staying with his great-aunt and uncle, he found a scarcely used little room full of books. It was an Aladdin's cave; there were sets of *Punch* and *The Graphic*. Lying, propped up on his elbows on the carpet, he read *Foxe's Book of Martyrs*. The image of Saint Lawrence with his gridiron gave him nightmares and a horror of cruelty that stayed with him all his life. In the bound copies of the *Illustrated London News* he read over and over again Rider Haggard's *Cleopatra*. One picture fascinated: an Egyptian priest staring imploringly up at the sky. The caption beneath read: 'He gazed at the sky with sightless orbs.' He was 'hypnotized' by the word 'orbs' and its sinister quality.[28] It was the same when he came across *Robinson Crusoe* in a battered volume in tiny type: a picture haunted his imagination – Crusoe clinging to a rock surrounded by breakers. Underneath were the words: 'I held my hold till the storm abated.' The word *abated* 'by its sheer musical conveyance of crisis and assuagement' meant more to him, he said, than the discovery of the savage's footprint in the sand. And later when he read in *King James's Bible*, 'And Moses was an hundred and twenty years when he died; his eye was not dim nor his natural force abated', he felt that throb of excitement again. It was perhaps an odd word to be so excited about, but the attention to the exact, evocative word was already there.

By 1890 Jonas was drinking heavily and gambling away the family money. When Jack was seven his father deserted Bessie and the children. He returned to Tavistock and practised as a vet, living in various lodging houses. There is no record of Jack ever seeing his father again; he is scarcely mentioned in his own accounts of his childhood.

There is, however, one strange remark that Jack made much later to Doll: 'Darling, we got the resolute fighter from our mother and the artist from our father.'[29] The first part was certainly true, but in Jack's imagination Jonas became for a moment a dark mythical figure of childhood inspiration, not the small-town drunk he really was.

After Jonas fled, Bessie was left with no money and no income. Ever resourceful and hard-working, she began to take in lodgers to support herself and her three children. She had a fine voice and mother and son enjoyed singing together. In the long dark evenings she taught him all kinds of card games – cribbage, piquet, solo whist, écarté and loo. Jack was brought up in this household of women and was 'much alone with my mother in my early days.' Later he felt that there were some drawbacks to this; there were many things he could not communicate and many secrets to be kept within the feminine walls of Princess Street.

Images of Plymouth were imprinted on his memory: Queen Victoria's first Jubilee – and being given a golden sovereign by a stranger who, to his five-year-old self, seemed eight and a half feet tall; the unveiling of the Armada memorial on Plymouth Hoe, with sister Dorothy hanging on to one of the nurse's hands and he on the other; Mr Gladstone speaking to a vast crowd of ten thousand from the balcony of the Grand Hotel; terrifying pictures of the Armenian Massacres on view outside a fairground booth; a Mermaid, and two Fat Ladies inside a stuffy tent dressed as Victorian little girls with shoulder ribbons and buckled white shoes. Or it was Handel's *Messiah* sung in the Guildhall beneath the thundering great organ, 'like a painted Giant's Causeway' by a massed choir all dressed in white with sopranos in red sashes and his mother among the contraltos in blue. Plymouth was a garrison town and its streets thronged 'with every other promenader in a blue jacket or a soldier in scarlet with a swagger cane'. Even the family's bootmaker was in a rifleman's green uniform, a shaving brush sticking up from his cap when he played his bugle for the volunteers. The world of his Plymouth childhood was as deeply vivid and important to Jack as Dylan Thomas's Swansea was to him.

As he grew older he began to explore the Devon countryside. Brought up within sight of Dartmoor, he thought it 'the kernel of Devon, granite and limestone the heart of the county and the cliffs the bastions.' The real Devon for him was not the softer lands to the east, but the wild landscape of 'the bogs, the fogs, the gorse and the heather, the boulders and the tors, the little torrents and the little trout.'[30] A resolute walker, he tramped the moor and loved the primroses, bluebells, lent lilies and stone walls sprouting wild geraniums and the ivory flowers of pennywort. Once he was old enough to ride a bike he could go further afield into east Cornwall. At Rame, just down the coast, he went bird nesting with an aunt. He was lowered down the cliffs by a rope to collect seabirds' eggs. Water was his element. The coast offered beaches full of shells, sea urchins and violet jellyfish. He dived into green water, translucent many feet down, with shells and pebbles inviting him to plunge ever deeper. Days were spent exploring rock pools with delicate anemones and darting little fishes. Jack's sense of the beautiful was already indissolubly linked to his sense of transience. As he remembered forty years later, 'There were sunsets over the sea which gave a child who had no words a pleasure that was married to pain and led to gropings about eternity and grief.'[31]

One of his best friends was the son of the curate of the Cornish village of Morwenstow. He spent dark winter evenings there 'in the lonely church by the sea, oil lamps hanging, singing "Through the Night of Doubt and Sorrow" and the steady melancholy crash of the breakers could be heard in all the intervals of the service.'

> Lord, I have seen at harvest festival
> In a white lamp-lit fishing-village church,
> How the poor folk, lacking fine decorations,
> Offer the first-fruits of their various toils:
> Not only fruit and blossom of the fields…
> But gifts of other produce, heaped brown nets,
> Fine pollack, silver fish with umber backs,
> And handsome green-dark-blue-striped mackerel,

And uglier, hornier creatures from the sea,
Lobsters, long-clawed and eyed, and smooth flat crabs,
Ranged with the flowers upon the window-niches…[32]

Jack was brought up by his mother as a regular churchgoer at the old church of St Andrew's in the middle of Plymouth. A shy child, he was at first too embarrassed to sing hymns in public and was always conscious of the rustlings of his sisters' skirts as they whispered and shuffled about during the long services. When he was nine, he struck a deal with his mother that he would become a chorister if he were allowed to give up the piano. The bargain was made and he spent many years singing in the choir. Thirty years on, his memories of St Andrew's remained intensely vivid: its tall bare granite tower darkened by centuries of rain, its three great aisles dim, with only the choir lit, and the organ booming out, his pew under someone's heraldic memorial. He knew his Bible very well, reading its fascinating strange tales and 'shocking bits' during long-winded sermons. Sunday afternoons were given up to 'Religious Instruction' in Plymouth, which involved brushings of hair, donnings of collars and gloves and the three children walking through the 'starched and prim Sunday streets' of the city. Sometimes they heard the Salvationist hymn 'Oh Father, stop and think, / Oh Father, stop and think, / Which is it you love the most, the children or the drink?' Everyone was in their Sunday best; 'dull and concrete men paraded slowly with their families and stiff soldiers walked with Sabbatised girls in their finery.'[33]

Organised religion and Sunday services may have meant little to him, but Jack was a religious child. Every night he prayed, kneeling on the hard floor at the side of his bed. He recited two prayers: The Lord's Prayer and an ever-expanding list for his family, maidservants and friends. As he remembered in 'Boyhood':

He looked awhile at the field all white
Glistening fair in the soft moonlight;
But the bells tolled the heavy midnight.

So he knelt him down beside the bed,
Folded his hands and bent his head
And the Devil smiled at the prayers he said.[34]

He had an image of God the Father as a full-bearded Patriarch with a broad brow and piercing eyes which showed he would stand no nonsense from little boys. Jesus was much more real to him. Prints and paintings showed him as a tall figure in white seamless robes, long fair hair and a beard. 'There was sorrow and rebukeful sympathy in the large eyes which looked straight at me from under their slow lids.' More than twenty years later he confessed, 'I have never been entirely free from his presence.' When he was confirmed he was so moved that he said he wanted to 'shout his assent' to the Bishop.

After church on Sundays Jack did not take part in the rough and rowdy games the choristers played after the services. He was an obedient child whose worst offence was smoking a clay pipe at the age of nine and making himself sick. No wonder that he decided to recall his childhood in an autobiographical fragment, 'A Good Little Boy'. He did not have far to walk from home to school in Park Street. A contemporary remembered him 'with a fine crown of thick wavy brown hair, studious face and wearing glasses; on his cap was the shield of the Corporation Grammar School'. At the age of thirteen, he wrote an essay on 'The Nile'; he had just been reading Ruskin and, adept imitator as he already was, caught the style. He was accused of cheating. No one believed him when he pleaded it was his own unaided work and then received the worst thrashing of his life that left him bruised in mind and body. 'Thereafter I do not recall putting forward my best paces for anybody. It horrifies me to think that Grammar Schools, masters and boys, can still be as loathsome as the Plymouth Grammar School was to me when I was small, the masters accusing me of cribbing when I wrote a good essay and the boys putting me on the rack.'[35] He left with bad memories and a permanent doubt about the value of education.

Despite this dismissal, he was in fact very successful at school. On

27 July 1900 his mother went to his final speech day in the Plymouth Guildhall. After listening to the march from *Athalie* and a fantasia on the theme of 'Men of Harlech' on the grand organ, she watched the Lady Mayoress present her son with the Holmes Prize for being the best student at the Cambridge Local Examination Centre, with distinctions in French, Mathematics, Physical Geography and English. He was the star pupil.

There were signs, however, that boded badly. A lonely child, he felt misunderstood at home and did not make friends easily. He developed a carapace of reserve and a habit of never saying what he thought. He often cried himself to sleep and became a regular sleepwalker; he could not stand on a train platform without retreating and clutching a pillar. He had a fear of heights: 'a terrible attraction which at once paralyses and draws to the inviting abyss'.[36]

As he grew older reading was a window into a more exciting world. Jack went through the then usual diet of boys' adventures and derring-do: J. M. Ballantyne's *Coral Island*, Captain Marryat's sea stories and G. A. Henty's tales of imperial adventure. More unusually, he also devoured works by the Victorian poets Mrs Hemans, Southey and Longfellow. Then he rediscovered a poem from his earliest memory. It was a revelation and was to haunt him all his life, another sea story – Coleridge's 'Ancient Mariner'. He did not know what an albatross looked like and had no idea of what the allegory might mean, but he was spellbound by the images: the glittering eye, the ribbed sea sand, the copper sun, the painted ship and the ocean.

His great-aunt allowed him free range of her attic. There he found a bound set of the *Illustrated London News* and read of the launch of the Great Eastern and the bloody battles of the American Civil War. He took back with him to read at home a whole set of Jones's 'Diamond Classics'. In these midget books with their almost unreadably tiny print (4.5 point) he read Pope and Cowper, *The Sorrows of Young Werther* and Blair's 'The Grave'. As he wryly remarked much later, the 'Diamond Classics' 'helped to send his eyesight on the downward path. He was also immersed in Dickens and *Tom Jones*, and borrowed from the library works by Montaigne, Rabelais, Sterne, Swift, and Malory. By any standard this was a serious course of reading for a teenager. All these books that were so close to young Jack he lost in the muddle and chaos of his life in the 1930s. But in 1939 he had still managed to keep with him a copy of the book that he said changed his life – Arthur Quiller-Couch's *Oxford Book of English Verse*. He bought it within a week of its publication in 1900 and read it from cover to cover: 'It fascinated, it saturated, it educated.' Night after night he pored over it in his bedroom by candlelight: 'It crystallized and carried on the taste of a generation,' he wrote. It certainly did for him.

By a stroke of good fortune an aunt left some money so that he could leave the hated Plymouth Corporation Grammar School. His mother offered him the choice of Blundell's School at nearby Tiverton, or Sherborne. As a good Devonian he felt bound to choose Blundell's and in autumn 1900 he joined the sixth form.[37] The school had recently moved just out of the town into Victorian Gothic buildings of mellow red stone. The tall square tower dominated a cluster of buildings; a long line of mullioned windows reflected sunlight and shade. There was an avenue of lime trees and the playing fields were surrounded by lawns and great high trees. On practice runs, half-holidays and weekends Squire explored the surrounding Devon countryside.

Like most public schools Blundell's devoted much time and energy to sport. Games of all kinds were played: rugby was the winter game and cricket the summer. There was rowing, fives, rifle shooting, tennis and swimming. A gym cup was awarded with colours and caps. Squire was introduced to this new world at Blundell's and he enjoyed taking part in all of it. Despite his short-sightedness, he played rugby energetically for school teams, but only reached the senior house team in the game that he came to love most – cricket. Every day he scrutinised the papers to see the scores and averages of county cricket. He once saw W. G. Grace bat and dreamed of making a century at Lord's. 'I could get no sort of thrill out of any triumph in literature comparable to the delight of striding out to an applauding pavilion after that hurricane century that saved the side,' he wrote.[38]

After the Corporation Grammar, Blundell's seemed a gentle paradise where, as the Boer War drew to an end 'in the last Golden rays of the Victorian sunset', he enjoyed a feeling of being at peace with the world. His closest friend at Blundell's was Willy Smith, an artistic, clever boy whose father was the Master of Sidney Sussex College Cambridge. He had won a scholarship to Blundell's the year before Squire arrived. They played cricket together for School House and had adjoining studies. Squire felt he had found a younger brother.

A notebook carefully dated 1900 contains an odd mixture of his earliest writing: a ghost story, a love poem and bloodthirsty tales spiced with ghoulish humour – the giant Polyphemus eats two Greeks and then carefully cleans his teeth. The theme of man's life set against the immensity of the world was in the first poem, 'The Weaklings,' where humans are 'puny worms with souls in a coffin of bones...' There were jokes and parodies, improved nursery rhymes and a historical romance describing the first battle between the Saxons and the Danes for the Ancient Country of the Free. It was a jumble – the work of an adolescent trying out different styles and subjects. But there was also a glimpse of the poet who might emerge: many of the poems were on a grand scale of cosmic drama, a visit to Hell on the Ship of Destiny prefigured all the images of voyages of his later poetry, the theme of mortality was ever present and the tone often melancholy.

He continued to read voraciously. In the sixth form room he hid copies of the Victorian popular novelists Rider Haggard and Henry Seton Merriman behind walls of more academic tomes. In the school library he came across poetry that shocked and intrigued him: Baudelaire's *Fleurs du Mal*. After lights out, he crept downstairs to his study in his dressing gown, carefully drew the curtain so that his housemaster could not see what was going on from across the lawn, and began to translate. In Baudelaire he found a mixture of realism and romance, a personality that 'stood in the mud and looked at the stars' and a distinctly un-Victorian 'marble purity of language'. For a while he devoured what he saw as the beauty and squalor of

Baudelaire's verse and all the 'grimmest literature' he could find – so unlike the approved reading matter of the school curriculum, and so unlike anything he had read before.

In the holidays he read Flaubert and the whole of Zola. Zola's view of the world was very close to Squire's own at the time, but one he later grew to hate: 'a repulsive man in a way; boringly Republican, Rationalist and Realist.'[39] To a sheltered boy of seventeen, and indeed to a young undergraduate, Baudelaire's poetry had the thrill of forbidden fruit. 'It is impossible to read him and forget him', he wrote later. He was to include some of his translations in his own first volume of poetry, *Poems and Baudelaire Flowers* in 1909. As he grew older and less rebellious he suppressed the book because of its 'falsity'. Nevertheless, sixteen of his translations were reprinted in his final work, the personal selection of poems he chose to be remembered by, his *Collected Poems*.[40]

'Sound is what the Old Testament was to me', he wrote. He loved the cadences and music of the Authorised Version that he heard every day in the school chapel. He loved too the narrative of the New Testament, but as he grew into adolescence, he began to examine the cruelties and 'Blackguardism' of the Old Testament. Cruelty of any kind was abhorrent to him and he found Jehovah a monster. At the age of seventeen he began to read atheist pamphlets and to call himself an agnostic. He refused to take the sacrament at Sunday Chapel – a powerful statement in the conformist world of the Victorian public school. After reading about Eastern religions in his last year at Blundell's he proclaimed himself a Buddhist, more as a pose calculated to annoy the 'clods and slaves' around him than a deeply held belief. He was beginning to show signs of intellectual revolt. He became secretary of the Debating Society, supporting liberal causes, opposing, for example, the motion 'This House deplores the education of the lower classes.' In his final summer term in 1903 he acted in a version of Aristophanes' *The Frogs* that he adapted and directed, for the school's Prize Day. He was singled out in *The Blundellian* as the life and soul of the performance for his comic role as the wily servant Xanthias.

As the end of his time at Blundell's drew nearer, he began to wonder what the future held. There was no money from home to support him. Perhaps a career in the Indian Civil Service beckoned with a tempting early retirement on a pension of £1,000 a year? Concern about his health made that unlikely. Or there was a riskier choice: a career in journalism? University was a possibility – but how could he pay the fees? Meanwhile he spent the summer holidays happily reading Dickens and Stevenson, fishing, sailing and ferreting. But he knew his childhood was over.

Chapter 2

Cambridge: The Rebel Heart

After he had left Blundell's Bessie wanted her son to join the navy. He told her he wanted to go to university. 'Very well, then, if you can get a scholarship you may go to Oxford,' she replied. He agreed that a scholarship was the only possibility, but he did not want to go to Oxford: Cambridge was his firm choice because it had produced so many poets and because he had supported the light blues in the Boat Race ever since he could remember.

On a December day in 'half fog' Squire took the train from Plymouth to London on his way to the interview. An eighteen-and-three-quarter-year-old whose only experience of a city had been Plymouth, he was shocked by the dismal, grimy backs of houses in Paddington. It was a misty day, very cold; a light rain fell He stood and trembled in the cavernous station, awed by the sheer size of the metropolis and the 'sharp coppery reek' of the railway terminus. He crossed London to Liverpool Street and the train to Cambridge. The rain had turned to snow and the wind blew icy from the fens. 'Death, Greef, Sadd and Pain', the Dickensian-sounding tradesmen's names on King's Parade, were not encouraging: 'It was, I thought, Hell.' For three days he stayed in King's and sat his scholarship papers to read history. Turned down there, he was awarded a foundation scholarship to St John's worth £40 a year. His success, he was told, was due to an essay he had written on the topic that a civilisation's

17

architecture was the best way of judging its character: a belief he held all his life.

So, in the autumn of 1903, Jack Squire arrived at St John's as an undergraduate. He had chosen a room high in the great mock-Gothic building almost overlooking the topmost branches of a vast spreading elm which filled the whole space of his window. On his first day he went to the Master's Lodge and, kneeling, put his hands into the Master's. Surrounded by portraits of bewigged worthies, he swore his loyalty as a foundation scholar, and signed his name 'Johannes Squire, Devoniensis' in an 'antique book, bound in thick leather-covered timbers'.

He looked lean and felt himself an outcast, a Dickensian waif, with a great tousle of black hair topping his pale features. 'After I finished my first scrappy meal, tucked away an aged violin-case, and stacked my clothes, I remembered I did not know a single soul in the College... I gloomily put a kettle on, and set the teapot to warm before the feeble fire made out of a few sticks and coals which the bed maker had borrowed from a Chinaman in the next room. I went to the bedroom, put on pyjamas, a dressing gown, and a pair of carpet slippers (I had induced my aunt to work me some, pea-green with pink roses) and came back to huddle over the ugly little grate and try to warm myself with tea...'[41] As midnight approached and rain spattered the windows, he was feeling lonely, provincial and cold. The oil lamp sputtered dimly. He felt he had chosen the wrong set with its grim workhouse staircase and its hundred stone steps and its horrible iron railings. Why, he wondered, had he gone for the howling green wallpaper that he would now have to live with? He reached for his tobacco pouch: empty. The fire was going out and he had not got a hot water bottle. Ever literary, as he heard the chimes of midnight carried by the gusting wind, he felt for himself the sorrows of Werther and the miseries of the prisoners of the Bastille.

At this point there was a quiet knock on the door. Who could it be at this hour, he wondered? Three men stood outside looking very grave and senior. 'We thought we'd call on you,' they murmured in unison. They entered and perched on two derelict chairs and a rickety cane-bottomed one from beside his bed. As they sat in a ring round him he leaned back in his dressing gown in a broken armchair. He could offer them nothing as refreshments and they were so shy that an awkward silence fell. Finally, they left and Squire retired to a cold bed, cheered by the thought that 'any rate there are some extremely pleasant human beings in this College, though of course, I shall never see them again, as they are very senior men.'[42] (The strict etiquette of the time, according to Squire, was that senior undergraduates would drop a visiting card into a freshman's rooms. The freshman then had to repay the call, after which a friendship might develop.)

After his first night his bedmaker arrived with kettles of hot water and put a hip bath before the fire. There was no gas or electricity in college; all light and heat came from oil lamps, coal fires and candles. A barber's in Cambridge offered a bath at a shilling in the back room of his shop. A kind invitation to make up a four to play bridge in Sidney Sussex College with Charles Smith, a friend from Blundell's, broke the social ice on his first full day in Cambridge. There he was formally introduced to his bridge partner: Mr Squire of St John's: Mr Wilkinson from this college.' Clennell Anstruther Wilkinson was to play a crucial part in his future life.

Soon he was asked to go to tea parties, which often quickly became prayer meetings. The question of religion was posed again at St John's, a very earnest low church establishment, as he remembered it. He found the arguments about religion unsophisticated and the Christian undergraduates dull – and he had to make his escape from their tea parties quickly. The claims of scientific materialism were more difficult to throw off. Arguments about evolution seemed to disprove the existence of God and for a while Squire, inspired by the then popular German scientist Dr Fraenkel, took on board the ideas of a mechanistic view of the universe. The intellectual snob in him felt gratifyingly superior to his fellow students, duped by Christianity and superstition, and he boasted he wanted to be seen as a rebel and to be viewed with both abhorrence and admiration.

For a while he relished his rebellion. Ostentatiously he drank champagne on Good Friday, enjoyed jokes about turning water into wine and composed a comic opera he called 'The Girls of Nazareth'. On the walls of his rooms he put blasphemous pictures and posters. One showed a picture of the Son of Man being pursued by an angry crowd that had not been satisfied by the tiny portions of loaves and fishes offered them. 'I would certainly have been rusticated had the Dean seen them,' he wrote. But it went against the grain of his character. As he drank the champagne of revolt he had an uneasy sense that Jesus was looking over his shoulder.

Some of the cruder advocacy of the atheists, tiresomely and absurdly showing him the bones of a dead horse to prove ideas of evolution, succeeded only in turning him back to a belief in something beyond the material world. 'The unknowable laughs at them,' he wrote. He felt there was something beyond, 'inspiring, purposive and vigilant whom those who perceive must obey', but he lacked a formula, a creed and a church. When he said, 'There is a God,' he said it as a protest against vain self-sufficiency and partly 'as an expression of certain cloudy feelings within me'. Reading Bishop Berkeley made him question ideas of time and space and the limits of materialism. 'The statement that there is no God repels me as indicating an earthbound mind.' He found it easy to accept miracles, as the whole of life seemed 'so great a mystery'. Unable to deny the Virgin Birth, he was equally unable to believe in it. His position was that of the reluctant sceptic: 'I would like to have faith, but I see no likelihood of obtaining it.'

Just outside Squire's room was a great elm that blocked all the roofs and walls from sight He was almost on a level with the top branches. On the far side of his room all he could see were 'the green caves and promontories of its branches. If he sat on the window-sill it was silhouetted against the sky. That autumn of Squire's first term in Cambridge the leaves of the elm outside his window turned gold. For seven days he gazed at 'something more beautiful than anything I had seen in my life'. He saw in their thin perfectly shaped golden leaves something weightless and insubstantial: 'The tree was a vision of that perfection that dwells always as a longing in some recess of the soul, that is scarcely ever realised in any material embodiment.' He was to keep the same rooms in college for his three years and each autumn waited to see the transformation, but never again did the tree turn into ethereal gold.[43]

It was one of those rare times when he felt what he described as 'a kinship with nature, a contact with something above the everyday world. These moments were essential to Squire, whether inspired by nature or love or poetry. But however important they were, they remained only glimpses, only hints – the nearest he could get to Eden. His sense of the 'something beyond' led him to moments when he felt the 'unreality of everything around me.' His poetry often charts these moments of fluidity, of dream, and reverie into a world where everyday reality slips away.

At Cambridge his hairdresser and tailor saw very little of him. There was a formal dress code; his disregard for the correct attire often caused difficulty. It was frowned upon to wear a soft hat, which he sometimes did, and even worse to go hatless, which he usually did. He claimed to have worn the first soft hat in 1903 Cambridge. Hair was worn short with a side parting: Squire wore his long brown hair parted in the middle in the bohemian fashion of the nineties. On Sundays a quiet lounge suit was appropriate, a bowler hat and a walking stick were carried. A very high stiff choker was generally correct. Soft collars were very much out – both he and Rupert Brooke wore them. It was not carelessness that made him disobey the conventions of dress: he wanted to be seen as different, a man who might have more than just sartorial change on his mind.

Squire became 'a most assiduous dodger of lectures'. He never saw the point of them and found the very few he attended did nothing to change his mind. He thought they were droning, dull, and full of points that would be better made in print. The historian of Byzantium, Dr Gwatkin, was a well-known example of the boring sort of lecturer, mumbling nearly incomprehensibly through his beard. He was noted amongst undergraduates for the remark: 'I went to the New Forest to look for beetles and there I found Mrs Gwatkin.' There were, however, a few lecturers that Squire did hear in the afternoons out of interest: the Trinity logician McTaggart on Hegel and the existence of God, Dr Inge on mysticism and Sir Martin Conway on early Flemish painting. He spent much more time in the Fitzwilliam Museum admiring images of feminine beauty than in the lecture rooms. He loved Palma Vecchio's 'Venus' and Millais's pre-Raphaelite 'The Bride'. Most special of all was Praxiteles' 'Aphrodite of Cnidos'; he made weekly pilgrimages to the archaeology department to gaze at the most beautiful thing he had ever seen.

Debating suited Squire's argumentative, witty and theatrical nature. In his first autumn term he paid two guineas that he could ill afford to join the Cambridge Union. At the freshman's debate in college he argued for the settlement of foreign citizens in England and became a regular member, speaking in favour of radical causes. He proposed the motion that women should be admitted to all the privileges that men enjoyed and was seconded by Willy Smith. He spoke along with his contemporary T. E. Hulme against the establishment of an English Academy, and against Hulme's proposition that the deterioration of the modern novel was a disgrace. He opposed allowing Chinese workers into South Africa as cheap labour and supported the idea that the state should interfere in the question of unemployment. In 1905 he joined the committee and started debating outside college at the Cambridge Union. There he first heard two visitors who were to become lifelong friends – G. K. Chesterton and Hilaire Belloc. Chesterton stirred his audience to laughter with his paradoxes and wit. Belloc too was a brilliant debater – and Squire, like many in the Union, only wished him to come to an end because laughter was hurting so much. He could not help but admire a man who stood 'foursquare against every modern trend in politics and morals'.

Squire's history tutor was J. R. Tanner, the Stuart historian and the future George V's coach on the constitution, 'a rich ripe chuckling sort of man' as Squire described him later. Squire told Dr Tanner his ambition was to be a journalist. 'I strongly discouraged him,' Dr Tanner said – and recommended the Civil Service. Methodical study for the Cambridge History Tripos did not suit Squire's mind or his inclination. Dr Tanner reported that his pupil had only 'trifled' with the long essay that was a key part of the course. Squire read out a stylish but dubiously relevant essay on Oliver Cromwell, pleased with sentences such as, 'Some men are born pious, some achieve piety and some have piety thrust upon them'. He read out another essay on King John that was, he felt, 'full of coruscating epigrams'. After he had finished, Dr Tanner left a long silence, smiled, and drew on his cigar: 'I think, Squire, you ought to have gone to Oxford.' What he did not know was that Squire had a blank file in front of him and had improvised the whole thing.

Squire did very little academic work at Cambridge, but he did read an enormous amount from the Union library. There were many other excitements to distract him from his books. Bar billiards was popular in the afternoons – so popular that it was banned at the rival university of Oxford. He got to know fashionable dons such as A. C. Benson who invited him to his rooms in Magdalene and was glad when he said he hated Kipling. 'A disgusting little man in private life,' Benson said. He enjoyed the social and sporting life of the college. He gave ten shillings to the college new boat house fund and treated his friends generously. In his rooms there was always a bottle of whisky (3s 6d) and champagne (5s) for special visitors and a box full of Turks and Virgins (Turkish and Virginia cigarettes). He was, he felt, still living in the last sunset rays of the Victorian heyday with income tax at ninepence in the pound and easy credit. But the undergraduate who could afford to entertain in style in Cambridge could not afford the train home.

When his second term was over Squire decided to walk home to Plymouth and take the first of his treks through England. On 4 March he packed his bag and left Cambridge. After stopping to admire the view of the city from Madingley Hill he then went on to St Neots, Bedford, Stony Stratford, Buckingham and Bicester. He stayed for a couple of days in Oxford where he met friends and played billiards and then continued west to Abingdon, Newbury and Amesbury. On the 23rd he rose early and saw the sun rising over Stonehenge. There was no traffic and very few people on the roads, apart from a few vagrants, often moustachioed veterans of the South African wars. By 26th he was in Tiverton and the following day arrived home. The journey of 300 miles had taken him a fortnight.

When Squire returned to Cambridge for the Summer Term he resumed his friendship with a remarkable contemporary. T. E. Hulme impressed him as 'a huge ham-faced, idle man, but one of great wit and lightning intellect'. At St John's he quickly built for himself a reputation for outrageous behaviour. He went up to read mathematics, but his interests soon turned to philosophy. He admired, and soon began translating, with the help of Squire, the work of the controversial French philosopher Bergson and the socialist Georges Sorel. Under Hulme's influence Squire began to read Auguste Comte and for a while became impressed by the agnosticism of the Rationalist Press Association. Hulme got into serious trouble with the authorities for brawling on Boat Race Night and was sent down with, according to Squire, 'the longest mock funeral ever seen in the town'. He lay in an open coffin surrounded by undergraduate mourners as it was slowly paraded through Cambridge. The following year, with the support of testimonials from Bergson and Squire, he was readmitted to St John's.

Squire respected Hulme as a philosopher and a wit and also admired his poetry, brief as it was, for its 'protest against woolliness and inexactitude'. These qualities were to become hallmarks of the imagist poets of which Hulme, despite his exiguous output, could claim to be a forerunner, if not a leader. Squire remembered three phrases, including 'The moon looked over the hedge / Like a red-faced farmer' – now well-known as an early example of imagist poetry – but, on the basis of five poems, could never see Hulme as an important poet and thought that he would have laughed at any suggestion of that kind. Hulme's second session at St John's did not last for long. The father of a sixteen-year-old girl found some indecent letters he had written to her and complained to the Master of St John's. Hulme was sent down again, setting a record, Squire thought, as the first man to be sent down twice from the same college.[44]

Squire was still wrestling with religious questions. His whole cast of mind rejected a materialist universe. For a while he called himself an agnostic but he was shaken by the argument that he could not call himself an agnostic because that belief implied a certainty that he did not have. After one of the many religious crises of his early life he was re-converted to Christianity by the idealist philosopher Professor Caird's argument that a sense of the presence of God was evidence of His existence. He wrote that he had never lost his faith in the immortality of the soul. But all was to change very quickly.

In late 1905 in Squire's final year a very different kind of thinker, who was to transform Squire's religious beliefs and his politics, arrived at Trinity College. Frederic Hillersden Keeling, unaccountably always called Ben, was years younger than Squire; Keeling, for a while, became his closest friend. Squire felt that they were most unalike as characters, but that Ben understood him better than anyone else: 'He has more soul than anyone I ever met.' Already a convinced Fabian at Winchester, he draped his turret rooms overlooking the Great Court with red flags. A huge poster showed the workers of the world advancing with clenched fists. 'FORWARD THE DAY IS BREAKING' in capitals underneath: the slogan was from one of Squire's favourite books, William Morris's *News from Nowhere*. Long-haired, wildly enthusiastic about the causes he cared for, Keeling soon became known throughout Cambridge as a charismatic leader of the opposition to the conservative majority. He effectively founded the university Fabian Club. Within a year of his arrival its membership had grown from a moribund group of six, with just one undergraduate member, to over a hundred.[45]

Keeling's political certainty put an end to all the religious crises in his friend's life: it was the faith that Squire had been trying to find and gave him the 'opportunity for the expression of the identical emotions that had plunged me into three or four varieties of Christianity at different times.' He became the keenest of Socialists and called himself 'an evangelical convert'. They were both members of the 'Fish and Chimney Club', whose motto was 'Drink like a Fish: Smoke like a Chimney', a small socialist play-reading group that was more serious than it sounded. It was led by Keeling and held weekly meetings to read and discuss plays by Ibsen, Sudermann, Shaw and Granville Barker, along with poetry by Swinburne and Yeats. In May 1906 Keeling proposed the motion at the Cambridge Union that England was ready for republican institutions, with Squire as his seconder. He spoke with Keeling against the motion that democracy had been a failure and against an ultra-conservative motion that 'the present system of parliamentary democracy ought to be allowed to die quickly'. He also opposed unpaid magistrates, 'relics of the feudal system', and argued against the motion that wars between civilised nations were never justifiable. Where he deviated from a radical agenda was when he spoke against the motion that public schools should be drastically reformed. (He stayed fiercely loyal to Blundell's and the public school system all his life: and thought its enemies were '(1) jealous people who weren't at one or (2) beastly little throw-outs who thought of themselves and not of team-work.')[46]

Keeling soon made his name among the senior Fabians outside the university. Beatrice Webb saw him as 'a fervent rebel... in his generous vitality and incontinent intelligence.'[47] She thought he was one of the two most promising young men at the university – the other was Hugh Dalton (later to become Chancellor of the Exchequer): 'The Cambridge men are a remarkable set, quite the most remarkable the Fabian Society has hitherto attracted – fervent and brilliant.'[48] H. G. Wells too was impressed and thought Keeling 'a copious, rebellious, disorderly, generous and sympathetic young man.'

Charles Hodges was another of Squire's close friends at St John's. At the end of his second year he invited Squire to join a group of actors to discuss a theatrical tour of East Anglia. The ostensible reason for the tour was to make money for East Anglian hospitals, but Hodges actually engineered the whole thing so that he could see as much as possible of a young woman whom he had fallen for. (The girl came chaperoned by an aunt, but the ploy worked – the thespians fell in love and later married.) The rest of the cast included a professional actress, undergraduates, including Clennell Wilkinson of Sidney Sussex College, and assorted friends and sisters.

Women were not part of College life but idealized representations of *Beata Beatrix* yearning with closed eyes hung on the sitting room wall of nearly all undergraduates. Dante's *Vita Nuova* bound in limp leather adorned the birthday table of all the betrothed. It was at that meeting in Charles Hodges' rooms on Saturday 7 June 1905 that Squire first met a very different kind of woman who was to change his life. Daringly unchaperoned and smoking in public, she was the centre of attention, talking to ten people at once. Attractive, dark-haired and spirited, she was the New Woman in person. She was Clennell's twenty-year-old sister: Eileen. She was shortly to show her independence by leaving the quiet vicarage of Hintlesham in Suffolk, where her father, the Reverend Anthony Anstruther Wilkinson, was rector, to work in London and join the suffragettes. Squire had never met anyone remotely like her and was instantly struck. Perhaps she knew that she had made a great impression because just a week after they first met she boldly sent him a letter asking for details of the tour's itinerary. He replied to 'Miss Wilkinson' in the first of more than four hundred letters he was to write to her.

The theatre tour itself took the Cambridge Comedy Company through Suffolk and Norfolk and lasted nearly four months from June to mid-September. They played at Hadleigh Town Hall, Sudbury, Stowmarket, Mildenhall, in the Abbey Gardens of Bury and at Thetford, Brandon and Swaffham. The cast learned what it was like to stand on cold, windswept railway stations and board in spartan theatrical digs. Once, as he traipsed along the road at night to the performance at Mildenhall, wearing unlikely beribboned dancing pumps, Jack Squire was arrested as a suspicious vagrant and spent the night in Ipswich prison in a cell infested with bed bugs. The Company performed in vicarage gardens, stately homes, halls and semi-derelict theatres. The plays were a medley including Sheridan's *The Rivals*, where Eileen played the lovelorn Julia, a vaudeville comedy *The Follies of a Night*, and *King Réné's Daughter* in which Squire (because of his swarthy complexion) played the part of an Arab physician and droned interminable speeches through a long white beard. On the tour they celebrated Eileen's twenty-first birthday. Another drama was happening behind the melodramas on stage...

After the tour was over, back in Cambridge, after a sleepless night, Squire went over again the whole summer's events from the beginning. He remembered it as a series of romantic moonlit scenes. After the performance at Mildenhall he knew that he had fallen in love but tried to talk himself out of it because he was afraid his feelings were not reciprocated. He failed. 'Agonising was no word for it,' he wrote. At Dereham he and Eileen spent Sunday evening together. As they gazed at the sunset he began to feel that she looked at him in a different way, but as their shoulders touched he did not dare to put his arm around her. On a hot summer's day they shared a rowing boat in the backwaters of Thetford and he tentatively put his arm around her waist. She told him that while 'men were the salt of life for women, a woman was never more than the sweets of life to a man', a remark he recalled months later and asked her to withdraw. If she was wary, he was full of passion:

> There was a day, when I, if that was I,
> Surrendered lay beneath a burning sky,
> Where overhead the azure ached with heat,
> And many red fierce poppies splashed the wheat;
> Motion was dead, and silence was complete,
> And stains of red fierce poppies splashed the wheat,
>
> And as I lay upon a scent-warm bank,
> I fell away, slipped back from earth, and sank,
> I lost the place of sky and field and tree,
> One covering face obscured the world for me,

And for an hour I knew eternity,
For one fixed face suspended Time for me.[49]

On Whit Sunday they lay together in a field as darkness drew on and only one star hung low in a green sky with a strip of yellow piercing it; their hands touched. The evening sunset made him recall a poem he had written when still at school at the age of sixteen: 'On the Moor (Evening)' seemed like a premonition:

Long lines of quiet rooks
Winging to their rest
Over where the trees stood black
'Gainst the yellow west.
Silent pool and brown moon
Peaceful as may be,
Fade and fade away, but you
Are all the world to me.
Ah! Lay your hand in mine
Till the last light dies...
Hush... a quiver?... Nay, love,
Tears in your eyes?

There followed another moonlit night when he felt that his love for her could be returned: 'That glorious wood at Brandon...We lay there for hours, hardly saying anything and I dared not kiss you.' Together they read Rossetti; 'The Blessed Damozel' was a favourite. They took photos of each other and enjoyed a night ride in a hansom cab, hiding their feelings from the rest of the cast by a front of laughter. At Saxmundham 'We went up a quiet street and saw the full moon behind that great black mill. I thought it was the second most beautiful thing in the world that night...' He remembered their exact words as they sat in a little wood near the town. 'Let's talk. Do you love me?' she asked. In reply he kissed her. 'That is the only answer you have for everything,' she said. The tour ended at Framlingham in Suffolk, a place he said he would never forget. They lay on the grassy moat with the background of the high walls of the castle and the shadowy trees caught in the moonlight or starlight as they read together some of Keats's love poetry. She leant back with eyes half-shut, smiling, as he held her face in his hands.

Eileen returned to London and tried to get a job working with children; Jack stayed with friends in Okehampton before walking from Devon to Cambridge and his last year at university. Nine months later she had written him seventy-five letters and he was staying up till dawn to read and reread them. One letter from Eileen was a monster of thirty-six pages. He dreamt of spending a whole day writing to her perhaps fifty, perhaps even a hundred pages. She described to him how she got his morning letters and curled up in bed to read them. When she had had breakfast she reread them carefully in her chair. He replied that he did exactly the same thing; he read her letters in bed as he breakfasted, and then put them on his neck for a quarter of an hour, 'infusing' them. When he had got up, he sat by the fire rereading them.

Chapter 3

You are my Sky

Squire returned for his last year in the Michaelmas term of 1905 and was desperately lonely without Eileen. He missed the company, too, of her brother Clennell and T. E. Hulme who had both left Cambridge. Back in London, Eileen was also feeling lonely. She had failed to get a job working with children and was working as a seamstress. She had moved from staying comfortably with an aunt to a one-room flat in a house she shared with other working girls in a shabby Chelsea Square. The reality of sewing blouses for the Shirt Company was not at all what she had imagined. When she saw the line of machines in the factory in Kensington she turned 'pea green'. The pay was poor too; she had to work a ten-hour day for fifteen shillings a week. Soon her fingers became sore and she developed bad eye strain and headaches. After Christmas another hour was added to her work and she began looking for jobs elsewhere.

Nearly every day he wrote long letters to Eileen; some days he wrote two, their frequency and immediacy making them feel like a conversational tête-à-tête. She replied in even lengthier letters; he collected them all and they became tokens of the affair where spaces were marked for her to kiss. He marked with arrows the exact spot on the letter where he had left a kiss for her. After five months his letters amounted in length to a substantial novel. He was capable of writing twenty sides in under an hour and always wrote from the same desk of the smoking room of the Union. She, amazingly, wanted his letters to be even longer and criticised him for the small size of the paper and the large size of the writing.

On 29 November he wrote, 'You say I have made life worth having to you. I cannot find an expression to say what you have made life for me. Morbidness gone – indifference gone – everything gone... I have never known anyone but you with whom I could have got through the reserve which always cloaks my actual self. I never even knew my real self until you brought it to the surface and made the nebulous forms take definite shape. You are (excuse the expression) the panacea for all my ills.' Again, 'I shall never cease to love you. You are the incarnation of all I have always looked for in a woman and never found.' He was a devoted and sentimental lover. He suggested *'je pense à vous'* should be written on the envelopes, he kept all the flowers that she had brought for him, he asked for a wisp of her hair which retained a faint scent of her presence to put in a bracelet – much more intimate than a ring, he felt. Every night in bed he reread the Rossetti poems they had read together and, in 'a mystic ritual', kissed her photo before going to sleep.

There were occasional visits to London but they were fraught with difficulty because Squire had very little money. Eileen was working full-time, making arrangements complicated. There was no private space for them; Jack could not visit her in her little room with the watchful eyes of her landlady and the other tenants upon them. They courted at night under a tree in Hampstead: both subsequently developed bad colds. Nevertheless, they enjoyed London Zoo and South Kensington Museum together where Squire admired the Constables. They saw the spectacular chariot race in an early film of *Ben Hur* at the Coliseum and the premier of Bernard Shaw's *Man and Superman* at the Court with Harley Granville Barker playing the lead. The choice between his wish to see Shaw's *Major Barbara* and her wish to see *Peter Pan* was a difficult one. He tried to avoid *Peter Pan* and suggested Ibsen's *Pillars of Society* at the Court as a compromise.

'The Devil take depression in the future. Love and work are enough to keep it off me.' Surprisingly he claimed that 'until I met you, dearest, I never felt the slightest desire to understand anyone or be understood by them.' Love not only released him from depression; together as a couple they might do great things. He sent her a poem that had first shown him what a woman's love was and told her to read Elizabeth Barrett Browning's 'Parted Presence' from *The House of Life* to explain what he felt for her:

Your heart is never away,
But ever with mine, for ever,
For ever without endeavour,
To-morrow, love, as to-day;
Two blent hearts never astray,
Two souls no power may sever,
Together, O my love, forever!

Perhaps they would follow in the steps of Robert and Elizabeth Barrett Browning in a partnership of poetry and love, or perhaps they would be like Sidney and Beatrice Webb, blending marriage with the advance of Fabianism and women's suffrage. Whatever the future, Squire had enormous self-confidence. He told Eileen that 'with a love like ours we can do anything'.

For all Squire's support for women's equality, the relationship was often that of teacher and pupil. In one of his first letters to Eileen he wrote, 'Forgive my mentioning it but the second page of the letter should be on the second page of the notepaper. If that is done it is the sign of a well-ordered and disciplined mind.' He told her it was bad form to leave a page unfilled. (She replied with half a page of kisses.) He corrected her style, grammar and spelling. He was ready to mock her 'abominably feminine' overuse of exclamation marks and her inability to spell *criticise*, *until*, *bracelet* and *Baudelaire*. His attitude to Eileen was sometimes patronising. He was the Cambridge University undergraduate and she was 'a modest little dressmaker'. He promised to put her straight on the topical question of tariff reform – he was a Liberal in favour of free trade – and told her she ought to accept his views solely 'on my word and recommendation'. On his side of the argument, he said, was nearly all educated opinion; the opposition were 'ignorant jingoes'. He sent her an assortment of books by his favourite author at the time, Gabriele D'Annunzio, along with works by G. B. Shaw, Baudelaire and Herbert Asquith, but he was dismissive when she sent him a book which she admired, H. G. Wells's *Revolutionist's Bible*. Under pressure, he eventually had to admit he had not read it. She accused him of never listening to her – a charge that evidently hit home as he rebutted it at great length.

What he confided to Eileen, and to no one else, was his ambition to be a poet. 'I honestly believe that there is something there, Eileen, and that I may possibly write something that the world will not willingly let die.' Five months later, in May 1906, he wrote to her, 'You must know that at the bottom of my indolence up here has been – Poetry! You can't serve Art and Mammon. You can't think of verse if you are concentrated on exams.'[50] He continued to write translations of Baudelaire and sent Eileen his own poems too. Proud to know that St John's had produced such poets as Sir Thomas Wyatt and Robert Herrick, he was reminded of the tradition every night as he swigged his ale in Hall sitting under Pickersgill's sober portrait of a red-nosed Wordsworth.

Influenced by Eileen and by Ben Keeling, Squire increasingly found Cambridge stuffily conservative. The days of billiards and bridge began to give way to more serious thought – although he still made a regular income of about five shillings a week from playing cards. In November he wrote to Eileen that he was becoming 'an ardent democrat and quite keen on social reform'. In the Christmas vacation he hoped to join the St John's mission at Browning Hall in south-east London. He promised her that he was not going to become a missionary but 'merely awaking to a sort of interest in the conditions amongst which we live'. As the year went by this vague awareness was to lead to more closely defined socialist politics.

He began to build a reputation for his weekly reviews of Cambridge Union debates for the university magazine *Granta*. In October he went on the attack, calling the latest debate 'the dullest thing I have ever struck'; he wondered if the paper would dare to print his piece. One cause he championed was that of an Indian student, C. R. Reddy, who stood for president when Squire stood for the committee. The opposition, mainly from Trinity, campaigned under the slogan 'Keep the Nigger out'. He found 'inane-looking bloods' walking up and down at the Union with complacent grins on their faces. Squire's views were too radical for the time and both he and Reddy were defeated. He got 127 votes – normally enough – but a record poll of 'brutes' kept him out. 'The colour feeling here is too strong,' he wrote to a friend. When he visited the Union afterwards, he noted there was hostility towards him and his supporters. The vice president of the Union called him the 'greatest blackguard in the University' – Cambridge seemed to be mirroring the increasingly bitter divisions of Edwardian England.

Squire was establishing a reputation as a powerful and witty speaker, a leading campaigner for radical causes in the university. A Fellow of Trinity offered money to found a rival to the establishment journal *Granta* and asked Squire to edit it, along with his friend Raglan Somerset. Squire was disappointed with the magazine's name; it was to be called *The Cam* – much too conventional a title he felt – but he leapt at the chance to upset the complacency of the undergraduates who had rejected him and Reddy. He promised Eileen that she would get the first number. He said he was poised to set out on a new adventure and overthrow any 'obsolete conventions, untrammelled by any sense of decency, sense of honour or sense of shame.' A career in radical journalism was beginning.

It was not only political and social conviction that led him to spend Christmas in a dormitory at the mission organised by St John's in Walworth, a deprived area of south London: he had only threepence to his name and could not afford a railway ticket home. The mission at least offered board and lodging, but the company of the serious young curates, the earnest debates and the round of church services were tedious. It was, he wrote, the dreariest place on earth and the Christmas holiday without Eileen was lonely and hard to bear. He wrote to her that his friends had gone off to divine service to worship their God and he had stayed behind to worship his Goddess.

After his spell at the Walworth mission, Squire and Ben Keeling went to Colchester, Keeling's home town, to support the Liberal campaign there in the 1906 election. At this time Fabians supported the Liberal party which, they hoped, would adopt a more socialist agenda. Unsurprisingly, Squire found the sitting Liberal member, Sir Weetman Pearson, too bourgeois for his tastes. He had 'a thick accent and no intellect' and his overdressed wife was, in the Cambridge slang of the time, a 'tout': Squire's socialist beliefs and social snobbery went hand in hand.

Nevertheless, he went canvassing for Sir Weetman and delivered a fiery fifty-minute speech full of the words *lie* and *liar*, which went down well. Afterwards, at one o'clock in the morning, Ben Keeling and he went round the town tearing down Tory bills. In one front garden they found a six-foot hoarding, sawed it down, took it into a side alley and smashed it to bits. The next day, he motored out to the Essex village of Frating where he spoke on behalf of the candidate for Harwich and roused his audience to cheers and hootings as he left. Back in Colchester he stuffed Liberal leaflets through letter boxes and tore out any Tory ones he could grasp. He stayed up till 2am to hear the result and said he was never more pleased in his life when both Liberals he had canvassed for won with healthy majorities. As he told Eileen, it demonstrated, as he had constantly told her, that the Liberals' policy of free trade, and not the Unionists' policy of protectionism, was what the country wanted.

The rest of January was taken up with speeches and canvassing in Rutland, Stamford, East Cambridgeshire and Newmarket. In February he was offered a job as secretary to the Liberal candidate for a Staffordshire division, but in fact his politics were changing fast with the times. Elated as he was by the Liberal success, he was beginning to turn away from the party. If they did not use their victory to put through radical progressive changes, then the socialist view that the Liberal hypocrite was just as bad as the Tory rogue was confirmed – and then, he told Eileen, both Ben Keeling and he were ready to desert the Liberals and join the nascent Labour party.

Squire prided himself on his enlightened attitudes to women and treated those who disagreed with contempt. There was nothing more loathsome, he told Eileen, than a phrase such as *wooed and won*: 'It implies an inferiority in the woman. It is in accordance with the conception of man as the hunter and woman as the quarry that he secures by spear or snare, by violence or by wiles.' He saw literature through the lens of the sexual politics of the day. Geniuses such as Shakespeare, and nearly all poets, he thought, knew that women were superior to men: Milton and Tennyson were second-rate exceptions. Tennyson never wrote any good love poetry because all he could think about were 'dainty girdles and slender feet'. Milton was even worse: Adam was 'an insufferable snob' and in *Paradise Lost* treated Eve like a domestic servant. Walt Whitman, on the other hand, was 'too fleshly'. He might have been the first poet to express the idea that physical desire was just as real as that of the spirit – but there was no need to stress what everyone knew already. Reading Whitman's *Leaves of Grass* was Squire's first encounter with free verse and he was immediately hostile. Whitman was guilty of unnecessary frankness and had a 'complete disregard for literary form'.

Squire was not nearly as liberal and free-thinking as he considered himself to be in his attitude to sex. Despite the bluster, there was something of the prude about him – he had been brought up with his mother and two sisters in a very sheltered Victorian household. Eileen was much more knowing and teased him in their arguments about women. She challenged him to name her undergarments, which he dared not describe in detail. She wrote about her petticoat bodice and he owned up to never having heard of one. He said he was familiar with the word *camisole* but had thought it was the same as a *chemise*. 'My education seems to be progressing,' he wrote. She enjoyed making fun of his 'delicate sensibilities' – a charge he was quick to refute.

Just after denying he was in any way a prude, in his next letter he wrote to say how the sight of a bird laying an egg would be 'positively nauseating' to him and he would be ill on the spot. He added that he hated dancing because he was horrified by the thought of putting his arms around another woman's waist and he often blushed when he passed a pretty woman in the street. His own coy and euphemistic language did not match his advanced views on 'the woman question'.

The couple negotiated their ideas about sex and love through literature. Eileen had a quite different reading list to the one Squire recommended. She too was reading the poetry of Walt Whitman, which she had in an expurgated edition – Squire warned her against becoming 'a complete Whitmaniac'. He nevertheless sent her a copy of his own, unexpurgated, edition. Not easily persuaded, she wrote that she admired 'Song of Myself', and 'Children of Adam'. Squire replied she would not like them nearly as much when the novelty had worn off. Keats's *Endymion* was another focus of disagreement. She thought Keats was mealy-mouthed; it was absurd of him to avoid the word 'naked' in the story of the love affair of Endymion and Diana and the descriptions of their lovemaking were 'ludicrous'. Squire admitted that he did 'beat about the bush' in those lines but on the other hand felt that the treatment of the Goddess of the Moon, like Whitman's poetry, was too 'fleshly'.

Eileen had also been reading the sexologist Havelock Ellis and was intrigued by his advanced ideas about polygamy and free love. Squire would have nothing of it: 'Avoid him as you would the plague,'[51] he cautioned her. He had not read the book she had recommended (*Sexual Inversion*) but heard that Ellis took 'a cold scientific interest in everything that is lewd'. He told her that it had been burned on the orders of the British Government and, according to one of his friends, who had read it, thoroughly deserved its fate. Polygamy, he explained, was mathematically impossible. He calculated that as the ratio of men to women was nearly equal there were just not enough to go round. And free love was morally abhorrent. The clinching argument was, however, a personal one: 'Would you like to share me with someone else?'

Marriage was not only ideal: it was just what he so desperately wanted. 'One wife is a scanty allowance,' she replied teasingly. Many men were unfaithful and many were rakes. Prostitution was the evidence for this. She suggested easy divorce would help women and noted that there were some tribes who held wives in common. She added that she was 'damned proud of her independence' and reluctant to let it go.

On the other hand, Squire told her that once women were educated, and became equal wage earners, prostitution would disappear. And as for the language of buying and selling, like prostitution itself, that was a product of commercialism, part of the world of capitalism which would disappear under socialism. Eileen had to 'forget her old cynicism' and look to this new world that they would build together. Their love was to be a paradigm of the way forward for society. 'You and I darling must do our small share towards bringing the race on to its ineffable destiny. No man can alter the course of Nature – but it is open to us to retard or accelerate her action.'

Eileen was less concerned about the destiny of the race and more worried about what would happen when she took Jack to the rectory to meet her father. What exactly did her fiancé believe in? Would he take Holy Communion? He reassured her that he would be happy to 'take breakfast with the Lord', just as he would with any other great man. He claimed to be a Christian although he did not believe in a personal God, incarnation, resurrection or redemption. All socialists were Christians, he told her, as they believed in loving their fellow man. 'We are all immortal!... We – or I – worship something, either the love of humanity in us, or the spirit of God in us, or the spirit of the universe in us.' Would she be able to marry in her father's church? Jack made it clear that 'honour' and 'obey' meant nothing in a relationship of equals but his redefinition of Christian faith meant that the wedding service itself was no problem. 'I believe a great many of the things I do and say are simply directed towards breaking down the barrier that existed when we first started our acquaintance. Absolute free speech and free thought is needed before we can build on it our perfect superstructure of love.'

Jack and Eileen spent three days of New Year 1906 at Hintlesham Rectory. It was the first time that he had met Eileen's parents. Their relationship worried the high Tory Anglican rector. It was altogether too hasty and the long-haired bohemian-looking Jack Squire did not at all look like the suitor he might have imagined or hoped for. His headstrong daughter was only twenty-one and just getting established in London. Over their stay nothing was said to reassure him about the young couple's relationship or intentions. He noticed that Jack now wore a ring which Eileen had given him, and a bracelet. What would happen if they behaved foolishly, he wondered? Squire had no money and unknown prospects.

After the New Year visit Eileen went up to see Jack in Cambridge and daringly, and quite against college regulations, visited him in his rooms in the Gothic tower of St John's. He asked her to carve her name deeply into the wood of the window frame. He kissed the teacup she had drunk from and wanted her to break some ornaments so that he could put their remains on his mantelpiece. After he had seen her off on the train he went back to his rooms wishing he had asked her to lay her cheek on his pillow. He kept his door shut to bottle in her invisible presence. His room became a shrine of dead flowers: January violets, followed by snowdrops, anemones and lilac.

Early in February, Eileen was expecting to receive the daily letter as usual. Instead, there was only one sheet: a love letter in verse form, and, unusually, Squire dated it: 12 February 1906. It began 'My bride, my wife, my life,' and ended:

Indeed I love thee: Come,
Yield thyself up, my hopes and thine are one.
Accomplish thou my manhood and thyself,
Lay thy sweet hands in mine and trust to me.

The words were from Tennyson's 'The Princess'. He had the words by heart and kept the violets she had given him as a marker on that page.

Their engagement was to be kept secret from both their families. It was only eight months since they had first met. Eileen's father, clearly concerned, sent Clennell to sound out the position. He told Jack that Eileen's pater was not against the match but was worried that Squire 'might do something rash'. As Jack suspected, the rector was also hurt that he had not made his feelings clear at New Year. He duly wrote a letter saying that yes, Eileen and he had come to an understanding, but both felt that it was not the time for a formal engagement as they had not yet got the means for settling down. It was possible for a couple in love not 'to play the fool'. The phrase caused confusion: the rector thought Squire to mean sex, but in fact he was referring to marriage. 'I wish I were in a position to marry you,' he wrote to her. The only problem was one that was to dog him throughout his life: money.

1906 was the year of the Liberal landslide; at the general election in February the Tories lost half their seats. It was not only a great victory for the Liberals, but, more importantly to Squire, the birth of the parliamentary Labour Party. Keir Hardie led the Labour Representation Committee, which won twenty-nine seats and for the first time became a serious political force, now renamed as the Labour Party. Squire noted that the socialist movement was gaining ground not only in England, but right across Europe. Carefully dating the poem 'February 1906' he wrote 'To the Continental Socialists'. The crusading flavour of his politics is caught in the hymn-like opening:

We who have but begun,
We who as yet are few,
Send out our hearts to you
Whose cause and ours is one…
Who, faltering not, have prest
Onward toward your quest,
O Comrades, noblest, best
Of all beneath the sun.[52]

In England, by contrast, 'faith was in the mire / And hope had shrunk and sickened / Till you within us quickened / The Dream and the Desire.' Like Wordsworth in 1789 hailing the French Revolution, he dreamed of a New World free from the tyranny of kings and priests, a world that would embrace not just France and England but all nations, the 'Holy Brotherhood of all beneath the Sun'. It was a dream that was closer to the anti-clericalism and anti-royalism of that Revolution than to any socialist utopia:

The land foreseen of old,
Where naught is reaped unsown
And human blood and bone
Are neither bought nor sold;
And earth where kings' oppressions
And prayers and intercessions
To priest-contrived obsessions
Shall be a strange tale told.

In February he wrote to Eileen to tell her he had been invited to King's to hear 'some great socialist buck' coming down from London to start 'a new Socialist (Fabian) Society'. He was one of about seventy members of the university, forty of whom were Newnhamites, who attended. He did not hold out any great hope for the meeting, which he expected would be attended by fools and poseurs, but came away astonished by its success and the number of women who were there. Under the leadership of Ben Keeling, they formed what was first called the Socialist, and then the Labour Club. Squire was elected as Secretary. He expected that in the future meetings would be held in the afternoons so that the Newnhamites, who were subject to a night-time curfew, might attend. Amber Reeves, the strikingly attractive daughter of Maud and William Pember Reeves, was elected as the first Treasurer and soon became a leading member of the Fabian 'Nursery', set up in April 1906.

The Fabians were the first Cambridge society to admit women as equal members and, in the days of the chaperone, offered chances that could not be found elsewhere in the university to meet the opposite sex and discuss political, social and sexual issues. To Squire's surprise, by the second meeting more Newnhamites than ever flocked to join the society, further outnumbering the men and even threatening to swamp them. He went to Newnham to hear Amber, 'our leading lady', read what he thought was an 'outstandingly witty and able paper'. She told him that they had already held a socialist dinner to celebrate May Day. 'Sporting lot, aren't they?' he commented to Eileen. He quickly became one of the many male admirers who found Amber dazzling. She was very enthusiastic and 'quite a humourist'. He looked forward to getting to know her better and to introducing her to Eileen. He did not imagine how Eileen, living a lonely life in her one-room digs, might take her fiancé's praise of the star of Newnham…

The questions about what the Liberal Party now stood for were very much in Squire's mind. Was it just another cover for the capitalism he hated? When the House of Lords threw out the Education Bill, Campbell Bannerman's proposals threatened to divide the party once again. Squire thought that kicking out the last remnants of the Liberal old guard was to be welcomed. The next stage, he thought, would be the disestablishment of the Church of England, which would get rid of all the bourgeois Wesleyans who would join the Tories. Then in open fight the reactionaries would 'go to Hell' if they opposed progressive reform.

The situation amongst the radicals was much less clear than his Armageddon scenario. The distinctions at this time between Fabians, Socialists and the Independent Labour Party are hard to make – and Squire certainly did not always make them. He was moving away from Liberalism and towards something newer and more extreme. He began to write to the luminaries of socialist thought, H. G. Wells, Keir Hardie, Bernard Shaw and Walter Crane, to invite them to speak to the club. He also invited 'Anarchy Brown' from Trinity College who was said to be in league with all the Continental anarchists. He also invited 'Anarchy Brown' who had attended secret meetings in London and Paris 'filled with wild-eyed Spaniards and Italians who shout and wave their arms' and was reputed to be the cleverest man in

Cambridge. Squire was pleased that Wells was going to speak to them in October and pleased too that he wanted to convert London Fabians away from being a philosophical debating society into a political force. Keeling and he both supported the idea of Fabian intellectuals working together with the Independent Labour Party.

Squire asked the secretary of the Cambridge ILP to his rooms in St John's to talk about collaboration: 'He was an ordinary workman, but very thoughtful and quite a wag... Several of us are joining the Cambridge Branch of the Independent Labour Party.'[53] The Labour candidate for Wakefield, Stanton Coit, came to address forty or fifty members in the room below Squire's and he spent the whole day organising the meeting. Typically, that week he was also giving a talk on Charles II at Queen's College, attending the Liberal Club Dinner and standing for the Committee of the Union...

As a newly converted socialist, Squire's letters to Eileen became more didactic. Politics now took centre stage. He promised to teach her that the only way forward was socialism: 'I will make of you a Radical of the most pronounced type before very long. You must be, you know.' After her education he told her she would not be able to read newspapers like the *Morning Post*, the Harmsworth Press or the magazine *Tit-Bits* without a feeling of revulsion. On the other hand, 'You positively <u>must</u> read a few elementary socialist things soon – William Morris & Ruskin to start on. You will realise that Socialism is far more a moral, ethical – even artistic movement than a political one.' He was now convinced that the Tories and Liberals were finished. 'The Tory and Liberal parties are merely sections of the bourgeoisie each aiming to prevent labour getting its just reward but we are moving quickly... You will see that Socialism is inevitable and moreover the right thing – when you understand what Socialism is – and to understand it you must have at least a cursory knowledge of history and social conditions since the dawn of history. Oh, dear girl, I am so keen to get you quickly started and knowing all the little that I know myself. As Ibsen says, world salvation is coming mainly from the women and the workmen...'[54] If so, Eileen clearly had to follow the reading list and do the homework that her mentor demanded.

As Squire's three years in Cambridge were coming to an end, he discussed his future with the two people closest to him: Eileen and Ben Keeling. If he were to get a First then a fourth year was very much a possibility. Keeling, 'my greatest friend on earth', generously volunteered to pay for it – and suggested that they should rent a cottage on the Essex coast and do some serious revision. Squire said he himself lacked ambition but felt Ben was ambitious on his behalf. He also felt that Keeling wanted him to stay on in Cambridge because he would be lonely without him.

As finals approached, work was not his main concern. The first week in March was typical. In the afternoons he played bridge. Evenings were taken up with writing letters to Eileen from the Cambridge Union. He was also busy editing and writing for *The Cam*. His first verse parodies of Union debaters appeared there in the styles of Keats, Wordsworth, Burns and Shelley. On 5 March he read a paper on Charles II to the History Society. In the evening there was the Blundellian Smoker: a bibulous affair at which he had got drunk the year before. Then on Monday there was the Liberal Club Dinner as he awaited the results of his election campaign for the Cambridge Union committee. A dangerous pattern had been set up of conflicting social, political, literary and romantic demands. Concentration on a single purpose went against his nature.

In April the reading party that Ben Keeling had suggested took place. He, Willy Smith, and Dudley Ward agreed that the rent of £1 would be divided between the four of them. They chose an isolated cottage at East Colne, on the Essex coast. The journey was not an easy one: a train to Colchester, followed by a motorbus to West Mersea, and then a three-hour walk. By the time Squire arrived at the cottage only Willy Smith was there. 'Colne View' was in a beautiful and remote spot on the marshes with the sea only a few yards away on three sides; trees grew almost up to the water's edge. The weather was 'ripping' and the days spent bicycling, bird-watching in hot spring sunshine and bathing, 'in a state of nature, I blush to say'. The reading party was really more like a holiday by the sea. Eileen joined the two men at the Easter weekend when she could get off work. There followed three idyllic days for Jack and Eileen: 'I never felt such a sense of happiness as in those nights in the cottage when you used to come in to me and snuggle up in my arms whilst you (quite awake) gradually brought me into a state of comparative wakefulness...'

May Week celebrations were something Squire had dreaded. They marked the end of his time in Cambridge. A full squadron of his female relatives was about to descend on his Cambridge world; he had to arrange rooms for them and look after their entertainment. But that was not what he chiefly feared. Eileen was puzzled that she had heard so little about her fiancé's family and began to question him about them. She suggested coming down to Cambridge for the May Week herself to meet them all and wrote to say how much she was looking forward to it. He was reluctant: 'If you are so keen to see my people, I suppose you must, but you will only have yourself to answer to it if you find them to be remarkably dull and very bourgeois. That's what irritates me – I like them all right but their hopelessly middle-class outlook, views, conversation – it goes very near driving me mad.'[55]

There were many farewell moments. The Fish and Chimney Club decided to take a punt and a picnic down the river and read a Shaw play as they ate and drank champagne. There was a party of French guests of the Union to show round Cambridge; there was a piece in *Granta* in which he reviewed a Union debate in the style of the much-mocked Poet Laureate, Alfred Austin; the final edition of *The Cam* came out. In the early summer sunshine Cambridge was at its most painfully beautiful. He enjoyed watching the boat races from the college punt, but the prospect of May Week and the meeting of Eileen and his mother and sisters loomed. He felt the need to warn her again and to distance himself from them: 'I am a remarkably exotic plant of that family,' he wrote. 'Personally, it seems brutal to say it – but the less I see of them – except my younger sister – the better I am pleased. I have a very deep affection for my mother, but I say it (for the first time and last) as you have to know – she gets on my nerves a little.' Eileen rebuked him for his lack of taste and he duly apologised. In the end he did his duty by the family, found them rented rooms, took them punting and to a May Ball at which he resolutely refused to dance – but he wanted only to see Eileen. His 'encumbrances' must have been very curious to know what was going on, but he told them nothing about her or their relationship.

Just after the ball, Squire received a letter from Eileen's father, still clearly worried. He was concerned that he might be blamed if he was seen to have encouraged the pair and it all went wrong. In it he said that his daughter 'was not the sort of woman for love in a cottage'. The letter sent Squire howling with derisive laughter at the idea he could not provide for the rector's daughter, or that he, as was hinted, might leave her pregnant. He took this as an insult and told Eileen that 'your sire' had 'the intellect of a provincial, bourgeois woman' – an extraordinary remark for a man who had a sophisticated sense of irony, and supported the women's cause.

Squire hoped that the examiners would like his style of historical essay, which was discursive and general, but feared they would want a catalogue of facts. After three years 'trifling', as his tutor put it, with reading history, Squire gained a second-class degree in his Finals. The revision and the 'reading party' had come too late. He had hoped for a First, but now any chance of an academic career was ruled out. He left a record of his final conversation with his tutor, Dr Tanner: 'Well Squire, now you're going down, what are you going to do?' 'I'm going to write, Sir,' I replied. The reply was frank: 'You are,' he said, 'eminently fitted for that, and eminently unfitted for anything else whatever.'[56]

Once term ended, as soon as he had taken his degree, he and Keeling took the train to Liverpool Street and then on to Lincoln's Inn to meet the secretary of the Fabian Society. He had promised Eileen he would put her name down too. He told her there were exciting meetings on Fridays at which Shaw and Wells often spoke and entertaining soirées to look forward to. She loyally signed up as a member for five shillings, which she could ill afford.

Squire's last year in Cambridge was the most exciting of his time there and he now regretted he had idled away his first two. Despite that, the future seemed to hold golden prospects for the couple. But he had no job and the contacts he had made did not lead to any paid work. Cambridge had sharpened the young man's intellect, but had also fostered his arrogance and a sense of social superiority. Pride came before a fall.

Chapter 4

Journalism

With his tutor's words ringing in his ears, Squire decided to try journalism. London beckoned. He was penniless as he searched for jobs. He had to sleep on twopenny rented seats on the Serpentine while the night drew on and long reflections of the lamps shone on the water. He went to a meeting at which Bernard Shaw, with a bright red beard, spoke, 'with a fine sweeping certainty about all things'. Then he tried his luck with various editors in Fleet Street, including the halfpenny dailies, and *Pearson's Weekly* where he came nearest to success as a judge of limerick competitions at thirty shillings a week. Nothing. Finally, he took a letter of introduction from an old friend to H. J. Massingham, then editor of the leading radical paper, *The Nation*. He asked Squire what he was prepared to write about. "'Almost anything," I answered, "but especially poetry." Massingham's lizard's eyes blinked behind his shining glasses. "They all say that," he said. They do. The wrinkled nutcracker smile was not unkindly, but there was a no in it. He saw young aspirants every day, no doubt. Years later we became acquainted and he evidently did not remember me; nor did I ever tell him that for a day I had pinned my last hopes on him.'[57]

Rejected by a London that he said would not be even a 'stony-hearted mother' to him, Squire crept back to the West Country in June. He worked off his anger and frustration by walking from London, through Winchester to Salisbury, in just over forty-eight hours. 'Chelsea at two; Guildford – with the gas-lamps shining melancholy on laurels outside – at half-past ten... Two nights out, sleeping rough by snatches, heaven knows where. I had never seen that road before, and now I know every turn on it.'[58] A train from Salisbury to Plymouth and he was back where he started, in his mother's lodging house at 1 Princess Street. The year that had been so promising ended with no career, no money and a fiancée over two hundred miles away.

There was talk of an extension lectureship: he offered a course on 'The Revolutionary Spirit in Nineteenth Century Literature', but it came to nothing. He applied for teaching jobs with no success. He was willing to take any job in journalism at a starvation wage on a local paper and even tried to use a friend's influence to get on the hated *Daily Mail*. If Lord Northcliffe had heard what he had said about him at the Union he certainly would not get the job, he told Eileen – but there were apparently no jobs going. He sold a microscope for £2 and a few books, including his eleven volumes of the historian Clarendon ('mere lumber'). His favourite edition of Swinburne went to his Cambridge friend Louis Wilkinson for twenty-five shillings; he carried on playing bridge for money and generally won, but he still had not enough even to buy stamps or writing paper for his daily correspondence with Eileen. He owed St John's College £50 and overdue bills began to drift in from Cambridge tradesmen. He was, however, still discussing a holiday with Eileen. His mother was shocked when she learned of the suggestion that Eileen along with her sister and two brothers might rent a holiday house together in the New Forest and invite Jack. 'It seems very lax to me,' she said. 'How conventional!' complained her son. In order to brighten his room, he decided to put up his Cambridge pictures, including some classical nudes. His mother told him to take them down as Doll might see them.

At home the atmosphere became tense. His mother and he were getting on badly; he lived rent-free and the idle life her son seemed to be leading must have rankled with the hard-working landlady.

In the hot summer of July he made trips into the country to escape. He thought little of walking twenty or twenty-five miles in a day. When he was staying at Okehampton with friends he decided to visit a place he had only distantly heard of, 'rejoicing in the name of Broadwood Widger'. The name of the place intrigued him. He had heard it was where his father's family came from. 'My paternal ancestors (God damn their Souls) were farmers and maltsters there for ever so many hundreds of years.'[59] However, the Devon yokels ('the bloodiest fools I have ever struck') from whom he asked the way could not give him directions and he never managed to find it...

The weeks dragged on. Plymouth was a 'God-forsaken hole, a sewer'. Autumn was very rainy and cold; he said it was the wettest place in England. He had few friends there and was finding the idle life boring. He filled his time reading Dickens, but thought that the author had no brains at all. The women characters were puerile or worse, and the men only a little better. The children were obnoxious – 'Another senile child of ten'. He did however admire Dickens's gift for description. And although he had no money for writing paper, he somehow found five shillings for his Fabian subscription.

'In a Chair', a poem full of absences, dates from this time of waiting:

The room is full of the peace of night,
The small flames murmur and flicker and sway,
Within me is neither shadow, nor light,
Nor night, nor twilight, nor dawn, nor day.

For the brain strives not to the goal of thought,
And the limbs lie wearied, and all desire
Sleeps for a while, and I am naught
But a pair of eyes that gaze at a fire.[60]

A journalist friend on the *Daily Mail* suggested that he should offer his services free to a local newspaper for a couple of months to see how the paper worked as a preparation for a London career. So, in desperation, he applied to the *Western Daily Mercury* where he was interviewed by its formidable editor and managing director R. A. J. Walling. The editor was in his mid-thirties; he had wide interests and had started a paper in Plymouth devoted to football, edited *Cycling News* and published a life of Sir John Hawkins. He impressed Squire with his energy and the fact that he had worked for the liberal *Daily News*, the national paper Squire read assiduously every morning. Although he was not a socialist, Squire thought he was one of the most extreme radicals he had ever met, an advocate of universal male suffrage and the nationalisation of land.

At first, Walling looked sceptically at the young Cambridge graduate, hatless, hair parted down the middle, wearing an effeminate wristlet watch and, most suspiciously of all, a gold bangle. Without much hope, he gave Squire some books to review. But when he had read what Squire had written he immediately offered him a month's unpaid trial. Squire would do all the book reviewing and the Saturday literary page. He would also have to 'rub up' his shorthand (non-existent) and report on everything from cattle shows to law reports, from the Petty Sessions to the Board of Guardians who administered the Poor Law and workhouses. He was also asked to do 'cemetery biographies' of Chamberlain and Sir Edward Clarke. Walling told him he ought to try everything to gain experience.

Squire was brimming with further suggestions: he offered to produce weekly letters purportedly from Oxford or Cambridge and pieces on Shaw, Wells and Kipling. He also promised a monthly column on the best poetry of the month: 'I want to puff any good stuff that appears.' He had to arrive at the *Western Daily Mercury* in Plymouth at seven o'clock in the evening, just as Eileen was returning home to her Chelsea lodging. He worked alone in the sub-editor's room throughout the night. A boy brought bread and cheese at 10.30 and cocoa at 2.30. He left the premises very early in the morning. Although he feared the paper was on the verge of collapse he was delighted finally to get a post.

Mostly it was work, and work at night; the machines drumming behind and below; the boys coming up for the little wads of copy; the scramble soon after midnight; the respite when all had gone down and it was now for the printers to finish the job; the wait for the first damp and sticky copy with everything miraculously sobered and strengthened in type, and miraculously fitting; the supper, or very early breakfast, of cocoa and cheese, under the lamps; the fearless mice who leapt on the littered table and sat up nibbling the fragments of cheese. It seems, in retrospect, charming and amusing.[61]

The *Western Daily Mercury* was a vital apprenticeship to the world of journalism and printing. Soon Walling was remarking on the impact his young recruit was having on the hard-bitten local journalists by the speed and accuracy of his work. Squire read an Anthony Hope novel in one evening and had his review ready for the morning paper, along with brief notices of 'Young England', the 'Child's Own Magazine' and 'The Making of a Motor-Car'. He had only twenty-four hours to review nine books and the following week he reviewed thirteen novels – 'fortunately they are all rubbish'.

Walling said Squire never stopped talking about politics when he was writing about sport or about cricket when he was writing about politics. Meanwhile there was the bread-and-butter work of daily journalism. He went to a Presbyterian Sale of Work, and then tea at a Wesleyan Chapel, hating every moment, but managed to enter into 'the bloody nonconformist spirit of the thing'. He heard lectures on British Coins, reviewed concerts, went to Parish Guild Debates, the Gleaners' Union Service and the Devonport Church bazaar; he reviewed books such as *The Golfer's Year Book* and *The Horse: his Ailments*. He even managed to write half a column on the Co-operative Society's annual accounts. He thought his old friends from the Cambridge Fish and Chimney Club would have cried with laughter to see his transformation.

Squire began to separate himself from the kind of liberalism the paper stood for. When he started canvassing for Labour in the local elections and was nominated in the socialist interest to be on the Board of Guardians he felt he had to ask the editor's permission because his views might conflict with the Liberal capitalism of the paper. Without hesitation, Walling agreed. After looking down on the *Mercury* as a small provincial affair, Squire began to see it as one of the largest and most influential journals of its type.

Walling introduced Squire to radical meetings in Plymouth and took him to the Unitarian Church on Sunday afternoon to listen to lectures and sing socialist hymns. It was more of a discussion group than a church; the minister was a keen socialist and the discussion advanced. Squire told Eileen that Unitarians were not Christians. Meanwhile she was dutifully attending Church with her father at Hintlesham, worrying about her fiancé's religious beliefs and what he thought about her church-going. In a long letter to Eileen in November 1906 he stated his position as an agnostic. He did not know about the divinity of Christ but was in no doubt that he was the greatest man who ever lived and his gospel was a socialist one. Squire recalled his experiences amongst the poor and had seen for himself the comfort that men and women got from their faith. He reassured her that they could take Communion on that basis.

Squire joined the newly started Plymouth Debating Society. The standard was, he remarked, infinitely higher than it had been at the Cambridge Union in spite of the fact that most of the members were tradesmen, shop assistants or clerks. Politics united them but he felt his 'hyper-aesthetic' ideas meant he was different from the workers. He continued reading Dickens and Walter Scott and carried on translating Baudelaire. He was also building up his first collection of poetry. When his friend Ralph Straus wrote to him about a new magazine he had started, published by the Samurai Press, Squire agreed to subscribe at two shillings a month. He hoped to get his verses published there. Eileen had persuaded him to read Jane Austen for the first time; he found *Pride and Prejudice* hilarious and hatched a plan that they should do a dramatic version of it together.

The political question was whether to join the more revolutionary

Social Democratic Federation or the Independent Labour Party. It was an initiation into working-class life at the local branch that led him to join the SDF. 'They are a splendid lot here. All working men however. Damned earnest chaps and they've all got a sense of humour.' He told Eileen he had been to a meeting where Shakespeare's influence on Tolstoy was heatedly discussed and a blind man had sung and played Wagner: 'Navvies, shoemakers and casual labourers. The more I see of them the more I marvel at them.'[62] Another meeting took the form of a lecture by a clever bootmaker on 'Socialism: Cataclysm or Evolution'. Squire was asked to address some outdoor meetings but, realising he lacked as yet any knowledge of the inner workings of a workman's heart and brain, turned the idea down.

Nevertheless, inspired by his own conversion and the friends he had made in the local branch of the SDF, he did begin to lecture to them on socialism. The lectures were to form the basis of his first work, *Socialism and Art*, a brief pamphlet published by the Twentieth Century Press for the SDF for a penny, and introduced by the well-known socialist artist Walter Crane. Squire's account is that of the Cambridge Union debater, full of the angry rhetoric of the newly converted Fabian. He advocated the kind of socialism that owed a great deal to William Morris and his belief that the Middle Ages allowed the artist and craftsman to thrive. In the twentieth century, by contrast, the only value was a commercial one and the result was a debased art. 'The imbecile suggestion' that socialism is the enemy of art is dismissed without argument. Fabians are told not to focus so much on economics but more on art and beauty.

The historian in Squire then traced art from the caves of Neolithic man to the present day. He concluded that art has been a necessary part of human life since records began: it springs from man's primal instincts. There is a universal delight in colour and form shared by the savage and a little child playing with skeins of coloured wool – as Squire had done himself. There had never been a society encouraging art for all, apart from Western Europe in the Middle Ages; medieval man decorated everything from a porridge pot to a cathedral. But when medieval craft was replaced by manufacture, or 'factoryfacture', cheapness and money became crucial. This led to a totally false conception of art and architecture. The artist became the servant of 'Mr Moneybags' – hence everything from the huge portraits of nonentities on the walls of the Victoria and Albert Museum to Kipling's Imperialism. 'There never was a system so noxious to Art as this of Capitalism.'[63] The ugliness of cities, the sameness and uniformity all around and the degradation of their inhabitants were the inevitable results. When, as Marx and a convinced socialist such as Squire believed, capitalism collapsed, art and artists would spontaneously thrive once more. He foresaw a communist society where every man followed in the footsteps of great artists of the past and cleared the way for the great artists of the future. The radical weekly paper, the *New Age*, welcomed the pamphlet as 'a breezy and outspoken lecture'.[64]

Much though he admired the members of the SDF, Squire was an exotic to them. He enjoyed singing some of William Morris's socialist hymns to the tune of 'John Brown's Body', and even playing charades and statues with them at Christmas. However, they jeered at the Fabians and they jeered at Squire for being one of them. The Fabians, they said, did not know what hunger was and, if they did, they would talk 'a little less ethics and a little more economics'.[65] Squire decided to set himself a serious course of reading and started on Adam Smith's *Wealth of Nations*. When he got to London he thought he would 'chuck' the SDF for the ILP. Nevertheless, it was through them that he learnt about real poverty and the 58,000 people who lived in squalid tenements in his home town, almost the worst in the country, he told Eileen.

As Squire was discovering the working class with whom he was sure the country's future lay, he was also meeting many middle-class people in Plymouth and the surrounding area. He was sent out to cover a Wesleyan luncheon and bazaar at Saltash, a suburb of Devonport, and found there everything he abominated, summed up in the word *bourgeois*. His account to Eileen has a Dickensian vitality. 'After some execrable speeches the diners tucked into a ~~nauseous~~ meal of huge chunks of veal and ham pie, followed by solid chunks of fruit with cream and then cheese. They indulged in heavy-handed facetious wit: "*Voulez-vous passer me le moustade.*" And things of that sort. If there was plenty of meat they ostentatiously pretended to be unable to move it round their plates with their forks. If they thought the portions too small they pretended to look at them through thumbs and forefingers as if they were looking through a microscope. They ate like hogs. After each course they made a great show of unbuttoning their waistcoats.' The moral was clear: 'The upper classes are not entirely irretrievable, the working classes are splendid, except the lowest and most miserable, but for those people and their likes I can see no fate but extermination.'

Squire was now a very different person from the Cambridge undergraduate who had enjoyed long idle afternoons playing billiards with Clennell. His violent hatred of men such as the millionaire William Whiteley energised his political views. 'Bourgeois' was a word that he increasingly used to attack the class enemy. Press barons such as 'Harmsworth and the Pearson gang', he said, ought to be drowned. They were 'narrow-minded swine' who could not see the need for change. He was full of hatred for 'touts' of all kinds; the rich; the middle class in general, Northcliffe, 'an utterly uneducated and uninformed man', the *Daily Mail,* all conservative newspapers, all Tory politicians, most vicars and the whole apparatus of capitalism. 'How I loathe and despise him', he wrote of Joseph Chamberlain. When Eileen said she was going to see a polo match between the Lords and the Commons he was appalled and suggested she should not go to an activity 'more or less symbolical of the filthy waste indulged in by the plutocracy'. He visited Swindon to see Clennell and found it full of disgusting touts with accents you could cut with a knife'. He told Eileen that the vast majority of Wells's readers were fools and 'not convinced of a single thing that is obvious to us'. Tactlessly he told Eileen, 'Parsons were hateful brutes mostly, except for the hypocrites.' He had become an angry young man, an Edwardian Jimmy Porter. Rupert Brooke, a fellow Fabian, diagnosed this cast of mind precisely;

he noted that violent hatred was an occupational hazard for the small, highly educated group of Cambridge Fabians: 'Of course, they're really sincere, energetic, useful people, and they do a lot of good work. But as I've said they do seem rather hard... They sometimes seem to take it for granted that all rich men and all Conservatives (and most ordinary Liberals) are heartless villains.'[66]

Socialism was now filling the space that Squire's childhood Christianity had occupied. Lonely in Plymouth, he found his only friends among the socialists of the SDF, or *comrades*, as he increasingly called them. He read the radical press with voracious enthusiasm; he read the *Daily News* every day along with weeklies such as *Justice*, *The Contemporary Review;* monthlies like the *Social Democrat and Fabian News*, and the quarterly *Westminster Review.* He continued to read William Morris whom he thought 'splendid, splendid, splendid'. He also read Shaw and Wells and Sydney Olivier's *White Capital and Coloured Labour.* He was active in local politics, canvassing in the municipal and district elections and becoming a socialist member of the Board of Guardians. On Sunday afternoons he was a regular speaker at the Plymouth Debating Society: 'My ambition is to become editor of a Socialist newspaper. Pray God I get the chance,' he told Eileen. As his politics became more passionate and all-absorbing, they also became more extreme and more virulent; he was becoming a revolutionary, looking admiringly towards the energy and growing success of socialists in France and Germany. When H. G. Wells threatened to split the Fabians and attacked them in a long and bitter speech, Squire applauded the idea of clear action as he feared that the Fabians might become merely ornamental in the struggle to come. But he made clear his absolute opposition to Wells's rejection of marriage and the family.

Both Eileen and he loved to argue and their differences were very clear. He had abandoned religion: she was still a regular churchgoer. He thought of himself as an intellectual: she claimed to have insight but no ideas. He loved H. G. Wells and she did not. There was one bitter controversial topic that dominated their letters in late 1906:

suffragettes. Eileen was a convert and fervent believer and marched to demonstrations in Trafalgar Square. Jack was intransigent and dogmatic. He had some sympathy for the suffragettes and told her the women's cause meant more to him than that of the workers. Women's 'gender tyranny' was even more harmful than the class tyranny, he wrote. But he could not accept direct action and, like his mother and sister, thought it did actual harm. 'Why can't they behave like women?' asked his mother. Opponents of suffragettes such as his mother and his Aunt Bertha thought the stories of dirty-haired women biting, screaming and fighting discredited the whole women's movement. The proper course of action was, he told Eileen, through politics, argument and the press. Having said how much he disapproved of the suffragettes' methods and how he feared emancipated women would become vulgarised women, Squire then seemed to retreat by saying how much he admired their throwing off convention. But by December he had come round to Eileen's view and promised to join one of the Women's Suffrage Societies as soon as he could get to London. And he also promised her that for once he would eat humble pie.

In October Eileen visited her father and persuaded him to support her engagement. He wrote Jack a generous letter wishing the couple well and inviting him to stay with them for Christmas as they usually made up 'a merry party'. From now on the engagement, which, in fact, everyone seemed to know about, was official.

That winter in Plymouth continued exceptionally cold and wet. A letter from Amber Reeves telling him that the Fabians had managed to get the former Prince Kropotkin to speak to them made him deeply envious. As he gazed down from his window he heard the Salvation Army brass band playing and thought of Cambridge where Eileen was visiting: 'Ah me! Probably you have just had tea and are smoking a cigarette in a fire-lit room and everyone there...' He said he would sell his soul for another week in Cambridge – with Eileen at Newnham! He had heard that the Union had hotly debated a Fabian motion till midnight and that 200 people had been present. He wrote that he could have delivered the speech of his life if he were still at St

John's. Meanwhile, Eileen visited Squire's friends and fellow members of the Fish and Chimney Club, including Ben Keeling. Keeling kindly arranged an introduction for her to Amber Reeves. Squire thought that she would be as attracted to her as he was. Eileen immediately disliked her, perhaps sensing a rival, and found her an 'impetuous child'. He was disappointed and wrote that you could not call a person of her brains and knowledge a child.

Walling asked Squire to do a Christmas piece for the *Mercury* and told him not to be cynical: cynicism was the other side of his idealism about Fabianism and his romantic love for Eileen. Squire replied that cynicism did not pay in the provinces, but you could not be anything else about Christmas – so confirming the charge. Not only was Christmas part of a religion which he now despised, but it was also a time of gluttonous bourgeois feasting: 'The ruddy festival arouses nothing but disgust in me.' His elder sister Nan's arrival for Christmas added to his displeasure; her grating voice got on his nerves and, all in all, she was 'one of those frightfully good-hearted people one prefers at a distance'. As for Eileen's uncles, the rich and successful Hornungs, Squire said he would rather cut his throat than be pleasant to them.

The first Christmas for the engaged couple was very difficult. It was a hundred days since he had held her in his arms, Jack wrote. He had to turn down the Rector's invitation to Hintlesham because he had to work over the holiday period and, besides, he could not afford the train fare. To his surprise his mother suggested that Eileen could stay with them in Plymouth. Eileen wrote boldly to ask Jack whether they could sleep together. The answer came back that his mother's old-fashioned prejudice would never allow it, but she would let them stay up late talking by the fire.

After a tedious journey from Hintlesham Eileen finally arrived in Plymouth. She and Jack went for long walks in the Devon countryside and did indeed stay up late by the fire. He said goodnight to her as he shut her bedroom door and went upstairs. She did as he had asked her to do at Cambridge and signed her name on his bedroom wall. Much to his surprise, his mother and Eileen got on so well that she asked for forms to sign up with the suffragettes. Eileen let him know that she was beginning to resent his criticism of her. He replied that at Cambridge he had got into the habit of thinking intellectual ingenuity the highest of virtues and on many occasions he actually agreed with her, but his combative and debating style did not allow him to show it. He took seriously the accusations from Walling, his mother and Eileen that he was becoming a cynic and said that he had taken the position as a pose, but it had become dangerously close to growing into the role. Now, he claimed, every day his whole outlook was transformed by his love.

Two days after Christmas Eileen caught the train back to London in a snowstorm. 'I can see you're going to live in an untidy house,' said Squire's mother. 'Why?' asked her son. 'Because she does not fold up her nightdress,' came the reply. Jack did not say that he already knew that.

Squire asked his editor if he could be transferred to the sub-editors' room, feeling that this would give him much more experience of journalism. By February 1907, only six months after he had started on the newspaper, he was writing leaderettes and obituaries for the 'morgue' (the stock of obituaries kept to hand by a newspaper). As sub-editor he wrote a regular column headed 'Notes by the Way'. After his trial period Walling told Squire he would make a brilliant journalist in a couple of years.

In January a surprising letter came to the *Mercury*. Walling called Squire in and asked him to deal with it. It was from a convicted house breaker, Charlie Livingstone, who had written the story of his life and his sixteen years in prison. Squire read the novel-length piece in bed and found it 'simply ripping', a marvellously human document written by a man with a keen sense of humour. It contained an account of Livingstone's meetings with West Country murderers who were lifers in prison. Squire met the author and was charmed. He also knew a good story when he saw one. He wrote the headings that soon appeared in the *Mercury*: SOMETHING UNIQUE; FAMOUS CRIMINALS; DEEP INTEREST.

Squire told Eileen it quickly became a hit with all the servants, domestics and nannies and aroused 'terrific interest' in Plymouth. A great correspondence poured into the office of the *Mercury* every day. He also promised that he would try to get it published as a book, hoping that it might make enough to set Charlie up as a mat maker. The story was, after all, 'something unique, the point of view of a low-class criminal'.[67] He duly sent off clippings for Eileen's comments. They were uncomplimentary: she did not approve of the story of drunkenness and thieving; Livingstone was, she thought, weak-minded. She was shocked when Jack replied he could understand any slum dweller becoming a thief and, furthermore, that theft from the rich by the poor was perfectly defensible: in fact, he would have done it himself had he not been in a funk about getting caught. At any rate, he had made Livingstone's name and a little money for him.

In January a deputation of working men approached the SDF about their plight. Squire spent the afternoon with some of them and was appalled by what he saw, as Fabianism had not prepared him for the sight of real poverty: 'The local Guardians are pleased to consider what they consider relief to seventy or eighty of Plymouth's unemployed. They pay them 8d a day (4s a week) for hard labour with pick and shovel. At present all the men are living on a few slices of bread and jam a day. If they are married they get 4d extra for their wives and 2d for each child. On Saturday they get 8d which has to last till Monday. They get two 4d beds for both nights and go hungry all Sundays and Mondays... Only, fancy 4s a week for 8 hours a day hard labour... Isn't it awful?' He found himself part of a group of the SDF branch that planned to meet the Guardians to try to raise their poor relief a little. Three days later Squire noted that the Guardians had refused to meet them.[68]

Violence was in the air. As the Women's Suffrage Bill approached in early 1907 Squire thought that those who opposed it made up for their lack of numbers with their malevolence. His politics were now an emotional crusade. The events of what came to be known as 'Keir Hardie Night' in Cambridge confirmed everything he felt about his old university's politics. Ben Keeling had invited Keir Hardie, the leader of the ILP, to speak. This was a controversial choice: a group of undergraduates decided to do everything they could to prevent him from addressing the meeting. Keeling organised two counterfeit Keir Hardies to act as decoys when the London train arrived. One of them managed to get up to Keeling's rooms where he and his friends, including Eileen, pretended to be enjoying a loud dinner party. Keeling himself escaped down from his rooms by rope as his opponents screwed up the door. Inside, his friends continued to imitate the sound of festivity. Meanwhile the real Keir Hardie had arrived by an earlier train and safely got to the Guildhall. There, he was confronted by a sea of drunken undergraduates anxious to drown him out. Trade unionists and Fabian undergraduates on the platform tried to hold back the mob and Keir Hardie managed to give his speech. Stink bombs were thrown and furniture wrecked. The riot was only quelled by the arrival of the Senior Proctor. Some £40 of damage was done.

Squire read of the events in the *Daily News*, the *Morning Leader*, the *Chronicle* and the *Telegraph*. Isolated in Plymouth from all the action, he yearned to know more and thought Eileen, like Delacroix's Marianne as Liberty leading the mob, must have escaped from Keeling's rooms and been one of the women who leapt over the reporters' table onto the platform. He desperately wanted to be with the comrades and wondered why the reactionaries in the Guildhall seemed so unopposed. He asked her to report exactly what had happened. The journalist in him knew that he had missed a scoop that would have paid handsomely. 'God! To have only been there on Saturday. I could have made a faithful account of the whole thing (from the inside) to the *Mail* or the *Express*. It would have made anything up to 10 guineas for a few columns.'

Squire wrote that the age before the war was a self-consciously open-air one. Cycling was all the rage, rucksacks enjoyed a steady sale and magazines for hikers and amateur tramps flourished. In late April he decided to take a month's holiday from the newspaper and to walk from

Devon to London in the guise of a penniless tramp. The project grew out of his meeting unemployed men in January. He thought he could walk the two hundred or so miles in a fortnight and return, stopping at friends' houses. His idea was to focus on the state of unemployment and on the casual wards which offered a bed for the night for destitute vagrants in return for hard labour the following day. He had discussed the scheme with Walling who thought it a good plan and wrote to the *Mail*, the *Mirror* and *Tribune* to stir up interest. If the papers took his articles he would be 'a made man', he told Eileen. The *Daily Chronicle* was already interested in his day-by-day account. He thought he could also add some 'newspaper verse' of the 'grim reality' kind.

Squire decided to use a bearded disguise to find out how the down-and-out live, following in the steps of the one-legged Super-Tramp, the poet W. H. Davies. On the way he would drop in on the comrades in Exeter, Bristol and Reading and then perhaps shock his tutor and his old friends in Cambridge by suddenly appearing in their rooms as a bearded tramp. He could certainly say goodbye to friends and perhaps give one final speech at the Union. He had never before spoken as a socialist and this was his chance to do so. At any rate, he was itching to leave Plymouth and get on the road. The trip would end in London with Eileen. He had his long hair cropped, gave up shaving, grew a bushy beard that he thought made him look a bit like Bernard Shaw, and put on an old white jersey and a grubby warm mackintosh. He assumed the name J. C. Wilkinson and the identity of a down-and-out 'clurk'. At midday 21 April, with eighteen pence in his pocket, he left home and started on the road east from Plymouth. The tramp did not go as planned. On the first night of his journey, having passed through Newton Abbot, he hoped to sleep on a haystack. No haystacks were to be found. He tried without success to sleep in the ploughed fields and had to spend the night crouched down miserably under the stars waiting for the dawn. In the morning he retreated to his great-aunt's house in Exeter where he found a bed and some sleep. He wrote to Eileen that he had already acquired a blister 'as large as a small tangerine orange and the same colour'.

At Cullompton he bumped into a friend from Blundell's and spent the night on the doorstep of his old school. The rain was terrible as he tramped on and his back was aching as he tried with no success to find a haystack. The next stop was Wellington and then Taunton where he hoped to pick up some letters from Eileen. As he was leaving Somerton three policemen converged on him, suspecting he was a shop assistant from nearby Winchcombe who had run away with the takings of three shillings and ninepence. He reassured them that he was a clerk from Plymouth who was on the road having lost his job. His story convinced the police. They said it was hard lines for a man of his sort to be on the road and he went on his way with their good wishes.

Moving on towards Castle Cary he had done twenty miles in driving rain and was exhausted, with a sprained calf and a swelling leg. No pubs would take him and the hostile locals told him he ought to sleep in the turnpike. He asked to sleep on a barn floor only to be rejected by the farmer: a policeman moved him on. He had walked for forty miles without sleep when he arrived in Bruton and wondered why tramps did not murder policemen, beerhouse keepers and farmers more often. Then he set out for Frome where he read Eileen's letters in the British Workman's teahouse. After a sleepless night, drenched to the skin, he was turned down by about a dozen places including the 6d-a-night rooms at a beerhouse. Finally, he found a bed at a temperance hotel for one and fourpence and slept for twelve hours. Eileen sent him five shillings and he told her not to worry as he really was a stoic by nature.

Time and time again he asked for work and found none. In towns he was told that times were hard and no work was available; in the countryside there was seasonal work in the autumn to get the harvest in, but nothing in April and May. Even for a skilled man it was hard to find work for someone on the road. He found the tramp's lot a most uncomfortable and unromantic one, 'sleeping in haystacks (a rat ran across my face in the dark), pheasant-copses (the rain dripping all night, the pheasants chuckling), and Casual Wards.'[69]

The focus of his story was to be a personal account of workhouse conditions. It was, however, not in Squire's nature to narrow down to a single purpose: his tramp was also to be a holiday. He visited old friends in Cambridge and dined with Ben Keeling in Trinity. Then he took a detour to Oxford where he shaved and borrowed clothes. He was an undergraduate again as he punted on the Cher, talked to a Rhodes scholar about Petronius, played a good deal of billiards and first encountered the writer and humorist E. V. Knox. Somehow, he acquired the fare to Reading, and, resuming the bedraggled mackintosh and the tieless collar, left the disgusted porter of Balliol behind.

After the digression in Oxford, Squire got back to his theme: the workhouse. 'I had walked from Maidenhead to Isleworth on a damp Saturday afternoon in May, and reached the workhouse when the lights were already being lit. My pockets were turned out according to the usual ritual; I informed the grim official in charge that I was a "clurk", and I waited my turn for the bath. Whilst I was undressing a tough customer with cunning eyes, a red nose, a black moustache, and a bristly chin, asked me if I had surrendered any money. "A few pence," I said. "You done wrong," he replied, "you should a' left it in the 'edge outside." The official, when I stepped into the bath, stood over me with a long-handled brush with bristles like stiff twigs. Observing that I did not need it, he demurred; and, realising that I could not be a professional, he gave me a few words of advice about not arriving at casual wards so late in the evening. I slept with difficulty on a thin blanket laid over large unresisting diamonds of wire that left red patterns on my thighs and back. The morning, as I had carefully arranged, was Sunday morning. No stone-breaking on Sundays: I was released early, after a plate of thin porridge, with a hunk of stale bread that I ate as I walked down the street. And I tramped from there to Chelsea where my best friend was to be found...'[70]

After the West Country, Cambridge and Oxford, the sheer size, dirt and ugliness of London reminded him of Cobbett's Great Wen and James Thomson's 'City of Dreadful Night'. It was the Victorian

London of Charles Dickens or George Gissing that struck him as he walked through the dirt and the crowds.

An unmitigated ugliness, it seemed: hideous shops, factories, gin-palaces, in endless succession, with here and there a gas-works, a railway station, or a Victorian Gothic church or chapel to relieve the misery with a change of misery; trams and buses all along the interminable miles, and the pavements crowded with shabby townees in their Sunday best. Size, squalor, lack of purpose, were the dominant impressions on one new to it all. Not one thing interested me the whole way: the dirt was too noticeable; it was all dirt... So depressed was I with the featurelessness of the new that I never noticed the presence of the old, seeing only the great gold and black fascias, the projected one-storey shops, the blackened front gardens, the groaning, creaking trams, the congested cross-roads, the wretched hordes of people...[71]

The two hundred and fifty mile walk over, after a journey which had in fact lasted more than five weeks, he finally arrived in Chelsea. Eileen was waiting for him. There, in the kind of ceremony he loved, she put on again the bracelet and ring he had worn for eighteen months and then sent on by post. They sat in the gallery to see the first suffragette play, *Votes for Women*, which had just opened at the Court, directed by Granville Barker. Squire strongly approved of the message but the title he thought crude. He suggested to Eileen other topical titles: 'Your Food will Cost you More – A Fact in one Act' (Tariff reform); 'It's your Money we Want – A Farce in Many Scenes' by Lord Northcliffe and C. Arthur Pearson, and 'A Closer Union with the Colonies– a Piece of Damned Nonsense.'

With a knapsack on his back and a toothbrush as his only luggage, Squire set off back home. He climbed Putney Hill and caught sight of the aged Algernon Swinburne. The roaring Republican had become a benevolent, almost dwarf-like creature, in an old rusty overcoat, tossing his great bulbous head left and right. Squire felt too embarrassed to make any contact and continued on his way. He covered more than a hundred miles to Salisbury in twenty-eight hours. Finally, back in Plymouth, he wrote up the story of his trip in six articles for the *Chronicle*. The best section, he was sure, was the one on the casual wards. He regretted now that he had not got thrown into gaol to add to the experiences of the down-and-out. He was an investigative journalist before the term existed, but he found that the story of his tramp was not as exciting as he had hoped. Only the casual wards section stood out, but the *Chronicle* published it. At last Walling came up with the first salary Squire had earned. He was paid a guinea a week and he was responsible for a column of notes on the day's events and issues, and many of the newspaper leaders. He was gradually taking on the role of the assistant editor.

Eileen was working ten hours a day as a seamstress in 'Madame Alys's' dressmaking establishment in London for £1 a week. She was looking for any means of escape, either as an art student at the school of reproductive art or a science student at Bedford College – or even as a sanitary or a factories inspector. She kept up Squire's contacts and Cambridge friends, especially Ben Keeling, and regularly saw all the plays at the Court her fiancé would have liked to have seen: Shaw's *John Bull's Other Island*, *The Doctor's Dilemma* and John Galsworthy's *The Silver Box*. In her little spare time, she was beginning to get to know some of the leading Fabians of the day. She was invited to lunch with Beatrice and Sidney Webb and met the Muggeridge family, Mr and Mrs Havelock Ellis and Mrs Jane Wells.

No doubt she was pleased to find that Beatrice Webb shared her dislike of Amber Reeves: 'She is a little liar, she is superlatively vain and she has little or no pity in her nature' – although she conceded that Amber had a fine intelligence and considerable willpower. Eileen's dislike grew more bitter: her letters to Jack were full of vitriol. Amber was, she wrote, a monster of perfidy; purely selfish; a gusher. Jack tried to plead that at least she was funny and was essential to keeping the Newnhamite socialists together, but he had to give up his plan to make the two like each other. He reluctantly came round to

Eileen's view that Amber was jealous of her as a rival for the role of the most attractive Fabian. He began to think that more was at stake: 'I suppose, really speaking, she is absolutely self-centred and wants to be the leading lady in the coming generation of Fabians and is afraid you may be.' It was a grave disappointment to him that Amber, a woman he had admired so much – and a Fabian woman at that – could be so unpleasant. 'Why, oh why, aren't people nice?' he bewailed.

The Whitsun holiday meant for Jack and Eileen a long-awaited fortnight together in Plymouth. Eileen was asked to bring her copy of *Pride and Prejudice* so that the two of them could get down to the task of dramatising it. When the fortnight was over Jack reluctantly took her to the station to go to Barmouth where she was to join the first Fabian summer school. Ben Keeling, generous as usual, had provided the money for Eileen to attend. The weekend was held in two or three houses on the remote and mountainous coast of North Wales near Merioneth. About a hundred Fabians and sympathisers, including many young, unchaperoned women, went to talk politics and economics, attend lectures and enjoy the fresh air. Squire was deeply envious and wanted a daily account of all the meetings and conversations. He urged her to make herself known to G. B. Shaw and his wife who were staying at a mansion nearby. But Eileen did not have the confidence to take part in the group and after the first day asked Jack for the train fare back to Plymouth. As neither of them had any money she had to stick at it for a fortnight.

With his first pay cheques Squire began to tackle his debts. For three months he continued to write for the *Western Daily Mercury* and tried to keep up with socialist friends from London and Cambridge. What was very frustrating was that his convert, Eileen, was now much more in touch with them than he was. He was in virtual isolation, while she saw Ben Keeling regularly. He offered to pay for her to read science at Bedford College. Squire, perhaps sensing Keeling's interest might not be entirely educational, told her she should not consider it.

Rupert Brooke had arrived at King's College in the autumn term of 1906, just after Squire left – 'the handsomest young man in England'

– according to Yeats, and, famously, 'a young Apollo, golden-haired,' according to the poet Frances Cornford. Already a published poet, he was soon to be elected as an Apostle (the elite intellectual society in the university) and lionised as a leader of the young. Squire first saw him in Green Street, Cambridge. Like so many of his contemporaries, male and female, he too was struck: 'His serenity and beauty made such an impression on me as I never received from any other man.' Brooke duly became President of the Cambridge Fabians. They met above a dairy in Bridge Street, sitting on grocery boxes and arguing about how to change the world. Squire met Brooke there 'in a window-seat above a crowd of gabbling people, who smoke and drink beer and coffee and talk about Keir Hardie, the Dolomites and Strauss.'[72] He met Brooke again in 1909, in King's Parade, when he was certain of a Fellowship, 'hatless and sunburnt, his fair hair ruffled, his grey eyes looking very direct and calm, a smile around his parted lips.'[73]

In Plymouth, away from the excitement of Cambridge, Squire's life now turned on politics, organising speakers, debating, attending meetings of Socialists and Fabians in Ruskin Hall or the marketplace. His social life consisted entirely of friends at the SDF. He spent a day talking to Frederick Rogers, first chairman of the Labour Representation Committee, often seen as the father of the Labour Party. He had lunch and then tea at home with him and thought he was a brilliant talker and 'the rippingest old man.' He also hosted H. M. Hyndman, the founder of Britain's first socialist party, the Social Democratic Federation. He was a steward at a huge socialist meeting of 3,000 at the Guildhall addressed by Hyndman, the Marxist Harry Quelch and Will Thorne, one of the first Labour MPs. Keir Hardie had to cancel because of illness, but Ramsay MacDonald did come – Squire thought him a poor substitute. The oratory of the young politician Philip Snowden, who spoke without notes to a huge crowd in Plymouth, inspired him. Each morning he read the national press carefully; he tried to make the socialist presence felt in the London County Council elections when he believed they had been rigged; he spent long hours addressing envelopes for the local elections of the

SDF and the Board of Guardians. He tried without success to convert Doll, Eileen's sister Nora and her brother Clennell to socialism. Every socialist, he told Eileen, should make three converts a year.

Nationally, all was not well with the Fabians. There was a public split between two of its leading figures: Shaw and Wells. Members were balloted; Squire was firmly on Wells's side. Wells represented his dream that the Socialists should all join together. He thought that the ILP, the SDF, the Fabians and some of the supporters of the *Daily News* had to form a unified front, as the Socialists (SPD) had done in Germany. Shaw on the other hand seemed most interested in the class that Squire himself belonged to, and the one he had come to hate most: the middle class. He believed that there were only two real classes: the employer and the employed. 'Damn the middle classes. It's no good mixing up an artificial social status with a real economic one.'

Eileen's letters were almost the only consolations in his exile. Her presence was in them and he read them through over and over again. He kept them in sequence, bound with ribbons, in an oak box under his bed. They were the holy writ of his new creed and had all the intimacy of her imagined presence:

'Shut your eyes
There?
Another?
There
Another?
There.'

He also listened to music, went to the theatre, played rugby and watched football on Saturday afternoons. But it was really a prelude; he knew that his future was not in the world of the provincial newspaper – and Eileen was waiting for him in London.

Chapter 5

Marriage and the *New Age*

'He was in those days already a very individual figure, slight but wiry, with pale complexion, strongly marked eyebrows, myopic eyes, hair worn longish and curling a little at the ends. Flannel trousers and a tweed jacket, of which the pockets were stuffed with old papers and other bulky things were his usual wear. And he was the only man I ever knew who, as an act of personal loyalty, wore a bracelet, though no man was ever less effeminate than he. It was perhaps a slight romantic flamboyance inherited with the trace of Spanish blood in him...'[74]

Squire's chance to begin his life as a London journalist finally came when, at the age of twenty-three he was offered a post to write articles and leaders for the *Sheffield Independent*. He left Plymouth and moved to lodgings in Markham Square next door to Eileen. He was not with that newspaper for long; his interest in politics led him to become a parliamentary reporter for the National Press Agency, where he worked from 1908 to 1912. He had to turn up at 9.30am, write a one-column article and leader and then sit in the gallery of the House of Commons, watching and listening to debates, which stopped at 11pm, or might go on all night, and then write his piece for the next day. It was hard work, made even trickier because the pieces appeared in both Liberal and Conservative papers, and he had to swallow his own prejudices to write impartial summaries of the debates. Nevertheless, it was a thrilling and dramatic time to be in the House of Commons. Squire reported on the key debates about Lloyd George's budgets, Irish Home Rule and the House of Lords veto. 'Did it kill me? No, far from that, but I cannot say I enjoyed it.'

On a grey winter's day at the end of November 1908, Eileen Harriett Anstruther Wilkinson and John Collings Squire were married in the church of St Nicholas at Hintlesham. She wore an exotic travelling dress, a white embroidered *djebbah* (a long tunic in the Moorish style, fashionable among Fabian women) with a mole-coloured velvet hat topped with blue ostrich feathers. In their wedding photographs he too looked exotic, out of place in a Suffolk village: his spectacles and long hair, parted down the centre, gave him the look of an earnest, almost supercilious, student. Eileen walked to the church from the rectory along a lane lined with well-wishers, and under three decorated evergreen arches. The church itself was richly decorated by the Head Gardener of nearby Hintlesham Hall with chrysanthemums and palm leaves. The cross bearer processed in scarlet robes; the choir, in purple gowns beneath their white surplices, sang the popular Victorian wedding hymn 'How Welcome was the Call'. Eileen's father took the service and led the congregation through the final hymn, 'O Perfect Love'.

The whole party went back to the rectory for the reception. The *East Anglian Times* gave a full column to the marriage, including photos of the bride and groom, the church and the rectory, and an extremely long list of all the presents on display along with their donors. Mr and Mrs Squire would never want for silver coffee and tea sets, tablecloths, silver spoons, or pictures. The Rector and his wife gave their daughter a travelling clock, and other gifts included a set of furs, silver buttons, silver egg cups, three toast racks, a brass coal scuttle, a hatpin, gold studs, and a mustard pot. What the young Fabians felt about this display of bourgeois wealth they did not say. The bride and groom spent their wedding night in Guildford and then on Sunday walked across the Hog's Back enjoying the views over the North Downs of Surrey. They visited the museum and gallery dedicated to the Victorian artist G. F. Watts and in the evening they returned to Chelsea and Markham Square. On Monday morning they were back at their desks.

Edwardian London seemed a glamorous new world. 'London was dominated by the bonhomie of Le Roi Edouard VII and the Man about Town, silk-hatted, full moustached, gardenia'd, still decorated Pall Mall...' Fashionable ladies wore extravagant hats, 'either towering like wedding cakes or undulant and plumy like the hat of Gainsborough's Duchess.' It was a world of prosperous town houses where the rich lived with hardly any income tax. There were horse-buses named The Monster, The Royal Blue and The Fulham White and the hansoms were 'speedy Atalantas'. Cars were rare and often broke down. There was real poverty too: 'The ragged and bare-footed urchins of Barnado's advertisements still infested the door steps of the slums.' Abroad there were threats from Ireland; the Russians looked dangerous for a moment but there was confidence that the young Czar would gradually liberalise the country which would become part of Western Europe. Perhaps the Sick Man of Europe would die and China might break up, but the clouds were small on the horizon. 'It was the calm before the storm; and its storms were storms in a teacup of Wedgwood.'[75]

After the stuffiness and respectability of living at home in Plymouth, London weekends came as a revelation. There was a freedom between men and women that Squire had never known before and a frank, even frightening, sense of liberty. He met again some Cambridge friends and contemporaries. Ben Keeling, who had come down with a First in history, was making his name for himself in the ranks of the socialists as an expert on poverty and Lloyd George's new Labour Exchanges: 'I see pictures of dreaming youth preparing for action. I see Frederic Keeling (for some forgotten reason "Ben") making statistics exciting in his rooms in the Walworth Road and his later rooms of Chancery Lane: bearded, flabby-lipped, wild, brown-eyed, much eye-lashed, tumble-haired, a man gone wrong but chivalrously wrong, voluble on blue-books, fierce about sex.'[76] Willy Smith was studying art at the Slade, Clennell Wilkinson was setting up as a journalist and T. E. Hulme was writing for the *New Age* and holding weekly salons for radical young artists and writers in Frith Street.

> It was the evenings and the week-ends that mattered… in all the circles of ardour and enlightenment there were as many women as men. They were not bobbed or shingled, but they seemed so. London in those days, and at that stage of one's life, was liberation. It was possible to talk to young women, who knew all about music and economics, on even the most alarming subjects, without feeling, or at any rate betraying, the slightest embarrassment. We went in throngs to the gallery at Covent Garden, where the knees of the row behind stuck into our backs; to the arena at Queen's Hall (smoking permitted), where Sir Henry Wood perspiringly whacked out "1812" and "Finlandia"; to meetings where Chestertons and Bellocs obstinately and too convincingly countered the Bee-hive Utopias to which we had too readily surrendered. We could be Utopian then, even in a cheap tea-shop… We sat about on the cushioned floors of studios and the bravely brown-papered walls of unfurnished lodgings (the lodgers often very poor), exchanging mature and crystallised views about Shaw and the Webbs, Debussy, Tolstoy, Maeterlinck, Charles Booth, Trusts, Combines, Cartels, the Stage Censorship, and the Czardom. Hardy, Bridges, and Housman were there in the background waiting for us, but we never talked of them. We argued, instead, that the Poor Law must be reformed, that the Liberals should force through Home Rule, that Women's Suffrage should be granted – lest worse befall. We were, obviously, sometimes right; equally obviously, we were often wrong. But we had an eagerness, a directness, a capacity for enterprise and the selection of essentials, peculiar to our age, and generally lacking in old men, who wait for death and merely wish, pending their demise, to keep the old pot boiling in the old way.[77]

However radical his political opinions, Squire's artistic heart beat to a more traditional rhythm. In the concert hall he loved Sibelius's incidental music to *Pelléas et Mélisande* at Covent Garden, but found Maeterlinck's plot and characters absurd. He associated it with 'young women, with mildly Socialist opinions and hair parted Madonna wise… yearningly playing in the candle-lit, brown-papered-walled drawing rooms of Hampstead and Chelsea those wistful mysterious piano pieces about cathedrals under the sea and rain falling on places that never were, full of the sounds of elfin horns, muffled bells and little winds wandering about the whole tone scale'.[78] Its moonlight melancholy was cloying and sounded etiolated, fin de siècle, pretentious. And so, when he went to the Queen's Hall again in 1908 to hear Debussy conduct short pieces including 'La Mer', he knew what to expect. The intensity of the conductor struck him most forcibly. His was the face of pre-Raphaelite agony, black hair contrasting with the pallor of an ivory complexion, deep sunken eyes and hollowed cheeks. The man and his music both bore the marks of 'illness, of incessant labour, of passionate exactitude'. To Squire it was the deathly masque of the 1890s. At Cambridge he had heard and loved Wagner's *Tristan and Isolde*, and joined his fellow undergraduates who rushed to hear the first London performances of *The Ring* at Covent Garden. He hated it: he heard in the music a 'Teutonic premonition of doom'.

What a contrast this music made with the first London production of Elgar's 'First Symphony', at the Queen's Hall in 1909 conducted by its composer rather stiffly in an old-fashioned frock coat. Squire never forgot its 'overwhelming' opening theme and what he called its superbly elongated ending. The composer himself, with his look of a handsome English colonel 'with haughty eyes, aquiline nose and a heavy grey moustache,' had nothing of sickly decadence about him. The audience gave it a rapturous response. This comparison of Debussy and Elgar reflected the polarities of Squire's criticism: a contrast between fin de siècle weariness against Edwardian swagger; the demanding and introverted music of the one and the confidence of the other; music appealing to the educated few, and music which thrilled the concert-goers; sickness against health. Elgar, Squire wrote, was the best English composer since Purcell.

Elgar was, nevertheless, Squire felt, not the greatest composer of his time. That honour fell to Sibelius. In 1906 he had heard Sir Henry Wood conduct *Finlandia* and never forgot the impression that it made on him, its crashing theme suggesting a nation on the march. (He visited the reclusive Sibelius in his Finland home and was at first turned away as he did not see visitors. 'Tell him that it is an Englishman who writes verse,' Squire said – and managed to get inside.) But he also admired the most 'promising composer alive,' a young Schubert according to his tutor at the Royal College of Music, Sir Charles Stanford: Ivor Gurney.[79]

The younger modernist musicians were even less to Squire's taste than Debussy. Just before the war he was pained to hear Béla Bartók play one of his own piano concertos. Squire was at the Queen's Hall when the 'bald and serious' Arnold Schoenberg conducted the first English performance of his own works in 1912. The audience responded with mocking laughter, ironic cheers and farmyard imitations. There was a cacophony of 'little twangings, grunts and groans, poppings of corks and gratings of cart-wheels,'[80] suggesting to Squire the Sydney cricket ground at its most raucous.

Eileen introduced Jack to A. R. Orage, a brilliant and influential figure in the Edwardian literary world. In 1907 he had relaunched the *New Age*, an iconoclastic radical weekly. Its masthead proclaimed it as an 'Independent Socialist Review of Politics, Literature and Art'. George Bernard Shaw gave £500 and regular contributions. The magazine was run on a shoestring – Orage himself nicknamed it 'No Wage'. Arnold Bennett, under the pen name Jacob Tonson, and T. E. Hulme became regular unpaid contributors. Squire began to send freelance work to the magazine and then more regular reviews. In 1909 he launched a series of 'Imaginary Speeches' of the leading parliamentary orators of the day whom he had heard when he worked for the National Press Agency – just as he had done with the speeches in the Cambridge Union. His witty versions of Lord Rosebery, David Lloyd George and A. J. Balfour proved so popular that he soon broadened his scope to include poetry. His literary reputation began as a master of the art of parody.

Soon, with a circulation of 20,000 at its height, the New Age became the leading radical magazine. It was daring, introducing thinkers such as Bergson and Freud to the English public. It reproduced frank nudes from Walter Sickert and discussions of free love. One distinctive feature was Orage's discovery of a much wider readership than magazines had found before – the magazine aimed to reach out to 'Board-school-educated teachers, lower-middle-class office workers and socialist autodidacts.'[81] Its success showed that there indeed was a newly educated public for professional journalism 'on a scale never known before.'[82] This mission was to echo through Squire's whole working life.

Alfred Orage made Squire poetry editor of the New Age to succeed the imagist poet and translator F. S. Flint. Writing for the New Age was not just a professional task: it was membership of a club of bohemians and radical thinkers. Squire was shocked to find himself among a group his sheltered background had not prepared him for. On Monday afternoons Orage met the contributors to Thursday's issue in the basement of the ABC restaurant in Chancery Lane. Discussions often went on into the night at the Café Royal or at his own flat. There were weekly meetings too at the Kardomah Café in Fleet Street and at T. E. Hulme's Tuesday evening salon at 67 Frith Street, the old Venetian Embassy off Soho Square, where 'that more dissolute version of Dr Johnson used to discourse to painters, poets and connoisseurs with a wit, profundity, perversity, variety, amplitude, imagery and irony which, alas for he was a big, lax, man, survives in but a few printed fragments.'[83]

Orage himself and the intellectual young critic John Middleton Murry were regulars, as was the patron saint of young writers and painters, Edward Marsh. Ezra Pound and Rupert Brooke were sometimes to be found there. These were noisy combative evenings with a cosmopolitan group of writers and avant-garde artists such as the sculptors Jacob Epstein, whom Squire was to champion, and the French Henri Gaudier-Brzeska with his Assyrian beard, along with the cubist painter C. R. W. Nevinson. Violence amongst the New Agers was never far from the surface and sometimes the evenings ended in fights. The hot-tempered Hulme carried a solid brass knuckleduster made by Epstein to reinforce his points. Once, Wyndham Lewis became fiercely jealous of Hulme and stormed out of a restaurant declaring he was going to kill him. As Hulme was coming out of Frith Street Lewis grabbed him by the throat. Hulme was much the stronger and bigger man and Lewis ended up hanging by his trousers upside down from the railings of Fitzroy Square.

Through his friendship with Hulme and *New Age* parties Squire met a little-known American poet who was to become one of the dominating influences of the century. 'Ezra Pound... would approach with the step of a dancer, making passes with a cane at an imaginary opponent. He wore trousers made of green billiard cloth, a pink coat, a blue shirt, a tie hand-painted by a Japanese friend, an immense sombrero, a flaming beard cut to a point, and a single, large blue earring.'[84] With his thick red hair, piercing green eyes, pointed beard, black cape and Stetson, Pound was a 'stunty kind of show' in person. Squire presented a very different face to the world. A sketch of him appeared in the *New Age* in April 1912, drawn by Tom Tit, the magazine's talented Polish cartoonist. It shows a serious bespectacled young man, ill-shaven, bareheaded and soft-collared. He wears the kind of 'Jaegerish' shapeless woollen jacket popularised by Bernard Shaw. His pockets are bulging with papers. Apart from the woollen jacket he has two distinctive features: he carries a walking stick upside down and he has a pipe in his mouth, also upside down. It is a picture of a young Fabian crossed with an absent-minded, other-worldly poet.

More sedate friendships with an older generation followed. Squire got to know the leading novelist and critic Arnold Bennett and the Irish journalist and essayist Robert Lynd, who both also wrote for the *New Age*. They acted as his sponsors for the National Liberal Club, the first of the many London clubs he was to join. Encouraged by Orage, he began to fulfil his ambition to print unpublished young poets. Many of the ideas that were to come to fruition in the *London Mercury* date from his time at the *New Age*.[85] One important lesson he learned was how quickly an editor could transform the fortunes of a magazine. In fewer than six years Orage had sent the sales of the *New Age* leaping upward and made many of its contributors' careers by what Squire called, 'the sustained brilliance of his own editorial writing'.

Squire was gaining a reputation as an advocate for the Female Vote. On Sunday 21 June 1908 the WSPU (Women's Social and Political Union) organised what was said to be the biggest political rally and demonstration ever held, which came to be known as 'Women's Sunday'. Seven processions marched through London to Hyde Park, banners streaming in the sunlight, brass bands playing, to hear speeches from H. G. Wells, G. B. Shaw and Emmeline Pankhurst. Squire marched side by side with a Liberal friend, Iolo Williams, in a mile-long crowd of nearly half a million supporters. Afterwards he began touring the country making speeches in village halls and schools to anyone prepared to listen. At least, he mused, they could not give him the usual barracking cry of 'Go home and mind the baby'.

Support for the suffragettes led him to spend the night of the 1911 census locked in a hall on the offices of the WSPU's Kingsway site, joining the militant women refusing to be counted in a census if they were refused a vote. The rafters were draped with the purple, green and white colours of the movement and a jolly party inside was held. Shortly afterwards Eileen was appointed to the teaching staff of the Working Ladies' Guild, a Victorian foundation whose aim was to 'Assist Unmarried or Widowed Gentlewomen in Need of Employment, or in Temporary Difficulty', where she looked for commissions for the gentlewomen and was paid wages that according to her husband were beyond the dreams of avarice – thirty shillings a week.

Squire's first volume of poetry, *Poems and Baudelaire Flowers*, was published in 1909 at his own expense by the New Age Press, and dedicated to Eileen. The first section was about his love affair with Eileen and contains some of the most confessional poetry he ever wrote. The second was made up with translations from Baudelaire. The two halves are loosely linked by themes of love and an overriding horror of death. Translation gave the cautious poet freedom to write about sex. '*Une Nuit que j'étais pres d'une Affreuse Juive*' (title untranslated) begins 'A hideous Jewess lay with me for hire / One night: two corpses side by side we seemed / And stretched by that polluted thing I dreamed / Of the sad beauty of my vain desire.' '*La Chevelure*' is a description of a siren and the 'delicious drunkenness' she arouses with her bare shoulders, billowing curls and the exotic scent of cocoa-oil and musk and tar. Another poem has the fantasy of frolicking over the body of giant woman – an erotic Brobdingnag

The poems to Eileen are more restrained, but still franker than he allowed himself to be later. The imagery often recalls the romantic mood of his love letters. Often the scene is set at dusk or at dawn. Moonlight casts its beams on the two lovers; night is their element. Squire wrestles with the conflicts of idealised love and desire. The opening poem, 'The Surviving Sense', begins with the couple locked in an embrace and talks of their 'sated lust' before asking how sexual love can be related to something more spiritual. Eileen is very much a flesh-and-blood presence in these poems: in the anatomical 'Pastoral', Squire sounds more like a dentist than a lover as he describes their kiss:

Twixt the even white lines of your teeth,
To your inner mouth and your throat
Where like water-anemones
Pink mounds of tendrils float
In silken salivan seas.[86]

And the poem 'Consummation' is just what it says it is, and opens;

On this cheek now and on this
Soft cheek that burns; now a mouth kiss.

We are near to swoon as lips meet lips
In ecstasy of deep eclipse of breath...
Let us inweave us in a mesh
Of twined limbs, together pressed...[87]

Like Rupert Brooke, Squire was trying to find a more honest language to treat sexuality and love in a franker way than Victorian poetry had allowed. 'This book will be strong meat to many persons,' warned F. S. Flint the poetry critic of the *New Age*.[88]

Along with the theme of love, there is a persistent fascination with, and fear of, death. The poems are littered with corpses, scaffolds and entrails. Baudelaire's shadow hangs over the Gothic horror 'To the Bodies of the Dead'. The poet asks the dead if there is any awareness of a past life:

Ay, nay! Though some of you in dank moist earth were laid,
Naught but a few thin boards for screens, which soon decayed;
Creeping and soft and quiet
They burrow rotting skin and flesh,
The worms hold silent riot
Eagerly writhing through, and lose
Themselves amid the coiling bowels' mesh
Pricking, and forth the sweet juices ooze
The which they suck...[89]

Not surprisingly, *Poems and Baudelaire Flowers* met with mixed reviews. Many of the criticisms focused on the carnality and 'the worship of the body'. *The Times* thought it 'Too fond of the morbid and macabre, and sometimes of the sensual.' The *Literary World* found it 'very original and striking, but unnecessarily unpleasant.'[90] The focus was on the 'daring frankness and intensity of the poems which would cause squint-eyed prudency to shrivel up.' F. S. Flint agreed that the 'fleshly love songs' would be 'strong meat to many persons.' He called Squire 'a poet of courage, power and virility' with a distinctive 'modern tone'. *Poems and Baudelaire Flowers*, however, was not a work Squire chose to remember. Shortly after its publication he bought up the remaining stock of 200 from the booksellers and destroyed them. He called it 'a bad little book of verse which I rightly suppressed because of its falsity, which I did not perceive until it was printed'.[91]

Squire turned from poetry to history. He had wanted to write on Charles II, about whom he had written a paper for the Historical Society at St John's – an odd subject perhaps for a young socialist – but he had enjoyed shocking his prim audience (although not Eileen) with tales of rakish behaviour at court. The publishers Methuen talked him out of it and suggested the much more respectable hero of Dutch independence, William the Silent. He started researching a biography which reflected admiration for William, and dislike of Philip of Spain and Catholicism. He worked in the British Museum on calendars, state papers and pamphlets. Clearly, he regretted that the times did not allow William to be a decent socialist, but he was the next best thing, a good Liberal. Squire's only historical work sold out, but failed in the circulating libraries, according to its author, because the ladies who borrowed from them were put off by the word 'silent'.

In 1911 Jack and Eileen decided to move away from shabby Markham Square to a six-roomed house not far away at 100 Chelsea Gardens. Eileen soon became pregnant. Perhaps this led Jack on his birthday to write down his thoughts in his unfinished 'Letters to Posterity'.[92] He began with the dream of his heart, a rural England scattered with small clean farms. This was a stark contrast to 'this England which today seems part of my body – disfigured by unsightly and disordered buildings'. This urban growth was perverted and monstrous. London was under a curse – 'the unacknowledged assumption that Midas was the happiest of men.' He drew a picture of the city as seen from the attic of his new home. The smoke and smog clear to give him a view over the trees to the Thames. Horses trot on the road below him; he hears women quarrelling and a boy goes by whistling; dust whirls and straw flies. The lonely writer in the garret looks beyond his perch to see the 'brickscape' which stretches north and east for miles and miles. He sees with horror the growing metropolis. England is becoming a 'Nation of troglodytes in a catacomb of bricks and mortar.' It was not just the ugliness and the pall of smoke: living conditions for the workers were squalid and the children pallid and weak. There were predictions, he wrote, that in three generations the London stock would become extinct.

London's population, Squire noted, was already larger than that of Scotland or Ireland. Its cancerous growth had spread to other great cities: Liverpool, Manchester, Hull and Birmingham. Towns were becoming linked by the development of metalled roads and a 'generous peppering' of villas and workmen's huts. No longer was England a land of town and country; it was becoming a land of huge towns, 'beads of coal on threads of slime', surrounded by suburbs. What kind of England would he leave to his children? Ever-growing towns or a return to the land? Squire decided that only drastic solutions were possible. A true patriot, he thought, would want a decline in population; a shrinking manufacturing industry; a central government restricting any further building of cotton mills or mines and the triumph of commercial rivals such as Russia or Argentina. The vision was that of William Morris; the practical solutions Squire proposed were his own. There was already town planning – now the time had come, he wrote, for Kingdom planning.

After they had moved house, Eileen and he decided to take a holiday to Holland to research his Dutch history and to enjoy the honeymoon that they had never had. They walked with knapsacks and travelled by canal boat, lowering the funnel to pass under bridges.[93] They visited churches and art galleries, admiring Vermeers and the 'marvellous' Hals groups at Haarlem. The trip and a visit to the beach provided the inspiration for a short story, 'A Summer's Day'. A newly married couple are enjoying their honeymoon spending a lazy afternoon lying gazing at the distant sea and the endless sands; the mood is one of complete erotic happiness on a beautiful beach. Away from holidaymakers and children, they inhabit their own world of dreamy content. 'They lie face downwards in the long grass of the sand dunes. To the hazy horizon the waters stretched away as smooth as satin but a few yards from shore long low ripples came into being to file placidly and evenly inwards and break with sleepy splash...' The lovers are in their own world. They cannot conceive of their ever parting and pledge their undying love for each other. 'I am sure no-one ever dies unless he wants,' says the young woman.

Then they see a man wading in the sea pulling towards him with his umbrella something white in a sheet. People begin to huddle by the shoreline. The black knot of the group by the seaside grows larger; ambulance men are called and it is revealed that there has been a drowning. Without an apparent change of mood the couple leave the beach and enjoy cutting through the sand dunes on the way back to their hotel. They are curiously remote from the drowning; it as if they are looking at a scene from a film, seemingly amused by the hustle and bustle. The story ends with Squire's spare comment:

> The sun sank, and quietly night came over. All the voices had drifted away, and the stars shone on the pale sands and the faintly washing margin of the sea. The two could have lingered all night with such beauty but they were hungry. They began walking back to the town. When they started they talked a little of what they had seen, and joked warmly about the optimism of the crowd but the air was fresh and the stars bright, and it was rather fun trying to take shortcuts amidst the sand hills, and they were feeling very happy and immortal. So very soon they forgot all about it; for use and good fortune will be served.[94]

What could have been a conventional romance becomes a version of what Squire called 'antinomies'; love and youth set against the raw fact of death.

Squire's sketches and parodies were republished in *Imaginary Speeches* (1912), which he dedicated to Orage who had first published many of them. The series offered a critical panorama of the verse of his day. 'The Exquisite Sonnet' was a parody of the excesses of late romantic verse and 'My-Oath-if-you only-knew-what-a-life-I've-led-Wheeze' a parody of the lurid confessional. For the rest Squire explicitly denied that he had a specific poet rather than a poetic school in mind, but the names were often obvious: 'The Hell-For-Leather Ballad' (Newbolt), 'The Hands-across-the-Sea Wish-wash (Kipling), 'The Poetry ought-to-be-freed-from all-Shackles Stunt' (Walt Whitman), 'The Other-Worldly-Spirit-of-Celticism-don't-you-know Lyric' (Yeats et al.), and what he called 'The Fine-Contempt-for-Civilisation-and-Geography-very-Fraternal-with-the-Elements-Plein-Air-Piece' (Walt Whitman et al.) *The Times* wrote that 'In a particular kind of parody Mr Squire is A MASTER, not that which guys the original and distorts it for fun, but the far more deadly parody which simply and suavely gives you something exactly like it but with the slightest touch of exaggeration – as one who should say "See what mannerism it all is and how easily turned out."'[95] The *Daily News* thought that Squire had a gift for parody beyond any other new writer and made it their 'Book of the Day'. He was proud enough of the reviews to paste snippets from them in his scrapbook: Mr S may be heartily congratulated… All are perfect… should be in the library of every politician with a sense of humour… an unqualified success.'[96]

Never slow to follow up a winner, in *Steps to Parnassus* (1913), Squire added parodies of contemporary theatre. The repertory drama section offered a mocking overview of the stage, which he increasingly felt was arid. He started with examples of 'The Higher Drama: Pelissier and Mariane' (Maeterlinck); 'Epigrammatic Comedy' (Wilde); 'Euripides up to Date' (Gilbert Murray); 'The Strife of the Blatherskites' (John Galsworthy); 'The Caged Eaglet' (Ibsen, a domesticated version of *The Wild Duck*); and 'The School of Rebellion and Stage Directions' (Shaw). Squire's gift for mimicry of the style and tone of his victims was combined with broad humour and farce.

In the next section of *Imaginary Speeches* Squire gave ironic tips about 'tricks of the trade' for writers, such as the art of borrowing. The plagiarisms of the young, though frequent, were not wholehearted enough. 'Be thorough' was his advice. If critics were to object that the narrative was tangled and some of the lines did not seem to connect with each other, then that was all to the good, argued Squire: 'I tell my brother-poets, with the most whole-hearted concern for their welfare, that obscurity and apparent discontinuity of parts will be all to their advantage. For if the critics cannot understand your argument or detect the junction of your images they will call you a symbolist. And that will be nice for you.'[97] The attack on obscurity was to become a major preoccupation of his criticism.

There was little to be said for Edwardian poetry, 'the lowest point in the long decline of English poetry,' as one critic has called it.[98] The Poet Laureate was Alfred Austin, and Alfred Noyes, Stephen Phillips, and Henry Newbolt presided over a poetic desert. Harold Monro, founder and owner of the Poetry Bookshop, called it a barren decade and 'an age of clipped wings and misty intelligences.'[99] Arnold Bennett wrote, 'There is a word… which rouses terror in the heart of the vast educated majority of the English-speaking race. The most valiant will flee at the merest utterance of that word… the most rash will not dare affront it. I myself have seen it enter buildings that had been full. I know that it will scatter a crowd more quickly than a hosepipe, hornets or the rumour of a plague. Even to murmur it is to incur solitude, probably disdain and possible starvation as historical examples show: that word is 'poetry'.[100] Squire summed up: 'Cambridge wrote it. Oxford edited it. And no-one read it.'

Squire felt that he had been living through a period of decadence. The Victorians had to create a fairyland to escape from an age that produced ugliness of all kinds: ugly buildings; ugly towns; ugly prose. They retreated to various versions of Tennyson's Palace of Art, just as the French symbolist poets had done. Squire often quoted Théophile Gautier's remark in the middle of the Franco-Prussian war, '*Moi, j'ai fait émaux et camées.*' 'How charming a perversion! How beautifully stated a blasphemy' he commented.[101] What followed Tennyson, Thomas Carlyle and William Morris was the decadence of the nineties. The work of Arthur Symons, *The Yellow Book* and the drawings of Aubrey Beardsley breathed a world of unhealthy sexual obsession that ended in disaster: 'Oscar Wilde (who went to prison), Aubrey Beardsley (who died young and repentant), Ernest Dowson (who was sick of an old passion and a good many other things), Hubert Crackanthorpe (who killed himself), late nights, late cafes, late hansom-cabs, feather boas, the swish of silk, pale faces, hollow eyes, absinthe and sins either sad or splendid or both.'[102] Squire's parody of Dowson caught that mood of Edwardian self-indulgence and weariness that he hated:

Ah me, ah me, the quiet end of evening fades
Nunc it per iter tenebricosum, to the shades
Where all the roses, all the roses, roses go,
Had it been otherwise, ah yea, I know I know.[103]

His attitude was never clearer than in his account of his friend, the publisher of *The Yellow Book*, 'The Nineties and John Lane'. The dominating mood then had been to escape to:

Anywhere, anywhere, out of a world of factories and limited liability companies. All artists and sensitives must abominate this civilisation, in which the towns spread, work is robbed of its interest and the corporation covers the whole country with its inhuman and loveless products… Temperamentally they were able to run away, turn their backs, and talk of sin, Cleopatra or Giotto; philosophically they saw no reason why they should do anything else.[104]

This was of course a gross simplification. Squire pointed out that the nineties was also the age of Conrad, Hardy, Henry James, R. L. Stevenson – and so on – but the mood of despair had to be resisted:

It is absurd to be driven by reaction into a futile whimpering; the sins of industrialism do not justify a recourse to the sins which shock the industrialists; man has to do the best with the circumstances in which he finds himself… it is better to die trying than to die bleating about them… any art is barren which is content to ignore the mass of humanity. Faced with a society like ours a man may refuse, or he may accept or may do his best to change what he dislikes, enormous though the task may be… but the greatest work has always been done by those who have accepted contemporary conditions and rejected contemporary conclusions.

But now in the Georgian Age Squire felt everything was about to change. Rupert Brooke published his *Poems* in 1911 and Squire reviewed it admiringly in the *New Age*. It was nothing less than the end of Victorian wooliness and Edwardian decadence and the beginning of something new. He began to read many other promising young poets – but the problem was that their voices could not be heard. The dismal reaction to Brooke's first book of poetry was a case in point. It was hard to get new work published, and, even if published, it was often ignored or treated harshly by the critics. Squire co-founded the Howard Latimer Publishing Company in 1912 with a Cambridge friend Howard Hannay with precisely this aim – to give young writers a start. One of them was Squire himself: his collection of parodies *Steps to Parnassus* and his second collection of poetry *The Three Hills* were both published in 1913.

It was as a publisher that Rupert Brooke tried to enlist Squire's help when they met for dinner in London. Squire was just as taken with Brooke as he had been on visits to Cambridge: 'He enters a crowded room in Lincoln's Inn, fair-haired, sunburnt, serene, straight-eyed, his collar is soft-blue, his suit fits loosely and perfectly; everybody is hushed by his appearance. I drink with him in a window of the National Liberal Club…' In the fading light they looked over the Thames and the Embankment and Brooke talked amusingly about the new 'sky-signs'.[105] He always had a magnetic attraction for Squire, appearing mysteriously as if carried on a magic carpet with 'a mild radiance' that dazzled him and many of those who met him. The meeting, however, came to nothing and the Howard Latimer Company collapsed after a year without publishing anything by Brooke.

One solution to the problem of publishing new writers came from a surprising source. Edward Marsh was Private Secretary to the First Lord of the Admiralty, Winston Churchill. A lifelong bachelor, he, like Squire, was under the spell of Rupert Brooke. He had inherited funds from the government paid to the descendants of the murdered prime minister Spencer Perceval and put together a fine collection of Old English Masters. Suddenly it dawned on him that his money would be better spent buying and sponsoring young artists. Soon his collection of paintings by Roger Fry, Mark Gertler, Modigliani, the Nash brothers, Walter Sickert and others extended all over his wall space on both sides of the bathroom door. A similar revelation came to him when he was introduced to contemporary poetry by the poet and suffragist Alice Meynell. He began to fund young writers such as D. H. Lawrence, Walter de la Mare, Middleton Murry and Edward Shanks when they hit hard times, as they nearly always did. Edmund Blunden called him 'our Maecenas'.

Marsh lived at No. 5 Raymond Buildings, Gray's Inn. Visitors climbed the stone spiral staircase to the top flat. There he held literary breakfasts; his devoted housekeeper Mrs Algy served up kidneys and bacon and China tea. Marsh, monocled, immaculately dressed, with flyaway eyebrows, talked in a squeaky falsetto and presided over his guests who tended to be young, good-looking upper-class men such as Rupert Brooke and Ivor Novello. He was, however, no snob: the working-class Isaac Rosenberg and Mark Gertler were two of his protégés.[106] During his breakfasts, new poems were read and then Marsh would set off briskly for work at the Admiralty.

In 1911 the great success of John Masefield's long (1700 lines) rollicking narrative poem *The Everlasting Mercy* came as an enormous surprise. It was a shocking tale for a genteel audience; set in pubs and back streets, full of swearing and coarse language. A bawdy, boozy poacher was the hero and there was a cast of prostitutes and down-and-outs. The story ended with Kane's conversion to Christianity. Masefield's poem combined everything Squire hated: he felt it was crudely expressed, overlong, cheaply sentimental and preaching a naive morality tale in which vice was finally redeemed by religion. The so-called 'realism' of the poem, he thought, amounted to no more than a collection of swear words. In 'The Merciful Widow' Squire was ready with mockery. He pictured the widow's daughter Hedda Lucrezia Esther Waters (a dig at the novelist George Moore's popular heroine and Ibsen's Hedda Gabler) with the modernists' bibles by her bedside:

And when she went to bed at night
She prayed by yellow candle-light:
'Six angels for my bed,
Three at foot and three at head,
Beardsley, Strauss, Augustus John,
Bless the bed that I lie on.
Nietzsche, Maeterlinck, Matisse,
Fold my sleep in heavenly peace.'[107]

Squire's version ended with an ironic twist: 'There is a poet up in London / Who, if we stray, / Will be quite undone. / Every crime that we commit / He makes a poem out of it.'[108] Kane had only turned to murder and rape so that he could keep a London writer comfortably in work: John Masefield. But whatever Squire thought of the poem it 'first made new poetry a rage'.[109]

On 9 September 1912 Rupert Brooke was sitting on a bed in Marsh's spare room chatting about English poetry.[110] They agreed that Masefield had shown that there was now an audience eager to read new poetry. The problem was that very few people realised that after the wasteland of Edwardian verse there was now a kind of poetic renaissance. Marsh wrote that there was a general feeling among the younger poets that 'modern English poetry was very good but sadly neglected by readers.'

Brooke thought up a 'brilliant scheme', a spoof anthology of six poets and six poetesses, masquerading under various *noms de plume*, all in fact to be written by him, in a selection of different modern or experimental styles. Marsh took up his friend's idea and refashioned it. The book would not be experimental (Marsh's pet hate) and it would not just feature Brooke's own work. It would be much better, he thought, to compile an anthology that would give a platform to talented young poets. His aim was very simple: 'To draw the attention of the general reader to the best new poetry.' An anthology, they thought, was just the right vehicle for an age whose strength was not in one or two towering figures but in the critical mass of poets writing exciting poetry.

The finances were to be arranged on a new and generous basis. Marsh wanted no money for his work: all profits were to be divided half and half between Monro's Poetry Bookshop and the poets themselves. With the recent coronation in mind, he suggested the title 'Georgian' to mark the end of the Edwardian poetic drought and to celebrate a new reign. Brooke thought the title too staid for 'for a volume designed as the herald of a revolutionary dawn' – many of the Georgians were seen in 1912 as 'dangerous literary revolutionaries'[111] – but Marsh had his way. He bequeathed his 'proud ambiguous adjective – *Georgian*'[112] to the world. So the word was launched in literary criticism on a twisting course as a description of an era, a type of poetry, a cast of mind – or simply as a term of abuse.[113]

Marsh's 'Prefatory Note' ringingly announced this new era: 'This volume is issued in the belief that English poetry is once again putting on a new strength and beauty... we are at the beginning of another 'Georgian Period' which may rank in due time with the several great poetic ages of the past.'[114] He would include only work published in the last two years. Brooke and he discussed the plan till well after midnight. 'In a fever of excitement, they decided to telephone Harold Monro first thing in the morning.'[115]

From then on events moved amazingly quickly. Marsh telephoned Monro inviting him to lunch at the rechristened 'Georgian Restaurant' at Harrods. He was signed up as the publisher. As editor of the *Poetry Review* and founder of the Poetry Bookshop he was to be a key figure. Marsh promised to stand guarantor for any losses the book might make and signed up for 200 copies to send to his friends. He gathered together his group of favoured poets for lunch at Gray's Inn and persuaded the most widely known of them at the time, John Masefield, to contribute. Ezra Pound was invited too – but nothing came of it. A. E. Housman replied that only a duchess or a relative could get poetry out of him – and as Marsh was neither he could not send him anything. Seventeen poets did accept, however, including D. H. Lawrence, Walter de la Mare, Rupert Brooke, W. H. Davies and G. K. Chesterton. Using all his influence and contacts, Marsh managed to get his anthology on sale to catch the Christmas rush. It could not have damaged the book's prospects that rumour had it that the prime minister's car was waiting outside Bumpus bookshop in Oxford Street on the morning of publication. By 20 December 1912 Marsh could not lay his hands on a single copy to send to Edmund Gosse. By Christmas the following year *Georgian Poetry* had sold over 9,000 copies.

In May 1913 Squire wrote enthusiastically about *Georgian Poetry* in the *New Statesman*. He noted that in four or five months it was already in its fourth printing. More good verse was now being produced and bought than at any time for many years. There was a 'great atmosphere of vigour' about the writing, seen, at its best, in de la Mare's 'The Listeners' and Rupert Brooke's 'Dining-room Tea'. They were original, direct works. There were weaknesses and omissions – and he hated the description of the grease, slime and spittle of sea-sickness in the notorious 'A Channel Passage' – but in short, he concluded, 'it is the best collection of the kind that has been or could have been published for decades.' For D. H. Lawrence *Georgian Poetry* was 'like a big breath taken when we are waking up after a night of oppressive dreams.' In Middleton Murry's *Rhythm*, he proclaimed: 'I worship Christ, I worship Jehovah, I worship Pan, I worship Aphrodite. [...] I want them all, all the gods. They are all God. But I must serve in real love. If I take my whole, passionate, spiritual and physical love to the woman who in return loves me, that is how I serve God. And my hymn and my game of joy is my work. All of which I read in the Anthology of Georgian Poetry.'[116] Even the conservative

Henry Newbolt thought it 'a new breath of poetic emotion' which would 'astonish' its readers.[117]

According to the young novelist Rose Macaulay, there was 'a kind of poetry-intoxication going on.'[118] It was an intoxication which Marsh's anthology both helped to create and tapped into. Harold Monro's Poetry Bookshop in Devonshire Street was launched in 1912 and thrived on profits from the sale of the five editions of *Georgian Poetry* for the next ten years.

Chapter 6

New Statesman

With all the contacts that Squire made through the *New Age* the literary world was opening up for him. His opportunity came when the *New Statesman* was launched in April 1913 by Beatrice and Sidney Webb with the financial and moral support of George Bernard Shaw.[119] Beatrice Webb thought Squire a most attractive young man, 'a picturesque figure with his warm Italian colouring, his slight well-knit and active form, his low but broad forehead set in masses of curly dark hair.'[120] Politically, he was 'a good collectivist' because he loathed money-making and instinctively always supported the underdog. But, crucially, he was not interested in 'political democracy or in administrative science', as Ben Keeling was. She thought that the two men represented the split among the Fabians between the artistic and idealistic wing, inspired by John Ruskin and William Morris, and intellectuals such as Keeling and the Webbs themselves who were more interested in economics and empirical analysis based on statistics. Blind to poetry herself, she nevertheless recognised it as Squire's strength and could not help admiring the 'melancholy mysticism of his philosophy, the rare beauty of some of his word pictures of nature.'[121]

She saw the contradictions of Squire's character. Whilst his Fabian politics looked to the future, he was also deeply emotionally committed to the past. 'He hates the destruction of anything which has charm or fine tradition. He is in fact a conservative of all that is distinguished because it is old, old faiths, old customs, old universities, old houses, and, last but not least, old books.'[122] She added that he pretended to be a bohemian, imbibing alcohol and tobacco to cover up the fastidious nature which would not allow him to enter a butcher's shop and had made him (for a time) a vegetarian. He was, she thought, in fact not bohemian at all but bourgeois, with a devotion to wife and family, loyal to all his friends and very hard-working: in short, a Victorian conservative with radical leanings.

The editor, the autocratic Clifford Sharp, was a 'massive man, red in the face, handsome, a glaring editorial hunk, full of drink.' Squire became his literary editor, responsible for the back half of the magazine. Both of them had learned their craft from Orage at the *New Age*. In the fissiparous world of socialist politics this was not just a change of job: it was also a rejection of the guild socialism of the *New Age* and a move towards the more international politics of Sidney and Beatrice Webb. In his first editorial on 12 April 1913 Sharp wrote that the *New Statesman* was a magazine that did not have a programme, but did have a definite point of view and an ideal to strive for. This was a growing sense of a corporate life and heralded a world movement towards collectivism which Sharp welcomed in his first editorial. The approach was not partisan or narrowly party political and would inspect and examine ideas 'in the same spirit in which the chemist or the biologist examines his test-tubes and his specimen'.

The experts of the time foretold disaster. In order to survive, the weekly needed to sell 5,000 copies. Shaw's name, it was estimated, would bring in between 500 and 1,000, the Webbs' between 300 and 500. Squire's followers were thought to be no more than 100. It was a risky proposition but at last it gave him a regular salary of £300 a year and meant that he did not need to depend on daily journalism. He now had the income to support a family.

The first half of the *New Statesman* was devoted to political analysis and comment. The Webbs, for example, wrote a densely argued twenty-part series on 'What is Socialism?', and the editor analysed the contemporary political scene in detail. Ben Keeling wrote analytic 'Blue Book Reviews' of sixteen pages a month which treated government publications as books. Sharp thought him 'the most industrious man I have ever met'. Squire called his columns 'Books in General' and 'Miscellany' and wrote serious literary reviews in a style that was engagingly witty and gossipy under a name that puzzled his readers: 'Solomon Eagle'. In response to their enquiries he explained, 'Solomon Eagle is not my legally registered name. But, strange though it may seem, there was once a person with the name. During the Great Plague of London (the temporary, not the permanent one) he perambulated the streets naked with a pan of burning coals on his head, crying "Repent, Repent." What better attitude could a sane man adopt? What became of him I forget. I think he died.'[123] His column too would be a kind of satirical fire which would burn off the abuses of the powerful and pretentious.

In one of his first articles, his 'Prologue, an Unwritten Letter to the Future,'[124] Squire imagined a remote descendent five hundred years on reading his words. In all his writing, including his autobiographical works, this was the only self-portrait he drew. He described himself as 'of middle age and condition, a man neither strong of temper nor, I think, violent or partial of judgement, a man with a certain deep-seated optimism, at which he can smile even while he clings to it, and with a preference for the joyous as against the gloomy and for the meditative as against the polemic.' He ended his 'Prologue' with a description of himself looking down from the window of his eyrie, a seer with only a pen to convey his message to the world: 'As I sit here at my window looking over tree-tops and the Thames which contrives to sparkle in spite of its burden of mud, I feel intensely and insistently alive. The blanket of smoke which usually folds over this capital city has blown off – temporarily. High above the trees small white clouds hurry from west to east across a clean blue spring sky. Horses trot along the road below me. A boy whistles as he passes…'

Squire had first made his name as a wit and humourist in the *New Age*. Now another series of parodies and shafts of humour added lightness to the weighty seriousness of the *New Statesman*. He published his first parody of Hilaire Belloc anonymously:

At Martinmas, when I was born,
Hey diddle, Ho diddle, Do,
There came a cow with a crumpled horn,
Hey diddle, Ho diddle, Do,
She stood agape and said, 'My dear,
You're a very fine child for this time of year,
And I think you'll have a taste in beer,'
Hey diddle, Ho diddle, Do, do, do, do,
Hey diddle, Ho diddle, Do.[125]

He admired the simplicity and directness of the Welsh poet W. H. Davies: 'He moves others because he has first been moved himself.'[126] His parody was an affectionate tribute. Virginia Woolf laughed at Squire's kindergarten version of the nature poet:

I saw some sheep upon some grass,
The sheep were fat, the grass was green,
The sheep were white as clouds that pass,
And greener grass was never seen;
I thought 'Oh, how my bliss is deep
With such green grass and such fat sheep!'

And as I watch bees in a hive,
Or gentle cows that rub 'gainst trees,
I do not envy men who live,
No fields, no books upon their knees.
I'd rather lie beneath small stars
Than with rough men who drink in bars.[127]

Pointing out its subtlety, Woolf noted there was 'an air of artless innocence only a little in excess' of Davies's own simplicity. She also admired the way that Squire caught the exact notes of the rollicking Victorian ballad style of Henry Newbolt:

It was eight bells in the forenoon, and hammocks running sleek
(*It's a fair sea running to the West*)
When the little Commodore came a-sailing up the Creek
(*Heave Ho! I think you'll know the rest.*)
Thunder in the halyards and horses leaping high,
Blake and Drake and Nelson are listenin' where they lie,
Four and twenty blackbirds a-baking in a pie,
And the *Pegasus* came waltzing from the West.[128]

Reviewing Squire's parodies in the *Times Literary Supplement*,[129] she suggested that the art of the parodist was to write something that was amusing in itself, but also recreated the world of the writer. First it made you laugh, then it made you think. She praised Squire for making a model poem, inhabiting it, and then by a few deft touches moving it into the sphere of the comic or absurd. His parodies were better literary criticism than many a dull academic analysis.

The elder statesman of English Letters, Edmund Gosse, was another admirer. The 'wicked sarcasm' of 'Numerous Celts' was one of the happiest pieces of mock imitation ever published,' he wrote.[130] It began lyrically and beautifully before descending into farce: only the title and the repetition of 'grey' warn that the poem is not to be taken at face value:

There's a grey wind wails on the clover
And grey hills and mist around the hills,
And a far voice sighing a song that is over
And my grey heart that a strange longing fills…
For I would be in Kerry now where quiet is the grass,
And the birds are crying in the low light,
And over the stone hedges the shadows pass,
And a fiddle weeps at the shadow of the night.

With Pat Doogan
Father Murphy
Brown maidens
King Cuchullain
The Kine
The Sheep
Some old women
Some old men
And Uncle White Sea-gull and all.[131]

For ten weeks the series continued with versions of John Masefield's back-street realism, G. K. Chesterton's ballads and 'The People who write in Secret what they Allege to be Folk Songs'. It ended with satiric versions of the writing of the two men most closely associated with the *New Statesman* – G. B. Shaw and H. G. Wells. Uncomfortably close to the truth, the latter was a spoof autobiography of 'Mr Bilgewater' who finds himself an exile after being ambushed by a bevy of his past mistresses, Astarte, Mary and Cecilia. His political career ends in scandal as he packs for the boat train… (Squire's account was scarcely an exaggeration. Amber Reeves's father was in fact waiting for the seducer of his daughter in the Savile Club, loaded pistol in hand.)

Squire, a lover of bad verse and absurdity, had a connoisseur's nose for sniffing specimens out. He started a competition in the *New Statesman*, inviting his readers to send him examples – and they poured in. The 'Lament of a Sick Gipsy Woman' was a favourite:

There we leave her
There we leave her,
From where her swarthy kinsmen roam
In the Scarlet Fever
Scarlet Fever
Scarlet Fever convalescent home.

As was:

Farewell, farewell, bonny St Ives,
May I live to see you again.
Your air preserves people's lives,
And you have so little rain.

The best single line Squire received was, he said, from the American poet James Whitcomb Riley: 'The beetle booms adown the glooms and bumps among the clumps...' He regularly added his favourite misprints to his column and was pleased, for example, to find a cutting about Mrs de Morgan Jones of Indianapolis lecturing on 'William Butler Meats and the Garlic Revival'. He noted that a critic writing on *A Midsummer Night's Dream* repeatedly referred to the character Hernia 'in a fine careless rupture'. He corrected the printer's 'Edmund Goose', but was reluctant to alter 'Hotairio Bottomley' as it summed up perfectly the editor of *John Bull's* jingoistic oratory.

To find material for his weekly column Squire used his contacts to the full; he published pieces sent to him by Rupert Brooke and Robert Graves, for which they were paid a guinea each. Edward Marsh passed on poems he did not need or felt were too daring for *Georgian Poetry*. His presence was felt throughout the magazine. He was the 'Admirable Crichton, constantly available and almost incredibly versatile'.[132] There was no part of the paper for which he could not write, except the City page. He was able to supply a political commentary, an article on anything or nothing, or a poem on demand. In the first number, for example, there were three very different contributions. Apart from the Solomon Eagle column, there was a short story about a love affair and the first of the series of parodies, 'How they do it'. At the printers he could scribble a parody in a few minutes or write a letter of just the right length to fill a gap, signing it H. B. de Winton. Many readers began to buy the *New Statesman* for 'the Eagle' alone.

The Eagle reported the death of the Poet Laureate Alfred Austin in June 1913. There was much debate about the role. A few, such as

Richard Aldington, Harold Monro and Middleton Murry, wanted to do away with the post completely, but most felt excitement about who should succeed Austin in this new age. Squire felt that the role made clear the importance of poetry in civic life. The interest in the laureateship was transatlantic – Rupert Brooke wrote from America that it was the chief topic of the literary world there. The three favourites were Kipling, the most popular poet of the time, the star of the hour, John Masefield, and William Watson, who could, according to Squire, write loyal odes on his head. Alfred Noyes, Henry Newbolt and Robert Bridges were also all in the running. A. E. Housman's pessimism ruled him out. The Eagle asked his *New Statesman* readers to imagine Housman writing about a new king's accession: 'Now treads Britannia new fields of hope, / For Empire dawns a brighter, happier day; / Cheer up, lads, there's still the rope / And a six-foot bed of clay!') Perhaps, after all, the post might as well be abolished.… The appointment he feared most was that of John Masefield. He was much relieved when the respected but little-known academic Robert Bridges was finally appointed.

The growing friendship with Edward Marsh was very important to Squire. Marsh had that very rare thing among young poets and painters: money. They began to dine together once a week. Marsh acted as friend and agent for writers as different as Rupert Brooke, D. H. Lawrence, James Flecker and Middleton Murry. He sent poems to the *New Age* and later to the *New Statesman* when Squire was finding poetry hard to come by. Lascelles Abercrombie was writing very long poems unsuitable for magazines; Lawrence had fallen silent and Brooke seemed to have disappeared to the South Seas. There were other difficulties: Marsh sent Squire a poem from Lawrence's collection *Look! We have Come Through* which, after three days, he had to return as he could not make head nor tail of it. Squire and Sharp howled with laughter at an anti-religious squib by Brooke but they dared not print it because it would lose the paper a hundred subscribers.

Squire began to rely more on Marsh's contacts to get good material cheaply for the *New Statesman*. (The going rate was a guinea a poem.) 'You have got me some of my best poems and I live in a lively expectation of favours to come,' Squire wrote to 'Dear Eddie'.[133] 'Why don't you write something for us?' he added. In return Squire reviewed *Georgian Poetry* and made a list of his favourite poems from the *New Statesman* for Marsh to include. He also introduced Marsh to some new names: W. J. Turner ('a scatter-brained kind of genius'), John Freeman and Edward Shanks. He tried to use his influence to promote people and causes: he suggested that Robert Bridges should get an O.M. (awarded in 1929); a Civil List pension for de la Mare, who was suffering under the drudgery of his work, and funds for the desperately poor Edmund Blunden. 'I cannot think of anyone more deserving and would benefit more by help than Blunden,' Squire wrote to Marsh.[134] Their friendship and desire to help struggling writers led to the founding of Britain's first literary prize – the Hawthornden.

Squire was also publishing his own serious poetry in magazines such as The *British Review*, *The Eye-Witness* and the *New Age*. At this time his poems were questioning, stark and designed to shock. Their conventional titles misled the reader: 'For Music', for example, is not about music at all: it is about a grim death at dawn;

Death in the cold grey morning
Came to the man where he lay;
And the wind shivered and the trees shuddered
And the dawn was grey.

And the face of the man was grey in the dawn,
And the watchers by the bed
Knew, as they heard the shaking of the leaves,
That the man was dead.[135]

The bareness of the diction and the paring of adjectives underlines the bleakness. 'Song' starts with fairies and builds up a world of pretty make-believe:

There is a wood where the fairies dance
All night long in a ring of mushrooms daintily,
By each tree bole sits a squirrel or a mole,
And the moon through the branches darts.

Light on the grass their slim limbs glance,
Their shadows in the moonlight swing in quiet unison,
And the moon discovers that they all have lovers,
But they never break their hearts.

Only to destroy it shockingly in the final quatrain:

They never grieve at all for sands that run,
They never know regret for a deed that's done,
And they never think of going to a shed with a gun
At the rising of the sun.[136]

The fairies are as heartless as they are beautiful. What began as a dainty Victorian poem ends as a suicide note. The title of 'Friendship's Garland' suggests a sentimental ladies' album of affectionate wishes and pretty compliments, but it is about the breaking-down of friendship and an alcoholic who ends his life drinking in a room isolated high in a tower. Fellow drinkers notice 'his twitching face and timid eye':

When they saw the eye he had
They thought, perhaps, that he was mad:
I knew he was clear and sane
But had a horror in his brain.

He had much money and one friend
And drank quite grimly to the end.
Why he chose to die in hell
I did not ask, he did not tell.

Perhaps most unsettling is Squire's refusal to offer any kind of response, feeling or explanation for the events he describes. At this time, under the influence of Hulme, he was cutting down his subject to its essentials. To the imagists this meant the hard purity of an image: to Squire it meant abandoning anything remotely 'poetic' or Victorian.

Willy Smith, Squire's best friend at Blundell's, suggested that they should rent somewhere together and in 1913 he found Swan House in Chiswick. It had a narrow brick-walled back garden with an acacia tree, two pear trees and a little grove of lilacs and flowering currants. Robins nested in the Virginia creeper on the back wall and thrushes sang in the tops of the ash trees.

From the front window Squire could see the road, a waterside garden, the osiers of Chiswick Eyot and the Thames and beyond that the rust-coloured sails of Thames barges carrying grain from Ipswich. He loved Swan House: 'I happen to live in a fragment of eighteenth-century London; Middlesex it then was. Little lawns behind palings slope to the river in front; the old brick houses have… trimly decorative doorways, occasionally a slender balcony; and inside white-panelled rooms and shutters that fold back into the walls…' He noted with pleasure that this part of the Thames had been unaltered for the past one hundred and fifty years. The house itself represented eighteenth-century values that his own age had scorned: 'The French Revolution passed, tumults and wars and rhapsodies passed, but this is civilization, this is competence, and a just harmony of the things most pleasant and pleasurable.'[137] Squire described the comfort of his sitting room:

The sofa then was blue, the telephone
Listened upon the desk, and softly shone
Even as now the fire-arms in the grate,
And the little brass pendulum swung, a seal of fate
Stamping the minutes; and the curtains on window and door
Just moved in the air; and on the dark boards of the floor
These same discreetly-coloured rugs were lying…[138]

As evening fell, he liked to look out from the windows of Swan House past the ash tree in the garden onto the Thames:

And a steamer softly puffing along the river passes,
Drawing a file of barges; and silence falls again.
And a bell tones; and the evening darkens; and in sparse rank
The greenish lights well out along the other bank.[139]

The view of the river and the docks with the sails of Thames barges furled up their masts at night filled him with a rare sense of peace and order.

Willy Smith and Jack Squire found a third tenant, Henry Wheeler, a shy Oxford bibliophile. He propped up booksellers' catalogues on the cruet every breakfast time and inspired Squire with a love of book collecting and bibliography. In their lunch hours they avoided the well-known second-hand bookshops on the Charing Cross Road but enjoyed foraging in the filthiest corners of the bookshops and the hawkers' stalls on Farringdon Road 'where you can get for 3d what you would have to pay 2/6 elsewhere'. For a shilling Wheeler seized a commentary on Plato signed, 'William Wordsworth. Rydal Mount,' with the owner's annotations, and a book by John Stuart Mill emended by the author. Squire found a copy of Callimachus that had belonged to the radical John Wilkes and bought for threepence a volume of Goethe's songs inscribed by Frau Goethe. Of course, there were very few 'finds', such as a Mazarin Bible or a First Folio of Shakespeare for sixpence, but if you were prepared to get very dirty in the obscurest corners of these shops, Squire wrote, you could still find good things going cheap.

The Squire family, now three in number with the birth of their son Raglan, enjoyed the company of a young bulldog brought by Willy Smith to complete the household. The dog was a character: it watched Raglan climb up and down a ladder and then managed exactly the same feat and lay contentedly on the top step. 'All boys together,' they played in the garden. Squire relished there the kind of domestic comfort he had never known and enjoyed the social life of Chiswick and his literary friends. There were always literary guests to invite to stay or to dinner parties. One of the least sophisticated was the countryman W. H. Davies who was amazed that the house had switches to control the electric lighting. 'It's magic,' he cried.

Sometimes, to the delight of young Raglan, the Thames would flood over into the little front gardens. Sometimes, their housemate Henry Wheeler would scull by and shout a friendly greeting from the river. May Morris, daughter of William, was a friend and neighbour in Hammersmith Terrace, only a few minutes' walk from her father's old home, Kelmscott House. The writer, wit and lawyer A. P. Herbert lived down the road. Raglan remembered that he became a neighbourhood joke as he cruised from Chiswick Eyot to Hammersmith Bridge, singing 'O Shenandoah...!' so lustily that he could be heard on both banks of the river. Squire himself bought a boat from a master craftsman, a follower of William Morris, and spent some of his happiest Saturdays sailing his ketch along the Chiswick waterfront, past Swan House, past the finishing post of the Boat Race, to Kew Gardens and beyond.

Back in Plymouth all was not well. A defensive and awkward letter to his mother from Hintlesham Rectory on Christmas Day 1913 tells a great deal about Jack's state of affairs. He apologised for not having realised that his mother had intended to visit him and his young son Raglan for Christmas in Chiswick. He did not prefer the rectory at Hintlesham to his mother's terrace guest house in Plymouth – it was just that he had not been to Suffolk for two and a half years. The letter is full of apologies and hopes. He had borrowed £250 (in 2019 approximately £5,500) from her in September on a short-term loan and now promised formally to pay her 6% interest. His present prospects were largely bound up with the publishing firm Howard Latimer, which would, he thought, succeed with another injection of more capital – the first of many promising ventures that he hoped would make the family rich. He apologised for his 'postponing habits' which he knew his mother would recognise. (He finally repaid the loan six years later.) Apart from money concerns, behind the letter lie her complaints that he never finds time to visit her and Doll in Devon. He ended on a domestic note, telling her that they had bought a young bulldog, a gentle creature, on whose back he was writing the letter. He enclosed a portrait of his little son 'who still refuses to speak but moves about with great vigour and understands everything his parents say to him.'[140] Perhaps all this helped to mollify her...

The Howard Latimer Company published *The Three Hills and Other Poems*, Squire's second collection, in 1913. Many of them had already appeared in the *New Age* and other magazines. It is full of arguments and questions and very much the work of a man trying to find his own poetic voice; there is no settled style or genre: very short poems which might be called imagist; a sonnet; poems set as dialogues; and a long conversational poem. The titles suggest how 'unpoetic' Squire was trying to be: 'The Roof', 'A Day', 'In a Chair', 'Town' and 'At Night'. 'The Mind of Man' begins with an anatomical view of the poet's own head, as if measuring it for a phrenological analysis:

My head is very small to touch,
I feel it all from front to back,
An eared round that weighs not much
Eyes, nose-hole and pulpy crack
Oh, how small, how small it is![141]

Again the 'scientific' approach and the stripped-down language show how far he had come from 'Victorianism'.

Many of the poems are set on a grand universal scale of opposites or 'antinomies': night and day, the sun and moon, the marsh and the good city. On one side is the leitmotif of Paradise, the Holy City, or the Palace of Art: on the other is a marsh through which the modern Thames 'runs slimy as the Styx'. The landscape of *The Three Hills* echoes Virgil or Dante; through this visionary landscape the poet-pilgrim has to try to negotiate his way. 'At Night' is about that mystery:

Dark fir-tops foot the moony sky,
Blue moonlight bars the drive;
Here at the open window I
Sit smoking and alive.

Wind in the branches swells and breaks
Like ocean on a beach:
Deep in the sky and my heart there wakes
A thought I cannot reach.[142]

The two longest poems are arguments. Squire dedicated his elegy 'A Memorial to F. T.', the poet and Catholic mystic Francis Thompson who wrote 'The Hound of Heaven'. To Squire he was a believer in a spiritual world and a dedicated craftsman, the type of the Parnassian poet; Squire's ornate style and elaborate metaphors pay homage to Thompson's own highly wrought verse:

For gone is beauty's votary apostolic
And are her temples now delivered over
To blindworms and libidinous goats that frolic
In places hallowed by that celestial lover.[143]

His poetry stands as a reproach to the 'fleshly' poets of Squire's day:

Iconoclasts, breakers of carven words,
Seekers of worthless treasure in the dung,
Mock images and cacophonous charlatans
And pismire artisans
Labouring to make
Such mirrored replicas of Nature's face
As might the surface of a stagnant lake.[144]

By contrast Squire, like Thompson, was sure that the material world was not the final reality, but what lay beyond could only be glimpsed or hinted at.

So, what kind of poetry could be written in this modern age? The long conversational poem, 'A Reasonable Protestation', is Squire's answer and a defence of his own poetry, presented as an argument with 'Frank' (Francis Burrows, Squire's friend from Blundell's days), who complained of his vagueness and lack of a clear philosophy. Squire replied that he cannot be more precise: it is the fault of the age. He cannot express the inexpressible when all Victorian certainty has gone:

> This autumn of time in which we dwell
> Is not an age of revelations
> Solid as once, but intimations
> That touch us with warm misty fingers
> Leaving a nameless sense that lingers
> That sight is blind and Time's a snare
> And earth less solid than the air.[145]

Squire believed he mirrored the philosophical cast of mind of his generation: 'Almost all thinking men are sceptics now.' It was not only the age that made certainty elusive, his own personality too was full of doubt. He might wish to be more definite, but he was not a seer or a mystic like Francis Thompson.

> I see what I can, not what I will.
> I see the symbols that God has drest...
> The wind that up my chimney sucks
> A mounting waterfall of flame,
> Sticks, straws, dust, beetles and that same
> Old blazing sun the Psalmist saw
> A testifier to the law.
> Divinely to the heart they speak
> Saying how they are but weak
> Wan will o' the wisps o'er the crystal sea;
> Yet stays that sea still dark to me.[146]

The conflict, or 'antinomy', is between Squire's need to believe and his doubt. The sadness and solemnity of the last line are underlined by the plodding heavy stresses and the internal rhyme. He has at least been honest. The poem ends on a contrast between his own poems and the dishonest aesthetes, self-indulgently 'gloomy modern men' who 'pose sad riddles to the Sphinx / With raven quills in purple inks... / Then send the boy to fetch more drinks.'[147]

The collection ends with twelve translations from Baudelaire. No wonder the critics found such a mixed bag hard to judge. *The Three Hills* did however earn much more praise and notice than *Poems and Baudelaire Flowers*. Walter de la Mare in the *Times Literary Supplement*[148] saw Squire as an intellectual pioneer, 'a latter-day Columbus who takes on the theme of man and the universe... This explorer of personality gropingly faces the unknown. Mr Squire's volume is a reiterated attempt to express the inexpressible.'[149] The *Manchester Guardian* found more than a touch of modernity in a poet who 'takes delight in uncouthness.' After his desertion to the *New Statesman* the *New Age* called him a difficult poet who evaded classification. Although he had 'a pretty lyrical gift' his poetry could often be 'repellent'. *The Spectator* praised him for having many gifts 'uncommon among our moderns – a thinker as well as a feeler.'[150]

Squire paid his first visit to Germany in May 1914, reporting for the *New Statesman* on what was intended as the greatest exhibition of the printed book ever held – the Leipzig Book Fair.[151] He made the twelve-hour journey from the Dutch port of Flushing to Leipzig over a long and dreary plain. In the French pavilion he admired the gorgeous old Morocco bindings. Most impressed by German printers and publishers, he noted that there were at least a dozen publishers in Berlin, Leipzig and Munich producing much more beautiful books than could be found in England. The way in which Germans managed to make their cheap books look presentable and readable was remarkable. Although it did contain some Shakespeare folios and examples from William Morris's Kelmscott Press, the exhibition in the fake Tudor British pavilion was, he thought, totally inadequate.

Enormous crowds from all over Europe would throng there in the summer. Officials promised him that 'August was going to be *the* month.'

Squire toured the Reichstag and took tea with members of the socialist party. His political allies were a disappointment: 'An uglier lot I never set eyes on'. The tea room was nothing at all like tea on the terrace of the House of Commons where men of all parties exchanged greetings. Instead each party had a long table and glared at their opponents. He was escorted into the Strangers' Gallery by the prominent socialist Dr Ludwig Frank and listened to a violent debate in the Chamber. The President rang his bell for order as men leapt up to speak against an angry roar. A demagogue was shouting interminably and shaking his fist at the chaotic scenes all round him. It was the 'wild Socialist Liebeknecht', the future Communist leader who was to be murdered in January 1919 along with Rosa Luxemburg.

If German politics were threatening, German art disappointed. To Squire it was summed up by the farce of the bust of Flora in the Kaiser Friedrich Museum. Dr Wilhelm Bode, the museum's director, had discovered and bought it in England for a small sum, convinced it was by Leonardo. Its discovery had caused a small sensation. Then 'a still small voice' in England revealed that it was in fact made by a well-known sculptor called Richard Cockle Lucas in Hampshire. So, by order of the Berlin authorities, the bust had to be examined and cut open. Inside were the remains of a loud check British waistcoat. The bust remained in place, however, and so did Dr Bode. Squire reported it was still there, twenty years on, labelled 'English C19', followed by a question mark.

Squire's dismissal of nearly all German art, romantic, impressionist and expressionist, was sweeping. Berlin's architecture fared no better in his eyes. The enforced height limit to buildings meant that there was a chaotic variety of facades. The Siegesallee, a long avenue of thirty-two patriotic sculptures erected by Kaiser Wilhelm, was so tasteless (and there many Berliners agreed with Squire) as to be funny. The exhibitions he visited were full of pale imitations of French modernists and 'hideous caricatures of local origin' – presumably German expressionists such as Kirchner and Kandinsky. The new Pinakothek at Munich, he thought, contained hardly a picture worth seeing. Modern painters such as Max Liebermann were third-rate and Rubens's 'writhing rosy nudes looked like fishermen's worms under a microscope'. In short, he felt, there had been no decent painting since Dürer and Altdorfer.

Squire was very aware of the nervous political situation. As a friend of Edward Marsh, Private Secretary to Winston Churchill, he nearly caused a diplomatic incident as he toured the dockyards looking at the latest warships with a note in his pocket from his friend, the dangerous socialist Ludwig Frank. He found a country united in its belief that the Cossacks were going to attack – as in fact they did in August 1914.

> Even the best of them seemed to be passionately convinced that that it was enough to be German to be right and that a guttural quotation from Goethe would make everything go down. Everywhere there were men in spurs; gigantic Prussians clicked heels when the Crown Prince went up the steps of the Kaiser's Palace; Zeppelins flew over Dresden.

In Munich he asked a friendly professor what all these preparations were for and what he was afraid of. He replied that the Germans were surrounded and that they were terrified of the Russians. Squire replied:

> Nobody wants to make a ring around you; we should like you to release your subject peoples in Poland, Schleswig, and Alsace; the Russians are incompetent; and nobody wants to attack you, although people in England are rather alarmed at your building up a great Navy, out of sheer vanity which may sever the vital cords of the British Empire. Encirclement and Cossacks was all I got in reply.[152]

Squire was pleased to be following in Rupert Brooke's footsteps to Berlin two years on. He did not, though, visit the bohemian Café des Westens, which had become a centre for artists and writers. There Brooke had penned 'The Old Vicarage, Grantchester', 'lightened its smoky bar with his cool radiance' – and argued with another visitor to Berlin, T. E. Hulme. Brooke had had many friends in Bavaria and was anti-Prussian, not anti-German.[153] Squire too distinguished between the Catholic and rural Germans of southern Germany and the military elite of Prussia. Like Brooke he felt nostalgia for England and was glad to leave Germany. He had found some individuals to like among the socialists he met, but he felt there was a deadening conformity and regulation about Germany. The German capacity for obedience was more a vice than a virtue. He echoed Brooke's sentiments about the contrast between a regimented and free society. 'The Old Vicarage, Grantchester', he wrote later, was light and amusing, but also an 'indictment of German Kultur':

> Here tulips bloom as they are told;
> Unkempt about those hedges blows
> An English unofficial rose;
> And there the unregulated sun
> Slopes down to rest when day is done.
> And wakes a vague unpunctual star…

Back at home in Swan House there was a growing family to enjoy. In May Squire's second son, Anthony, was born and Eileen devoted herself to bringing up her babies and entertaining her husband's friends. Despite money worries and the shadow of war this was the most settled and happy period of Squire's life.

Revolution and rebellion were in the air. As poetry editor of the *New Age* Squire had been part of the group of artists and writers who were in the vanguard of change. When the Italian Futurist poet Marinetti paid a visit to London, Monro held a dinner party for Squire, Aldington, de la Mare, Flint and Sturge Moore. More establishment figures such as

Marsh, Newbolt and Chesterton were invited but did not come. After the dinner they decided to call on Yeats nearby in his Woburn Buildings flat. 'All I can remember is that the room was hung with brown paper and lit with candles, that some of us sat on the floor, that the atmosphere was rather hieratic, and that now and then, after an expectant hush, Yeats, in the manner of one delivering an incantation, would begin quietly intoning some mystic tale with the words: 'I had a dream.'[154] Squire admired his 'almost impeccable craft', but hated his tone of melancholy tiredness. The visitor was then asked to read. Marinetti, 'a flamboyant person adorned with diamond rings, gold chains and hundreds of white teeth', threw off his coat. Squire listened as he declaimed 'The Siege of Adrianople', consisting largely of lines like 'Boum! Boum! Boum! Les Canons! Les Canons!'[155] Sweat poured from his forehead and his voice became hoarse from imitating the boom of the Bulgarian guns. He was only halted when the neighbours began knocking on the party ceiling to ask for peace. Performance poetry was born.[156]

On a July day of suitably violent thunderstorms, Richard Aldington, 'a man at war', according to Ezra Pound, published the Vorticist magazine *BLAST: A Review of the English Vortex*, an angry, funny, anarchic outburst against the establishment. The contributors were many of Squire's old colleagues on the *New Age*, the artists and writers of the avant-garde immediately before the war: Rebecca West, Ford Madox Hueffer (later Ford Madox Ford), Ezra Pound and Aldington himself. *BLAST* contained two manifestos, short stories, and artwork by Henri Gaudier-Brzeska and Jacob Epstein. 'Everything about it was belligerent, from its shocking pink-magenta cover to its typography and its abstract illustrations,' wrote Solomon Eagle.[157] He was very impressed by the startling cover, but found the inside disappointing. It listed those to be *Blasted* or *Cursed* and those to be *Blessed*. Many of those whom Squire admired and liked, including A. C. Benson and Dean Inge, the cricketer C. B. Fry, musicians such as Edward Elgar and the 'clan Meynell' – were of course put in the *Blasted* category. Perhaps as a joke, that pillar of the establishment Henry Newbolt was to be *Blessed*. Robert Bridges was certainly blasted – he could not even manage to produce a snowstorm in his verse and could only muster 'a faint drizzle'. G. K. Chesterton was the target of Pound's jibe in 'The New Cake of Soap': 'Lo, how it gleams and glistens in the sun / Like the cheek of a Chesterton.' Squire detected the 'cloven hoof of Walt Whitman' in Pound's poetry. He was either silly or incomprehensible. 'L'Art, 1910', he thought, was the former:

> Green arsenic smeared on an egg-white cloth,
> Crushed strawberries! Come, let us feast our eyes.

Squire was quick with his parody: 'Vers Libre' was subtitled 'If a Very New Poet had Written the "Lotus-Eaters"':

> Bring me six cushions
> A yellow one, a green one, a purple one, an orange one, an
> ultramarine one, and a vermilion one,
> Colours of which the combination pleases my eye.
> Bring me also six lemon squashes
> And
> A straw...[158]

Squire treated *BLAST* and everything it represented with scorn: it was not even new. English Vorticism was simply Italian Futurism dressed up. 'We haven't a movement here, not even a mistaken one; all we have is a heterogeneous mob suffering from juvenile decay tottering along (accompanied by the absent-minded Mr Hueffer in a tail-coat in reach-me-down fancy dress uniforms, some of them extremely old-fashioned), trying to discover as they go what their common destination is to be.'[159] He concluded that they should be arrested and let off with a caution.

Squire's was the kind of patronising mockery that provoked his opponents to fury. He saw it as simply puncturing pretension. 'It is to be hoped that that the appearance of the first number of *BLAST* will put an end to the Futurist movement in England,'[160] Squire wrote. Futurism in the end amounted, he wrote, to no more than an intellectual game rather than art, an illegible scrawl to which no one had the key. He thought Marinetti an extremely clever writer, but his worship of violence was 'the kind of egoism that men discarded when they threw away their bows and arrows'.

Squire was much more sympathetic to experiments in sculpture and painting however than in poetry. He admired Epstein's sculptures, paintings by the Nash bothers, Kandinsky and the cubist art of C. R. W. Nevinson. Unlike T. S. Eliot, he was sympathetic to Picasso's work. In 1913 he had visited Modigliani's studio in Paris with Epstein. He called the artist that 'poor proud talented man' and was upset that he could not afford the £50 for the vast painting by Paul Gauguin that he tried to sell him.

On 25 July 1914, Solomon Eagle began his poetry reviews in the *New Statesman* with *Rhyming Thirds,* a volume of poetry written by the boys of The Perse School, Cambridge, and was full of praise for the boys and their teacher. The review was followed by a very brief comment on the first of the imagist anthologies and a landmark of modernist poetry: Ezra Pound's *Des Imagistes,* published by Monro's Poetry Bookshop. Squire found the thirteen-year-old boys of The Perse just as imaginative and able as Ezra Pound's group. These revolutionaries, he noted, used the same classical references to Phoebus, Proserpina, pomegranates and roses as their reactionary elders. He praised Flint for 'The Swan', and 'a strange and rather moving' poem from Pound, 'The Return'. However, the '*vers très libre*' of *Des Imagistes* was not organic to their poetry and there was nothing else of note about them.

In his first year at the *New Statesman* Squire had dismissed *BLAST,* the Vorticists, Marinetti, the Futurists, along with Pound and the imagists. What annoyed him more than the poetry was the timidity of the critics who took them seriously; the nervous failure of critics to speak out was a sign of the times. They were in 'a blue funk', scared that they might be following the footsteps of the first critics of Wagner and impressionist painting. 'This timidity in the face of the laughter of posterity was', he wrote, 'the truest sign of decadence.'[161]

Chapter 7

The Great War: The March

'It seemed on that Sunday that a golden age had lasted till yesterday and that the earth had still had to hear news of its ending,' wrote the *Times* journalist Arthur Clutton-Brock. Squire quoted his friend's words admiringly in the *New Statesman*.[162] When war against Germany was finally declared on Tuesday 4 August 1914 his mind went back to the Leipzig Book Fair just three months earlier. He remembered the crowds who thronged to see the exhibits on display as oompah bands played, steins were filled and pretty dirndl-clad young girls danced. 'And now the cheerful male members of the Bavarian Peasants' Band have taken off their green hats and put on helmets, left the women behind, and gone off to burn villages like their own and disembowel sunburnt French peasants as naturally amiable as themselves.'[163]

In the *New Statesman* Squire published Rupert Brooke's 'An Unusual Young Man', an account of how he heard the news of the war. Just returned from his Samoan romance where Germans were often the butt of jokes, he now found himself imagining for the first time an England invaded. It was the soil, the landscape of England, he felt compelled to defend: an instinctive, not a carefully considered or rational decision. His main feeling was one of relief, and even joy. Squire did not share the joy, but he echoed Brooke's instinctive feeling about defending his country's soil. On 10 August 1914 he met Brooke in the street hurrying from recruiting office to recruiting office. He asked Brooke what all the rush was for: 'Well, if Armageddon is *on*, I suppose I should be there,' came the reply.[164]

There was an almost light-hearted mood as Squire's Cambridge friends – poets, painters and philosophers – joined up straight away and started forming fours and shouldering arms in London's drill halls and open spaces. There was a race to get into khaki. Ben Keeling drilled in an Officers' Training Corps with Rupert Brooke and joined the Duke of Cornwall's Light Infantry. True to his Fabian sympathies, he refused a commission. Willy Smith enlisted in the Royal Field Artillery. T. E. Hulme signed up as a private in the Honourable Artillery Company. Rupert Brooke was drafted into the Hood Battalion, Royal Naval Division by December. When you had been a long-haired aesthete at university it was amusing, wrote Squire, to take on the role of the square-shouldered Army Man and start growing what the Germans called 'an Englisher toothbrush moustache'.[165] He himself was turned down immediately because of his bad eyesight, as was Middleton Murry and, initially, Richard Aldington. Harold Monro tried to join the Motorcycle Corps but was told he could not because he had arrived at the recruiting office on a motorbike with the wrong sized engine. He turned up the next day but was rejected again as there was now no more room.

Squire gave up books and read only newspapers, fourteen a day, nearly a hundred a week as he estimated. There was no time for serious poetry, and he wrote nothing but satirical verse for the first two years of the war. What frustrated him was a lack of any reliable news. Although there were eight pages of 'war news' in the dailies, the indisputable facts would scarcely fill a paragraph. He felt the day of the war correspondent was over; there was no eyewitness reporting. There had never been a war, he told his *New Statesman* readers, when information had been so scarce.[166] Rumours, though, were plentiful: Squire noted the resurrection of the sinister Doctor Death who had put cholera molecules into wells in the Franco-Prussian War and was now busy again in Belgium and France.

In the Savile Club Squire saw at first-hand how rumours spread. The evening paper reported that Aberdeen doctors had gone to attend some wounded men at Cromarty, off the Scottish coast. Five minutes later this became a brush between English and German destroyers. Five minutes after that the incident involved flotillas. And then, within the hour, the club servant told Squire that there had been a great naval battle in the North Sea and the British Fleet had suffered a terrible disaster... A history of war rumours, he thought, would make good reading. In September he did get one piece of definite news: his socialist friend from Berlin, Dr Ludwig Frank, had been killed in a battle near Lunéville. Only four months earlier he had had tea with him at the Reichstag and Dr Frank had led him to listen to the debate in the Strangers' Gallery of the House.

If news was scarce, patriotic poetry was plentiful. On the morning of 5 August, the day after war was declared, Henry Newbolt's 'The Vigil' appeared in *The Times*.

> England: where the sacred flame
> Burns before the inmost shrine,
> Where the lips that love thy name
> Consecrate their hopes and thine,
> Where the banners of thy dead
> Weave their shadows overhead,
> Watch beside thine arms to-night,
> Pray that God defend the Right.

Each of the four stanzas ended on the same line. 'The Vigil' was to be the first of a torrent of patriotic verse of all kinds: a sonnet by William Watson appeared on the following day. Two days later the Poet Laureate was published in the paper. Even the academic Robert Bridges wrote poetry which sounded more like a recruiting slogan:

> Up, careless, awake!
> Ye peacemakers, fight!
> ENGLAND STANDS FOR HONOUR!
> GOD DEFEND THE RIGHT!

By the end of September, one month after war had been declared, Squire had received two anthologies, 'Poems of the Great War' and Sonnets for England'.

German poets of 1914 were equally sure that God was on their side. Ernst Lissauer composed a slogan which had an immediate propaganda impact throughout Germany and Europe: '*Gott strafe England*'. Squire was now an agnostic and religious calls on God's aid from both sides met with a sarcastic reply. In 'The Dilemma' – 'quoted and re-quoted all over the country' at the time, but rarely attributed – he pointed out the tragic absurdity of priests on both sides invoking the same God:

God heard the embattled nations sing and shout
"Gott strafe England" and "God save the King!"
God this, God that, and God the other thing –
"Good God!" said God, "I've got my work cut out!"[167]

Whatever the war was, Squire knew it was not a crusade. In what he was sure was the temporary stunt of 'war poetry' William Watson had poems published in *The Times* and the *Daily News* on the same day. His account of a naval battle contained the 'atrocious jingle', 'We bit them in the bight, / The bight of Heligoland'. He should have titled it 'The bighter bit', commented Squire.[168] The journalist and writer Harold Begbie was also a particular target. Squire was appalled when his poem about the German invasion of Belgium, 'By their Fruits', was published by *The Times*. 'Prussian Vulture / Screams Culture / To the wounded you have killed / To the maiden / Heavy laden / With the lust your butchers swilled. / Prussian Vulture / Screams Culture / O'er the slaughtered priest and nun / Mutilation of a nation / Not so cultured as the Hun!'[169]

Squire wrote his own anti-war-writers' piece in which he mocked Begbie and the whole range of his fellow poets in verse of deliberate awfulness:

Did even the voice from Rudyard Kipling's shelf
Say anything it had not said before?
And was not Stephen Phillips just himself?
And was not Newbolt's effort on the war
Distinctly less effective than of yore?
And would not German shrapnel in the leg be
Less lacerating than the verse of Begbie?'[170]

At the same time as Begbie's poem, Squire's own, very different, 'Christmas Hymn – 1914', appeared in the *New Statesman*. He had an edition of fifty published as his radical Christmas card. Under the heading 'Patriotism for the Pauper Children' *The Times* reported that the Guardians of the Lambeth poor had decided that they would have to discontinue their custom of giving each child in their care an egg for breakfast on Christmas morning. It would be better to give them nothing rather than 'a shop egg'. This provoked an attack of almost Swiftian savagery. Why, Squire asks, stop at eggs?

Guardians mine, so far so good
This adjustment in the food;
But, my Guardians, why, I beg,
Go no further than an egg?
If you'd have them not ignore
All the grave effects of war,
Sell their beds and let them freeze
Like the Belgian refugees;
Go the whole instructive hog,
Shell the workhouse, burn and flog.[171]

Squire's anger and pity emerge in the biting satiric rhymes: 'Peace on earth and mercy mild, / And Christ forgive a workhouse child.' In the final stanza the Guardians retire to their comfortable homes in Alexandra Row and Chatsworth Terrace, 'The Den' or 'The Manse' or 'River View', to eat their fill of Christmas dinners 'Justly proud of what you've done / To repel the hated Hun.' Squire's poem had an immediate effect; the Guardians were suddenly overwhelmed by letters of protest. Eggs were reinstated.

Solomon Eagle gave a do-it-yourself guide to writers of patriotic poetry. 'What is wrong with most of these patriotic versifiers is that they start with a ready-made set of conceptions, of phrases, of words and of rhymes, and turn out their works on the formula. 'Put England down as "knightly", state her honour to be "inviolate" and her spirit "invulnerable", call her enemies "perjured" and branded with the "mark of Cain"... summon the spirits of Drake and Grenville from the deep, introduce a "thou" or two, and conclude with the assertion that God will defend the Right – and there is the formula for a poem.'[172] He said he was like a bat within a cave trying helplessly to explain how so many people managed to write exactly like one another.

Apart from the 'official' poetry, readers submitted their own poems to magazines and newspapers. According to Solomon Eagle in 1914, *The Times* received as many as a hundred poems a day, and the *Daily Mirror* about sixty – it had to ask its readers to send in no more. Squire quoted a typical example, 'Old Bobs', from a correspondent in North Shields: 'Who was it Cronje's ribs did dig / And pleaded hard for army big / to save us from the Hunnish Pig?' Leader writers quoted Kipling *passim*. Young poets like Alfred Noyes (dubbed by Squire 'The Noyse of War') were prolific, and poets as different as Henry Newbolt in *The Times* and Jessie Pope in the *Daily Mail* were widely read. Advertising hoardings became recruiting posters full of jingles: 'What will you lack, sonny, what will you lack, / When the girls line up the street... / What will you lack when your mate goes by, / With the girl who cuts you dead?' Squire mocked the sentimental treatment of the war in popular songs. As he looked into a music shop window on Upper Shaftesbury Avenue, he noted two typical titles: one was 'Only a Bit of Khaki that Daddy Wore at Mons' and 'The Little Irish Red Cross Nurse'.[173] Anthologies were rushed into print: less than two months after the declaration of war Squire had already reviewed two of them.[174]

Crude attacks on German 'Kultur' were the order of the day. German music was (briefly) prohibited at the Proms, hardly anyone would drink German wine and a woman taking her dachshund for a walk down Piccadilly might well be scowled at. Squire hated the casual ubiquity of the word 'Hun' and deplored the excesses of anti-German feeling. His position in London was a difficult one. He and many of his Fabian friends supported the war – but he hated jingoism. He hated the *Times* sets of cheap patriotic broadsheets sent out to soldiers and sailors with titles such as 'Deeds that Won the Empire', forcing them to read what they neither wanted nor needed. Much better, he wrote, send an illustrated comic paper with 'no comment about the war except wagging'. Socialism was an international movement and the repeated mantra of *England* and *Empire* did not come easily to him.

Squire's socialist sympathies were with the ordinary soldiers. The real poetry of the war, as he wrote in the *New Statesman*,[175] came from the songs of the men in France and Belgium, songs which arose from the spontaneous feelings of soldiers in the trenches. They received nothing like the publicity of newspaper 'war-poems', but sometimes he heard a snatch in the street and sometimes his friends posted the words to him from the Front. An Irish correspondent sent him '*What did I come to Belgium for?*' A 'Sergeant of the Line' (Ben Keeling) wrote to him in September 1915 that he was glad he was writing about soldiers' songs and enclosed the best one – an unprintable version that he and his men had sung as they crossed the Belgian frontier. (Squire said it would burn a hole in the paper if he printed it.) He also sent a specimen of another that he had often heard on the cobbled roads of Flanders:

Kitchener's Army,
Shillin' a day!
Stuck in the guardroom,
Lose all your pay!
What shall we do boys?

Let's run away!
Kitchener's army,
Shillin' a day.

He added that he had heard an interesting variation on the last two lines which originated in his own battalion: 'Join the Canadians, / *Dollar* a day!' This was evidence for the German view that the British Expeditionary Force of 1914 was full of mercenaries attracted by the money, he added. In fact, discontent about the pay and conditions of the soldier's life was another common theme amongst the soldiers' songs:

We work all day, we work all night,
We work all day on Sunday,
And all we get for our time
Is 'Don't get sick on Monday.'

Keeling wrote to Squire noting that repetition of the same line was characteristic of the New Army's songs. The American gospel hymn 'When the Roll is Called up Yonder' became:

When the beer is on the table,
When the beer is on the table,
When the beer is on the table,
When the beer is on the table I'll be there.

He taught his men to sing a French version of the words ('*Quand la bière est sur la table / Je suis la*') and a Dutch one ('*Als het bier is op de table / Ik ben daar*'). As they went from the reserve dugouts into a large field that was to be their rest camp someone started to drone to a hymn tune, 'Forty days and forty nights, / Forty days and forty nnights / Forty days and forty nnnights...' After eight days at the Front, Keeling brought his weary and wet detachment on the long march back to camp, hot tea and a dry 'kip' to the words of 'Isabel':

Farewell, Isabel, Isabel!
I got to leave you, I got to go.
You know very well, Isabel,
I got to leave you to fight the foe.
You know very well, Isabel,
As the battle I go through,
I shall do my best when I'm in it to win it
As – I – won you.

When the war was over, he told Squire, he would call his next daughter Isabel...[176]

The historian and novelist Maurice Baring, serving in the Royal Flying Corps, wrote to Squire saying that one of the most beautiful songs ever written, 'It's a Long Way to Tipperary' was no longer the soldiers' favourite. They had become sick of it and never sang it. 'But it will always be the song of 1914.'[177] The most popular song at the Front, he said, was 'Annie Laurie'. An officer of a fusilier battalion – Willy Smith – also sent Squire his men's favourite, sung in lusty cockney to the tune of the music hall star Florrie Forde's 'Hold Your Hand Out, Naughty Boy':

Hold your head down, Fusilier,
Hold your head down, Fusilier,
There's a bloody Great Hun,
With a bloody great gun
Who'll shoot you
Who'll shoot you
There is a sniper up a tree
Waiting for you and me
If you want to get to your home any more,
Hold your head down Fusilier.

Willy Smith also sent what he called a pleasant ditty: 'Send out my mother, my sister, and my brother, / But for God's sake don't send me.' He also wrote about a song he had heard from soldiers under his command that had a very quaint and dismal tune: 'I don't want to go to the trenches no more...' Willy Smith said that his men would sing that melancholy tune very quietly while grooming their horses. He had never heard anything in his life which moved him more.

> I want to go home, I want to go home.
> I don't want to go in the trenches no more,
> Where whizzbangs and shrapnel they whistle and roar.
> Take me over the sea, where the Alleyman can't get at me.
> Oh my, I don't want to die, I want to go home.

('Alleyman' was trenches slang for German, from the French *allemand*.) Squire wrote of the 'utter fed-upness' that the song expressed.

'The greatest interest lies in these queer, unique songs – whimsical, ironical, grumbling – which have come into being in the Army during the war and exist in many versions in the true manner of folk-poetry.' They were the real voices of the young men at the Front rather than the pompous heroics of the "England, I consecrate to thee school," made up by, he thought, bald-headed gentlemen living at Shepherd's Bush or Folkestone. The songs were truly English: 'The Germans would never countenance lack of reference to the Fatherland and the French would think a revolution was near if they heard the words "I want to go 'ome."' Squire was one of the first writers to notice and print the songs from the trenches. [178]

Unable to join his friends in uniform, the best Squire could do was to carry out guard duties outside Buckingham Palace with other war rejects and senior civil servants. Night after night, and year after year, they turned out, with challenges, salutes and torches flashing, and then retired to the King's Stables for cocoa, biscuits and bridge. Squire felt it was a pointless and sometimes farcical exercise, but at least it meant comradeship and kept a little at bay his feelings of guilt about not being at the Front.

He continued to lecture on behalf of the Fabians and it was at one of their meetings that he met Virginia Woolf for the first time. On a snowy January day in 1915 a public discussion of the 'Conditions of the Peace' was held at Essex Hall, the favourite Fabian meeting place. Virginia Woolf was appalled, she wrote, by the earnest drab-looking women and the shock-headed young men, in tweed suits. The Fabians were well worth hearing and seeing, she added with some distaste. Leading liberals such as Beatrice Webb and Sir Sidney Oliver spoke, but the only speech worth anything, she wrote, came from a man who stood out by his bright blue shirt and his 'amusing appearance': Jack Squire.[179]

In April Virginia Woolf was invited to tea at Swan House. Squire himself was not at home and she found Eileen patronising as she brought out her husband's collection of first editions for admiration. The two young children, Raglan and Anthony, were 'common lumpish brats', too young to talk. It was the kind of family scene she disliked intensely. Undaunted, in December the Squires invited her again, this time to dinner. 'O my God! What an evening! All the lights went out, dinner an hour late, pheasants bleeding on the plate, no knives, tumblers or spoons, poor Mrs Squire thought to laugh it over, but became distracted; Squire ferocious. Strange figures wandered in and out, among them Mrs Hannay, an artist – Pike an inventor, Scott a don. Stove smoked, fog thick. Trains stopped.[180] Virginia Woolf's diaries and journals became full of vituperation. Squire was an 'omnivorous and callous-throated Eagle, that cheap and thin-blooded creature.'[181] He belonged to the 'stinking underworld of hack writers'. Sometimes her remarks were more analytical, but always hostile: 'Jack Squire has imposed another false self upon his true self which is sensitive, unhappy. He dresses up as Dr Johnson, but a Johnson without the power of speech.'[182]

James Elroy Flecker, a contemporary of Rupert Brooke's at Cambridge, was a contributor to Marsh's anthologies. Squire had come to admire his distinctively oriental poetry which he thought had the musicality and the exoticism of the Parnassians. He never met

Flecker but had published his poems in the *New Statesman*. Flecker's 'The Burial in England' was, he thought, one of the few decent poems the war had produced so far. After reading his letters, Squire had come to feel that he knew and liked his candid and exuberant character. In January 1915 he received a bundle of poems ending with a puzzling message: 'This is the last batch I will trouble you with as I am sending all my MSS to the Author Alliance.'

A week after the poems arrived Rupert Brooke's voice on the telephone came as a surprise. He told Squire the bad news: Flecker had died from tuberculosis in a nursing home in Davos, Switzerland. He was thirty years old and the first of Squire's close contemporaries to die. Squire immediately published the last poems Flecker had sent him in the *New Statesman*. He praised Flecker for some 'imperishable lyrics' and his verse play *Hassan*, which promised a dramatic breakthrough 'unsurpassed by any similar dramatic work since the Elizabethans, which isn't saying much'.[183] He told Flecker's widow that he would set about editing her husband's *Collected Poems* immediately and suggested to Marsh they might do it together.

Brooke visited Squire to commiserate. Then he recounted his own war experience of the retreat from Antwerp where he had lain in trenches for three days under German shelling before leading his troops out of the besieged city. Outwardly debonair and amused by the comedy of the chaos, he felt for the suffering of the nocturnal flight of endless streams of refugees carrying children and a few poor goods along roads lit up by blazing houses.[184] He promised Squire that he would write a full account for the *New Statesman* and determined that the same thing should not happen to England.

It was to be the last time they met before Brooke went to the Dardanelles and his death on Shakespeare's birthday, St George's Day 1915. A heartbroken Marsh wrote at length to Squire: 'No doubt you have received the dreadful news, which has just been telegraphed from Turkey, that our beloved and admired Rupert died yesterday in the French hospital-ship. I know how much you will feel this blow, which falls not only upon us who loved him, but upon English literature.

He was our Marcellus and I see no one, all round, from whom more could have been reasonably expected than from him. I am very much agitated to-day, because I dreamed about him over and over again last night (of course because of yesterday's bad news). He appeared to me in his usual guise, but with an expression insufferably sad. He seemed in an agony to say something, but no sound whatever came from him, and I woke not once, but twice in the agony of trying vainly to help him to speak. I rarely dream, and the vividness of this vision has quite unmanned me.'[185]

Brooke's death led to an outburst of national mourning. Winston Churchill wrote his obituary in *The Times* and Dean Inge praised him from the pulpit of St Paul's. John's Masefield's wife Constance wrote to Marsh, 'It is impossible to believe that Rupert is dead. Something most beautiful has passed out of life.'[186] Squire himself was deeply affected: 'He died and his death was the signal of the death of something in all his contemporaries.' A week later Squire wrote about him in the *New Statesman*. It was impossible not to call him glamorous, with a smile in his grey eyes as he brushed back his fair hair to tell of the escape from Antwerp, but he was a much more complex person. Brooke, he wrote, would have been amused and felt awkward at being called a soldier-poet. 'He was in love with life, but willing, for what England meant to him, to leave it.' His only published volume was sometimes crude, but at his best he reminded Squire of Donne. No one could say how he would develop as a writer, but Squire had no doubt that Rupert Brooke's death was a great loss to the world of literature. He ended on a personal note: 'What his death meant to those who knew him one would rather not attempt to express.'[187]

Two months later Solomon Eagle reviewed his *1914 and Other Poems* in the *New Statesman* of 26 June. He especially admired Brooke's gift for 'verbal music'; he could almost make music out of meaningless syllables. Alert to the irony that his Fabian friend had become a canonised patriot, he was reticent about Brooke's war sonnets. Squire noted, he had already become a symbol, a blend of General Gordon of Khartoum and Tennyson, rather than the ironical, witty person whom he had known, the author of 'Grantchester' and a poem on the theology of fishes: 'Brooke's name a few weeks after his death is known to a public a hundred times more numerous than that which knew him in life. A myth has been created: but it has grown around an imaginary figure, very different from the real man.'

As some critics began to question Brooke's character and reputation Squire stayed loyal. He felt that Brooke was being maligned by intellectuals – always a pejorative word for him – and 'the silly reactions of fashion, the current jealousy of people who had hearts and died in the war, the smiling denigration by living dogs, some of whom had known Brooke, of dead lions...'[188] Two of the dogs were Virginia Woolf and Middleton Murry. Another was Ezra Pound whose satirical poem about Brooke appeared in the wartime *BLAST*. It portrayed him as the lustful suitor of a Tahitian beauty who had to climb a coconut tree to escape his advances. It could not have been worse timed. Squire added Pound to his private 'Chamber of Horrors.'

There was a Yank humbug called Pound
Whose verse was – I won't say unsound –
But it rotted and stank
With an odour so rank
You could smell it for twenty miles round.[189]

The war brought more losses. Denis Browne had been the *New Statesman*'s music critic and joined the naval section with Rupert Brooke. He too died in the Dardanelles two months after his friend. Another friend of Brooke's and a fellow Fabian, Charles Lister, fell in August 1915. The artist Gaudier-Brzeska, twice decorated for gallantry in the French army, was killed at Neuville St Vaast in 1915, aged twenty-four. Squire's brother-in-law Clarence was killed that year and the ever-gallant Clennell was invalided home with the remains of a shell inside him and was never the same again. Thinking of his Oxford and Cambridge contemporaries, Squire wrote: 'My own generation either died in the war or were left scarred and prematurely aged; my generation did little except die.'[190]

His natural melancholy combined with the growing casualty lists of his friends led him to solitary despair. 'Fragment from a Memorial Ode' contrasts the peace of Swan House as evening falls with the world of war and death.

So you are dead like all the other dead...
You are not here, but I am here alone;
And evening falls, fusing tree, water and stone
Into a violet cloth, and the frail ash-tree hisses
With a soft sharpness like a fall of mounded grain.
And a steamer softly puffing along the river passes,
Drawing a file of barges; and silence falls again.
And a bell tones; and the evening darkens; and in sparse rank
The greenish lights well out along the other bank.
I have no force left now; the sights and sounds impinge
Upon me unresisted, like raindrops on the mould.
And, striving not against my melancholy mood,
Limp as a door that hangs upon one failing hinge,
Limp, with slack, marrowless arms and thighs, I sit and brood
On death and death and death. And quiet, thin and cold,
Follow of this one friend the hopeless, helpless ghost.
Death chasing hard on the heels of creating life.
And I, I see myself as one of a heap of stones
Wetted a moment to life as the flying wave goes over,
Onward and never returning, leaving no mark behind...
There's nothing to hope for.[191]

It was cowardice, however, Squire felt, to give in to this tragic vision, overwhelming though it might seem. On 1 May 1915 Solomon Eagle's piece in the *New Stateman* was 'On going to the Music Hall.' It was said that in France church attendance had shot up. In England too it might well have risen on Sundays, but for the rest of the week

Londoners caught taxi-cabs to see the American singer Elsie Janis at the Palace or George Robey. The Victorian music hall, with its red-nosed parody of life, was enjoying another heyday. Now, not without a trace of guilt, Squire became a habitué of its smoke-filled halls. He roared out patriotic choruses such as— 'It is the Navy, the British Navy / That keeps our foes at bay' and 'Sons of the sea, / All British born, / Sailing every ocean, / Laughing foes to scorn.'

Solomon Eagle wondered how he and his fellow Londoners could be enjoying this sometimes coarse, sometimes silly fun in the middle of a European war. His reply went to the heart of his character. He felt deeply what he himself called the 'antinomy', or the conflicts in his own nature. On one side were the forces of despair: 'To the completely tragic imagination the world is a place through which the black procession of funerals never ceases to wind. Its very dust is mixed with the crowds of the dead... We cannot build without digging in the dust of generations of men and beasts and insects and trees and flowers. The world wears death like a garment. If we are happy it is only like children playing among the tombs.'

His dark side met with a balancing energy. As he had described himself in 'Letters to Posterity', he had 'a certain deep-seated optimism with a preference for the joyous over the gloomy.' Comedy, he thought, was the expression of this refusal to give in; he was fond of quoting George Gissing's remark, 'We needs must laugh in the presence of suffering; else how should we live our lives.' The human spirit fought against the tragic vision: 'There is something in the human mind, however, some comic and reasonable element which entirely denies this black picture. It rejects this conception of life as the triumph of worms... Consequently, there is a comic revulsion against the dark poetry and a tendency to mock them... a rebellion of today against eternity.'

That was the reason why when all Europe was a slaughterhouse that the Oxford music hall was packed to hear Wilkie Bard, disguised as a beautician, sing the ridiculous nonsense of 'Stewed Prunes and Custard' and laugh at the gross false teeth of Mr George Graves.[192]

Squire's inner conflict meant that he was 'Fat Jack' and everyone's friend to those who did not know him well, but he seemed a conflicted near-tragic figure to intimates such as Pryce-Jones – his jollity was the bright side of the darkness of the warring sides of his personality.

Squire's fellow Londoners shared his resilience. The day after the first Zeppelin raids on London in May 1915 he saw little girls in the park change the raid into a game. One of them threw herself down on the grass crying in rich cockney, 'Look Mummy, look, I'm shot.' He was sure that the war could destroy buildings but not the spirit of the country, or even its defiant commonness. Londoners continued to read about the 'Brides in the Bath' murderer and went about their normal business of 'drinking, seducing and profiteering'.[193] There were no signs of panic: 'People bathed in submarine infested seas and slept peacefully under the Zeppelin infested clouds.'

On his way to work he saw the effects of another Zeppelin raid. There was almost a holiday mood. Beer drinkers stood on the pavement outside the pub; policemen stood in a row outside the almshouses where the bombs had fallen. They were still standing, but 'the slates of the roofs were scattered like a pack of cards flung loosely on the table'. Within half a dozen yards of where the bomb had fallen a bed of geraniums lay fresh and scarlet and untouched. Squire followed up a side street where hawkers thrust ugly little memorial cards at him. 'One penny. In loveen memory of the pore victims. Buy a mimowrial card.' A file of people crowded in at the door of a working man's brick dwelling. 'He had suffered nothing but broken windows, but over the back wall of his garden you could see a hole where a bomb had burst among the hollyhocks and scarlet runners and near it a gap in a terrace where a little house had been – like a gap in a jaw when a tooth has been knocked out. The workman who owned the garden stood in his shirtsleeves and discoursed on the tragic drama of the ruined house. He declared it had been inhabited by a family, a father, a mother and four children who had come for safety to escape from air raids in the East End the day before the Zeppelins had come and killed them all. It was one of those stories that made one believe in destiny, Squire thought. At this point a woman who lived closer still to where the bombs had fallen emerged. She told him that in fact nobody had been hurt and the whole family had scrambled to safety...[194]

Half a mile away he found another site where the back walls of the houses had been smashed into rubble and went in by the side of the house and out through the front door. The pub landlord asked all the sightseers, many of whom were in khaki, to give the Kaiser a punch and two punches from him – and appealed to them all to use the collecting box on the way out. Collecting boxes seemed to be the rule to visit ruined houses or gardens or get a good view, Squire added. He ended his account:

> Outside in the streets young girls went about in the casual sun in
> the vanity of white shoes and children ran after hoops and played at
> soldiers and got in the way of motor-bicycles.

Sometimes a Zeppelin floated by Swan House and, Raglan recalled, the whole family, clutching mugs of Horlicks or Bovril, took refuge in the cellar. 'Airship over Suburb' is about one such moment:

> A smooth blue sky with puffed motionless clouds.
> Standing over the plain of red roofs and bushy trees
> The bright coloured shell of the large enamelled sky.

> Out of the distance pointing, a cut dark shape
> That moves this way at leisure, then hesitates and turns:
> And its darkness suddenly dies as it turns and shows
> A gleaming silver, white against even the whitest cloud.

> Across the blue and the low small clouds it moves
> Level, with a floating cloud-like motion of its own,
> Peaceful, sunny and slow, a thing of summer itself,
> Above the basking earth, travelling the clouds and the sky.

The poem absorbs the airship into the summer scene as one of the clouds in the sky. Unspoken is the knowledge, all the more powerful for never being stated, that this messenger of summer is a weapon of war.

As so many of his fellows and rivals were away at the Front, London offered a tremendous opportunity for a young writer. Squire was making his name as literary editor of the *New Statesman*. His weekly articles were unpredictable, partisan and witty. The subject matter was whatever struck him at the moment – one of the attractions for the reader was the surprise of what might be this week's offering. Another was the companionship of the implied persona of the writer. He was a learned guide who could introduce the most obscure English and foreign writers – when writing about 'Table Talk and Jest Books', for example, he noted a lost work *De Jocis Ciceronis*, before quoting the Florentine writer Poggio – but he was no stuffy intellectual. He invited his readers to share his sense of the comic and the absurd. His collection of bad verse ('The Beauties of Badness') was so successful it was followed by another – ('More Badness') – based on readers' suggestions. He was a journalist who was up to the moment too in his pieces on the popular novelist Mrs Barclay, the young James Joyce and the popular songs of the war. There was plenty of book talk too and gossip; an account of his trip to the Leipzig; crooked dealers' rings in the salesroom and songs from the music halls. Sometimes he sounded like George Orwell looking at seaside postcards; listing favourite music hall subjects, he noted, 'Throughout history any reference to bad smells has moved the Englishman to tears of laughter'. Sometimes his mockery has a bitter twist. He suggested, for example, that Parliament should punish poets who wrote on neoclassical subjects, King Arthur or the Holy Grail: 'Any poet writing on Tristan and Iseult shall have his eyelids cut off, be smeared with honey, nailed to the ground, and connected by a trail of honey with the nearest heap of large ants. Perhaps a little too severe, but just right for a House of Commons which finds forcible feeding a subject for entertainment.'[195]

Squire was appalled by the state of wartime literary criticism. Serious reviewing of books by daily newspapers almost ceased during the war years and was often seen as a waste of space; short notices became the rule of the day. After surveying the reviews, a reader would, he thought, conclude that England was full of the most distinguished writers and that bad books were never published. The customary politeness of reviewers was a fault, but 'log rolling', the practice of good reviews for books advertised, was deplorable. The deference to public men and their reputations was absurd and a damaging feature. Solomon Eagle, living up to his namesake, prescribed a much less polite treatment of them. 'If we think a man is a pompous dolt or a flamboyant charlatan, we should make our position clear.'[196]

Squire certainly made his position clear again on Futurism and Vorticism when the second (and final) wartime issue of *BLAST* came out a year later: 'Just before the war that vivacious Southerner, Signor Philippo Tommaso Marinetti, introduced us to the type-page which consisted of capital letters and notes of exclamation tumbled about in apparent confusion. The first large enterprise of the Futurist-Vorticist-Cubist kind was (though it contained normal patches) the magenta magazine *BLAST*. It succumbed after a hostile critic looked up the word in his *Webster's Dictionary* and found the definition: *Blast... a flatulent disease of sheep*. But it died only to give place to countless smaller magazines and books containing bewildering designs and extraordinary poems.'[197]

He lived up to his promise again in a literary quarrel that was a prologue to the many conflicts to come between him and the forces of modernism. In November 1915 copies of D. H. Lawrence's *The Rainbow* were seized. 'Utter filth,' the magistrate called it. The book was not banned, but the police removed all the copies they could find from the publishers. There was much consternation and anger; questions were raised in the House of Commons and the publishers were prosecuted. Lytton Strachey and Clive Bell wrote to Squire to enlist his support in the *New Statesman*. Squire wrote that a 'good deal of hysterical nonsense' was aired in court. He thought the charge was absurd; D. H. Lawrence was no pornographer, but he could not support the novel. He disliked and also needed to be reassured that the book's lesbian scenes, of which he disapproved, had nothing to do with the seizure. It would be quite impossible he felt for the *New Statesman* to defend perversity of that kind. 'Damn his eyes!' wrote Lytton Strachey. But Squire finally agreed and wrote that the law was not framed to attack literature, but to ban pornography. His reply did not appease Lytton Strachey, or make Squire like the novel any more.

> It is a dull and monotonous book which broods gloomily over the physical reactions of sex in a way so persistent that one wonders whether the author is under the spell of German psychologists, and so tedious that a perusal of it might send Casanova himself into a monastery, if he did not go to sleep before his revulsion against sex was complete. I think it a bad novel: and it contains opinions unpalatable to me and tendencies that I personally believe to be unhealthy... it is doing Mr. Lawrence common justice to protest against the way in which his name has been dragged through the mud.[198]

He ended his column by quoting a very different account of love, a poem from the hated Lord Northcliffe's *Weekly Dispatch*: 'Every day, late or early, / Take an armful of girlie; / When you've found her, / Just cuddle round her, / Do a little loving every daa-a-a-y.' 'That is how we really like it put,' he concluded.

By contrast, on Christmas Day 1915 Solomon Eagle in the *New Statesman* reviewed the second *Georgian Poetry*. He noted what a revelation the first volume had been and praised the 'very devoted and self-effacing' editor (Marsh always signed his preface 'E. M.'). Now, running into its thirteenth printing, it had totally disproved the view that anthologies of contemporary verse would never sell. The second volume was dedicated to the memory of R. B. (Rupert Brooke) and J. E. F. (James Elroy Flecker). Squire thought the selections from the two were perfect. Seven of Brooke's poems, including 'The Soldier', were included. It was Marsh's farewell gift to the man he had loved devotedly. Brooke's name became the tutelary spirit of the whole series and his glamour ensured even greater sales. There was, Squire thought, every reason to think that the second *Georgian Poetry* would prove just as popular as the first. He was right: within a few months it had sold 19,000 copies. 'E. M.' gave a platform where the latest verse could find its public. It was, he wrote to Marsh, '*vital* that the editor, should continue his work.'

Squire had one major reservation about the anthology. He thought that it was weakened by *King Lear's Wife*, a long poetic drama by Gordon Bottomley. It was Marsh's favourite, honoured by its prime position. Squire made his objections clear in two long letters. He hated the crude realism of the cleaning of the dead Goneril's body by a corpse-washer. The song of the louse who had lost its home was just repulsive. It was so morbid that it made him want to compose 'a rollicking tune and sing it.' He felt the play had no psychological truth and the characters were approached in a too-detached way. If their creator thought of them so objectively how could a theatre audience react with any sympathy or interest? No play could be a masterpiece unless it engaged feelings.

Marsh argued that Squire only liked poetry that made a clear moral statement. Squire replied that he did not think that poetry should be didactic, but that if a poet responded to his deepest feelings it inevitably had a moral effect. 'I do believe that the finest artistic work always does by a certain nobility, move the heart and elevate the mind.' It was not enough to be on the right side: bad democratic, pacifistic, anti-conscriptionist verse had to be condemned no matter how much Squire might agree with those views. 'Really great art can't help being morally useful, but certainly the notion of teaching is the wrong one to start with. A man must start from a deep emotion in himself... and express himself as nearly perfectly as he can.'[199] He went on to say that the only defect of Marsh's anthologies was that his selections all came from published work. What he wanted to see was a more adventurous selection of unpublished work by little-known writers.

Chapter 8

They Thought War was
an Evil Thing

'The England of one's dreams, which was revivified when one thought it might be a Liberal war, carried on by Liberal people, slowly fades. I wish to Christ they would clap Harmsworth in jail,' he wrote to Marsh.[200] Squire attacked armchair generals, politicians and journalists. Horatio Bottomley, editor of *John Bull*, was always a favourite target: 'a cynical criminal… most vehement and rapacious of patriots.' The *Daily Mail* and the Northcliffe Press were also under constant attack. Squire and Clifford Sharp campaigned against Lloyd George as the leader of the careerists who were using the war to make their own reputations and fortunes. As the *New Statesman* put it, 'He has struck many a shrewd blow for national dissension, as a step to personal power, never one for national unity.'

Outraged by the ostentatious wealth in London when many of his friends were in the trenches in France, Squire wrote an angry letter to the *New Statesman* complaining of the luxury that he saw paraded everywhere: private cars crowding the London streets; shop windows full of luxuries; fashionable fur coats costing £20 each – and all the jewellery that went with them. In reply Beatrice Webb suggested that everyone should give a proportion of their income to a national war chest. Squire disagreed: as a socialist he did not want the poor punished any further. He wanted the rich to give up their luxuries, their servants sent to munitions factories, and all surplus incomes conscripted. There was class hatred in his remark that the pain caused would be compensated by the pleasure of watching the rich reluctantly having to disgorge their goods.[201]

'A Hymn for Lambeth' set the angry tone for Squire's next volume of wartime poetry – *The Survival of the Fittest, and Other Poems*.[202] Squire dedicated it to 'W in the trenches' (Willy Smith): 'You live with Death; yet over there / You breathe a somewhat cleaner air.' The brief collection was a bitter attack on the England that Squire's friends were fighting for. Often a press comment from Northcliffe's *Daily Mail* or *Evening News* or a headline from the *Star* or the *Morning Post* was the spur that aroused Squire's protest.

The title poem, for example, took as its epigraph the editor of *The Spectator* J. St Loe Strachey's statement 'without war the race would degenerate'. War was often seen as a positive Darwinian process to weed out the weak and enhance national vitality. Squire knew his friends went out to France with entirely different ideas of what they were fighting for:

> They thought War was an evil thing, and fighting
> Filthy at best. So thus deluded, they,
>
> Not seeing the war as a wise elimination,
> Or a cleansing purge, or a wholesome exercise,
> Went out with mingled loathing and elation…[203]

They did not have any idea of social Darwinism, but nor were they followers of Rupert Brooke's idea of war's purifying effects; they fought for their country 'so that Europe should be free', with a combination of feelings of duty and horror; they fought:

> Only because there towered before their eyes
> England, an immemorial crusader,

A great dream-statue, seated and serene,
Who had seen much blood, and sons who had betrayed her,
But still shone out with hands and garments clean…

Romance and Rhetoric! Yet with such nonsense nourished
They faced the guns and the dead and the rats and the rain,
And all in a month, as summer waned, they perished.
And they had clear eyes, strong bodies, and some brains.

. . . .

Strachey, these died. What need is there to mention
Anything more? What argument could give
A more conclusive proof of your contention?
Strachey, these died, and men like you still live.

The last line was the most bitterly personal that Squire ever wrote. Far from being one of the fittest, Strachey has become one of the most contemptible. (In later versions Squire deleted 'Strachey' and substituted the fictitious 'Thompson'.) Squire sent Marsh another bitter snippet as a postscript to a letter – not for publication:

O to be in Flanders
Now that April's there
Where the water's drying up in the trench

To make more room for the summer stench
With General Joffre and Marshal French
In Flanders now.[204]

Smug religion too gave its approval to war. An Anglican dean had written that conscription was 'a step towards the Higher life' – a suggestion that Squire found both absurd and hypocritical. 'The Higher Life for Clergymen' began with a description of the Crucifixion and the priests Caiaphas and Ananias who had sacrificed Christ in the name of Moloch, God of War, and ended with a biting couplet:

When the last worst war is done,
And all mankind lies rotting in the sun,
High on the highest pile of skulls will kneel,
Thanking his god for that he did reveal
This crowning proof of his great grace to man,
A radiant, pink, well-nourished Anglican.

Other poems in *The Survival of the Fittest* broadened the theme of corruption at home. Politicians and press barons such as Lord Harmsworth urged war at all costs, even poison gas; the press cried for widespread bombing of German cities and the troops were duped by the combined force of the *Daily Mail*, *The Times* and the propaganda of the Lloyd George, Minister of Munitions.

Customs die hard in this our native land;
And still in Northern France, I understand,
Our gallant boys, as through the fray they forge,
Cry 'God for Harmsworth, England and Lloyd George!'

Ambitious politicians like the conservative Sir F. E. Smith (later Lord Birkenhead) and the Fabian economist Sir Leo Chiozza Money rose through unearned military promotions; new millionaires such as Lord Devonport ('Lord Underweight of Margarine,' according to Hilaire Belloc) urged cuts in soldiers' pay. In 'Bridging the Gulf or The Union of Classes' Sir Roger Trepan was 'very much moved by the war / It made him aware of a number of things that he never had thought of before.' Though crippled by the new super-tax he determined to brighten the lives of less fortunate folk. With this in mind he 'ran a few gee gees', shot grouse, attended dances for the Belgian Red Cross and drank champagne to support the French farmers. 'All Hail to the war for the blessings it brings!' Sir Roger and his likes had '... at last seen the sense of the Gospel / That they should not be selfish like hogs, / That the children may eat till they're round and replete, / But they must leave some crumbs for the dogs.' Meanwhile the working class were no better: anti-German riots in Peterborough and elsewhere led to thefts and raids on butchers' shops and were praised in the press as a great outburst of popular indignation and were tacitly supported by police and magistrates.

Squire's satiric poems about the Home Front were the counterpart to Sassoon's from the trenches. *The Survival of the Fittest* painted a picture of a decadent England torn by class divisions, profiteering and hypocrisy. It was published by George Allen and Unwin – the only publisher brave enough to print such an attack, one of the first condemnations of politicians, newspaper tycoons, bishops and millionaires in the war. It clearly touched a nerve as it was reprinted three times in 1916. 'Liberalism never had a better sharp-shooter,' wrote J. B. Priestley.[205] The Scottish newspaper *Forward* was full of praise and, under the heading 'Socialist War poets' applauded the rapier thrusts of Squire's attack: 'Clear hitting and effective, it was worth reams of heavy treatises.'[206]

Ben Keeling wrote to Squire about his life at the Front, approving his war poems and adding some of his own. Against all army regulations, he had refused to shave off his beard, a mark of his socialism – and his power of persuasion. Squire admired the way his friend revelled in being on 'the weakest side in all things' and carried on as journalist, editing the regimental magazine, the *Red Feather*, but he had one reservation. 'He talked, the last time he came on leave to see me, about his privates betting on louse-races – for, until he entered the Army, he had never really (for all his slumming) got in touch with the ordinary Englishman.'[207]

Keeling himself felt very differently. For him the sergeants' mess was the family he had never had. 'I have certainly never felt more at home among any body of men than I have in my regimental sergeants' mess. If it is my good fortune to come back safe and sound from over the water after the war it is the sergeants' mess which will form the centre of my memories of my military past.'[208] He was killed on 18 October 1916 on the Somme in the fighting round Delville

Wood. Squire agreed to edit a selection of his friend's letters, but found he was too busy to do so and H. G. Wells took on the task. The following year another friend from St John's died. T. E. Hulme fell just after his fortieth birthday. He had served in France and Belgium as an artilleryman and under the name 'North Briton' wrote a weekly column for the *New Age* from the Front. Wounded in 1915, he returned to France the following year, and was part of the advance towards Passchendaele when, as his comrades had knocked off for lunch, there came a sudden and unexpected burst of shellfire falling on the gun lines. Hulme was blown to pieces.

The loss that Squire felt the most, however, was that of Willy Smith. After his friend left Swan House to join the Royal Field Artillery Squire kept his room just as he had left it, with paintings, paint and easels ready for his return. When he first came back from France on leave, the bulldog they shared gave him such a greeting that Squire had to hold the dog down as Willy Smith divested himself of his military greatcoat. Willy filled his pipe, stretched his legs, gazed into the fire and asked, with a yawn, 'Well, when do you think this damned war will be over?' That first winter of the war they talked of art and the landscape round Ypres which,

> Reminded you of Chinese paintings
> The green plain, striped with trenches,
> The few trees on the plain
> And the puffs of smoke sprinkled over the plain.
> You said, when the war was over,
> That you would record that green desolation
> In flat colours and lines
> As a Chinese artist would.
> That is what you were going to do.
> The plain is still there.[209]

Twice Mentioned in Despatches, Willy Smith took part in the Battle of Arras and survived two years of some of the deadliest battles on the Somme. He watched from a ruined tower as his gunners fell around him in terrible fighting at Longueval, just west of Delville Wood. But on 22 April he and his artillery were in a comparatively safe place, an observation post behind the lines. Rising to get a better view, he was hit in the back of the neck by the fragment of a stray shell splinter. Apparently unwounded, he died as he was being carried by the stretcher bearers to the first-aid post, giving the poem its bitter subtitle: 'The Fluke'.

> A casual shell has come
> And pierced your head,
> And the men who were with you, uninjured,
> Carried you back,
> And you died on the way.

The flat style and the conversational voice let the moment speak for itself. The poem ends with frankness that has almost forgotten to be poetry in its broken grief.

> How many days we spent together!
> Thousands. And now I would give anything,
> For another, or even for one hour:
> An hour, were it only of aimless lounging,
> Or a game of billiards in a pub.[210]

In one of his best-known poems Squire remembered Willy Smith's last visit on leave in Chiswick, a moment 'before time stopped', through an address to 'Mamie', the dog they had shared: 'To a Bull-dog'. (*W. H. S., Capt. [Acting Major] R.F.A.; killed April 12, 1917.*)

> We sha'n't see Willy any more, Mamie,
> He won't be coming any more:
> He came back once and again and again,
> But he won't get leave any more.

We looked from the window and there was his cab,
And we ran downstairs like a streak,
And he said 'Hullo, you bad dog,' and you crouched to the floor,
Paralysed to hear him speak,

And then let fly at his face and his chest
Till I had to hold you down,
While he took off his cap and his gloves and his coat.
And his bag and his thonged Sam Browne.

We went upstairs to the studio,
The three of us, just as of old,
And you lay down and I sat and talked to him
As round the room he strolled.

Here in the room where, years ago
Before the old life stopped,
He worked all day with his slippers and his pipe,
He would pick up the threads he'd dropped…

But now I know what a dog doesn't know,
Though you'll thrust your head on my knee,
And try to draw me from the absent-mindedness
That you find so dull in me.

And all your life you will never know
What I wouldn't tell you even if I could,
That the last time we waved him away
Willy went for good…

And though you run expectant as you always do
To the uniforms we meet,
You'll never find Willy among all the soldiers
In even the longest street,

Nor in any crowd; yet, strange and bitter thought,
Even now were the old words said,
If I tried the old trick and said 'Where's Willy?'
You would quiver and lift your head,

And your brown eyes would look to ask if I were serious,
And wait for the word to spring.
Sleep undisturbed: I sha'n't say *that* again,
You innocent old thing.

I must sit, not speaking, on the sofa,
While you lie asleep on the floor;
For he's suffered a thing that dogs couldn't dream of,
And he won't be coming here anymore.[211]

From the start Squire was not sure about the poem. There was no doubt about its sincerity: Raglan, then aged five, remembered that his father wept the whole day when he heard the news. Squire told Marsh he could not classify the work at all – 'it came out of me too raw and spontaneous. I can't look at it as a poem.' Perhaps he thought it too personal, perhaps too much like a sentimental Victorian ballad. Edward Marsh, on the other hand, loved it and knew how popular it would be. He requested it for the next *Georgian Poetry*: 'I want the Bull-dog frightfully. I see you don't put it very high on your own list, [Squire had put it bottom of his list of suggestions], but I think it's a wonderful thing.' Others agreed with him: 'Few of the "in memoriam" poems of the war touch the heart as does that poem, with its moving close,' wrote Robert Lynd. Arthur Waugh, the publisher father of Evelyn, thought it 'exquisitely poignant' and 'almost intolerably sincere'. The reviewer in the *Aberdeen Daily Journal* called it 'the most sincere and bravest of all the poems inspired by the Great War.'

Not everyone agreed. In his attack on contemporary English poetry as a whole the South African poet Roy Campbell singled it out for mockery. 'Dog was GOD for all of them', he wrote. They were led by Squire at his sentimental worst in 'To a Bull-dog'. Squire was a self-indulgent and sad character, the 'forlornest of the undone.' Jack Squire through his own tear drops sploshes / In his real, flat, trochaical galoshes.'[212] 'To a Bull-dog' continues to divide readers in its new life on *YouTube*.

Chapter 9

Wars and Rumours

As the casualty lists grew and more stories of German atrocities circulated – stories he might well not have believed at the start of the war – Squire's sympathy for Germans evaporated. Reports of the epidemic at Wittenberg Camp in 1916, which left British prisoners to die in appalling conditions, and the refusal to allow the prisoners food or medicines appalled him. There was no excuse for this inhumanity. 'Their brutality is self-conscious, incredible, unashamed, official – and rewarded with the Iron Cross.' The maltreatment of prisoners of war was an infamy that Squire thought had been banished from Europe for centuries. The Prussian tradition of militarism, he wrote, had infected the whole nation.[213]

In January 1917 Squire published his last selection of parodies in *Tricks of the Trade*, which was reprinted three times.[214] Squire dedicated it to his Robert Lynd, now literary editor of the liberal *Daily News*, with the words 'These final essays in a not altogether admirable art'. He felt queasy about publishing them because he felt that this kind of writing was not what a serious poet should be doing in wartime. 'I am fed up with parody. It is too sterile,' he wrote to Marsh.[215] When he came to putting together his *Selected* and his *Collected Poems,* he left them all out – but he never stopped writing doodles, billets-doux, parodies and poems for friends in letters, on the backs of envelopes, menu cards or theatre programmes. He continued to use fragments of parody to develop literary arguments and for the sheer delight of comic invention. They came as naturally and easily to him as serious poetry was elusive and fitful. When it was suggested at the Savile Club that there ought to be a companion epigram to Pope's couplet on Isaac Newton, 'Nature and Nature's laws lay hid in night: / God said "Let Newton be!" and all was light.' Squire asked for a pencil and paper and scribbled: 'It did not last: the Devil howling "Ho, / Let Einstein be," restored the status quo.'[216] He added a postscript:

A curious family is Stein.
There's Gert, and there's Ep., and there's Ein.
Gert's poems are bunk;
Ep's statues are junk;
And nobody understands Ein.

In the summer of 1917 Squire was at Victoria Station when a train of casualties was brought in. As the stretchers were wheeled out and the men disembarked, many bandaged or on crutches, he heard the command, 'Make way for the wounded!' The wounded became their ghosts in 'The March':

I heard a voice that cried, 'Make way for those who died!'
And all the coloured crowd like ghosts at morning fled;
And down the waiting road, rank after rank there strode,
In mute and measured march a hundred thousand dead.

A hundred thousand dead, with firm and noiseless tread,
All shadowy-grey yet solid, with faces grey and ghast,
And by the house they went, and all their brows were bent
Straight forward; and they passed, and passed, and passed, and passed.

But O there came a place, and O there came a face,
That clenched my heart to see it, and sudden turned my way;

And in the Face that turned I saw two eyes that burned,
Never-forgotten eyes, and they had things to say.

Like desolate stars they shone one moment, and were gone,
And I sank down and put my arms across my head,
And felt them moving past, nor looked to see the last,
In steady silent march, our hundred thousand dead.[217]

In the summer of 1917, an ancient acacia tree came into flower in Squire's Chiswick Garden and inspired him to write a poem that is both delicately observant and, like Andrew Marvell's 'The Garden', a celebration of survival and fulfilment in time of war.

All the trees and bushes of the garden
Display their bright new green.

But above them all, still bare,
The great old acacia stands,
The solitary bent black branches stark
Against the garden and the sky.

It is as though those other thoughtless shrubs,
The winter over, hastened to rejoice
And clothe themselves in spring's new finery,
Heedless of all the iron time behind them.

But he, older and wiser, stronger and sadder at heart
Remembers still the cold winter, and knows
That in some months death will come again;
And, for a season, lonelily meditates
Above his lighter companions' frivolity.

Till some late sunny day when, breaking thought,
He'll suddenly yield to the fickle persuasive sun,

And over all his rough and writhing boughs
And tiniest twigs
Will spread a pale green mist, of feathery leaf,
More delicate, more touching than all the verdure
Of the younger, tenderer, gracefuller plants around.

And then, when the leaves have grown
Till the boughs can scarcely be seen through their crowded plumes,
There will softly glimmer, scattered upon him, blooms,
Ivory-white in the green, weightlessly hanging.[218]

At home in certain weather conditions Squire could hear the distant boom of the guns from across the Channel. 'On Hearing Flanders Guns in Chiswick, 1917', retitled 'August Moon – Chiswick, 1917', starts with just the kind of crepuscular scene that he loved, a picture of calm, stillness and moonlit tranquillity. The tide is full; a Thames barge is moored by the bank, and, in the bows, the bargee is smoking his evening pipe:

Silence. Time is suspended; that the light fails
One would not know were it not for the moon in the sky,
And the broken moon in the water, whose fractures tell
Of slow broad ripples that otherwise do not show...

I have always known all this, it has always been,
There is no change anywhere, nothing will ever change.

But then the poem suddenly moves dramatically away from the peaceful moonlit scene.

I heard a story, a crazy and tiresome myth.
Listen! Behind the twilight a deep low sound
Like the constant shutting of very distant doors,
Doors that are letting people over there
Out to some other place beyond the end of the sky.[219]

How could he reconcile the cosy life at Swan House, the garden, the Thames flowing by, the only sound the splash of a dog going into the river, with 'the deep low sound' of war. What had the domestic image of doors shutting and letting out the visitor, to do with the unimaginable reality of 'some other place beyond the end of the sky'? This antinomy could only be 'a crazy and tiresome myth'. 'The colossal insanity, the awful intrusion of war has never been more effectively dramatized', wrote J. B. Priestley.[220]

It was impossible to forget the grief of wartime. In 'The World: 1918' Squire imagined what his friends at the Front were enduring. Once again, the poem is based on a dramatic contrast. 'How curious and lovely and terrible is the World!' it begins. Swan House is a picture of comfort: he is sitting at his desk at midnight with a glass of beer, the only sounds those of distant bells and a mouse scratching somewhere; Eileen peacefully sleeping with the children in the countryside 'safe from every harm'. Then the poem turns as he imagines the Channel and the trenches:

Dark is the land and dark the farther sea
Where wakeful warships wander secretly,
And dark that coast and dark the fields within;
But then there comes a zone of fire and din
Where very small and slow beneath the night
Men sweat and labour in the ghastly light
Of shells and flares and rockets, wait the roar
Of something that will end them evermore,
And trembling in the dark men creep to kill
An enemy that shares their every ill
With equal suffering. Some may sleep but none
May sleep unguarded, till this night is done.[221]

Arnold Bennett arranged Squire's first meeting with Siegfried Sassoon. They had lunch together on 9 May 1917, the day after *The Old Huntsman*, his first collection of mature poetry, came out. The book contains graphic and brutal accounts of the war and some of the most bitter denunciations of those who stayed at home to send the young out to die. The meeting was awkward: Squire respected Sassoon but could not endorse the violence of his anti-war attitudes and poetry. The army officer's first impression of Squire was of 'a vegetarian sad-looking type of poetical person with hair rather long brushed tidily over right eye-brow. Slouching gait, hands in pockets. Distinct charm in face when lit up. Looks more like an actor. Seemed amused by some of my remarks (pacifist cussedness about the effects and conduct of the war.)'[222] The two men had a lot in common, but Squire's objection to the kind of war poetry that Sassoon wrote was fundamental. He wrote to Gosse complaining about what he called 'the mud and blood school' and the horrors of 'sodden buttocks and mats of hair'. They agreed that Sassoon and others would write very fine poetry 'when the foulness of this war has been left behind and he can write of the things he loves instead of the things he hates.' Later he was to denounce 'the lavatory school' which dwelt unremittingly on the horrors and cruelty of war.[223]

Edward Marsh too found some of Sassoon's images of amputated limbs and broken minds too powerful and too horrible to include in *Georgian Poetry*. According to Sassoon, he preferred 'more idealized soldier poems'. Robert Graves agreed that poets should have 'a spirit above wars' Marsh and Squire both felt that a year of war had left writers too stunned to respond: 'The whole thing is too filthily ugly and monotonous in that expanse of mud, devastation and scientific slaughter.'[224] Men at the Front became acclimatised to it and realised that brooding would not help them. Squire believed that the few good poems that had emerged so far were often poems of escape. Poetry could be found in 'Stray beauties, such as the stars on a fine night, or flowers on a parapet, or in a ruined garden'. 'Home Thoughts in Lavantie' by the young Grenadier Guardsman Edward Wyndham Tennant was one of his favourites. He especially admired the poetry of Edmund Blunden who also used pastoral imagery as a contrast to the horror of the trenches. Blunden ended his chronicle of his war years *Undertones of War* as 'A harmless young shepherd in a soldier's coat'. Squire wrote: 'He sees the war most clearly as a cruel disturbance of rural peace and he is continually driven to exhibit its vileness by contrasting it with the natural beauty which it destroys...'[225]

In 1917 Squire received two poems from 'Edward Eastaway', Edward Thomas's pseudonym. Squire thought his treatment of the countryside was very different from other writers who tended to select dramatic scenes and moments: sunsets; ripe cornfields; seas very rough and very blue; moonlight rather than the diffused light of an ordinary cloudy day. By contrast, Thomas, like Blunden, was a poet of the ordinary, the typical. 'He might write a poem about anything one might see at any time of day in a walk across the South of England.'[226] One of the poems he sent Squire was written just before war broke out and was revised three years later in the trenches. It did not mention the war directly, but its presence coloured every word. 'Adlestrop' ends with a chorus of all the birds of Gloucestershire and Oxfordshire. Thomas was killed on 9 April 1917 and Squire published the poem three weeks after his death.[227]

The satire of Sassoon and the realism of the trench poets were not the only ways to respond to the horrors of the war. The staple of Georgian poetry, the love of the English countryside, became the expression of permanent values, of sanity and tradition in a world of destruction. 'Men at the Front developed the habit of writing about home, trees, the stars and anything except fighting.'[228] The soldiers valued the English countryside as 'the kindest and loveliest thing in the world'. 'The return to Nature' was their way of blocking out the man-made destruction and horror of the trenches, a vision of the possibility of a better world. It was escape, not 'escapism'. Squire did not think offering images of the countryside provided protection against reality; quite the contrary: 'he in fact felt that they would intensify our awareness of things ...'[229]

Wartime allowed no space to contemplate. Like Wordsworth, Squire believed that poetry demanded distance and tranquillity. War was inimical to art, but lent itself to journalism. He acknowledged that there had been plenty of vivid wartime writing, but there had been little 'pure literature'. It would take some years before poets could write about the war with some perspective.[230] Unlike Yeats, however, who notoriously refused to publish any war poems at all in his *Oxford Book of Modern Verse 1892–1925* because 'passive suffering is not a theme for poetry',[231] Squire continued to publish Sassoon, Owen and Graves in the *New Statesman*.

Chapter 10

Georgian Poetry

In 1917 Squire was outraged by a scandal. The world of Oscar Wilde and the nineties came back to life with a private performance of a version of his verse drama *Salome*. Maud Allan, a dancer and actress, gave one performance of her version of the play which contained near nudity, lust and murder. The Independent MP Pemberton Billing linked its 'depravity' with German attempts to corrupt the army by homosexual activity. In his newspaper *The Vigilante* he claimed to have 47,000 names of 'sex traitors'. Maud Allan sued for libel. When Lord Alfred Douglas, Wilde's lover, spoke on her behalf he unwittingly turned it into a second trial of Oscar Wilde and homosexuality. At a time of war weariness the trial was a press sensation.

Prompted by *Salome,* after two years of poetic silence Squire had 'an outburst' of writing. As he explained in his Prologue to 'The Moon' it was not so much the play itself he disliked – although he did hate its 'artificial; / tinsel magnificence and limelight horror' – as the decadent world the prosecution revealed. He took it on himself to defend 'the beloved and insulted moon', in *Salome* linked to madness, sex and murder. 'Certain earthworms out of Harley Street, / Proclaimed that any inclination to the Moon / Betrayed the pervert.'[232] Squire took the alienists' and psychiatrists' view as a personal affront to his deepest sense of himself: images of the mystery and beauty of the moon and darkness were deeply embedded in his mind. His poem celebrated beauty rather than ugliness, romance rather than sex, order rather than madness. The moon was hymned for the inspiration it had given to poets from Sidney to Shakespeare and Keats. The poem was a kind of manifesto, a calculated attempt to make new a traditional poetic trope.[233] So many poets had written brief lyrics about the moon and two-line references were everywhere, but no one, Squire thought, had written at length about it. He promised Marsh another original verse title – 'Ode to Spring and other Verses'.

It had taken him a year to find the right stanza form and metre to create 'the moon-like march' of the verse. His long (170 line) poem was the most carefully crafted he ever wrote. He chose an intricate pattern of thirty-one ten-lined stanzas, 'a poem with each stanza like a moon… / That evenly progresses in the sky.'

Within the fixed decasyllabic verse form there is variety and movement. The poem begins:

> I waited for a miracle to-night.
> Dim was the earth beneath a star-swept sky,
> Her boughs were vague in that phantasmal light,
> Her current rippled past invisibly.
> No stir was in the dark and windless meadows,
> Only the water, whispering in the shadows,
> That darkened nature lived did still proclaim.
> An hour I stood in that defeat of sight,
> Waiting, and then a sudden silver flame
> Burned in the eastern heaven, and she came.[234]

In the final couplet the iambic beat gives way to a stressed word outside the pattern: 'Waiting'. It is followed by a break – and then the enjambment gives a sense of the thrill of 'the miracle' as the moon rises. Squire thought it 'by 10,000 miles the best poem' he had written.[235]

'The Moon' was welcomed by most critics who felt that it showed Squire as a man of the twentieth century who blended the classical and the modern. Its most important feature was that it was a reaction against the 'new Georgian style'. Many agreed with the reviewer who concluded, 'it is more satisfying than any poem or series of poems of this century'.[236] By contrast, no poem could have been calculated to outrage imagists such as F. S. Flint more. He had fallen out with Squire because the press refused to print any imagist poems and filled pages with 'illiterate Irish poems'. Squire replied that it was not his fault: the press did not print them because they did not like them. In response Flint wrote an essay on 'The Art of Writing' which he called 'a manifesto for modernism', making his argument as a series of numbered points. The focus was a comparison of 'The Moon' with the imagist poet H. D.'s 'Sea Gods'. In every way Squire came off worse. Flint found 'a lack of artistic cohesion, lack of poetic rhythm, clumsiness' that pervaded Squire's whole work.[237] Squire put him in his private notebook as part of his 'Chamber of Horrors'.

There was a poor fellow called Flint,
Who of intellect had just a hint,
But he found the worst balls
That were written by Gauls
And translated and put them in print.

Harold Monro, publisher of *Georgian Poetry*, homosexual poet and owner of the Poetry Bookshop, was opposite in temperament to Jack Squire. According to Squire, he was 'a delicate depressed man, frail, pale, dark moustached and pathetic-eyed who felt happier in a hushed chamber away from the rush and roar'. The over-sensitive Monro seemed to personify the kind of other-worldly poet whom Squire hated. He liked his poets to be more robust. He noted that Blunden, 'though light as thistledown', was a first-rate soldier and cricketer, as was Siegfried Sassoon; Tennyson was a fierce swarthy old gipsy; Hardy had the look of a vivacious plumber and Housman resembled an ancient Colonel and would only talk about the navy and wine. His hero Dr Johnson was enemy to 'the priggish, the sceptical, the haters of heartiness, and jollity and size, religion and patriotism.[238] In his portrait of G. K. Chesterton, Squire outlined the kind of poet and poetry he believed in:

> Must not a poet (the illusion dates from the Romantic Revival) be remarkably unlike other men in all respects, unfailingly solemn, remote, ecstatic? Some of the Victorian artists played the role well... Some of our own contemporaries have achieved the same result, quiet men with no impulse, and no need, to write a line which is not quintessential. But there are others, journalists by profession, or propagandists by calling, who cannot keep out of the market place, and forfeit respect because of the very fullness of their humanity and the very comprehensiveness of their zest for life.[239]

It is not surprising that Squire and Monro soon fell out about *Georgian Poetry*.

Public recitation of rousing poetry such as Tennyson's 'The Revenge' had become common in music halls, but the idea of a public reading of one's own poetry was very new. Squire was suspicious of the vogue; it was generally felt, he noted, that there was something ridiculous about standing up and reading poetry in public and, besides, often poets did not read their verse well. The worst had was yet to come: 'From the professional reciter, God save us all.' Monro began to host weekly poetry readings on Tuesdays and Thursdays at six o'clock in the candlelit barn at the back of the Poetry Bookshop. Marsh described it as a kind of loft which looked as if it ought to store apples and be reached by ladder through a trap door. Squire read there himself, but only once; he hated the almost ecclesiastical atmosphere in the darkened room. He thought it was, like its proprietor, too reverential.

In 1916 Elizabeth Asquith, the daughter of the prime minister and a great charity organiser, had held a grand and successful evening of poetry readings for the Star and Garter Fund, which cared for injured soldiers. Four hundred guests paid a guinea apiece to hear ten or twelve poets. A large crowd watched the famous poets arrive:

Sir Henry Newbolt, Yeats, Walter de la Mare, Hilaire Belloc and W. H. Davies, 'looking like one of his own woodland creatures', were greeted almost as if they were the rock stars of their day. 'Parnassus in Piccadilly' was the headline Squire read in his paper. The following year she tried to repeat the success in the black and gold ballroom of the Grosvenor Square house of her friend Mrs Leeds, a fabulously rich American heiress. On 21 June eleven poets read to an audience of 150 aristocratic ladies for the Scottish Women's Hospitals. Edward Marsh helped Elizabeth Asquith organise the event and persuaded a reluctant Squire to take part. He decided to read from his small collection, *The Lily of Malud and other Poems*. He began with 'Prologue: In Darkness', which introduces the title poem. It sets the theme of the mysterious inspiration that lies behind poetry. The wearyingly long-drawn-out couplets enact his frustration about his wartime poetic drought: 'With my sleeping beloved huddled tranquil beside me, why do I lie awake'/ Listening to the loud clock's hurry in the darkness…?' But in the final couplet dawn breaks and there is some hope that there will be release:

Can it be that from this, when tonight's gone from memory, there will spring of a sudden, sometime,
Like a silver lily breaking from black deadly waters, the thin-blown shape of a rhyme?'[240]

The imagery recalls Squire's 'In my First Flower-Time' where at night the 'the lily broke its sheath' and 'each day brought surprise from the dark lake underneath.' Imagination, dream and vision are fused.

Squire's poem that struck the audience most strongly that evening was also visionary one, set in a mysterious tribal village. The first line, read in 1917, spoke directly to its time and audience: 'The lily of Malud is born in secret mud'. But at the poem's heart is, not an image of the trenches, but a vision of beauty. Once a year in the middle of the night the lily in the dark forest surrounding the village comes into flower. In moonlight the maidens in a trance-like state make their way through the forest and watch in silence as the flower unfolds. Then they return to the village and their huts to sleep. They recall it as a miraculous dream, but it is also unsettling and 'gives a rare shade of trouble in their eyes.' The men are ugly and incoherent: 'Unaware of the vision they chip and grunt and do not see.' But the women stay in their huts pondering and…

> … try to remember
> Something sorrowful and far, something sweet and vaguely seen
> Like an early evening star when the sky is pale green:
> A quiet silver tower that climbed in an hour,
> Or a ghost like a flower, or a flower like a queen:
> Something holy in the past that came and did not last.
> But she knows not what it was.[241]

Only the women see the lily burst into flower and they cannot fully understand the experience. They are troubled with the uncertainty of 'Something sorrowful and far, something sweet and vaguely seen'. They have one of those moments of vision, epiphanies that Squire felt belonged to childhood but could only very occasionally be glimpsed in later life. The sight of the blazing autumnal leaves of the tree outside his rooms at St John's had been one such moment, and the moment of falling in love with Eileen was another. These flashes were sudden, unbidden and overwhelming and left the seer/victim in a state of bemused wonder. For Squire, who found the inspiration to write poetry the most important, but the most unreliable, part of his life, the flowering of the lily was just such a revelation, the muse itself, a mystery nourished in darkness.

The Grosvenor House reading got a poor press: the ticket price of two guineas was far too much. The opulent setting of enormous electric chandeliers and red and gold gilt chairs, with a grand marble staircase leading to the recital room, seemed to intimidate the poets. The ladies did not listen but gossiped in groups round the chamber. The poets did not impress: John Drinkwater read fairly well; Harold

Monro and W. J. Turner were too quiet and hesitant; Yeats beat time to his quavering voice; Walter de la Mare seemed weary and apologetic. Maurice Hewlett was the worst of the lot. 'One of our greatest living poets who has written some of the best poems on the war' was there – but 'Bob' Nichols had not been chosen to read. He yawned effectively. It was not helpful either that the evening's takings were being loudly counted in an adjoining room. 'Poets who write but cannot read' was the subheading the following day in the *Weekly Despatch*.

It was the first time Squire had recited one of his own poems in public. He was the only one to emerge from the evening with credit. He did not read as the others had done, but spoke the more than 150 lines of 'The Lily of Malud' from memory in a low rapt voice so convincingly that the audience did not detect his improvisations when he forgot the words. 'His was the most remarkable performance of the evening,' was the press verdict. 'Jack Collings Squire will become the most distinguished literary man of the twentieth century,' a notable society dame told Beatrice Webb afterwards. He had become the darling of the duchesses.

Acclaim for the poem was not confined to Grosvenor House. Edward Marsh wrote to an unconvinced Harold Monro that it was a masterpiece – 'Quite unlike anything else, in vision, in metre and in using rhyme and to my mind ravishingly beautiful.' Under a broodingly Byronic photo, the *Tatler* called Squire 'one of the rising poets of the younger generation.'[242] He even looked a little like Rupert Brooke. In their 'Books of the Day', the *Observer* noted that his reputation was already made but if it were not 'this thin paper-bound book would make it'. The poem, promised the *Westminster Review*, would be as famous as Keats's 'Lamia'.[243] And the *Express* felt that Squire would easily figure in everybody's list of the six most prominent figures among the younger school of literary men and women. Virginia Woolf was, naturally, unimpressed: 'It seems to me a hot, sentimental, blundering poem; thick-handed as usual.'[244] Most surprisingly of all, T. S. Eliot called it 'an original and rather impressive poem which deserves better company'.[245]

Squire's appearance in the third *Georgian Poetry* marked his recognition as a serious poet. He had nothing published in the first two issues, but Marsh wrote to say that 'The Lily of Malud' was one of the few poems that made him want to do a third in 1917. Squire immediately replied, very pleased that Marsh had liked 'my lily', and fearing that he might give up: 'I do hope this doesn't mean you had thought of stopping the series. It seems to me your bounden duty to literature. Readers 200 years hence will be hunting up the Georgian books as we do the old song books and miscellanies, only more so.'[246]

Harold Monro, on the other hand, was disillusioned. Reluctant to publish the third *Georgian Poetry*, he urged Marsh to wait until he had better material. Marsh and Monro began to fall out. The divisions between them were not entirely about poetry. They had worked closely together and now a third person, Squire, was making his voice felt. He disliked 'The Lily of Malud' and resented the new faces that Squire introduced to Marsh. He was hurt as he felt he was being shouldered out. Monro implored Marsh to include more of his own poetry. Anxious to placate his friend and publisher, Marsh allowed him a generous eleven pages. He also agreed to publish the poets in reverse alphabetical order so that Herbert Asquith's patriotic poem 'The Volunteer' – which Monro hated – should appear last, but he stood by his choices and his timing.

Georgian Poetry 1916–1917 was the first to take note of the war and included poems by Siegfried Sassoon, Robert Nichols and Isaac Rosenberg. The Australian music critic W. J. Turner, whom Squire had discovered and first published in the *New Statesman*, was there too. Squire himself appeared with three poems: 'The Lily of Malud', 'A House' and the poem Marsh had wanted so much: 'To a Bull-dog'. Within a fortnight *Georgian Poetry* had sold more than two thousand copies. Squire looked with admiration and some surprise at the achievement. At Christmas 1917 he wrote in Hilaire Belloc's weekly *Land and Water* on 'The Poetical Revival'.[247] He stressed that it was not, as some thought, a product of the war, but predated it. After the great Victorians led by Tennyson and Browning, there had set in a decadence when Squire was growing up: art lost touch with life and mutually self-admiring groups led to a public lack of interest and respect for poetry. Now everything had changed. The habit of verse had died but was now reborn. 'A new exuberance and enthusiasm, in individuals and the generality. And you got a new generation of young men just before the war: an imperceptible alteration had taken place.' Squire thought it was his responsibility as an editor and critic to give direction to this new age. He thought he was doing nothing less than recording a defining moment in the history of English poetry.

Georgian Poetry 1916–1917 was a turning point for Harold Monro too. He had lost sympathy with Marsh's choices and was sure that the third *Georgian Poetry* was the worst one. He urged further delay before the publication of another edition. He was not alone. Some key poets such as Graves, de la Mare and Sassoon decided they no longer wanted to be associated with Marsh's anthologies. Sales too were declining; the third *Georgian Poetry* could not match its predecessor's massive 19,000.[248]

Monro reluctantly did publish two more volumes, but at the same time launched a surprising, bitter attack on the whole group of Marsh's Georgians. The epigraph of his survey *Some Contemporary Poets* was from Coleridge: 'Swans sing before they die – 'twere no bad thing / Should certain persons die before they sing.'[249] Squire was his main target: the epitome of the worldly and commercial. 'In J. C. Squire we have an interesting example of the modern professional poet.' Monro noted Squire's development from politics to journalism. His career path was linked to the deterioration of *Georgian Poetry*. Beginning as a fortuitous and informal group, he felt it was 'transformed into a form of literary tyranny, demanding of its disciples a complete conformity to certain standards and seeking to exclude altogether those who refuse to do homage to those laws.'[250] Monro coined the term *Neo-Georgian* to separate the brave first two volumes of *Georgian Poetry* from what he felt were the inferior Squire-influenced ones that followed.[251] In private, Squire added him to his 'Chamber of Horrors':

There was a man called Monro,
Who wrote one good poem or so
But his average page
Would most fitly engage
The attention of Madame Tussaud.[252]

At the *New Statesman* Squire was much more than the literary editor. He was often called upon to stand in for the editor, Clifford Sharp, when drink had got the better of him. In 1917 the prime minister, Lloyd George, finally lost patience with Sharp's hostility and his anti-war stance and had him conscripted into the Royal Fusiliers and sent to Scandinavia. For the last two years of the war Squire took over the role of editor. Lytton Strachey looked on appalled as the 'Eagle fluttered to a higher perch'.[253] As befitted his new position Squire had his long hair cut and bought a new suit. Every Tuesday he had lunch and a discussion with the Webbs. He received detailed comment, criticism and advice in a weekly letter from Arnold Bennett on every issue. 'I think you have been running the paper excellently,' he wrote.[254] Bennett thought him 'an A1 chap. But he is a vegetarian & he doesn't understand life either. And either he or his wife doesn't understand shirts!'[255] Squire asked him to gather material on the Russian situation and they became firm friends.

Few readers noticed the change of editors, but Squire later claimed he had turned the *New Statesman* into a patriotic journal.[256] It seemed strange to some that the urbane 'not too serious gentleman essayist of the rear half of the magazine could become the hard-minded Fabian liberal of the front half', but it reflected the same kind of complexity of character that Beatrice Webb had seen. Squire was not jingoistic, but he certainly wanted to make sure that Germany was beaten. Victory in the war to end all wars was, he told his readers, the only way to ensure that all the losses could be justified.

As editor he continued the attacks on Lloyd George, fiercely opposed conscription and in 1917 defended the liberty of the press after Massingham's magazine the *Nation* had been banned abroad by the Government – but his political beliefs were changing fast. Shaw was no longer his hero. Under the title 'Common Sense about the War' he had written a supplement to the *New Statesman* in November which had caused an uproar.[257] Shaw did not see the war in simple patriotic terms, but as a natural consequence of two rival imperialisms: Britain and Germany. As a result, *Heartbreak House* and the *War Playlets* were banned during the war. Squire reviewed them in one of his last reviews for *Land and Water*. 'A worse volume has never appeared under the name of a man of reputation, and seldom under any name at all.'[258] He now saw Shaw as a traitor and declared that the author ought to be tarred and feathered. *The Nation* called his attack 'an outrage on Mr Shaw'.

Squire's attitude to the war had hardened. He began to see Germany as the source of all the cruelties of war. Their tearing up the treaty of London, which guaranteed the neutrality of Belgium, was the beginning of the destruction that haunted the twentieth century. It was the sin of Cain. It coloured his politics and destroyed his youthful Utopianism, as he wrote thirty years later in the *Illustrated London News*. One pacifist, the conscientious objector Lytton Strachey, was appalled at the way that in November 1917 the *New Statesman* dismissed Lord Lansdowne's proposals to end the war with a negotiated peace. Strachey's hostility dated back to their arguments about *The Rainbow*. Ever since then he had disliked 'that little worm, Jack Squire'. In the summer of 1918 Squire invited him to write again for the magazine. He replied that the *New Statesman* was 'a filthy rag' and his own contributions in the past had only been for 'filthy lucre'. He could not now write for a magazine that was openly jingoistic and supported the Northcliffe press with their wicked policy of ending the war with a knockout blow. In fact, Squire was, he said, in a precisely directed insult, a Northcliffian. He could find only one word to describe the scorn that Squire had poured on Lord Lansdowne's head: 'blackguardly.'[259]

Beatrice Webb felt that Squire had tried to follow in the editorial footsteps of Clifford Sharp, but was sorry that he had shifted the magazine's balance away from politics and towards literature. However, she praised both editors for attracting a younger readership; they had done the trick whilst the elder statesmen Shaw and Wells had been a dead loss. Despite never making a profit, she was pleased to note that the *New Statesman* under Squire was becoming much more widely read (6,000 and rising in 1918) and influential.

As the war dragged on Squire's elegies for his friends became a lament for a lost generation.

> There was a time that's gone
> And will not come again,
> We knew it was a pleasant time,
> How good we never dreamed.
>
> When, for a whimsy's sake,
> We'd even play with pain,
> For everything awaited us
> And life immortal seemed.
>
> It seemed unending then
> To forward-looking eyes,
> No thought of what postponement meant
> Hung dark across our mirth;
>
> We had years and strength enough
> For any enterprise,
> Our numerous companionship
> Were heirs to all the earth.
>
> But now all memory
> Is one ironic truth,
> We look like strangers at the boys
> We were so long ago;
> For half of us are dead,
> And half have lost their youth,

And our hearts are scarred by many griefs,
That only age should know.

('A Generation: 1917')[260]

The war that Squire felt as so destructive and terrible was also a beginning for him. During its four years he was at his most productive and made his name as editor, journalist and poet. In March 1918 he published *Poems: First Series*, containing fifty poems that he had written between 1905 and 1918. They were 'all that he did not wish to destroy' from the four volumes he had already issued. The title, he explained, promised that there was more, and, he hoped, better, to come. The collection began with 'In a Chair', written when he was twenty-one, and ended with a love poem to Eileen: 'Envoi':

And when belief was dead and God a myth,
And the world seemed a wandering mote of evil,
Endurable only by its impermanence,
And all the planets perishable urns
Of perished ashes, to you alone I clung
Amid the unspeakable loneliness of the universe.[261]

Robert Lynd hailed the achievement. It was now possible, he said, to see the poet learning to fly. Squire's refusal to have anything to do with the merely poetic, and his demanding imagery, reminded him of John Donne. Squire had begun as an X-ray realist in poems such as 'The Mind of Man', and a master of 'disgust' in 'Ode in a Restaurant'. His was rugged intellectual verse: 'Now that these poems have been collected into a volume it is possible to measure the author's status. His book will, I believe, come as a revelation. A poet of original music, of an original mind, and an original imagination, the author has now taken a secure place among the men of genius of today.'[262]

The publisher Arthur Waugh was equally impressed: 'When a poet begins to sift and weed out his poetry we see for ourselves that the day of his maturity is at hand,' he wrote.[263] Squire was important as 'a modern of moderns.' The cast of his mind was always critical and led him to question and test his own emotions, analyse and reject prettiness and sentimentality. He was an iconoclast in revolt against the technical graces and ease of his predecessors. Waugh thought that none of the younger poets had experimented so boldly. Squire rejected any slavish adherence to rhythm or rhyme; his greatest gift was to encourage a new prosody of 'suppleness and variety'. He rejected too the 'stooky and wainy' views of rural life that 'Georgian' at its worst came to represent. For Squire Nature meant a crowded civilisation, not fields and fells. Finally, Waugh argued that his work was a total contrast to the Victorian dreamers and Lotos-eaters. This picture of a tough-minded iconoclastic poet striving to 'purify the language of the tribe' is the opposite of his reputation today.

The friendship with Edmund Gosse was leading Squire into the heart of the literary establishment. Born in 1849, Gosse had been on friendly terms with the great names of Victorian literature, Arnold, Swinburne and Tennyson. Still a prolific writer and critic, to many of the younger post-war writers he now seemed a pompous relic. Osbert Sitwell said that young writers were not so much introduced to him as brought up to be presented.[264] Evelyn Waugh thought he was like Mr Tulkinghorn in *Bleak House* and wished that 'some demented ladies' maid would make an end to him'. Virginia Woolf saw 'the little dapper grocer' as 'the ornament on the teapot', the emblem of Victorian respectability. Squire, on the other hand, came to admire and like 'the doyen of English critics, the official head of English Literature over which he exercised a benevolent tyranny'. Despite the difference of age (thirty-five years) and politics there developed a real bond between the two men. 'I have a strong feeling that if you will let me say so I have found a friend,' Gosse wrote. He even began to subscribe to the *New Statesman* 'in order to shudder weekly at your blood-curdling sentiments'.[265] Soon he was writing, 'You are a poet of a high order and a mind in curiously close sympathy with me. I feel myself singularly in tune with you. I understand exactly what you say. It is so rare.'

The Birds and Other Poems was another product of the last months of the war. The title poem was dedicated to Gosse. Only one poem in this tiny (eight poems) collection directly refers to the war, but the elegiac note is pervasive. The long narrative poem 'The Birds' takes as its theme the contrast between man's brief life on earth and the birds who have been there 'in the dark backward and abysm of time'.[266] The immensity of time and a world where man has never trod is a theme deeply embedded in Squire's imagination and gives power to his sinewy lines:

O let your strong imagination turn
The great wheel backward, until Troy unburn
And then unbuild, and seven Troys below
Rise out of death, and dwindle, and outflow,
Till all have passed, and none has yet been there:
Back, ever back.[267]

In its use of formal rhyming couplets, the poem was a tribute to the traditionalist Gosse:

A dizzying tangle of gulls were floating and flying
Wheeling and crossing and darting, crying and crying,
Circling and crying, over and over and over
Crying with swoop and hover and fall and recover.
And below on a rock against the grey sea fretted,
Pipe-necked and stationary and silhouetted,
Shags stood in a wise, black, equal row
Above the nests and long blue eggs we know.[268]

The rhythm brings the shrieking chaos of the gull colony and their 'dizzying tangle' to life, and comes to a halt with the stationary, solid row of shags. Gosse called the quatrain about the gulls 'SUPERB', stretching the heroic couplet to its limit without breaking it. 'Pure 1760', he purred, on reading the final octave. With this poem, he wrote, the classic age of poetry needed never to have come to an end: 'You make me proud. I am immensely pleased to see my name pinned to the cover of your noble and original poem... After this, you should be capable of anything.'[269] The poem was already a classic: it would, he promised, last as long as anyone reads English.

The period at the end of the war was Squire's most productive and some of his finest poetry was written then. 'Winter Nightfall' describes a deserted Regency house with peeling stucco and a garden that has become a wilderness of 'dusty dark evergreens'. The last person to live and die there was an old retired colonel, 'Some Fraser or Murray', but Squire does not know the name.

Was it wet when he lived here,
Were the skies dun and hurrying,
Was the rain so irresolute?
Did he watch the night coming,
Did he shiver at nightfall,
Before he was dead?
Did the wind go so creepily,
Chilly and puffing,
With drops of cold rain in it?
Was the hill's lifted shoulder
So lowering and menacing,
So dark and so dread...
Perhaps. But he's gone now,
He and his furniture
Dispersed now forever;
And the last of his trophies,
Antlers and photographs,
Heaven knows where.
And there's grass in his gateway,
Grass on his footpath,
Grass on his door-step;
The garden's grown over,

The well-chain is broken,
The windows are bare.

And I leave him behind me,
For the straggling, discoloured
Rags of the daylight,
And hills and stone walls
And a rick long forgotten
Of blackening hay:
The road pale and sticky,
And cart-ruts and nail-marks,
And wind-ruffled puddles,
And the slop of my footsteps
In this desolate country's
Cadaverous clay.[270]

'Cadaverous clay' was a phrase full of resonance in 1918.

'Winter Nightfall' was John Betjeman's favourite, an example of what he admired most in Squire's poetry: the power of evocative description. It also set a pattern for his own 'Death in Leamington', first published in the *London Mercury*, and, much later, even Philip Larkin's 'Mr Bleaney'. The atmospheric 'Fen Landscape' was another of Betjeman's favourites and as near to an imagist poem as Squire ever got:

Wind waves the reeds by the river,
Grey sky lids the leaden water.
Ducks fly low across the water,
Three flying: one quacks sadly.

Grey are the sky and the water,
Green the lost ribbons of reed-beds,
Small in the silence a black boat
Floats upon wide pale mirrors.[271]

On 19 October 1918 in the *New Statesman*, 'Onyx' (Squire)

A Victorian family. From left, Dolly, Bessie, Jack and Nan.

(Left) Jack at Plymouth Corporation Grammar School.
(Right) Jack at Blundell's School.

Elizabeth (Bessie) Collings Squire.

*(Left) Willy Smith at
Cambridge.
(Above) Jack the
undergraduate.*

'You Are My Sky'. A young Eileen.

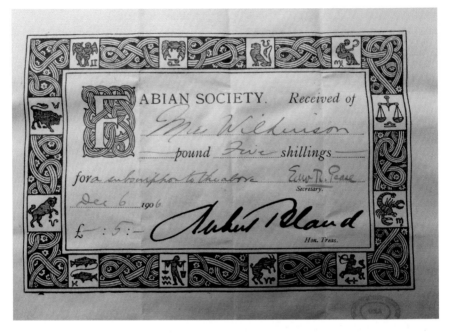

Eileen the Fabian.

(Left) Wedding Day.
(Above) The young intellectual.

MR. JACK COLLINGS SQUIRE.

(Left) Tom Tit's cartoon in the New Age.
(Above) The bull-dog, Willy Smith, Jack and son Raglan

FRAGMENT FROM A MEMORIAL ODE?

SO YOU ARE DEAD LIKE ALL THE OTHER DEAD...
  You are not here, but I am here alone;
  And evening falls, fusing tree, water and stone
  Into a violet cloth, and the frail ash-tree hisses
With a soft sharpness like a fall of mounded grain.
And a steamer softly puffing along the river passes,
Drawing a file of barges; and silence falls again.
And a bell tones; and the evening darkens; and in sparse rank
The greenish lights well out along the other bank.
I have no force left now; the sights and sounds impinge
Upon me unresisted, like raindrops on the mould.
And, striving not against my melancholy mood,
Limp as a door that hangs upon one failing hinge,
Limp, with slack, marrowless arms and thighs, I sit and brood
On death and death and death. And quiet, thin and cold,
Following of this one friend the hopeless, helpless ghost,
The weak, appealing wraiths of notable men of old
Who died, drift through the air; and then, host after host
Innumerable, overwhelming, without form,
Rolling across the sky in awful silent storm,
The myriads of the undifferentiated dead
Whom none recorded, or of whom the record faded.
O SPECTACLE APPALLINGLY SUBLIME!
  I see the universe one long disastrous strife,
And in the staggering abysses of backward and forward time
Death chasing hard upon the heels of creating life.
And I, I see myself as one of a heap of stones
Wetted a moment to life as the flying wave goes over,
Onward and never returning, leaving no mark behind...
There's nothing to hope for. Blank cessation numbs my mind,
And I feel my heart thumping gloomy against its cover,
And my heavy belly hanging from my bones.

J. C. SQUIRE?

Ode from the Magazine Form.

Broodingly Byronic

Anti-Vivisection protest outside the House of Commons.
From left, Harold Monro, Ralph Hodgson and Jack

The young editor

The family. From left, Jack, Raglan, Maurice, Eileen, Anthony, at Swan House.

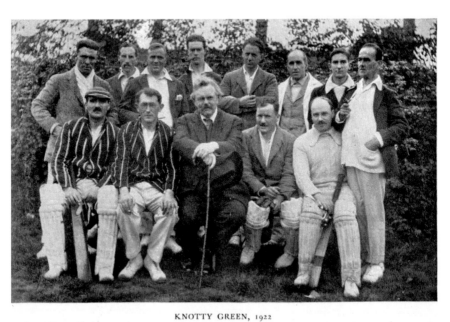

KNOTTY GREEN, 1922

R. Berkeley N. D. Bosworth-Smith C. Palmer A. G. Macdonell C. Bax M. Pike R. Austin R. H. Lowe

R. Straus J. C. Squire G. K. Chesterton R. Richards E. N. da C. Andrade

The Invalids.

Edmund Blunden and Sir John

Talking tactics.

LEDGER—PHILADELPHIA, FRIDAY,

ON "HUMORESQUE TOUR"

On the left is shown A. P. Herbert, editor of Punch, and beside him
J. C. Squires, editor of London Mercury, who are in Philadelphia today
as part of a tour of the country to study, among other things, American
humor.

Jack with A. P. Herbert.

Mr. & Mrs. J. C. SQUIRE.

GENERAL ELECTION 1924

Brentford & Chiswick Division.

Election Address
OF
MR. J. C. SQUIRE
PLEASE READ THIS CAREFULLY.

To the Electors of the Brentford and Chiswick Division.

**LIBERAL CENTRAL COMMITTEE ROOMS,
211 HIGH ROAD, CHISWICK, W.4.**

LADIES AND GENTLEMEN

13th October, 1924.

I have the honour to ask for your votes as Liberal Candidate in the forthcoming General Election. I have for many years lived in the constituency and I believe I can genuinely represent it. The Election has been rushed, and there will not be time for me to meet you all personally. I therefore earnestly ask you to read every word of this rather long Address. I think I may claim that it is the result of my own honest thought, and that there is no vote-catching clap-trap in it. We have had enough of politicians who think they need do no more than fling about vague phrases about Empire, Progress and Prosperity.

THE ELECTION AND THE THREE PARTIES.

I am standing in the conviction that the country at this juncture can only find salvation with the Liberal Party, which unites idealism and common-sense, as neither of the others do. The Conservative Party lacks enterprise, is too bound up with vested interests, and gets all its ideas second-hand from the Liberal Party about ten years too late. Recent experience has shewn us that, however moderate many of the leaders of the Labour Party may be, its constitution puts them too much in the power of " wild men " and impracticable

Election Address, 1924.

(Right) Thursley. Jack and his Alsatian.
(Above) A dapper Thomas Hardy at Thursley.

Amateur theatricals at Thursley. Eileen is fourth from left.

Invalids v. Eskimos, BroadHalfpenny Down, New Year's Day 1928.

Teams in front of the 'Bat and Ball', 1st January 1928.

Drawn by Hubert Williams

THE MERCURY'S NEW OFFICES: 229 STRAND

Three upper floors of the Mercury's new offices.

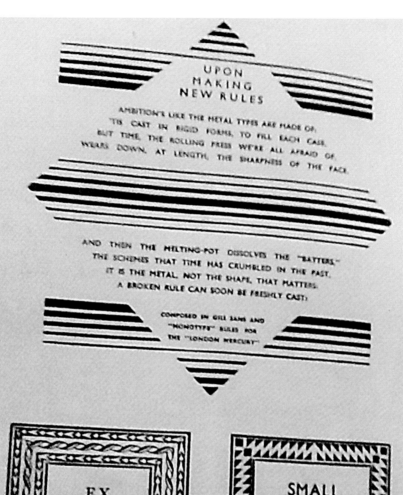

A PAGE OF "MONOTYPE" RULES

Monotype Rules from the London Mercury.

finished his account of the war as seen through soldiers' songs:

> Some of the soldiers on leave tell me that the effect of the dawn of victory on the Army has been most remarkable. Its fighting mettle has never declined, but there have been long periods when it has plugged on in a very dismal if dogged way. One symptom of the universal boredom was the total disappearance of the singing habit which was universal in the early stages of the war. Men – whatever the correspondents might say – have never sung much when going up to the trenches, but during the last twelve months they have never done much even when marching out again. All this has changed, and the regiments of the advancing Army go into the line laughing, singing and whistling in a manner unprecedented. The melancholy folk-songs of the Army have gone; they tramp to the latest rag-time. On the German side music at the moment is conspicuously absent.

When the war finally ended on 11 November Squire was one of the special constables who were detached from their normal duties at Buckingham Palace Gardens to assist in controlling the huge and exuberant crowds. His beat was the Mall, Trafalgar Square and Pall Mall. Far from the reported orgies that hit the news, 'all I saw, except for a small attempt to light a bonfire in front of the nose of a Landseer lion, was a crowd of soldiers who were dancing because the killing was over with girls who were dancing because the soldiers were not going to be killed.'[272] He reported patriotic rejoicing and cries for vengeance: 'Kill the Kaiser', 'Bleed the Huns', 'Make Germany Pay', 'Expel them all' and 'Lloyd George won the war'. He did not accept a word of it and summed up what the war had meant for him in one of his last *New Statesman* pieces.

> It was the end of a sodality… all thought of school friends and college friends in that far time before an end was made of our youth – the end of young manhood, the end of a world. To people who were fifty when the war broke out it came as an interruption, however

long, terrible and fraught with change. To us, who were thirty or less it came as an end. We had no careers, or long associations behind us... The war broke us, destroying, invalidating. Our youth went prematurely, we were scarred before our time by the griefs of age, we had to face a new world when we were just beginning to acclimatize ourselves to an old one. And for half of us the parting from youth was more bitter and final, for to those bones there is no return, even in imagination, to lost things; no remembering, with every pang and outline softened in the gold-dusty air of illusion, the joys and sorrows that were, and the faces, serious or laughing, of those who strayed through courts that strangers now inhabit and by streams that still so brightly and indifferently flow...[273]

Chapter 11

Peace

It was time to think of a post-war future. In June Squire 1918 Squire had written 'Mr Wells and World Peace' in *Land and Water*, favourably reviewing a tract that showed the necessity for 'A league of nations.' He told his readers that, 'If we do not get rid of war, war will get rid of us.' Now he became one of the founder members of the League of Nations Association, the parent of the League of Nations Union and served on the committee drawing up the first constitution. 'Another war would not only involve the hideous suffering and waste that the last war involved but would be the end of European civilization.' He was accused of being an imperialist when he urged the principle of 'one country, one vote' should be modified according to its size. He thought it was vital that Germany should be part of the League along with America. At the time of the Versailles Treaty he 'piped up' and argued for an agreement between the Western European powers to include Germany. They could and should have been coaxed and coddled into an agreement. As it was, Germany was left out, only to become a dangerous enemy.

A new world beckoned. Squire's third son Maurice was born in September and the family set about enjoying their life together in Swan House. Social life resumed with the usual round of dinners, literary parties and fundraising events in Chiswick. Jack and Eileen played their part in local politics. On behalf of the Chiswick branch of the League of Nations Eileen performed dramatic sketches and Jack played in a string quartet. She entertained his colleagues and friends, but was not a natural cook. When Harold Nicolson and his wife came for dinner they were greeted with anguished cries from the kitchen of 'What an effluvium!' as she retrieved from the oven the smoking remains of a duck. Undaunted by her previous experience of the hospitality of Swan House, Virginia Woolf went to dinner with the Squires in May. Looking forward, she told Lytton Strachey, to an evening of wild dissipation, she found her host 'more repulsive than words can express and malignant into the bargain' and his wife a garrulous bore: 'Yes, I give these parties because they are cheap,' she reported Eileen as saying, 'continuing in that style in a draught and without respite for ¾ hour'.[274]

Cricket resumed. In late Victorian and Edwardian England no sport had gripped the public imagination more than cricket. Its iconic figure was the stoutly bearded W. G. Grace, wearing the bacon-and-eggs, red-and-gold-coloured cap of the MCC. A gentlemanly and not too serious form of the game had also flourished since mid-Victorian times. J. M. Barrie captained the Authors (which he called the Allahakbarries under the mistaken impression that the Arabic meant 'God Help Us.') Among its players were Arthur Conan Doyle, H. G. Wells, P. G. Wodehouse, Rudyard Kipling and E. W. Hornung, Squire's uncle-in-law, and the creator of the character of the gentleman thief and deadly spin bowler A. J. Raffles.

After the war ended Hornung told Squire that his brother J.P. had his own cricket ground at West Grinstead Park and suggested that his nephew might bring along a team of writers and artists to play the village team. It was agreed and on August Bank Holiday Monday 1919 the match took place. At first Squire called his side the 'Old Age Pensioners', but as they contained many friends and colleagues who had fought and been wounded, they quickly became the 'Invalids' and adopted the colours of officers' hospital pyjamas, blue and gold; their crest was a pair of crossed crutches. Squire's eleven included a man whom he had just met at 39 Half Moon Street with Siegfried

Sassoon, who shared his love of cricket and poetry: Edmund Blunden. Squire had immediately invited him to play and to send his poems to the *Mercury*. Blunden, a bona fide veteran who had twice been reported killed in action, played in the first match and opened the batting padless. The team included Squire's brother-in-law Clennell, and the wartime artist the Hon. Neville Lytton. They held on for an honourable draw aided by a shower of rain and 'an excellent and prolonged luncheon'. The captain was less successful himself. The scorecard read 'J. C. Squire b. Hornung (Capt. G) 0.'

In his final pieces for the *New Statesman* and *Land and Water*,[275] Squire took stock of the literary landscape. He gave an overview of the literary scene as it had evolved since Solomon Eagle had begun writing his column in 1913. His heroes of his Fabian days, Wells and Shaw, had both lost their appeal. They shared a kind of evolutionary optimism which Squire increasingly rejected. He did not believe, as they apparently did, that the majority of men were looking for a genuinely scientific religion. He mocked Wells's idea of utopia as a group of highly educated engineers who play bar billiards on board smoothly running trains and discover how to fly to other planets. He found Shaw's idea of creative evolution in which man developed into pure spirit equally absurd. Both tried to write Bibles for their new religions – and both failed. Squire thought that they both failed to relate two things: 'Time and Eternity, neither of which we can comprehend.'[276]

He remembered how before the war the theatre had been the standard-bearer of progressive thought. Shaw, Ibsen, Granville Barker and the suffragette plays at the Court had heralded a New Age. But now everything had changed. The theatre of social issues, 'the Age of Drains', as Squire called it, was over. 'Realism' had been the pretext for 'a scene or two showing a young woman in a djibbah reading a Blue-book while her obscurantist parent (male always) asked her what that nonsense was all about.'[277] The vogue for Schnitzler, Wedekind and 'that gloomy lunatic Strindberg' had passed. Depression and monotony were the marks of Galsworthy's dramas that had now taken over the commercial theatre. His plays gave Squire the impression that it was the duty of a serious contemporary writer to be 'horrifying, unpleasant and disgruntled'; they always made him feel he was in some cheerless seaside lodging house on a wet day.[278] 'They would invite you to witness in five acts the squalid meals of a clerk and his wife in Brixton, into which an acuter pain was introduced: drink, adultery or unemployment'. Now 'Repertory plays' and misery had had their day. Yeats, Squire thought, offered the exciting promise of a drama of poetry and imagination – but the spirit of the time was against him. The theatres themselves were, Squire thought, dismal dying places and the drama had become a living corpse. The music halls were much better – and he could smoke there. He was looking forward to a revival of drama – and at its best and most serious that was always poetic drama. This revival was long overdue.

The novel seemed to Squire 'temporarily dead'. Hardy had given up writing novels; Joseph Conrad was past his best; Henry James was dead. Squire admired D. H. Lawrence as a poet, but hated his novels as phallocentric and gloomy. He praised James Joyce as 'a realist of the first order' who might discover a new form of writing – but *A Portrait of the Artist as a Young Man* was not a novel as Squire understood the word. It showed a gift for poetry not prose. 'It is doubtful if he will make a novelist.'[279] So far Virginia Woolf had published only one novel. 'The deflation, temporary perhaps, of the Novel has been proceeding for some years; the absence of even tolerable new novelists has been too nearly complete to be attributable to the peculiar war conditions. The novel of "psychology", the novel of minute observation, the propagandist novel are still produced in quantities; but the best literary brains are not going into them.' Squire had hoped for young novelists to emerge, but none, he thought, had. Some had enjoyed wide popularity for a while but then disappeared. There was of course popular romance or what Squire called the 'sex novel' of Ethel M. Dell, Mrs Barclay and George Egerton. He suggested a common opening for this kind of fiction: 'Rain drifted from a lilac sky. Miss Jones felt the child stir within her...'

The general weakness was the kind of realism that presented a world of grim surroundings and sad characters who dominated the novel just as they had the theatre. Squire felt that there had been no happiness, no fun, no laughter in the novels of the past decade. Their characters faced terrible endings – 'dead, disgraced or dipsomaniac – and lucky if they escaped suicide in the end.'[280] 'Realism' was the sentimentality of misery – just as escapist as any sugar-coated world of happy endings. It neglected love, happiness and laughter. By contrast George and Weedon Grossmith's *The Diary of a Nobody* was a book he read and reread. He felt the comedy of lower-middle-class suburban life contained more truth to life and more humour than any novels of the so-called realistic school. Sociologists of the future, he thought, would find it much more revealing than Zola and much more useful in its portrait of middle-class life in the 1890s than George Gissing. 'If any man really wants what the critics used to call a slice of life, here it is,' he wrote in his introduction to the 1940 edition.

Squire felt that the underlying reason for the failure of novelists and playwrights was their lack of understanding of the mood of post-war England. No epic or tragic literature could be written: 'A generation of thorough and often conscienceless scepticism followed by a breakdown of civilization has produced a mental and moral chaos.' The painfully realistic seam had been worked out: 'The modern novel is as temporary as the steam engine.' He guessed that a new kind of novel would emerge – but he could not imagine what it would be like.

The poets, though, did understand. Squire called his Christmas article in the December 1917 *Land and Water* 'The Poetic Revival'. 'Ours is a lyrical age,' he proclaimed. It was true, he argued, there were no towering figures and no long philosophical poems, but 'you had a great crowd of youths willing to expose the best and truest in them and spontaneously aware they must do it in musical language...' He developed the theme later in the *London Mercury*:

It is a matter of a change in attitude towards life; a return on the broader emotions; a desire to acknowledge and praise the things men love and find beautiful rather than to labour at analysis and at speculation—not to mention sophistry. It is mostly lyric poetry that men are writing; and it is one of the results of the war, which had intensified our awareness of the old familiar things around us, which were in a sense threatened for all, and the loss of which was imminently before millions of individuals, that much of it is poetry of the English landscape and especially of the English landscape as a historic thing.[281]

Georgian Poetry was a beacon of hope. Squire felt that the Georgian was on a par with the Elizabethan and the Romantic ages. He was sure, 'Should our literary age be remembered by posterity solely as an age during which fifty men had written lyrics of some durability for their truth and beauty, it would not be remembered with contempt. It is of no use asking a poetical renascence to conform to type for there isn't any type.'[282] Now poetry had a position and a prominence that it had not enjoyed since the time of Tennyson.

The war had transformed Squire's thinking: it had given him a suspicion of the new, a distrust of foreign art and a reverence for tradition. The main feature of the past decade had been 'sections of artists in all countries from France to Nicaragua running amok, inuring us to every kind of lunacy and incomprehensibility with subcutaneous connections with the European soul and mind.' He did not name them, but clearly, they were the heirs of Futurism, Vorticism and post-impressionism. Opposed to them was a sane mainstream. The struggle between the two forces was of crucial importance: 'We are in the middle of a critical battlefield, of a conflict between beliefs and working assumptions which to some of us mean sanity, vigour and health, and beliefs and disbeliefs, passions and manias, which might, were they to spread, mean the death of ordered civilisation and of literature with it'…[283] English society stood at a crisis point: on one side was Culture, and on the other Anarchy. Having uttered these warnings, Solomon Eagle fell silent.

Squire had become a leading figure in literary London. Alec

Waugh remarked that in 1914 he was little known, but by Armistice Day he had arrived. Edmund Gosse arranged his election to the National Club at 12 Queen Anne's Gate so that they could easily meet there and then proposed him as a Fellow of the Royal Society of Literature. He was seconded by Henry Newbolt and in June 1919 he was elected unanimously. Through Gosse's friends and contacts Squire also made contact with the world of high politics. He admired and liked Viscount Haldane, then leader of the House of Lords, and spent evenings dining with him and afterwards drinking coffee in the study and smoking one of the millionaire Sir Ernest Cassell's gold-encased cigars.

Edward Marsh invited Squire to meet Winston Churchill for lunch at the Savoy. In his pre-war days he had thought Churchill a 'wrong un'. When they met in September, Squire was still on the executive committee of the Fabian Society. He was surprised to find Churchill fascinating: 'I have met many politicians; this is the first one who is alive.'[284] He added that Lloyd George was also alive, but he wished he wasn't. Churchill had many qualities and the primary virtue of courage. Other politicians were 'mostly cynics and cowards'. He still had his doubts; he thought Churchill's weakness was 'sentimentalism' and disagreed with his view that Lenin's treachery summed up the Russian situation. What remained of the socialist in Squire could not accept the dismissal of industrial unrest by calling British munitions workers well-fed malcontents. Melodrama and overstatement, he felt, coloured Churchill's politics.[285]

Despite growing doubts about socialism, Squire decided to stand as the first Labour candidate for the University of Cambridge. The constituency returned two members, generally two unopposed Conservatives. 'At that rate the Manx cat has a chance,' commented Virginia Woolf.[286] His manifesto showed him to have modified his utopian views, in line with official party policy. It was a dutiful account of Labour policy but it lacked Squire's own personality and style. It read like, and seemed copied from, the official party manifesto. He emphasised that the state had to play a much more important role than in the past. He demanded the immediate nationalisation of railways and mining; a national minimum wage; shorter working hours; state supervision of farming; the building of new houses and a Ministry for Health. More personally, he told the voters that he had already supported the suffragette campaign and would continue to favour equality of opportunity and equal pay. Finally, he appealed to his electors in the university with the message that they had to reform. They had to think again about the dominance of Classics. And they had to admit women on an equal basis to men – or face the prospect of being controlled by outside forces. Squire's radical agenda did not win over the university electorate: he polled only 641 votes and lost his deposit. At least he could now begin to focus on his main strength – literature.

Tired of politics and politicians, and disheartened by his failure at the Cambridge election, Squire was to exclude politics entirely from the new magazine he was setting up. Now he had a clear enemy within his sights to replace the fat bourgeois of his Fabian days: the young modernist. *New* was the word of the moment. 'Make it new,' commanded Ezra Pound. Periodicals trumpeted the adjective – the *New Age*, the *New Statesman*, the *New Coterie*, the *New Weekly*, *New Numbers*, the *New Republic* and the *New Witness*. The precocious schoolboy Brian Howard wrote a piece called 'The New New' for the *Eton Candle*. Behind Squire's suspicion lay the shade of Dr Johnson's neoclassical belief in universality: 'The chief emotions of mankind are the same in all parts of the world where man exists, and they are the same as far as we have been able to discover where man has composed.'[287] He followed Johnson in believing that at the heart of literature were the great commonplaces of human nature, 'sentiments to which every bosom returns an echo'. Modernism was based on entirely false premises:

That tendency to think that art and thought began yesterday; that all history before yesterday left only a few relics worth preserving which were 'modern' before their time; that a thing is necessarily great if nobody has ever said it or thought it worth saying before:

that anything which is abnormal must be good and that nothing is interesting unless it is bizarre and preferably violent.

By 1919 the more or less peaceful coexistence of artists and writers of different outlooks that had thrived before the war gave way to bitter literary arguments. What kind of literature would best reflect the post-war world? Rupert Brooke, the name everyone knew, was dead, as were Wilfred Owen and Edward Thomas. Futurism, Vorticism, and perhaps imagism too, were over. The forces of modernism in England had dispersed. Pound had left London for Paris, Joyce was in Trieste, Lawrence had begun his wandering exile and Eliot was still known only to a select few who read the little magazines. In 'Post-Georgian Poet seeks a Master', the American Douglas Goldring wrote of his dilemma:

> In those blithe days before the War began
> Ah me I was a safe young Georgian!
> Now all is chaos, all confusion.
> Bolshies have cast E. M. from his high throne:
> Wild women have rushed in and savage Yanks…
>
> I don't know where I am or where to go…
> Can Nichols be relied upon for a lead?
> Or should I thump it with Sassoon and Read?
> Or would it not be vastly better fun
> To write of Nymphs with Richard Aldington?
> Or shall I train, and nervously aspire
> To join with Edward Shanks and Jack Squire
> A modest 'chorus' in a well-paid choir?[288]

The 'wild women' are H. D. and Amy Lowell. Shanks, by now Squire's deputy editor at the *London Mercury*, and Squire himself are marked out from the rest as well-heeled professionals. Unnamed in the list are Pound and Eliot, although they are probably the 'savage Yanks'.

Squire's relations with Eliot both as critic and poet were always complex. They had met for the first time when in March 1914, recently arrived in England, Eliot had sent Squire a review at the *New Statesman* and tried to fix up a lunch. There followed a moment of nervous geniality when he offered as a special treat the promise that 'There will be beer – and whiskey!' Three months later he sent another review and corrected proofs in Squire's office while the busy sub-editor was on the telephone to the House of Commons. Eliot wrote to his mother to say how pleased he was that he had had his articles accepted by the *New Statesman*. Squire promised him introductions to the American magazines *The Dial* and *The Century*. (Ironically enough, it was Squire who published Eliot's seminal essay 'Reflections on *Vers Libre*' in the *New Statesman* of March 1917.) Eliot asked Squire to write a testimonial to recommend him for the Quartermaster Corps of the U.S. Army. In August Squire cautiously reviewed *Prufrock and Other Observations*: 'Certainly much of what he writes is unrecognisable as poetry at present… and it is only fair to say that he does not call these pieces poems. He calls them "observations" and the description seems exact [because] we do not pretend to understand the drift of the "Love Song of J. Alfred Prufrock".'[289] When the war was over Squire tried to recruit Eliot for the *London Mercury*, but he replied with polite caution and nothing came of it.

It was time for modernists such as Eliot to regroup. Their arguments became theatre at the Conference Hall, Westminster. The Arts League of Service, an idealistic group formed in October 1919 as a parallel to the League of Nations, organised an autumn programme of four talks on 'Modern Tendencies of Arts'. The programme was itself a modernist statement. Designed by a friend of Eliot's, the poster artist Edward McKnight Kauffer, it showed the stylised figure of an outsize man spanning a bridge. On one side was a medieval town and the other a modern industrial city. The message was obvious: man was about to step heroically from the world of the past into the future.

Wyndham Lewis gave the first talk on 'Painting' and on 28

October more than 300 poets, artists and musicians packed the hall
to hear the thirty-one-year-old American poet and critic T. S. Eliot
give the second lecture: 'Modern Tendencies in Poetry'. 'Strange as
it seems now it is a fact that to admire his poetry in 1919 was daring
and revolutionary,'[290] wrote Richard Aldington. When he suggested
writing about Eliot's poetry he was cautioned, 'But he's a wild man.'
The audience contained many of the 'Athenaeums' including Edith
Sitwell, the music critic Edward Dent, the modernist novelist Sydney
Schiff and his wife Violet, and Middleton Murry. Laurence Binyon
was the Chairman and the Georgians were out in force too, led by
Squire, Shanks and Abercrombie.

Laurence Binyon introduced Eliot. 'He was a middle-aged poetic
celebrity who knew nothing about me except I was supposed to be the
latest rage,' wrote Eliot to his mother. He seemed to attack Eliot's ideas
in his lecture before he had heard them. With what he thought was a
hostile chairman and a hostile audience, Eliot was careful not to praise
Ezra Pound or criticise Rupert Brooke. Afterwards he wrote that he
was very anxious to avoid putting his foot in it or 'saying anything
that might bring popular fury on to myself'.[291] In his lecture Eliot
developed the idea of the impersonality of poetry with the analogy
of the work of the poet to that of the scientist. Like science it had to
grow and develop from the discoveries of the past. Poetry could no
longer be the 'mere ebullition of personality'. To illustrate the way the
poet's mind worked he compared this process of depersonalisation to
chemical catalysis.

> When you study the life's work of a great scientist, you recognize that
> the man accomplished what he did not through a desire to express
> his personality, but by a complete surrender of himself to the work
> in which he was absorbed... The great scientist submerges himself
> in what he has to do, forgets himself. But if he is a great scientist
> there will be... a cachet of the man all over it... His personality has
> not been lost, but has gone, all the important part of it, into the
> work... There is the same inevitability and impersonality about the

work of a great poet… the greater the poet, the more evident his hand in every line, and the more elusive his personality.[292]

These were new and challenging ideas. Squire listened to Eliot as he developed an analysis which was completely foreign to his own romantic and traditional view of poetry as the expression of feelings. He was both puzzled and sceptical. Whereas Eliot talked of impersonality and science Squire felt that the more personality the better and he had little interest in science. After his lecture there were questions. Eliot faced 'the heavy fire of heckling' from Squire and his friends, but he responded in philosophic style by countering questions with more questions. He wrote to his mother that his lecture had been a great success.[293]

Middleton Murry's marriage to Katherine Mansfield, friendship with D. H. Lawrence and admiration of T. S. Eliot helped to make him a central figure in the world of the modernists. He had no doubt that the lines were drawn up ready for a fight for survival. He described what was at stake to his wife in gladiatorial terms and signed himself 'Tiger': 'The anti-Athenaeums – Munro [sic] Jack Squire etc. – present in force. There's no doubt it's a fight to the finish between us & Them – them is the "Georgians" en masse: It's a queer feeling I begin to have now: that we're making literary history. But I believe we are going to. More than that, in spite of the London Mercury and all its réclame, I believe we've got them on the run. They're afraid.'[294]

Murry's attack was much less abstract and much less cool than Eliot's lecture; his anger boiled over. He derided the 12,000 readers of the latest Georgian Poetry as being as ignorant of poetry as they were of the theory of relativity and launched into an assault on the 'charlatans who form a strange group with self-deceivers to exploit the taste of the tasteless. J. C. Squire sprawls on the artistic horizon attended by an assiduous claque which knows the rising star. They roll each other's logs. They are filled with noble patriotism. They toady with LG [Lloyd George] and dine with Winston. Jolly old England!… and now the same clique-claque has a fat orange review full of sound sentiment and fake art to show how fine and prosperous and noble they are and how degraded and envious and bitter is the fruit sold on the way.'[295]

He was of course wrong about Lloyd George (whom Squire loathed) and wrong too about Squire's dinners with Winston. The hatred that Murry felt for Squire, the *London Mercury* and *Georgian Poetry* became something obsessive. Behind the disagreements about poetry and art there was something else. Murry wrote with the kind of fury that came from personal hurt. For him the life of a writer and editor had meant poverty and threats of bankruptcy. By contrast Squire and his friends seemed to lead a well-fed, all-powerful establishment which had rejected him. 'That gang [Marsh and Squire] has tried to crab us long enough. I begin to feel angry. I want to lash out and kick their heap of dry bones into the gutter...'[296]

Chapter 12

'The London Murkury'

'The London Mercury constituted a mediator in a field of periodical production… It was savvy enough to negotiate the commercial concerns of a successful periodical as well as take an aesthetic stand about literary modernity. As we see in Woolf's work, the London Mercury's proximity to the emerging modernist highbrow made it a tempting site of publication; modernists almost necessarily derided its central positioning while still profiting from it. Its importance in the field of periodical production cannot be underestimated since it was a force that successfully negotiated the divides of the modernist print market until the late 1920s. What Squire endeavoured to promulgate was a wider view of culture than elite modernist coteries allowed. What he achieved in his magazine was an often-disputed, but hard-won middle ground.'[297]

'Little magazines' of all kinds and sizes flourished in the years before and during the war. Most started their lives with great hopes and clamour and then fizzled out. Money was nearly always the issue. In England Middleton Murry hoped to write novels and poetry, but knew that magazines were where a writer had to begin his career. He had edited *Rhythm*, an Oxford undergraduate magazine in Autumn 1911. Avant-garde in its approach to literature and art (it printed the first drawings by Picasso to be published in England) it became a mouthpiece for progressive ideas and ran for two years before it went bankrupt. *Signature* was a short-lived collaboration with D. H. Lawrence. Murry had grand plans for a clubroom in Bloomsbury for his salon of writers and collaborators. Two issues and one month later it collapsed and he had to flee to Paris to escape his creditors.

Other magazines followed the same pattern. In 1914 the Georgian magazine *New Numbers* managed to last only a year. In wartime England *BLAST*'s two numbers also spanned only a year. Harold Monro's *Poetry and Drama* survived for three years and that 'Citadel of Modernism', *The Egoist: An Individualist Review* began in 1914. Comparatively long-lived, it started with a readership of 2,000, but five years later when it finally collapsed it had fallen to 400. Wyndham Lewis's the *Tyro* ran for only two numbers. These magazines were natural channels for experiment and modernism; many key works saw the light of day in them. Ezra Pound found a home in *Poetry*; James Joyce's *Portrait of the Artist as a Young Man* and *Ulysses* were both published serially in little magazines; T. S. Eliot's *The Waste Land* first appeared in the *Dial*. Despite small circulations, shoestring finances and mayfly lifespans, the little magazines were where modernism began.

After the war ended a host of jostling rivals entered this already crowded magazine world. Harold Monro produced his *Monthly Chapbook* and two Oxford University students started *Coterie*. The first number came out on May Day 1919 with contributions from Eliot and Aldous Huxley. After struggling with poverty throughout the war Middleton Murry was suddenly offered £800 a year to edit the re-formed *Athenaeum*. In April 1919 he launched it with an impressive list of contributors – a serious challenge to the *TLS* – which immediately gave away 10,000 copies in response as an advertising scheme. *John O' London's Weekly* magazine, launched in April 1919, costing only twopence, aimed at a more popular readership and enjoyed enormous sales of up to 80,000.

Robert Graves was quick to join the post-war fray. Still in uniform, he wrote to Squire from the training camp at Rhyl in September 1918 announcing a new magazine that he was going to set up with his father-in-law, the artist William Nicholson. It was to be called *The Owl*, a miscellany of poetry and art from the best people, old and young: 'Between us we know the real good ones.' After the grim years of wartime, *The Owl* was to exclude politics and consist of 'good work, healthy minds and good fun'. Graves's beautifully produced and very expensive magazine (ten shillings and sixpence) emerged in May 1919. He knew that it would have to compete with yet another newcomer, Arnold Bennett's *Life and Letters*, but thought, in the language of the trenches, that would prove only to be a 'stunty sort of show'. 'I hope we can count on your moral support, if not your help', he wrote to Squire.[298] To suit the new mood Squire sent one of his most assured love poems, 'Song':

You are my sky; beneath your circling kindness
My meadows all take in the light and grow;
Laugh with the joy you've given,
The joy you've given,
And open in a thousand buds, and blow.

But when you are sombre, sad, averse, forgetful,
Heavily veiled by clouds that brood with rain,
Dumbly I lie all shadowed,
I lie all shadowed,
And dumbly wait for you to shine again.[299]

The second number of *The Owl* came out in October. Once again Graves asked Squire to contribute. He sent another love poem, 'The Happy Night':

I have loved to-night; from love's last bordering steep
I have fallen at last with joy and forgotten the shore;
I have known my love to-night as never before,

I have flung myself in the deep, and drawn from the deep,
And kissed her lightly, and left my beloved to sleep.
And now I sit in the night and my heart is still:
Strong and secure; there is nothing that's left to will,
There is nothing to win but only a thing to keep.

And I look to-night, completed and not afraid,
Into the windy dark where shines no light;
And care not at all though the darkness never should fade,
Nor fear that death should suddenly come to-night.
Knowing my last would be surely my bravest breath,
I am happy to-night: I have laughed to-night at death.[300]

In August 1918 Squire had resigned from editing *Land and Water* and decided to fulfil his ambition to produce his own literary monthly. Ten years earlier he had told Eileen his dream had been to edit a socialist paper.

'I had an opportunity of doing what I had long wanted to when in 1919 there came my chance to establish the *London Mercury*. When I was a young man I made up my mind that if I ever got into a position of any power I would start a paper with the main object of printing young people. I knew that to make it go I had to put the old ones in too, but my entire purpose was, while telling nobody about it, to give youth its opportunity.'[301] With the end of the war his ambition had changed: one area that the magazine specifically did not cover was the world of politics. Squire had spent the last two years writing about it for the *New Statesman* and knew that there was no longer any appetite for it after the exhaustion and failures of the Great War.

'A fantastic situation had arisen,' wrote Alec Waugh. Squire had acquired the best network of friends and colleagues of any of his magazine competitors. Edmund Gosse gave him easy access to the *Sunday Times*; Edward Marsh was a close friend and associate; on Wednesday afternoons he took Turkish baths with Arnold Bennett; Edward Shanks, Squire's assistant editor, was sub-editor at the *New*

Statesman; W. J. Turner wrote theatre reviews. Squire himself still wrote occasionally for *Land and Water*, edited by his friend Hilaire Belloc, and *The Outlook* whose literary editor was Clennell Wilkinson, who also reviewed for the Saturday *Westminster Gazette*. In the autumn Squire became the chief literary critic of the *Observer*. No wonder he called himself a centipede with a foot in a hundred camps.

Squire had learnt a great deal from *Georgian Poetry*. It was clear to him that there was now a real appetite for new writing and that a magazine could even make money to reward its contributors. From his mentors Walling, Orage, Sharp and Marsh he had learnt the importance of one guiding editor to direct the whole magazine. Just as Orage controlled the *New Age* and Marsh's hand was everywhere in *Georgian Poetry*, so Squire shaped the *London Mercury*. He had watched so many magazines flourish and die (including the strange quarterly *Form*, which he had edited) and was ambitious to start his own on a much longer-term and more stable basis. He set up the *Mercury* in a way that he hoped would not depend on a monthly or quarterly purchase; he found the capital to invest in his venture from 'thousands of subscribers' who were prepared to support him without ever seeing the magazine. They included his wife's rich uncles J. P. and E. W. Hornung and the Liberal grandee Aneurin Williams. He already had been promised poems for his new magazine by Hardy and short stories by Conrad and asked Edward Marsh if there was anything of Rupert's available: 'It would be a great thing for No. 1. The *London Mercury* <u>shall</u> be the best thing there is,'[302] he promised.

The first number came out in November 1919. A brilliant orange cover proclaimed its arrival into the monochrome magazine world. For an annual fee of thirty shillings it would be sent post-free to all parts of the world from its editorial base at Windsor House, Bream's Buildings, EC4. Unlike the 'little magazines' the *Mercury* was big – it ran to 148 pages. At 2s 6d it could almost have been thought a bargain. Unlike its high-minded rivals, it welcomed advertising. Sixteen publishers advertised in the first number, together with an assortment of rare book dealers, stockbrokers and a salesman of fishing rods. The

Mercury's advertisements were given over largely to publishers, fine presses, and businesses associated with the print trade.

The format was to remain much the same for all of Squire's editorship. He used the editorials to speak directly to his readers. The tone was set by the tone of the editor's voice. Increasingly this became one of the main attractions. A selection of new poems followed, headed in the first number by two unpublished poems: Thomas Hardy's 'Going and Staying', and Rupert Brooke's 'It's Not Going to Happen Again', duly sent by Edward Marsh. There were poems too by Siegfried Sassoon, W. H. Davies, Laurence Binyon and Walter de la Mare. Then came a short story by Robert Nichols and a critical essay by Edmund Gosse. Squire certainly had brought up the big guns. After this there was a features section which contained longer critical articles, short fiction and essays.

In his first editorial he defined the magazine and its purpose.[303] He began by noting the precarious and difficult business of launching it in the uncertainty of the year after war ended: 'It might have come in more tranquil and comfortable days.' He feared that paper might be unprocurable, printing impossible and distribution from hand to hand. 'We have had a glimpse into the abyss, but', he concluded, 'the more uncertain and darker the future the more obvious the need for periodicals to hand on the torch'. Not only was the ambition grand, it was also unique. 'We may say that there never has been in this country a paper with the scope of the LONDON MERCURY,' he boasted. Squire felt he was a pioneer in bringing together original poetry and criticism. Whatever he had said about the main purpose being to publish young poets, his emphasis was slightly different in 1919: 'The chief function was the examination of conditions likely to produce in the past and the future artistic work of the first order and the formulation of critical standards.' The world of literature, and the arts more generally, were in a state of ferment. His conservative analysis of that ferment led him to become the best-known editor of his day – but also to his downfall and near oblivion.

Squire saw the literary world as divided between a sound and sensible mainstream which included Thomas Hardy, Joseph Conrad, Robert Bridges and A. E. Housman – and numerous sects who went in for various meretricious 'stunts', often to disguise their lack of ability. They included Futurists such as Marinetti, imagists such as H. D. and Ezra Pound and Dadaists such as Tristan Tzara. He insisted that he was not dogmatic and not against any type of art, provided it was genuine: he was not against free verse (and of course wrote it himself). He wrote that he was prepared to support an artist who drew on papier mâché with a red-hot poker. Emphatically, Squire claimed, the *Mercury* was not a coterie magazine: it aspired to include the best that was written, regardless of where it came from. Unlike the modernists, he wanted to attract as wide a spectrum of readers as possible.

Many young writers, he felt, had lost their way. They needed to remember the old saying: 'Look into your heart and write.'[304] Many were simply too intellectual and dry. Then there was the issue of difficulty and obscurity. 'All good writing will carry at least a superficial meaning to the intelligent reader.' At present, 'disconnected words and images, meaningless and even verbless' counted as poetry. There was a vogue too for cynical and cheap mockery. In the past a young simpleton of a poet would only need to utter 'vapid nonsense about moonshine and roses' to be applauded. Now the same simpleton only needed to become 'incorrect, incomprehensible and incoherent'. The poor state of criticism had allowed this to happen. Faced with the work of the young, older critics found it difficult to spot genuine new talent and to sort out the gold from the dross. If poets could not find understanding from critics, and if they could not find publishers, then magazines were the only way to survive. And that was exactly what Squire felt that the *Mercury*, with its blend of sound criticism and the best new poetry, could achieve. That was its mission.

Unsurprisingly, the *London Mercury* received a mixed reception. Edmund Gosse spent what he called an enchanting evening reading the first number from cover to cover and was quick to congratulate the editor: 'You have succeeded superbly. No such good "first number" was ever launched. But how will you keep it up? The effort is Herculean!'[305] The novelist Elizabeth Bowen called it the dominating magazine of its time. Others were less enthusiastic. Rose Macaulay felt it was 'too crabby', but admired the courage of the Editor's Notes. The *New Age* noted sourly how it was impossible to pick up a journal that was not full of praise for the *Mercury* and Jack Squire. The editor acknowledged that Squire was sometimes a good poet and parodist, but he was not a sound critic. So far, he was 'not even a dark horse in his stable'.

As editor of the *Athenaeum* Middleton Murry was becoming acknowledged as the spokesman for the modernist group of critics and writers he published, Eliot, E. M. Forster, Lytton Strachey and Virginia Woolf, and a bitter opponent of the Georgians. 'The Squire crowd hate the *Athenaeum* as so much poison,' he wrote to Katherine Mansfield. Now, only a few months after he had taken on the editorship, the crowd had launched a hostile competitor to considerable acclaim. He saw the *London Mercury* as a deadly threat and wrote to his wife of a 'new monthly (run by the awful Jack Squire) which announces a list of contributors, including nearly all ours, except you and me. So, we shall have to pull hard this winter and make the paper as good as can be.' Even though Murry dismissed the *Mercury* as the opposite of the *Athenaeum* there was evidently a considerable overlap between the two magazines and both editors competed for the favours of Eliot, Thomas Hardy, Aldous Huxley and Virginia Woolf. Murry's real fear was that Squire would poach all the good writers. He hoped Squire's magazine would prove a one-year wonder. 'Squire will have to produce something infinitely better than that to frighten me. And frankly I don't believe he's got it in him,' he wrote to Katherine Mansfield.[306]

Squire was anxious to recruit Virginia Woolf to write for his magazine and, despite the frosty atmosphere of the previous visits, invited her again to dinner in February 1920. It did not go well. This time she found Mrs Squire 'even more repulsive' than her husband, a picture of odious maternal happiness: 'a sort of indecency... in her passive gloating contentment in the armchair opposite... a jelly fish

– without volition, yet with terrifying potentiality'. By comparison Squire himself came off almost favourably. Although Virginia Woolf hated his generalities about 'love, patriotism and paternity', she found she could speak her mind to him. He tried to dissuade her from writing for Middleton Murry. The *Athenaeum*, he told her, was winning a bad name for its sceptical tone about everything; it was the frost of death to all creative activity. Virginia Woolf said she loathed 'that slop pail of cold tea', the *Mercury*, and declared she stood for honesty and high standards. Squire replied that his magazine stood for poetry and enthusiasm. In the end she decided she could write for both of them – plus Desmond MacCarthy's *New Statesman* – proof, she said, of her 'catholicity or immorality, according to your taste'.[307] (Squire was to publish two of her short stories, 'An Unwritten Novel' in July 1920, and 'Lives of the Obscure' in January 1924.)

Squire's position was further strengthened later in 1919. The success of the *Mercury* led to him being appointed by J. L. Garvin, the editor of the *Observer*, to write a long (1,500 words) weekly literary column on a subject of his own choosing. In the age of the Squirearchy, Garvin said, the paper could only profit from having the Squire himself. He paid a generous fifteen guineas a week. With his friend Gosse as chief reviewer on the *Sunday Times* the two friends had Sunday journalism's literary pages covered for the immediate future.

In the *Observer* Squire continued the literary war vigorously. He made a frontal attack on imagism and the abuse of free verse. In 'The Elements of Poetry', he argued that rhythm and music of some kind were essential to poetry. Imagism was an American movement alien to the English tradition – 'an imported, not an important thing'. 'The Revolting School' were publicity seekers. He quoted examples of bad verse by imagists such as Richard Aldington:

> The defect of Mr Aldington and his Imagist friends is that, although they are quite right, though not original, in emphasising the need for concrete language, they do for the most part lack that rhythm

that makes poetry what it is and rememberable. It is not that they write in free verse. Rhyme is no necessary part of verse, and nobody in the world ever contended that all the lines of a poem should be of standard lengths. But a poem in free verse should have a continuous rhythm other than that of prose, and *will* have it if it is written by a man who is strongly moved and has the gift of musical expression. Mr Aldington may have that gift, but if so he represses it.[308]

The attacks provoked a swift and angry reply from F. S. Flint who defended his imagist friends. Imagism, he claimed, was not a foreign import. It was started in London by Richard Aldington and others and exported to America where it flourished in anthologies. Squire's selection of bad verse ignored all the good poems they had written. Flint catalogued the failings of Squire and his circle. 'It was they and not the imagists who sought publicity: they edit reviews in which they print their dull and unimportant works side by side with famous authors; they get themselves posted on every coign of vantage where they sing one another's praises; they found literary prizes and award them to each other and call the newspapers in to report proceedings; they stick at no sort of manoeuvre that will keep them in the public eye and others out of it.'[309]

Flint's view seemed confirmed when Squire's growing influence extended to his control of the first important English literary prize, the Hawthornden, named after the Scottish poet William Drummond of Hawthornden.[310] Alice Helen Warrender, the philanthropic daughter of a Scottish baronet, encouraged by her friend Lady Randolph Churchill, had the idea of awarding a prize for imaginative literature. She sought advice from Edward Marsh about how to set it up. He recommended his friend Jack Squire for the selection committee of four. Squire was delighted to join and proposed that the prize should be awarded for the most imaginative literary work of the year written by an author under the age of forty. The first panel consisted of Laurence Binyon, Edward Marsh, Jack Squire and the donor herself. Miss Warrender soon fell out with Squire but Marsh reassured her that 'from his influence and energy he was by a long way the most useful member of the committee and does more for the prize than the other three put together.'[311] They were to become good friends all her life.

The Hawthornden Prize for Literature was awarded for the first time in 1919. The prize was a cheque for £100 (in 2019 worth about £15,000) and an inscribed silver medal, but the real prize was the recognition it gave as 'the most important literary award made in England'.[312] The committee decided unanimously that Edmund Gosse should present the prize, as otherwise he might do everything in his power to damage its reputation. It came as no surprise to Squire's enemies such as Osbert Sitwell that Edward Shanks, then Squire's deputy editor, was named as the first winner. In Sitwell's 'The Death of Mercury' the Goddesses of Dullness and Mediocrity unite:

Praise Squire from whom all blessings flow,
Oh, may he prosper! May his brood increase,
And death to all who are not Dull as he is!'
Up from glad Earth the chorus swells again,
'Praise Squire, Praise Squire,' we hear the swift refrain
That leaps like fire from every school and college,
From stately London home or Cotswold Cottage,
Wherever poet meets a poet brother
(Or makes an income by reviewing each other).

The echo alters to 'We never tire / Of hearing Squire on Shanks and Shanks on Squire.'[313]

Next year Squire told Marsh he hoped the prize would be given to someone completely unknown to them. In fact, it went to John Freeman, a keen if little-known nature poet. Squire's friend W. J. Turner described the scene. On the platform at the Wigmore Hall the Georgian judges were out in force – Edward Marsh, Laurence Binyon, Professor Gilbert Murray and Squire himself, 'wearing a bright grey suit with the air of a man who was going straight down to Goodwood and was on a sure thing'. Murray gave a speech, but did not seem to know who had won the prize. As no one had thought to provide steps John Freeman had to stand on tiptoe to receive his cheque from the platform. As darkness fell on the nearly empty hall Chopin's *Funeral March* could be heard from next door. Marsh called it a nightmare afternoon.[314]

Squire and Middleton Murry were at odds again when both the *London Mercury* and the *Athenaeum* reviewed Marsh's fourth anthology. Neither Squire nor Shanks could write a review, as they both had poems published there. The *Mercury*'s anonymous reviewer praised E. M.'s pioneering scheme: 'an act of faith, based on an act of divination'. Georgian poetry could not yet be defined. United by community of spirit and attitude rather than common style, the movement was gradually realising itself. There was praise for Harold Monro, W. H. Davies, Walter de la Mare, John Freeman and Robert Graves. To Marsh, credit should be given, the reviewer argued, not for naming or discovering a group, but for seeing so early the liveliness of the writers and publishing and nurturing them.

The *Athenaeum* naturally took a totally different line. Murry wrote a frontal attack. He wanted to title his article 'Marshmallows' – as the Georgians were all 'soft, dry and stodgy'. Much admired by the young F. R. Leavis, 'The Condition of English Poetry', as his review was eventually titled, was the most influential thing Murry wrote. He contrasted *Georgian Poetry 1918-1919* with the latest 'cycle' of Edith Sitwell's magazine, *Wheels*. The situation, he felt, was analogous to the war that had just finished. The Georgians were the coalition government with all that this implied about good honest citizenry and patriotism – Murry was at this time a pacifist. *Wheels* was the opposition. (Edith Sitwell had set up her slim magazine during the war as a riposte to *Georgian Poetry*. Reviewing the third 'cycle' in the *New Statesman* in Christmas 1918, Squire had written of her 'tiny talents'.) Murry's tone was drily sarcastic and demeaning. Dog lovers (Squire), fish lovers (Brooke), bird lovers (all) – the Georgians were derivative and lacked passion. They wrote poems to order. The *Wheels'* poets on the other hand were rebellious and much more interesting. They were striving to find new expressions for the new times they faced. The essence of poetry, he wrote, was the expression of feelings – and here he found the Georgians lacking:

> The negative qualities of this *simplesse* are the most obvious; the poems imbued with it are devoid of any emotional significance whatsoever. If they have an idea it leaves you with the queer feeling that it is not an idea at all, that it has been defaced, worn smooth by the rippling of innumerable minds... There is nothing disturbing about them; they are kind, generous, even noble. They sympathise with animal and inanimate nature, they have shining foreheads with big lumps of benevolence... And one is inclined to believe that their eyes must be frequently filmed with an honest haze, if only because their vision is blurred. They are fond of lists of names which never suggest things; they are sparing of similes. If they use them they are careful to see they are not too definite, for a definite simile makes havoc of their constructions, by applying to them a test of reality. But it is impossible to be serious about them...[315]

'Blurred eyes' was Murry's catty reference to Squire's short-sightedness. He ended on a topical and bitter word: treachery. It was the duty of the writer in troubled times not to be muddled or false. As Edward Marsh's biographer noted, 'From this moment E. M.'s anthologies ceased to hold their position as the acknowledged vehicle for the best in contemporary verse and the spokesman for this new trend in literature was John Middleton Murry.'[316] What was true for the Georgian Anthologies was, of course, true for J. C. Squire.

Murry knew that he had written the most damning indictment. He wrote to Katherine Mansfield that he had been 'terribly severe' and feared the Squire clique would seek its revenge. He knew too that he might well lose the friendship of his old friend and patron Edward Marsh (who had sent him a cheque for £100 and bailed him out of bankruptcy more than once) over the issue, but felt that he could not do anything else. It was too important a task to allow anyone else to do, but the effort had shaken him: 'It's a terrible thing, I'm almost frightened of it myself.'[317] The article effectively cleared the ground for Georgian poetry's successors.

Murry was therefore unsurprised, but nervous, when he was summoned round to the *Mercury's* office the day after the review was published. He was faced by the deputy editor Edward Shanks. Shanks told him that Squire had indeed been terribly upset by the review. Apparently, his bulldog Mamie had died two days before and he considered the passage about dog lovers unfeeling.

In his 'Sonnet to a Friend' Squire continued his attack on Murry and destructive modernist critics. The anonymous subject of the poem might have been a critic, 'Had he not chosen to remain instead / One of those vulgar fools with hearts and souls.' The sestet ends:

He might have talked of mind; he might have minced;
He might have made Parnassus Mount a morgue
Of eunuchry and logic and Laforgue,
And shrunk in sour disfavour from the big,
Squeaking, 'I fear that I am unconvinced.'
In fact he might have been a modern prig.[318]

His targets are clear: the obscure French poet Laforgue, an important influence on T. S. Eliot; Lytton Strachey, well-known for his sardonic squeaky voice; 'mincing' and 'eunuchry' were digs at the Sitwells' sexuality as well as the sterility of their work. The leading 'prig' was, of course, Middleton Murry. But the attack was not just personal: it was on the whole movement of dry intellectualism that Squire associated with the 'modern', the enemy of those with heart and soul, the killer of true poetry. This emphasis and the denial of the musical led to 'a small public getting the dry unmelodious, intellectual husks it wants, the great public consoling itself with "Annie Laurie" and the hungry sheep in between... who look for guidance where there is none...'[319] Hugh Walpole and many of Squire's friends agreed that the *Athenaeum* was indeed 'a gloomy pretentious affair written entirely by cranks'.[320] When Squire reviewed Murry's *Poems 1916– 1920* in the *Mercury* he took his revenge and dismissed the poems as 'the fatigued product of a man in a blind alley of what we used to call fin de siècle. It merely irritates.' Not only were the poems no good: they were old-fashioned.

In reply, and in private, Squire composed his squib, 'To the Athenaeum':

Little prig who made thee
Little prig God made thee
He who made the goat & pig
Made thee also, little prig.

Long thy ears, loud thy bray,
Imbecile the things you say
Striking the likeness, can it be
That he who made the ass made thee?

What immortal hand and eye
Dare frame thy sheer fatuity
And thy imbecile conceit
What dread hand and what dread feet?[321]

The critic Robert Ross saw the dug-in positions clearly: 'For most poets [in the 1920s] it was simply a case of fight or die, coterie warfare or poetic oblivion. The slow, often halting development of the individual poetic along lines determined by its own uniqueness, which had been the prize jewel of English poetry for generations, seemed by 1920 to have become a thing of the past, a sacrifice to the collectivist urge and the relativist urge of the onrushing twentieth century genius.'[322] Edith Sitwell described the groups or 'Coteries' in the *Sphere*.[323] There was the Squirearchy and its house magazine the *Mercury* on Fleet Street; the 'Bloomsberries' headed by Lytton Strachey and Virginia Woolf in

Gordon Square and 'a group of virile young men calling each other Pete'. And, of course there were the Sitwells themselves. Squire's friend the Irish critic Robert Lynd described the mutual hostility: 'The latest collection of Georgian verse has had a mixed reception. One or two distinguished critics have written of it in the mood of a challenge to mortal combat. Men have begun to quarrel over the question whether we are living in an age of poetic dearth or of poetic plenty – whether the world is a nest of singing-birds or a cage in which the last canary has been dead for several years.'[324]

A few poets, such as Thomas Hardy and Robert Bridges, had reputations and positions that pushed them above the fray. Others such as D. H. Lawrence were original enough to evade classification. Some publications and editors had feet in both camps. Harold Monro, strangely bracketed with Squire as an anti-Athenaeum by Middleton Murry, published the *Georgian Anthologies* but also the *Monthly Chapbook* with a clearly modernist slant. Readers of all kinds, schools and ages mixed promiscuously at his Poetry Bookshop. It was convenient for all parties in the literary wars to define their own identities by using simplistic oppositions: Georgians versus modernists; tradition versus experiment; rhyme versus vers libre; the *London Mercury* versus the *Athenaeum* – but the factions were often more alike than they allowed, 'an intricate, casual and shifting network of friendships' as Peter Howarth called it.

Squire's most influential critic and detractor was T. S. Eliot. In Squire's autobiographical journey, *Water-Music* (1939), his canoeing companion William Bliss finds an adulatory review of Eliot's poetry and tosses it to his friend for his comment, quoting the phrase 'the damp souls of housemaids' and the comparison of the sunset to a patient lying anaesthetised on a table. "As if God Almighty made sunsets for that!" exploded Bliss: "Damn it all Squire, you've read these and I haven't; what the devil do they do it for?" "Don't lump them all together just because the press does," I said, "those sentences at least are not obscure and pretentious gibberish. And they aren't really typical. They date from his early period when he was a depressed and frustrated romantic. He is a churchwarden now. Anyway, the proper way to regard it is as urban and local, a sort of peevish *vers-de-société*.'" Bliss will have nothing of it and suggests 'the chap ought to have a good dinner or go canoeing or something.' Squire's reply shows he thought Eliot different from other modernists and was ready to defend him against his friend's blimpish attack – even though his defence was of a most peculiar kind.

Eliot's more or less friendly relations with Squire ended with the war. By 1921 Eliot seemed to hold Squire entirely responsible for *Georgian Poetry*. It was not only a question of poetry: it was a question of class. Squire had become the epitome of middle-class philistinism.

> The dullness of the Georgian Anthology is original, unique; we shall find its cause in something much more profound than the influence of a few predecessors. The subtle spirit inspiring the ouija-board of Mr J. C. Squire's patient prestidigitators is not the shattered Keats but the solid and eternal Podsnap himself. This party represents, in fact, the insurgent middle class, Mr Monro's General Reading Public...[325]

It is hard not to see this as a version of the snobbery that Eliot deplored in the middle classes. As yet there was no such derogatory term as 'middlebrow', but that is what Eliot described:

> What I wish to comment on is the extreme lack of culture on the part of a number of writers in prose and verse; and when I say this I hear already the repeated epithets of 'elegant anguish,' and 'dusty face,' and '*précieux ridicule*' with which my efficient clipping-bureau has lately refreshed me... But it is doubtful whether culture is perceptibly developed by a busy life of journalism. A literature without any critical sense; a poetry which takes not the faintest notice of the development of French verse from Baudelaire to the present day... Culture is traditional, and loves novelty; the General Reading Public knows no tradition, and loves staleness... The Georgian public is a smallish but important public, it is that offensive part of the middle

class which believes itself superior to the rest of the middle class; and superior for precisely this reason that it believes itself to possess culture.

Eliot was clearly a wounded man, sensitive to the insults and slights of the press; his 'efficient clipping-bureau' was his own memory storing up grievances. When Sydney Schiff's poetry was turned down for the *Mercury* with Squire's woundingly throwaway comment, 'it doesn't bowl us over', Schiff complained furiously to Eliot. 'There is no truce possible with such people when everything out of the ordinary produces a sneer,' Eliot replied.[326] He was looking for revenge for what he called the plain stupidity of Shanks, Squire and Turner.

The quarrel was ultimately a battle over the nature and future of poetry and the ways in which it could reach its readership. Magazines were, Eliot knew, the power blocks of poetry. His main target was the *Mercury*. He felt that Squire had a godlike control over five or six influential outlets. The only exceptions were *The Times*, the *Athenaeum* and *Art and Letters*.[327]

God from a Cloud to Squire spoke
And breath'd command: take thou this Rod
And smite therewith the living Rock;
And Squire hearken'd unto God.

And Squire smote the living rock,
And Lo! the living rock was wet –
Whence issue, punctual as the clock
Land and Water,
The New Statesman
The London Mercury,
And the *Westminster Gazette*.[328]

In January he wrote to his American colleague John Quinn: 'The *London Mercury*, which started with a great deal of advertisement, will I hope, fail in a few years' time. It is run by a small clique of bad writers. J. C. Squire, the editor, knows nothing about poetry; but he is the cleverest journalist in London. If he succeeds, it will be impossible to get anything good published.'[329] From Eliot the phrase 'cleverest journalist' was, of course, not praise.

There were only two contemporary poets Eliot felt worth reading – Wyndham Lewis and Ezra Pound – and they could not find a publisher in England. He had used his influence to secure a niche for Lewis in the *Athenaeum* but there was nobody willing to take on Pound. Squire had in fact reviewed Pound's early 'Canzoni' very favourably in the *New Age* and had initially thought him 'a genuine artist with eyes of his own and brains of his own'.[330] He had been amused too by Pound's summary of Housman in his *Canzoni*, ending, 'I hope we shall all be dead pretty soon.' Pound, on the other hand, dismissed Squire as just part of the literary establishment of 'the buggers, bastards, Squires, Geeses (Gosses)' he had to crush, along with 'the wet dung of the London Murkury'.[331] Eliot feared that if there were to be no more reviews Pound's poetry would be killed by silence. No one, he wrote, thought well of Osbert Sitwell's poetry, but he was published and reviewed everywhere. 'In London a man's first work would command attention but 'when he has enemies later it is essential he should establish connections with at least one important paper.'[332]

One important magazine did collapse in 1921. The *Athenaeum* went bankrupt in March having lost £10,000 over two years. In his *Mercury* editorial Squire was generous to a man and a magazine which had been relentlessly hostile to him: Murry, he wrote, had made a gallant attempt to restore the magazine to its former prestige and the paper was interesting and well edited. 'That we did not always share its views about contemporary literature makes us all the more regret that it has gone.'[333]

The next thing for a successful young English writer was to look to new horizons and conquer the lucrative market of America. He was already making plans.

Chapter 13

Approaching America

One feature of the *London Mercury* from the start was its openness to America and American writers.[334] Squire discussed American copyright issues and how they punished foreign writers. 'We scarcely publish a number without one or more American things in it,' he wrote. It was the first of the many campaigns that the periodical ran. He invited the young poet Nicholas Vachel Lindsay from Springfield, Illinois to England. 'Bryan! Bryan!' was the leading poem in the *Mercury* of February 1919. Squire thought that Lindsay was the American poet who truly mattered, the distinctive voice of his day. He accepted the invitation and Squire took him round his old college, St John's, and showed him the Chapel and the Tudor Hall with its hammer-beam roof. 'It looks very much like the railway station at Springfield,' said Lindsay.

Undeterred, Squire went ahead with his plans. He insisted that the room should be packed full so that the audience could feel the full force of Lindsay's roar, which was 'not all like a sucking-dove'. His instructions were followed and about eighty undergraduates including women from Newnham and Girton colleges, along with their chaperones, heard Lindsay declaim the old gospel tune 'Go Chain the Lion Down'. The performance was a far cry from the politeness of an English poetry reading. 'He strides, leaps, crouches, he swings his arms, tensely clenches his fist, he uses his face as if it were rubber.'[335] The audience joined in the choruses, growling the 'Daniel Jazz' to the tune of 'John Brown's Body', recreating a cross between a revivalist meeting and Wilkie Bard's music hall. 'And the Lord said to Gabriel, Go down the Lion's Den' had even respectable elderly dons shouting, stamping their feet and imitating the beat of the tom-tom. Cambridge had seen nothing like this before. Squire contrasted Lindsay's poetry with that of his compatriots Ezra Pound and T. S. Eliot who, he said, were 'a little too fancy for me... I prefer the unpolished, the enthusiastic, the definitely musical.' For his part Eliot noted with distaste Lindsay's 'apparent Americanism' and thought his 'Y.M.C.A. morality represents something more remote than a massacre in Armenia. His verses have appeared in an English periodical...'[336] Much to Eliot's annoyance, Squire continued to publish Lindsay's poems in the *London Mercury*.

Following in the footsteps of Dickens, Thackeray, Trollope, Gosse, Rupert Brooke, Hugh Walpole, Bob Nichols and, most recently, Siegfried Sassoon, who had all seen in America a largely untapped readership for their work, Squire decided to set out there on a six-week lecture tour. On 15 October 1921 he boarded the *Albania* in Liverpool.[337] The aim of the whole enterprise, to be financed by lectures on American and English poetry, was to contact publishers, write weekly reports, encourage sales of the *Mercury*. Squire also hoped to publicise some of his own books and enlivened the trip by inviting his friend the writer A. P. Herbert to join him. Herbert wrote up their journey in half a dozen humorous articles commissioned by *Punch* under the heading 'Across the Pond'. The pair were surprised and pleased to find the American writer Logan Pearsall Smith on the same boat.

The *Albania* was more like a floating boarding house than a luxury liner. Herbert suggested it should be renamed 'Sea View' or 'No. 1 Marine Parade'; Squire suggested 'the good ship Dipsomania'. The eccentric-looking trio soon attracted the notice of their fellow passengers; it was rumoured that Pearsall Smith was the Bishop of Bermuda and Herbert his private chaplain. They enjoyed singing together; Herbert had a fine voice, Squire a mellow baritone and Herbert happily shared the part songs and madrigals he always carried in his luggage. Squire also won 2,996 farthings at piquet from an American millionaire and was amused by a ladies' game of bridge when, after playing for a halfpenny a hundred points, they ordered a small bottle of Bass and four glasses.

Squire had already imagined the collision between the old world and the new in a much-anthologised sonnet, 'The Discovery':

> There was an Indian, who had known no change,
> Who strayed content along a sunlit beach
> Gathering shells. He heard a sudden strange
> Commingled noise; looked up; and gasped for speech.
> For in the bay, where nothing was before,
> Moved on the sea, by magic, huge canoes,
> With bellying cloths on poles, and not one oar,
> And fluttering coloured signs and clambering crews.
> And he, in fear, this naked man alone,
> His fallen hands, forgetting all their shells,
> His lips gone pale, knelt low behind a stone,
> And stared and saw and did not understand,
> Columbus doom-burdened caravels
> Slant to the shore and all their seamen land.[338]

The 'discovery' is also a loss as the 'doom-burdened caravels' spell the end of the world that the Indian had known conveyed by the solemnity of the sestet and the final two lines' funereal beat. In 'Approaching America' by contrast Squire charted his own excitement at his approach to the New World.

> Came first five hundred miles from port,
> A perching bird of homely sort,
> And next in tumbling waters grey
> Nantucket's gallant lightship lay

Rocking, lonely, small and black,
A moment's friend upon the track.

Through the porthole the travellers first caught sight of America, which appeared as 'a strange planet reach'd through space'. And then they saw an English autumnal scene, brown woods from which peeped 'a cosy spire'. No longer was the land so alien; a 'confederate kindness' linked Britain and America, Staten Island and the Solent. As dawn broke, New York's skyscrapers began to rear into sight:

Each up its slice of skyway goes,
Windows in thousand chessboard rows;
Pointed and lean and broad and blunt
Behind the rusty water-front
In random rivalry they climb
The oddest pinnacles of Time.[339]

Prohibition – and its avoidance – were immediately evident. On arrival in New York at 6.30am a steward smuggled in three whiskey and sodas under a cloth. After filling in immigration papers for what seemed like hours and the awful formalities of landing, the trio were met by representatives of Alfred A. Knopf, the publishers, and the press. They were also met at the wharf by a man with a bottle of whiskey, which was carried secretly to their hotel to be opened with a screwdriver. Later they visited the firm of George H. Doran, which became Squire's American publisher. Plans were also made for an *American Mercury* under the editorship of the humourist H. L. Mencken. It duly emerged two years later in bright green covers as opposed to Squire's orange ones, but preserving the same format. Herbert and Squire booked into the Albert Hotel on 42 East 11th Street, which Herbert described as 'cheap, God-forsaken and miserable', as it would not serve him early-morning tea.

New York immediately impressed them with its pace. They were struck by the recently built Woolworth Building, then the tallest in the world, and Fifth Avenue with its sky-signs (neon lights). 'No Loitering. Keep Moving' commanded the road signs. They played the role of two English clubmen, dressed in Savile Row suits, blue patterned soft shirts, grey hats with black silk bands worn steeply angled, canes trembling in the sunlight, as they exchanged witticisms. The *Philadelphia Evening Public Ledger* asked why they had decided to come to America. 'I say, Herbert, let's go to America,' said Squire. 'Right you are,' replied Herbert. 'And here we are.' They were asked about what became a theme of the tour – alcohol and prohibition. 'You don't mean to tell us that this country has prohibition! My word! But of course, they may have made special efforts to keep us supplied so that we might feel at home,' replied Squire. The reporter was impressed by Squire's 'smooth smiling countenance which reflects goodwill on all the world'. 'Two London editors on the trail of jokes' was the misleading headline of the *Philadelphia Ledger* on 4 November 1921.

The companions visited Philadelphia, Baltimore, Louisville, Lexington, St Louis and Chicago, impressing their hosts and the American Press. The *Illinois State Journal* wrote of 'their charm of manner, their lack of affectation and huge enjoyment of life', and the *Daily North Western* was taken by Squire's disarming smile and 'his artless-little-boy-who-has-got-into-a-jam look'. The most frequent questions they were asked were, according to Herbert, 'What do you think of the way the New York women look?' and 'What do you think of the skyscrapers?' 'Hodge', as Herbert called Squire, had two beautiful answers prepared: the answer to the first question was: 'They remind me of my mother.' The second was 'I think they look best on a foggy day.' Unfortunately, he got them the wrong way round.

Squire delivered his lectures with practised style and humour. Margaret Duthie, the young reporter from the *Daily Northwestern*, was fascinated by the appeal of an 'unfathomable Englishman with dancing eyes and a disarming smile, wearing long-legged dinner clothes' and a Pickwickian collar and tie. Much more hostile was Harriet Monroe, editor of the modernist magazine *Poetry*, who was lying in wait for him in the audience at Northwestern University. She challenged him to read his own poetry; he declined, saying that he had only read in public twice. She then engaged him in a battle of words: Duthie observed that she was the only person who seemed to get the better of the lecturer's charm and repartee.[340]

For the most part, however, the trip was a great success. The pair met publishers, poets, academics, millionaires and senators. Into his scrapbook Squire pasted a newspaper cutting. The headline read: 'We nominate for the Hall of Fame.' Underneath a romantic photo of the black-haired, pipe-smoking, calmly gazing young Squire, the caption reads: 'Because his parodies have been as critical and amusing as any of our generation; because he is one of the best known of the Georgian poets; because as a critic he is the most able young man in England, devoted to upholding conservative standards; because he is the editor of the *London Mercury*, which under his direction has become the most successful literary magazine in England: and finally because he is now, happily, on a lecture tour of the United States.' A headline in the *Chicago Tribune* which Squire kept and had framed read, 'Squire Stays Sane: Other British Poets Seem Opposite.'[341]

Meanwhile in London another editor, T. S. Eliot, looked on with dismay as Squire invaded his home territory. In March he wrote to dissuade his friend John Quinn from publishing in the *American Mercury*: 'It is a despicable volume, but it is well arranged and its appearance is attractive.' He warned another friend, Scofield Thayer, against any involvement that would damage the reputation of the *Dial* by connecting it with a magazine disliked 'in the eyes of the better English writers…'[342]

Squire specially wanted to meet Vachel Lindsay again. He visited him at his home in Springfield, where they discussed another English trip. He spent some time too with Robert Frost and at Princeton with the young poet and critic Schuyler Jackson. He had lunch with the famous book collector Dr Rosenbach and stayed with Judge Bingham, the future United States Ambassador to Britain. In the columns of the *Illustrated London News* Squire recalled a highlight of the stay: 'a midnight in Kentucky nearly twenty years ago… I went to bed late, under a full moon, and there came in, wafted from far away… the strains of "The Moon Shines Bright on My Old Kentucky Home", and I thought to myself, Schubert would have liked this.'

Squire pencilled a diary of the whole trip along with a daily 'drink diary' which revealed that prohibition had been a stimulant rather than a deterrent. The entry for 3 November was typical:

1 Large whiskey at Darans

Lunch: I large double Bronx

5-45. 3 Vast Cocktails at Devos

10-12. 6 Six gin and orange Delums.

Several of their law-abiding hosts had stocks of whiskey, gin and wine hidden away; sometimes they had to hold frantic searches to find where they were. Squire found the topic amusing enough to write about. 'I was never compelled to drink so much in my life. The whole place is stiff with illicit saloons.'[343] The speakeasies were, he felt, the heart of America. When Herbert and Squire visited Logan Pearsall Smith in hospital he noted of the pair: 'They are having a roaring time & their talk is all of the evasions of the Prohibition laws… The sweetness of forbidden fruit seems irresistible.'[344] It was three weeks into their trip till they first had a dry day. Squire's 'Ballade of Soporific Absorption' became very well-known:

You may drunk I am think, but I tell I'm not,
I'm as sound as a fiddle and fit as a bell,
And stable quite ill to see what's what.
I under do stand you a surprise a got
When I headed my smear with gooseberry jam:
And I've swallowed, I grant, a beer of lot –
But I'm not so think as you drunk I am.

Along with the drink diary and occasional ballades Squire was writing a series of poems mapping his journey; *American Poems and Others* was published on his return to England. What most struck him was not the newness of the country, its skyscrapers and its heavy industry, but its vast spaces and the primordial age of its landscapes. He urged fellow travellers to follow his steps to Western America where few tourists had gone before. 'The Unvisited' (Western America)' offered a vision of Arcadia:

> Dream-prairies spread with flowers that never grew,
> And breezes balmier than ever blew,
> A fiercer wilderness and mightier mountains
> And deeper woods than traveller ever knew,
>
> And mellower fruits and bluer lovelier bays
> And warmer starrier nights and idler days,
> No pain, no cruelty and no unkindness,
> Peace and content and love that always stays.[345]

After rural California Los Angeles came as a shock. Squire was shown around the film studios that were just beginning to spread around the city. Unimpressed, he thought film-making nothing but a crude way of making money, the spirit of commercialism once more taking over from the world of innocence and beauty. In the fall the travellers visited Washington where they went to the cinema and shook hands with President Woodrow Wilson as they left.

Squire was entranced by the colours of the Fall and leaves that were subtly different from an English autumn, not 'crimson or brown', but 'paler tints', coral spray and lemon and golden green. The final stanza of 'Autumn: Outskirts of Washington' set the idea of earthly paradise against the awe-inspiring wastes of time and emptiness:

> It seems unreal: a world of youth,
> So new and innocently gay,
> The mind will scarce accept the truth
> This land was not made yesterday,

That through those years of Asia's kings
Or ever Greece was glorified,
Here also flowered all the springs,
Here all the autumns burned and died.[346]

The Niagara Falls impressed both travellers. 'Niagara' begins as they approached the Falls, seeing first the river's low shore and rocks, then a mist joining grey sky to grey water, then the trees of Goat Island and then the 'Avalanches of wheeling water unceasing'. Squire gives a sound picture of them in all their power. The poem changes direction in its final stanza: its perspective becomes timeless in a description of a post-apocalyptic world that frustrates all man's dreams:

America empty again, and beasts astray,
The forests growing again, the cities gone,
Fall'n, moss'd over, Niagara sounding on,
In a region where stilled are the voices of all our day;
Not a house, not a fence or field from the lake to the ocean,
No chimneys on the horizon, no smoke-trails hovering,
Only brushwood and grass, spreading and covering
The broken proofs of our race's old devotion.[347]

The most striking poem to emerge from the American trip was very different. It came from a visit to Chicago and describes a journey to the stockyard of Messrs Swift and Son, Meat Packers. It is a remarkable poem, a complete anomaly in Squire's work, one of his few narrative poems, the longest and most graphic he ever wrote. A reader meeting it for the first time would never guess its author: irregular in metre, grimly realistic, it is the least 'Georgian' of poems. 'I could not help writing it. It was on my mind till I did,' wrote Squire.

Squire dedicated 'The Stockyard' to Robert Frost whom he had just met, and its conversational opening and spare style owe a great deal to him.[348] The yard itself is approached by a journey on an icy grey day through thin snowflakes and 'waste spaces, heaps / like the litter at top of mines / Scabrous cottages, dirty forlorn little shops, / Railroad crossings, canals and telegraph poles...' – the Thirties poets did not have the industrial landscape entirely to themselves. There is a contrast between the aseptic offices, the rows of clerks and pretty young typists – and the abattoir. Squire dares not look, overcome with the smell of blood, and then hears:

> A sound of perpetual scraping, a warm wet stench...
> And then, still steaming, moved evenly into a hall
> A line of pinkish-white pigs, atrociously naked,
> Their unders gashed with a wound from tail to head,
> Suspended parallel, a quivering pattern of trunks
> And dangling snouts and smooth flapping pointed ears...

They were next shown cool chambers where the beasts were cut up, cured and the joints wrapped in paper by aproned girls who reminded him of storybook dairy maids. But there was worse to come. The cattle were led into the largest shed of all and a man wielding a hammer killed the beasts.

> But some I saw that, dazed, fell to their knees
> And needed a second blow, and one
> That came to its knees and looked with uplifted head,
> Bewildered, appealing, as against a dread mistake,
> And the loud crack drove it down, and it lay like the rest...

The realism demands our pity. The poem ends:

> And I thought no longer of only Chicago
> But of all our haunted race and its world...
> And I saw in a chasm of infinite darkness
> Killing, devouring, and charnel smoking,
> Writhing, flames and a rain of blood...[349]

'Won't you stay to lunch, after you've seen the sticking?' asked the genial old treasurer of the firm, Mr Cotton, 'proof of the pudding, you know.' The travellers declined.[350]

J. B. Priestley felt that the poem was more effective than half a dozen realistic novels on the same theme. 'The Stockyard' was more than a poem about the cruel slaughter of animals. It was a journey into the heart of darkness or, as Squire called it in his journal, 'the Inferno'. Edmund Gosse told him: 'It is appalling – but vivid, real even majestic. It beats all that you have hitherto done.' He added that his praise meant more as 'The Stockyard' was 'in subject and form counter to everything I have learnt to admire... magnificent.'[351] To a later critic it spoke of another slaughter: 'No poet after Passchendaele could have thought only of Chicago,'[352] wrote Philip Larkin.

The rest of the day was spent sightseeing, chatting about books and shopping, but Squire could not get the smell of blood out of his head; when he went to the opera in the evening behind the operatic choruses he heard a 'desolate lowing'. A pastoral ballet followed with all the 'lovely fairyland world' of the stage – shepherds, shepherdesses and pan pipes, an Arcadian scene of harmony and music. But still he could not forget the stockyard and its 'inveterate miasma of death'.

The poem caused considerable resentment. 'Mme X' wrote in the *Chicago Daily Tribune* that it was outrageous that a British meat eater who had met some of the city's most prominent people and been shown the sights of Chicago and its opera house should only have remembered it as a nightmare of slaughter in a 'long, rhymeless, metreful moan'. She ended: 'So that's the way we appear to Mr J. C. Squire of England. We are a smelly, noisome, blood splashed folk.'[353]

Apart from the stockyard visit, the trip to America was a great success. Herbert's only regret was that he had not seen 'a real darky crap-game' in Harlem, but Squire and he did the next best thing and saw the first all-black American musical, 'Shuffle Along', which had become a Broadway hit. In 1924 the *London Mercury*'s cousin, the *American Mercury*, was launched and was soon selling 75,000 copies. The publishers were pleased and Squire delighted: the Americans were the kindest people on earth. 'America, if one visits it, is in a thousand ways inspiring. I propose next year to breathe that exhilarating air again.'[354]

Six weeks after they had embarked, on 17 December, the travellers returned to a cold England.

Chapter 14

Best of Editors

After disastrous evenings at Swan House it was surprising that Virginia Woolf invited the Squires for a weekend to her Sussex home, Monk's House in Rodmell, 'that little lost village under the South Downs'. She was beginning to feel besieged by Georgians: Hilaire Belloc, J. B. Morton, D. B. Wyndham Lewis and Clennell Wilkinson – all had houses there. By one of life's little ironies Edward Shanks had bought Charne's Cottage, next door to the Monk's House garden and separated only by the church path. 'Our garden becomes a suburban garden. Anything would be better than a poet – one of Squire's poets,' she wrote. She shuddered to hear Mrs Shanks shouting over the wall to her husband asking how he'd like his cocktail mixed.[355]

An Australian interloper, J. M. Allison, had also come to live in Rodmell. He owned the Field Press, and published both *Land and Water* and the *London Mercury*. In her rural retreat, he built walls and gates and restored cottages and invited the villagers to tea in his barn. He even had a telephone. Worse still, he was a great friend of Squire who often enjoyed his hospitality, his parties and his wine. Allison threatened to build on the meadow just over the wall from her garden and invited visiting teams there to play cricket against his side. Squire's Invalids made their unwelcome presence felt in Virginia Woolf's fastness. In fine sunny weather on the last day of August 1920 she looked over her wall to see Squire and Siegfried Sassoon batting.[356]

The captain of the Invalids was, of course, the very last person she wanted to see. She had a nightmare vision of 'Jack Squire in a poetical villa within a hundred yards. As it is, I see Shanks's paper stand at his cottage window. The truth is, Rodmell is a colony for Georgian poets & though I am all for living and let live and not reading their works, it is hard, and even intolerable that I should have to let them live next door to me.'[357]

To her dismay Rodmell became the favourite village ground for Squire and the Invalids, and one where they began to play an annual fixture. The cricket square was well prepared, but the outfield was a jungle of longish grass – runs came in singles or sixes. Cows grazed happily in the meadow as the game went on. The thought that Virginia Woolf might be gazing with disdain over the garden fence added a touch of piquancy to the game. Despite all her misgivings, the following year she invited the Squire family for the weekend. However, she could not resist an ironic dig in her invitation: 'I think you know how to get here. Indeed, I saw you being bowled out not so long ago on the meadow.' She did warn the implacably hostile Lytton Strachey to keep well clear. The Woolfs began to look at house advertisements. In 1928 they bought the meadow.

Away from Sussex-by-the-Sea, post-war Britain faced a series of political and economic crises. When the miners went on strike to oppose the denationalisation of the pits in 1921 there was talk of a general strike led by the railwaymen and the transport workers. In May the *London Mercury* noted, 'Like everyone else we were forced to contemplate at one moment the possibility of an industrial breakdown, and even of a revolution.' But by May the dangers seemed over. 'We don't mind being over-political enough to say that we believe that with luck these things will be avoided in this country.' In the final analysis some kind of compromise between the governing classes and the working class will 'avert a mess that scarcely anyone wants.'[358] How changed he was from angry young Fabian before the war! The one thing Squire promised his readers was that in the event of a general strike he would make an heroic effort to keep the magazine going. If necessary, he would reduce it to a typewritten sheet or two and deliver it by bicycle. The more chaotic politics were, the more important it was to keep traditional culture alive. In fact, as he was pleased to tell his readers in August, the circulation continued to grow despite the slump and the coal strike.

Squire decided it was time to form a private company to purchase the *Mercury* from the Field Press and run it himself... The 'London Mercury Limited' had a nominal capital of £15,000. The preference shareholders put up the necessary capital and included Eileen's uncle J. P. Hornung, Alice Warrender, Iolo Williams and the rich American writer Logan Pearsall Smith. Squire was given a ten-year contract as managing director and Iolo Williams was made his co-director. He was in command and his fortunes were now indissolubly linked with those of his magazine.

The *Mercury* moved from Windsor House, Bream's Buildings in September 1921 to a ramshackle building in a little blind alley, just off Poppins Court. It was the last court off Fleet Street, just opposite the Law Courts. Moving to Fleet Street was a gesture of confidence, but it was the name 'Poppins Court' as much as anything else that attracted Squire. He found it charming, noting that it came from 'Sign of the Popinjay', a wooden bird for shooting practice that had once decorated the spot. With his usual love of street signs as folk art that brightened the dull monotony of the city, he decided to restore the sign and spent some time wondering whether a parrot or a green woodpecker would be more authentic. Below the office was the Red Lion. There in the long bar every weekday between half past twelve and two, Squire and his regular contributors would be joined by Robert Lynd, Hilaire Belloc and J. B. Morton. It was there that J. B. Priestley heard 'the liveliest talk I ever remember hearing'. But he also told 'Beachcomber' that 'the trouble with the whole lot of you is you never do any work'.

Squire had met Thomas Hardy for the first time just after the war in J. M. Barrie's flat. He was the poet Squire admired most of his generation, 'a great representative spokesman'. 'Going and Staying' had introduced the *London Mercury* and eight more new poems followed in the 1920s. Hardy congratulated Squire on maintaining the high level and interest of the *Mercury*. In 1921 Squire took the Invalids on a tour of the south-west to Dorchester, dropped in on Hardy and invited him to play for his side. Hardy, aged eighty-one, said it was a great many years since he had played cricket but he might umpire.[359] Squire was introduced to Hardy's wire-haired fox terrier 'Wessex'. The dog was a notorious visitor biter – and he was lucky to get away unharmed.

After this there were annual visits to Max Gate, Hardy's Dorset home. The aged poet and the young editor became very good friends. In 1923 Hardy had been 'inveigled into setting up Wireless' – and did not know what was about to happen. To his surprise he turned the set on and heard Squire lecturing on poetry. He found that he could hear every word beautifully delivered and ended his letter of congratulations: 'P.S. Our dog listened attentively'.[360] This was quite a compliment, for Wessex, Hardy told Squire, enjoyed the music, but could not stand 'the Talks'.[361] He would not allow his master to leave the room without hearing a few minutes on the wireless and yapped furiously until it was turned on.

Hardy showed Squire the signatures of German prisoners who had worked in the garden shed and was taken to St Michael's in Stinsford ('Mellstock' in the novels) to see the family graves. He asked Squire what he thought of the lettering and added, 'If you ever want a good monumental mason, just you drop me a postcard and I'll send you the name of one.' Soon he trusted Squire enough to allow him to alter any poems he sent to the *Mercury*. In the evening Mrs Hardy went up to bed and her husband asked if he could stay down a little to chat. She agreed so long as it was only a little. He then produced a bottle of claret and they went back into the dining room and talked until two o'clock about the songs and legends of his Dorset youth. The late-night session was so successful that Mrs Hardy told Squire that he could come again – but in future he had to stay in a hotel.[362] Back home, Squire sent Hardy a copy of his *American Poems and Others*, which he had dedicated to the older poet. Hardy replied that he reread 'A Stockyard' and wrote of the 'paralyzing attraction of that terrible piece', and said he had much enjoyed 'A London Sunset', 'The Lover' and 'The Journey'.[363]

The friendship with Edmund Gosse also continued to grow. He accused Squire of ruining his old age by regularly putting into print in the *Observer* exactly what he wanted to say before he had a chance to get his own article out in the *Sunday Times*. Nevertheless, 'I have a strong feeling that if you will let me say so, I have found a friend,' he wrote from the pier at Bournemouth during the railway strike, imagining Squire thoroughly enjoying the 'Revolution in shouting, struggling, striking London'. 'Evasive creature, how can I chase you over your barricades? God knows when, if ever. What a wonder you are.' Gosse's admiration had a romantic homoerotic tinge.[364] There was no doubt that he found Squire attractive: 'I long to see you… you fill me always with a certain anxiety when I reflect how precious you are. I shiver at the thought that you overstrain the machine.'[365] He wrote to the poet and novelist Maurice Baring, 'I hope to see the good, the peerless Squire this evening. What a pearl of a man he is! I do not think there could be found a better specimen of the Intellectual Man. *C'est presque le plus bel exemplaire de l'homme de lettres qu'il m'était donné.*'[366] Squire was the anointed heir. The admiration was mutual. Squire wrote him more than a hundred letters, nearly all of which are lost, including a long verse letter on Viscount Haldane all on one rhyme. 'Monstrously clever, Squire is,' reported Gosse.

Gosse knew how perilous Squire's finances were and wished that some millionaire would endow him with £1,000 a year. He was concerned too about the amount of work that Squire took on and his lack of focus. When Squire complained about his poetic drought, Gosse was ready to diagnose the problem: 'You are squandering your precious powers. I am not surprised that the poetry comes slowly, its current is choked up by your cares and worries.'[367] He needed to concentrate on the task in hand and not get waylaid: '<u>You are doing too many things. Stick to business.</u>'[368] He gave fatherly advice about the world of the theatre to which Squire was beginning to pin so many of his financial hopes, pointing out that only J. M. Barrie and Bernard Shaw made a living out of the stage, let alone a fortune. There were shoals of heart-breaking failures, including men of genius such as Henry James. It was advice that Squire ignored. He did have one moment of startling success. Eileen and he worked together on a four-act version of *Pride and Prejudice* which had a charity premiere on behalf of Bedford College for Women at the Palace Theatre, London. Ivor Novello played Mr Bingley and there was a walk-on part for the seventy-four-year-old Ellen Terry. The Queen herself, in her role as patron of the college, clapped till it seemed her gloves would burst. To insistent cries of 'Authors, Authors', Mr and Mrs Squire were presented to the royal party. But after one performance the play was never seen again.

In November 1919 Edith Sitwell and Jack Squire had met at a party given by Edmund Gosse where she enjoyed goading him. Surprisingly, though, she wrote afterwards to the poet Robert Nichols: 'I can't help liking him personally, though I know the feeling is not returned.' But this was only a temporary lull in hostilities. Relations between Squire and the Sitwell family were always going to be operatic and the language high-pitched. Their tastes were aristocratic, experimental, avant-garde and given to what Squire called derisively 'stunts'. The relationship was further poisoned by his review, a month after they had met, of the fourth 'cycle' of *Wheels* in the *London Mercury*. Most of the poetry, he wrote, consisted of disconnected strings of statements which showed no sense of metre or music. Squire dismissed Edith Sitwell's own poetry: her verses 'though incomprehensible, contain a good deal of vivid detail, pleasant because it reminds us of bright pictures.'[369] He included nothing from her in his 1921 anthology *A Book of Women's Verse* or in his unappetisingly-titled *Cambridge Book of Lesser Poets*. She felt boycotted by the Squire-controlled press: 'It is irritating, for I *know* Squire is no good as a writer; one has only to compare him with the poets whom he imitates. Meanwhile, he is preventing any new work obtaining a hearing in England.'[370] He called her brother Osbert 'an ordinary immature writer of verses'.[371] *Ordinary* was a well-directed insult. Osbert replied in kind in 'The Death of Mercury'. He first mocked the image of the god that appeared on the cover of Squire's magazine: 'He looks to see the name, alas! there leers / His face, his own, that once spelt speed and joy / – Drawn on the cover by the office-boy!!' and ended with a flourish:

The Messenger of Gods rests where he read,
In awful peace. For Mercury is dead,
As dead can be, as dead as Anne-the-Queen,
– Or as that dullest, deadest magazine.[372]

But, in fact, it was not the *Mercury* but *Wheels* that died. In November 1921 the Oxford publisher Blackwells refused to publish any more cycles and *Wheels* collapsed. Much to everyone's surprise, Edith Sitwell then took the meek Georgian poet John Freeman under her wing – and told him how much she despised Squire's poetry.

The Hawthornden Prize became the focus of the Sitwells' revenge. In an article titled 'Jolly Old Squire and Shanks' Mare's Nest'[373] Osbert, as 'The Major', a racing tipster, set out the runners and the odds for the next 'Hawthornden Stakes'.

Mr Freeman writes for the *London Mercury*.
Mr J. C. Squire is editor of the *London Mercury*.
Mr J. C. Squire is chief literary critic of *The Observer*.
Mr Iolo (I. O. U.) Williams, a poet, writes for the *London Mercury*, of which Mr J. C. Squire is editor, and reviewed Mr J. C. Squire's book of poems for *The Observer* of which Mr J. C. Squire is chief literary critic. Mr Squire has now written a preface to an anthology edited by Mr Iolo Williams.
The Major, writing from Newmarket, advises sportsmen to back Mr Iolo Williams as a future Hawthornden Prize Winner.

The Sitwells decided to present a literary prize of their own – a spoof of the Hawthornden: a stuffed owl awarded for the dullest literary work of the year. The event was a piece of the kind of satirical theatre at which the Sitwells excelled. The dead owl was the Sitwells' hit at the Eagle himself and all the rest of the bird-loving Georgians. The first recipients of the stuffed bird were Jack Squire himself, Edward Shanks and Harold Nicolson. (When the supply of owls ran out Nicolson was awarded a stuffed mangy cat and a few diseased mice under a huge glass dome.)

The Prize continued to stir up arguments and resentment. An infuriated Murry wrote to Marsh of his disappointment and hurt when in 1922 it was awarded to Edmund Blunden's poetry and not to *The Garden Party*, his wife Katherine Mansfield's volume of short stories. Virginia Woolf on the other hand was pleased that Squire doubted Mansfield's genius as much she did. She looked on her friend with admiration tempered by jealousy; 'So I have some cause for pleasure,' she admitted.

In the battle of insulting nicknames Osbert Sitwell called his opponents 'Mammon' poets because they were powerful and made money; Squire called his opponents 'Asylum poets' as they were fit only for the madhouse.[374] The *London Mercury* with its broad readership and its appeal to the educated middle classes was not sympathetic to the Sitwells. Squire began to include the cartoons of Will Dyson, which captured the superiority and snootiness of the Sitwells and modernist writers with wit and accuracy.

Osbert Sitwell put his case again in the pamphlet *Who Killed Cock Robin?* The cover shows a robin redbreast in a bowler hat looking fearfully at an arrow aimed straight at its heart. Its title page promised a sequel: 'In Preparation: A Study in Evolution, a comic history of the Squire-archy, by Augustine Rivers' – the first use of that term.[375] He hated the Georgians' clichéd poetry of 'larks in the trenches' and sentimental views of the English countryside. 'Affected lark-lovers, rhymsters and dunces,' they stood for all that had been wrong with Victorian poetry. Their present representative, he wrote, 'a direct descendent, one imagines, was born in 1884 on, or shortly after 1st of April, went to Cambridge, has edited many periodicals and written verse...' He then gave a two-line summary of Squire's poetry: 'A Whistle! A kick! A rush, a scrabble, a scrum! / And now I'll go home and open a bottle of port.' The following year Sitwell continued the attack in 'The Jolly Old Squire. Or Way-Down in Georgia,' a mime-drama supervised by the Goddess MEDIOCRITY. The heroes are 'Jxck Sqxxre' and 'Edxxxd Shxxks', editors of the *English Hermes*. The curtains open on a cricket ground strewn with empty ginger beer bottles and currant buns, with wickets broken and half a bat in the foreground.[376]

The word that he had coined stuck: 'Squire-archy'. It lost its hyphen and soon took on its own impetus. Like the word 'Georgian' it spread to mean any group of writers that opposed modernism or was traditional or backward-looking: a poetic mafia. And finally, it became a more or less empty insult.

The truth is that it is thoroughly misleading. Squire hated labels and hated labelling poetic movements; he believed in poets, not poetic fashions, or *isms* as he usually called them. Unlike the imagists and Futurists, Squire and the Georgians did not constitute a movement with an agenda: they issued no counter-modernist manifesto. With the exception of 'Dick' Shanks, Squire had no poetic followers. As he wrote to the critic H. E. Palmer, 'I never had, as you seem to think "a gang". I merely spent the best years of my life, usually without pay, trying to keep the poetic flag flying by printing what I thought good... I had no school. Some of the good writers I disliked personally, some of my dearest friends I refused to print.'[377] None of Squire's friends acknowledged the existence of a squirearchy or even a Georgian identity. Squire wrote: 'If anyone accused any member of the group in a pub of belonging to it, he would fall into a frightful passion and deny it with hysteric oaths.'[378] Marsh himself, also annoyed by the charge, also denied that there was a group identity of any kind:

I should like to make a mild protest against a further charge that *Georgian Poetry* has merely encouraged a small clique [Eliot's phrase] of mutually indistinguishable poetasters to abound in their own and each other's sense or nonsense... to my fond eye those who have graced these collections look as diverse as sheep to their shepherd, or the members of a Chinese family to their uncle; and if there is an allegation which I would *deny with both hands*, it is this: that an insipid sameness is the chief characteristic of an anthology which offers – to name almost at random seven only out of forty – the work of Messrs. Abercrombie, Davies, de la Mare, Graves, Lawrence, Nichols and Squire.[379]

In the autumn of 1922, as a counter to what he saw as the philistinism of the *Mercury*, T. S. Eliot decided to set up the *Criterion*. Just as Squire had proclaimed his intent by putting one poem by Hardy and another by Brooke to head the first number of his magazine, so Eliot gave *The Waste Land* pride of place in the opening number of the *Criterion*. It was a gauntlet thrown down. The *Mercury* announced its rival's birth with a three-line entry in the 'Literary Intelligence' section. After praising a 'delightful piece' by George Saintsbury, it noted without comment the appearance of 'a long poem', ('The Waste Land') by T. S. Eliot and concluded: 'The cover is attractive and the type good.'[380]

Although they were very different magazines in terms of their scope and their readerships, Eliot saw the *Mercury* as a rival to be defeated. In a letter to Harold Monro, he contrasted the apparent luxury of a well-supported magazine with his own hand-to-mouth existence. 'The *Criterion* has to be better in every way than its competitors. It has to compete with reviews which have an editor and a sub-editor, paid and devoting all their time, a business manager and secretarial staff. The *Criterion* is run without any office, without any staff or business manager, by a sickly bank clerk and his wife after a boring and tiring day and subject to a thousand interruptions. People thought him a lunatic for doing all this without a salary.'[381] He did not mention that it was bankrolled by Lady Rothermere. His rival had no wealthy patron to offer financial security. Eliot's quarrel with the *Mercury* was not entirely about literary standards: envy and self-pity played their part.

Eliot continued to attack Squire's magazine with a mixture of arrogance and snobbery. His American friend Scofield Thayer was thinking of setting up a London version of the *Dial*. Eliot cautioned him against the idea and told Thayer that the idea that he could attract four thousand readers was unrealistic. There were only three or four hundred people who were intellectual enough to understand it. The English would not take to the idea of a subscription. He would have to be very careful to avoid the contagion of the *Mercury*: it was 'a despicable volume but by comparison with most literary magazines it was well arranged and its appearance is attractive.' The different coteries of pre-war London seemed to have simplified into two warring camps. 'You must understand that writers here are divided into at least two groups, those who appear in the London *Mercury* and those who do not. The *Mercury* has no standing among intelligent people, and the paper appeals wholly to a large semi-educated public. It is socially looked down upon – a point which is difficult to explain at a distance but quite evident here.'[382]

Eliot's criticism that, for a time in the 1920s, too much power and influence was vested in one man has some force, and it is easy to understand how frustrating and annoying Squire's dominance and control of literary periodicals could be. But the argument that he only published a narrow range of the work of his own supporters and friends has no basis in fact. As for the accusation that Squire had a deadening and restrictive effect on publication, his aim, constantly restated, was to publish and bring on new young writers.

Henry Williamson was one young writer who owed Squire for his start. They had first met at a party in 1921. It was Williamson's first encounter with the literary establishment. After having seen some of the worst fighting of the war in the trenches, he had read Francis Thompson and found him inspiring. Shyly he asked Squire if he thought Thompson was as great a poet as Hardy or Byron. 'One should not try to rank poets in order of greatness,' came the reply. Squire was much more encouraging when he remarked: 'You must write what you saw and know.' He added, 'By your face you are a writer.' Williamson remembered that remark fifty years later when he wrote that 'Jack Squire was as generous as he was intuitive.'

Henry Williamson was awarded the Hawthornden Prize in 1928 for *Tarka the Otter*, an award and a book that made a career. The novel had been initially published in a limited edition of only 150 copies and distributed to only a few friends. The prize gave Williamson immediate publicity: 'It means unlimited kudos and marked rises for untold stories etc. In fact one arrives,' he wrote. Squire gave him the seal of approval by recommending him for the Savile Club. Later in the year, in October, Squire praised his war novel *The Pathway* in the *Observer*. 'It is a very remarkable book, and the man who could write it was born to be a novelist… It is about a young man of genius whose war experiences have left him restless, neurotic, visionary… it is about nature and man in North-west Devon… There are very fine glimpses of the war, particularly one of the Truce of Christmas 1914. There are soaring and blissful passages about nature and fierce outbursts against war…'[383]

Edward Davison, another ex-serviceman, was also just the kind of young poet to appeal to Squire. When serving in the navy he had sent some poems to the *New Statesman*. After the war ended he had no money and was at a loose end. He wrote to Squire and told him about his ambition to go to Cambridge. Squire suggested his old college and a degree in history and began to support him financially at St John's. He was the poorest and most generous of patrons: 'At the moment I am overdrawn at the bank – so don't show them this letter – but I will let you have £15 for them next month.' At Cambridge Davison became close friends with another young ex-serviceman, J. B. Priestley, whom he introduced to Squire. Priestley thought Squire's talk was full of large statements which he could not accept: Squire was unused to blunt Northerners. Within half an hour Priestley found himself contradicting the formidable editor. Despite the lack of warmth between them, Squire asked Priestley to send something to the *Mercury* and recommended him for his first job as a reader to the Bodley Head publisher John Lane at £6 a week. In the *Bradford Telegraph and Argus* he remembered, 'When most doors were closed to any contributions of mine – and shut so tight that I was never allowed a glimpse of a human editor working behind them – the *London Mercury* suddenly opened its broad and bright orange gates, and I found myself not only in print but among the best living company in print.'

The novelist Stella Gibbons too was first published in the *Mercury*. She sent three poems with the message, 'None of these is any good'. Graham Greene was unknown when his first poems were published in July 1927 in the *Mercury*, as was John Betjeman. Alan Pryce-Jones had his first poems published by Squire. He also published work by Ivor Gurney and Edmund Blunden when they could not find an outlet. The case of the poet Gwen Clear showed him at his best. Her niece wrote: 'My aunt Gwen was I think only 22 when in 1927 Longmans published a volume of her poems called *The Elder Sister*. She had been writing verse for some time, with the encouragement of Squire, though how he first came upon her I do not know.' Her father was a wheelwright in the East End and money was scarce. At some point in her late teens Squire came to tea with the family, to the huge pride of her father, who died very soon after. The poems are dedicated to Squire and a signed photo of him was among the papers she left.[384] Betjeman later wrote that there were hundreds who owed their start in literature to his encouragement. And for Squire's team of sub-editors, often straight from university like Pryce-Jones and a harem of red-haired young women, the *Mercury* was ' Jack's kindergarten'.

Eliot was right in seeing Squire as the most influential editor of his time. Between the end of the First World War and for ten years afterwards no literary figure seemed more important in England than did John Collings Squire. 'The best critic going,' according to Siegfried Sassoon.'[385] 'The least tyrannical of rulers, who, for a period, acted as the chief arbiter of English poetry,' according to Alan Pryce-Jones, later editor of the *Times Literary Supplement*.[386] The critic Frank Swinnerton was sure that he was 'the most successful of those representing the younger generation – our chief reputation maker.'[387] Squire's poetry was also widely admired. Edmund Gosse, Edward Marsh, Edmund Blunden and Robert Graves all led a chorus of approval. 'What modern poetry ought chiefly to be,' according to Arnold Bennett.[388] 'Like all good art, half-strange, half-familiar, and altogether beautiful and satisfying for generations,' according to J. B. Priestley.[389] Harold Monro wrote, 'No one could doubt the 'impressiveness of the position which Mr. Squire has come to hold as arbiter and foremost representative of modern English Poetry.'[390]

The years immediately after the war were some of the busiest, happiest and most successful times for Squire. He was enjoying life in Chiswick with his growing family. He had come out of a dry period and was now writing some of his best and most mature poetry. His American tour had been a great success. The *London Mercury* had been greeted with acclaim. He had been anointed by the Victorian grandees Edmund Gosse and Henry Newbolt as a Fellow of the Royal Society of Literature. His control of periodicals, magazines and newspapers meant that any young poets he favoured 'need not to fear being snubbed, drubbed or neglected by the Press'.

And all this when he was only in his mid-thirties.

Chapter 15

London: Back to Work

Squire still had political ambitions. The war and the loss of friends such as Willy Smith, Ben Keeling and Rupert Brooke began to shape his politics. The anniversary of Willy Smith's death revived Squire's bitterness about Lloyd George and the politicians of the 1920s who betrayed the promises of a better world, a world for which Willy Smith had given his life. This is the theme of 'April 22, 1917–1922':

Five years ago to-day, old thing,
Five years ago to-day
They bent above you and found you hardly breathing
When the smoke had blown away.

There was no blood upon your coat,
No bruise upon your brow,
But a shell had burst and killed you: a war was raging
The war is over now.

Three years ago they ended it,
They silenced all the guns,
And said you had left a better world behind you
For us and for our sons.

Perhaps: we must give it time to settle,

The wrangling time to cease:

But O that harmless you should die in battle

For these to live in peace.[391]

Ivor Gurney was a terrible reminder of what war meant. His second volume of poems, *War's Embers*, had failed to sell and he found his work rejected by publishers. Soon after the war ended he had written to Squire the first of many appeals: 'An English War Poet cries for rescue… I have suffered enough…'[392] He was writing furiously but there was no one to listen: 'He had no readership, no audience and no publisher.'[393] Squire was his only supporter. He replied that he could do no more than 'publish your poetry on occasion and make your genius known'.[394] When Gurney sent him a draft he wrote encouragingly, 'There is a fine poem in this but I don't think you have completely excavated it. Do come on Thursday…'

He helped to get Gurney a job as a pianist in a cinema, but he fled after only a week. After this Squire wrote patiently: 'The real point is to find out exactly what will best serve your interests. Do tell me precisely and fully what you think about it.' Gurney used to wander in and out of Swan House and play the piano, sometimes accepting a bed for the night, sometimes disappearing into the darkness. He was finally incarcerated in the City of London Mental Hospital in Dartford where he spent the last fifteen years of his life. Squire wrote to the Ministry of Pensions and tried to ensure that he had a piano there. He wrote to Walter de la Mare: 'I wish we were rich enough to give him a cottage and a keeper. I publish his verses – they are good enough anyhow. I think I will suggest that some of his songs be published in the *Mercury*. The worst of it is that he sees through it all and knows that these are only little sops to please him. He is a man of genius and it is awful to think of him down there.'[395] Squire was caught in a dilemma. When he summoned up the courage to visit him Gurney would become terribly disturbed, go down on his knees, weeping and pleading for his release. On the other hand, if no visitors came, he felt lonely and deserted.

Gurney wrote to Squire weekly from hospital. At one point he made his escape and walked the twenty miles to Chiswick. He suddenly appeared at Swan House. Squire found his friend distressingly sane except for momentary intervals: 'We longed to keep him with us but it was no good; he might kill himself at any moment.' That was the last time they met. The correspondence of Squire and Gurney at the University of California, Los Angeles is a heap of half-charred letters in Gurney's heavy black ink, the characters more carved than written, memories of Gloucestershire interspersed with Hebrew, apocalyptic quotations from the Bible, cries for death's release and the words 'Eloi, Eloi, lama sabachthani' over and over again. His letters addressed to Squire and Dean Inge are a terrible picture of a mind at sea. Squire wrote: 'There, more than in any graveyard, is the ghastly face of war.'[396]

Squire was in Cologne for the Dadaist exhibition of 1921. He was appalled. European modernism was more extreme and more experimental than anything he had met before. He was truly shocked: 'Having entered the exhibition through a public lavatory, you found yourself in a gallery where a young girl in a white Communion dress stood reciting obscene poems. In accordance with the Dadaist plan that audiences should be incited to behave violently hatchets were hung around for the use of visitors who wished to attack the works of non-art on the walls.' He thought Dadaism the *reductio ad absurdum* of experiment; the Dadaists were like the Cubists and Futurists in desiring a clean sweep of the past. They parted company with them at the point where construction turned into destruction. They did not want to construct a new Art, as did the surrealist Apollinaire. They did not want Art at all.

But if Squire thought he was writing the obituary of modernism he was wrong. 1922 was the *annus mirabilis* of modernism in England with the publication of two of its defining works: *Ulysses* and *The Waste Land*. Both stirred up violent antagonisms and the reviews were deeply partisan. On the one side, defending Eliot's poem, stood the *Times Literary Supplement*, Clive Bell, Harold Monro, Ezra Pound and Bloomsbury. On the other were much of the literary establishment, most reviewers, the fellows of All Souls College, Oxford who turned down Eliot as one of their body, American critics such as Louis Untermeyer and John Crowe Ransom – and, of course, Jack Squire and the *London Mercury*.

Squire began his review in the *New Statesman* by admitting that after several readings he could not make head nor tail of *The Waste Land*.[397] Any open-minded person, he wrote, would accept that Eliot at least meant something and had been 'at great pains to express himself'. In the honest belief that he was exploring 'a new avenue' he had merely ended up going down a cul-de-sac. Eliot's notes were no use in explaining the function of the learned mish-mash of quotations, references and drab pictures. Finally, Squire came out with one of his most notorious judgments: 'Conceivably, what is attempted here is a faithful transcript, after Mr Joyce's obscurer manner, of the poet's wandering thoughts when in a state of erudite depression. A grunt would serve equally well; what is language but communication, or art but selection and arrangement? I give it up; but it is a pity that a man who can write as well as Mr Eliot writes in this poem should be so bored (not passionately disgusted) with existence that he doesn't mind what comes next or who understands it.' Eliot wrote to Robert Graves on 9 October 1925 that he was actually rather pleased with Squire's comments as, unlike some of his fellow reviewers: 'The man is honest.'

Squire's criticism was all of a piece: he felt the underlying principle was that reader and writer were bound together. If Eliot and modernist writers failed to respect that bond then the whole point of literature was lost. 'I hate publishing anything that I cannot understand even in details. The paper is not allowed to rise above the level of my intelligence.'[398] (He lived up to his word: he once implored Yeats to write something for him, and then had to send the poem back because he could not make anything of it.) Eliot and Joyce thought obscurity and difficulty were intrinsic to writing of their time; they were keywords of the modernist aesthetic. To Squire they were anathema. The strength of his position was that it looked towards a broad literate readership: 'I am a commonplace man and I know what commonplace men think,' he boasted. The weakness was that it could become a tendency to dismiss anything that could not be readily understood at the time.

*

First Interlude: 'The Man Who Wrote Free Verse'

Squire published a satiric dissection of modernist poetry in the short story 'The Man Who Wrote Free Verse'.[399] It is a collection of parodies and a fable with echoes of Evelyn Waugh's *Vile Bodies*.

Two young men about town, Adrian and Reginald, are enjoying a weekend in the country with their hostess, Lady Muriel, and her husband. (Shades of Lady Ottoline Morrell and Garsington Manor.) They start to argue about poetry. Reggie defends the new poetry his hostess likes by arguing that a new society needs a new kind of verse. Experiment is the style of the times. The Russian Revolution and Cubism go hand in hand. His cynical friend Adrian disagrees strongly. The only reason that the revolutionaries espoused Cubism, he states, was to upset the bourgeois sentiments of the reactionaries. The argument turns on whether the new art forms are legitimate expressions or just empty fakes. To settle the issue Adrian suggests a bet; Reggie should write as a poet of the advanced school and see how well he does. He should adopt a nom de plume of an imaginary second cousin, the advanced poet 'Sydney Twyford' (a dig at the fashionable patrons of modernism, the rich couple Sydney and Violet Schiff). Both men know that this practical joke has a serious point. If Reggie succeeds then this will prove Adrian right: modernist poetry is a trick and its readers are bamboozled and deluded. If he fails, then there may be something in it. The first test is for Reggie to write an imagist poem. Over lunch they survey the results.

Reggie has sweated hard to write nonsense and found it much harder than he expected. He gazes over the slate roofs and chimney cowls from his room – an allusion to a poem that Squire felt illustrated Richard Aldington's weakness as a poet: 'The chimneys, rank on rank, / Cut the clear sky…'[400] Reggie's first effort is in the style of early imagist poetry:

> The chimney cowls
> Gyrate
> In the
> Wind
> There is a blot of ink
> On my paper.
> I am going to have lunch
> Before long
> And I am glad there is
> A
> Lobster.

Adrian congratulates his pupil on a good start, but has some 'faults' to point out. The poem is written in sentences which have a flow to them, and in another place a genuine emotion is stated: he is glad to have the lobster. He suggests an improvement which would simply cut out the connectives and end with exclamations:

> Gyrating cowls
> Ink!
> My God a lobster!

Then he sets Reggie the task of writing in four different modernist or experimental styles. His first try is:

> Chimney cowls
> Cut
> Against sky
> Excruciating, torturing, abominable
> Lobsters

Claws like saws
Goggle-eyes, pins, tentacles
Goggle eyes at goggle-eyes
Fat men dining at
The Ritz.

Reggie promises that the first lines begin with lower case letters, alternate lines are printed upside down and that the word Ritz is printed in very large capitals followed by a line of exclamations and question marks (playing with typographical conventions was a hallmark of Futurists and Vorticists). The next poem is in conventional rhyming quatrains, but their simplicity is countered by polysyllabic and 'fearsomely obscure' diction. It begins:

Apocalyptic chimney-cowls
Squeak at the sergeant's velvet hat
Donkeys and other paper fowls
Disgorge decretals at the cat…

And the final quatrain reads:

Autumnal abscesses relent
The twilight of ancestral days
But, smiling at the parsnip's scent,
The Nubian girl undoes her stays.

Here the target is the Eliot of the quatrain poems. Peculiar syntax, use of obscure words ('decretals'), a narrative that seems to hint at meaning and then refuse it, and finally the exotic and decadent sexuality of the foreigner, black or Jewish – all these can be found in 'Sweeney Erect', 'Sweeney Among the Nightingales' and 'Burbank with a Baedeker'.

Adrian is delighted with this, but says he hopes that the next one will not rhyme. Reggie apologises for another rhyming poem, worried that it might not be obscure enough. It starts with the usual chimney-cowls but now they are 'chequered':

Jewelled parakeets arise
Making many a silver noise
Round the chequered chimney cowls
Whilst the old Marchesa's owls
Blinking in the glaring day
Flit like fans from far Cathay…

The ink is no longer a bare noun, it is a 'glittering ink which sheds bleak incense / on the poodle's stifled sense.' And the lobster has become 'crimson-armoured'. In the background is an exotic jumble of 'oleanders, asters, / Prim pagodas, jet, wax-fruits, / Crinolines of Dresden queens / And indecent salmon tins…' 'Who, oh who can this be meant for?' asked Edith Sitwell.[401] Adrian knows only too well, and asks his friend if he has managed to include the word 'crystal'. Reggie promises it will come later along with the jade and the unicorns.

Reggie found that one so easy to write that he could not stop. The final poem is 'the Classical'. Reggie's rhapsodic Greek imagery mocks the classical references that Ezra Pound, Richard Aldington and his American wife H. D. used freely and often obscurely. He insists that proper names are spelt in the modish way with 'good hard "k" sounds and "os's" instead of "us's"'.

Chimney cowls,
Cut
Against sky.
O Phoibos Albanios
The white limbs
Of the nymphs
On Hymettos
Io Pan, the honey

242

Acrid
In the nostrils
Io, the purple
Of the vats of Herakles
On the cliffs
By Akrokeraunia
Hard and bitter
The shells
But the flesh
Ah Zeus!
Ah good!

Adrian is impressed but suggests Reggie has still missed out one kind of advanced writing: the revolutionary. He has only once hinted at class hatred – rich fat men dining at the Ritz. His verse has been fine, but too tame. He has dissolved grammar, but not words. He has not stated his Futurist desire 'to destroy society, to burn libraries and pictures, to bombard churches and turn the almighty from his throne.' He hasn't even expressed the wish to be a tiger or a motor-car.

Squire pictures the coterie that encourages modernist 'stunts': upper-class ladies such as Lady Muriel who preside over a group of six middle-aged women and six fawning young men lunching in her 'jazz dining room' at Upper Brooke Street, Mayfair. Their husbands are noticeably absent. This combination of leisured ladies and callow youth is the audience for advanced art. 'The women at a glance seemed all to have white faces and red hair; the young men had white faces and either no hair or too much; tortoise shell spectacles were generally worn; voices were pitched high and any indecency was welcomed by titters of appreciation.' The talk is of Art, Brazilian painters and pornography. Here is the Bloomsbury group: Clive Bell on Art, Lytton Strachey of the squeaky voice, and a shared sniggering approach to sex. The young men are not sure where to place the poetry of Sydney/Reggie. They all felt Cubism and Futurism were too narrow to describe his work; they agreed Electrist, Early Victorian, Deliquescent, Sadist, Universalist, Psychoanalyst and Communist all failed as well. A myopic youth assures his hostess that her favourite Teddy's latest 'Convulsions in Blue Flat Minor' are *vieux jeu* and that 'Sydney has got much farther'.

For two years Sydney Twyford earned great success. His 'Collected Poems', titled 'Ourang-outang', (nodding to Eliot's 'Sweeney Erect' rising from his bed of steam with 'a gesture of orang-outang') gave him fame and fortune. So far Adrian has been proved right: Reggie has shown the emptiness of the advanced school of verse and the folly of its readers: the point of the fable is all too clear. But Squire has a twist to his story. Reggie is woken from his bed by three dirty hirsute men, pistols in hand, to be told that now the revolution has happened he is to be Poet Laureate of the British Bolshevik revolution. His experimental verse has been taken in its anti-bourgeois stance to be just the right literature for the cause exactly as Squire had predicted.

> There is something pathetic about the way in which, wherever the political Bolsheviks get into office, they print the verses and cartoons of the artistic anarchists. They don't understand them; all they know is that the bourgeois dislike them; so in Munich last Easter, and (we daresay) in Moscow now, there is an excellent opening for those who, for all anyone would be able to say to the contrary, have only to scratch out the old titles of their interlocked triangles and write underneath "Uprising of Proletariat," or some such thing.[402]

Adrian and all his friends are exiled to the newly formed monarchy in St Petersburg where he teaches dancing and English and sells peasant embroidery. They have failed to see where the new literature and art might lead. They might have been amused by the art of revolution, but others were not. The irony is not only directed at fashionable modernism but also against Adrian and his too easy, too cynical dismissal of its link with bolshevism. Experimental art and social revolution go hand in hand. Adrian pays the price for his naïveté.

*

After the runaway success of its predecessors the fifth and final *Georgian Poetry* only managed 8,000 sales in 1922.[403] The series had run its course and sold more than 70,000 copies. In its ten years it had straddled the Great War and made poetry the focus of public attention that it has not been since. Robert Lynd summed up its role in a literary civil war that he felt was ultimately healthy:

> It means that poetry is interesting people sufficiently to make them wish to argue about it. Better a breeze – even a somewhat excessive breeze – than stagnant air. It is good both for poets and for the reading public… with all its faults, *Georgian Poetry* still remains the best guide we possess to the poetic activities of the time.[404]

Squire praised Marsh's achievement in the *London Mercury*: 'From 1912 Mr Marsh has done far more than any other writer or anthologist to attract attention to good modern verse.'[405] Squire, still convinced that he was living in a time of a poetic renascence, decided to carry on Marsh's work with anthologies of his own. His *Selections from Modern Poets* appeared in May 1921, just before the final *Georgian Poetry* was published, and was reprinted twice in that year. By 1941 it had gone through fourteen impressions. He excluded anyone born before 1870. The date was, he admitted, somewhat arbitrary but he had to fix on some starting point: 'my object was to illustrate what many of us think an exceptional recent flowering.' This meant cutting out some of the great names such as Kipling, Hardy and Yeats. In his anthologies Squire did what *Georgian Poetry* did not do: they became a channel for unpublished work.

The war figured largely in Squire's selection. Rupert Brooke, Robert Graves, Julian Grenfell, Ivor Gurney, Robert Nichols, Siegfried Sassoon and Edward Thomas were all there. Many of the predictable names of *Georgian Poetry* were there too, but Squire included two poems by James Joyce, one by D. H. Lawrence and several by lesser-known Irish poets. Gosse enjoyed teasing his friend for the excessive number of 'Hibernian poetasters who ought to have been left to stew in their own juice (or joyce).'[406] He reported that he had 'just bought the anthology of Modernist Poets', and praised Squire for putting 'modernists in a remarkably favourable light'. For many of the older generation and many of Squire's contemporaries 'modernism' did not mean Pound, Eliot or Joyce, but Rupert Brooke, John Masefield, Siegfried Sassoon, Walter de la Mare and Squire himself.

Two more of Squire's anthologies were to follow, the first in 1924. *Second Selections from Modern Poets* advanced his starting date to 1875. Squire had to acknowledge in his preface that there was now less eagerness to welcome the work of the younger poets than before. It was therefore all the more important to call attention to their work. It was also true that 'younger poets' such as Alfred Noyes, Harold Monro and W. W. Gibson were not so young any more. Some, such as Robert Graves, refused to be part of Squire's anthology and some had to be cajoled. There was more from poets whom he had come to appreciate – Wilfred Owen, Ivor Gurney and three poems by D. H. Lawrence, written in the freest of free verse – 'Man and Bat', 'Kangaroo' and 'Snake'. (Squire viewed Lawrence as 'undoubtedly a man of genius, a passionate, brooding, glowering, worshipping man'.)[407] Along with these however there was an increasing sense of reliance on friends, colleagues and cricketers. The voices of the Invalids' opening bat, the poetical Professor E. N. Da C. Andrade, Sylvia Lynd, the novelist wife of his colleague, his old friend Iolo Williams and Edward Shanks, are not powerful ones. 'Keats and water', the critic Vivian de Sola Pinto called Squire's selection, with some justice.

Siegfried Sassoon echoed this uncertainty. He heard news from his publishers Martin Secker that Squire wanted to include six of his poems in his *Second Selections* and decided that he did not want be hauled into the limelight of this company: 'It will probably contain a lot of the dull stuff which Squire prefers to the genuine poetry of E. Sitwell and C. Mew' – and refused. In reply Squire wrote an eight-page fan letter saying that his book was propaganda for the best modern poetry. He enjoyed every word Sassoon wrote and his anthology would be crippled without him; he was relying on Sassoon to give him examples of the best. Sassoon relented. Six of his poems (although not the ones Squire had chosen) duly appeared at three guineas apiece. Sassoon noticed the irony: seven years earlier he had been 'hanging his tongue out' for a favourable review from Squire of his *The Old Huntsman*. Now it seemed that the tables had turned.[408] The series still sold well and earned praise in the press: the *Scotsman* wrote, 'In the plethora of anthologies that crowded the book market Mr J. C. Squire's is easily the best.' But the heyday of the anthology was nearly over. The anthology that had been the best showcase of Georgian talent was itself becoming a target of abuse. Robert Graves told Squire that letting a poem appear in anthologies was tantamount to losing control of it and any money it might make. (Later, in 1928, he wrote 'A Pamphlet against Anthologies' in which Squire was the arch-villain.) It became a word of abuse: 'They call us Anthology poets. Damn them,' wrote Edward Shanks.

In the *London Mercury* Squire reviewed side by side two very different works that came out in 1925 – Blunden's *English Poems* and Eliot's *Poems (1909–1925)*.[409] Naturally, Squire gave his friend the pride of place. The contrast was pointed. Blunden was 'as incorrigibly English as the wild rose'; he was the heir to a tradition of nature writers from Wordsworth to John Clare, William Barnes and Hardy. (Blunden's edition of Clare had brought his poetry back to life after years of neglect.) His own work reflected the village life that Squire was beginning to enjoy in Thursley, the farms, ploughland, barns, church, and cricket matches. Squire thought his poetry was as traditional as the country ways it described and hailed him as the central figure of his time, unmistakeably a man of genius 'at the heart of his poetic generation'.

Eliot was an American whose character and poetry continued to puzzle Squire. He respected Eliot as a critic and generously wrote that his magazine the *New Criterion* would be welcomed wherever serious criticism was read.[410] Some of Eliot's poetry he admired. But he could not understand Eliot's reserved character and was sure his 'muted dejection' was not likely to produce good poetry. Squire thought the more full-blooded emotions of hate or love or passion were the stuff of poetry. Eliot's poems seemed to him an 'elaborate expression of disgust', 'Baudelaire without the guts', recalling the fin de siècle poets he disliked so much. Why on earth should Eliot bother to write at all, he wondered. All he could produce was 'a vagrant and fatigued sequence of images of the exhaustion of our civilisation'. Perhaps he was experimenting with automatic writing... He certainly failed the test that Squire always set: comprehensibility. 'Unhappily Mr Eliot has very little regard for the reader.' At any rate, wrote Squire, Eliot's poems were Double-Dutch to him. 'Why to the Waste Land add a Valley of Peculiarly Dry Bones?' he asked.[411]

Edith Sitwell, outraged by the review, wrote to Eliot: 'I am determined that Squire shall be punished *now*, – if he isn't, we shall have him teaching the Archangel Gabriel how to play his trumpet in Heaven.'

In 'Piebald Unicorn' Squire continued to mock both of them:

Under the hyperthyroid moon
Seated, I shall eat caviar with a spoon
While Mr Nokes, that melancholy man
Will cool my heated features with his fan
The ghost of sainted Elagabalus
Will sometimes come to drink his tea with us,
Gazelles and eunuchs, crystal as a leaf,
Will pace the rose-beds to assuage my grief.
I shall applaud their steps, and when I please,
Lean forth to stroke their thin anatomies,
While Mr Nokes, that melancholy man,
Discourses gentle music with his fan.[412]

The coffee spoons with which Prufrock measured out his life now were full of caviar; the obscure reference to 'sainted Elagabalus' (most dissipated and useless of Roman emperors) like Tiresias in *The Waste Land* half-man, half-woman, hits at Eliot's 'cobweb of obscurities' and his interest in the obscene. The knowing reference to Mr Nokes, 'that melancholy man', alludes to the way Eliot introduced his characters as if they were familiar friends. Exotic names such as Mr Apollinax, Princess Volupine and Grishkin give way to the very ordinary English Mr Nokes. Edith Sitwell does not escape: her poetry is full of imagery of mythical and gracious beasts – unicorns and gazelles. 'Crystal' was the one word that summed up her bejewelled world for Squire. The surreal title itself might well have been a song from Sitwell's *Façade* and the poem mocks the world-weary ennui that Squire always loathed.[413]

Despite Squire's scorn, as Middleton Murry had predicted, the modernists were taking over. Eliot began to occupy the commanding position that Squire had held just after the war – he was now the centipede with a foot in a hundred camps. The victors wrote the history and the reputation of Squire and the Georgians continued to decline. Their achievement was however remarkable: the creation of a popular audience for poetry that has never been recaptured.

Chapter 16

Hassan and the Theatre

Squire felt that the post-war commercial theatre was drab and repetitive. He said he had seen ten thousand plays about cabinet ministers and their rebellious daughters set in drawing rooms, involving blackmail and adultery. He told Blunden that 'the theatre is given over to a gentleman called Coward, of whom you will not have heard; he writes more or less smart plays in in the eighteenth-century manner'. None of them was worth anything compared with 'this one creation of a young poet who died'.

On 20 September 1923 James Flecker's *Hassan* had its first night on the London stage at Her Majesty's. It was, Squire, wrote, a work of genius, the renaissance of the poetic drama that he had long hoped for. Produced by Basil Dean, *Hassan* was hauntingly beautiful to look at and listen to – the incidental music was by Delius. But it was not for those that Squire urged his readers in the *London Mercury* to see it. He noted that the major plays that lasted from the great ages of Classical and Elizabethan theatre were poetic. *Hassan* was of such importance that he devoted his editorial to the play: 'If there is any life in English theatre, it will have to develop on Flecker's lines,'[414] Squire promised. Yet the play was deeply rooted in the language of the past; its ornate verse seemed to belong more to the 1890s than post-First World War England. The Prologue begins:

We who with songs beguile your pilgrimage
And swear that Beauty lives though lilies die,
We Poets of the proud old lineage
Who sing to find your hearts, we know not why,

What shall we tell you? tales, marvellous tales
Of ships and stars and isles where good men rest,
Where nevermore the rose of sunset pales,
And winds and shadows fall toward the West.

And how beguile you? Death has no repose
Warmer and deeper than that orient sand
Which hides the beauty and bright faith of those
Who made the Golden Journey to Samarkand.

The theme of the journey on the Golden Road had an especial resonance for Squire. It was the voyage of the Ancient Mariner; the heroic quest for something vital and yet unknowable, which is a leitmotif of his poetry: Eden; The Lily of Malud; America; Death.

We are the Pilgrims, master; we shall go
Always a little further; it may be
Beyond that last blue mountain barred with snow
Across that angry or that glimmering sea.

By contrast, he hated the first London production of *The Seagull*. The theatre of Chekhov was a blind spot. Squire praised the dramatic skill by which the plot emerged naturally from characters and situations, but asked: 'Does anyone care when Konstantin kills himself at the climax of the play?' His reply was simple: 'Nobody turns a hair. Nothing has died because nothing has lived.' The fundamental weakness was that the whole set of characters lacked any kind of vitality and a Russian gloom settled over the play. 'They are all out there by that lake, disappointed with love and hankering for what they lack, self-centred, humourless, devoid of volition, much less a sense of obligation. There they sit, bleating in antiphony. If the whole lot had shot themselves we should have been purged neither with pity nor terror.' Squire was at his most Victorian in his criticism of the ennui and rootlessness of the play. As so often in his most damning reviews he ended with a throwaway dismissal: 'As for the Seagull itself, it was no true gull, but at heart half a Wild Duck.' He added that the programme note said that 'Seagulls supplied by Watkins and Doncaster 36 Strand WC2.' 'So now, if you want a seagull, you know where to go.'[415]

Squire continued to hope that he could turn around his own fortunes with a play. *Robin Hood*, 'a comic pastoral farce', had one performance outdoors in 1926. Alan-a-Dale became an affected young man sent down from Cambridge. With make-up he bore a remarkable similarity to the author. When asked why he got sent down he replied that he had 'read a great deal in a solitary and discursive way. But not on the lines of the syllabus'. Squire forbade amateur performances, but despite broad hints to Basil Dean, the play was not performed again. Another play, *The Copper Gypsy*, a romantic comedy with the thinnest of conventional plots, never saw the stage. The Prologue gave Squire a chance to air his views on the theatre of his day while latecomers drifted in:

We all feel that verse is slightly artificial and pompous, don't we – and so unnecessary. But our author, who is one of those hopelessly unpractical people, insists that he cannot do without it altogether. There are some things which cannot properly be said except in verse. Of course, we all know he is talking nonsense. My own experience does not bear it out at all. I have produced my comedies all about tea parties and adultery, a play about a municipal contract and several scathing indictments of our social system, and in not one of them did I find a single line of verse was called for. I have discovered silence is more eloquent than speech, relied on the unspoken word, discarding prose itself, leaving it in fact for an audience to imagine the play themselves, working on certain clues provided by me.[416]

Squire had predicted the theatre of Harold Pinter. It is very easy to guess what he would have thought about it.

Like Aldous Huxley and Henry James, other doomed would-be dramatists, Squire continued to hope that he could make his fortune with a West End theatre show. *Berkeley Square* was based on an unfinished story by Henry James. Squire had co-written the play with the American John Balderston. On the opening night he sat in his box with Eileen and G. K. Chesterton. His greatest hope was that it would transfer to America, but the reviews were middling and complained about a complex plot that was too hard to follow. The play that Squire had hoped would make his family's fortune ran for five months. He set about rewriting it for a future production. Then he sold all his rights to his fellow author for cash so that he and his family could take a holiday in Switzerland. Ironically, a year later it enjoyed a very successful run in New York and was afterwards broadcast several times on the BBC. It was billed as written by John Balderston; underneath were the words: 'In collaboration with J. C. Squire.'

As Edmund Gosse had warned, the commercial theatre proved a terrible disappointment to Squire both financially and artistically. He argued that theatres were so expensive to run that they could not risk experiment or innovation and therefore stuck to well-tried favourites. How were the best writers to emerge? It was the same as the problem with publishing young poets – only even worse. If it took eleven years to take on a masterpiece such as *Hassan* what chance was there? Squire pinned his hopes on the formation of theatre clubs or societies which would be less affected by the overheads of commercial theatre and could put on plays of merit. At least the situation was not as bad as it had been in the 1890s. Meanwhile there was only disappointment for the playwright hawking his plays round to various theatre impresarios, who kept them for an age – and then rejected them. His description of the process was full of his own disappointment and frustration.

*

Second interlude: 'This Bloody Turf'

A short story, 'This Bloody Turf',[417] dissected the new theatre, just as 'The Man who Wrote Free Verse' had dissected new verse.

Stanley Gudgeon's career started at university where he developed a taste for 'Art, Aubrey Beardsley and Modern Theatre.' Thanks to the enthusiasm of some young women, a University Dramatic Society was formed, of which Stanley soon became chief actor and producer. His career began with a production of a play by the Victorian dramatist Henry Arthur Jones. This was very popular, but clearly 'not the sort of thing for a pioneer'. His next productions showed the progress of his pioneering: A. A. Milne and James Barrie gave way to George Bernard Shaw and Euripides. The committee of the dramatic society did not allow Gudgeon to produce Ibsen's *Ghosts*, but did let him to do the latest German expressionist play. The audience sat for three solid hours 'staring at a number of cubical designs and listening to a disjointed variety of hammerings, rattling and cryptic interjections.' His last play of all at the university showed that he had reached the 'penetralia of the Dramatic Renaissance'. The penniless Stanley played Czczcz, a railway clerk, in a Lithuanian drama, 'challenging the Almighty on behalf of all mankind'.

Mrs Grunt, the wife of a very successful ironmaster in the North East, was the Queen Bee of the local Mummers. She took seriously the idea that the world could and should be reformed by the Drama and invited lecturers from London to talk about Strindberg and Wedekind. She was also part of the London Mummers, 'the most chic and unsuccessful of London play producing societies' – lack of success was a guarantee of quality. Weekend guests found on their dressing table in their bedrooms at the Grunt household, 'odd volumes of Hauptmann, Sudermann, Hudermann, Brudermann and Still von Rudermann.'[418]

Infatuated by the attractive young man, wearing his hair fashionably long and with a centre parting (just as Squire had done), she persuaded her husband to buy a London theatre to launch Stanley's career. Her protégé put on three Lithuanian plays before happening to go to a performance of the Victorian favourite comedy *Charley's Aunt*. He hated it himself, but noting how the very mixed audience rolled about and wept with laughter (as Squire had done himself at the age of twelve), he put the play on. It was an enormous success; Mr Grunt bought four more theatres and made half a million in two years.

Now Stanley decided that it was time to take a serious interest in the 'Art of Drama'. There were three possibilities: ancient plays, including Shakespeare; 'plays by bewildering modern foreigners', and new poetic tragedies, preferably in blank verse, by neglected British geniuses. He therefore decided to set up a competition for the best poetic drama and promised to put the winner on in one of his London theatres. Mrs Grunt and he finally settled on a play by Robert Slater called 'A Stain on the Shield' as undoubtedly the best on offer. It proved to be a splendid success: 'Every dramatic critic in London, even the most carping and cautious, even the most theoretically exacting, saluted this new author, who had at last done what nobody since the Elizabethans had done, written a play in verse which was so thumpingly dramatic that the gallery could enjoy it as much as the stalls.' Mr Gudgeon was praised for restoring poetry to the stage: 'All London, temporarily tired of 'strained wit, pyjamas, the conflict between callous youth and puzzled age, bedrooms, revolvers, chintzes, cocktails and Chinamen', flocked to the play. (The list covers the whole range of popular West End theatre from Oscar Wilde and G. B. Shaw to Noel Coward, bedroom farce and the smash hit musical comedy *Chu Chin Chow*.) 'This is new', everybody said. 'This heralds a reaction.'

But the success of the 'Stain on the Shield' was not to last. A Cambridge undergraduate found that the play was, word for word, taken from Robert Browning's forgotten verse tragedy *A Blot in the 'Scutcheon*. Gudgeon was quick-witted enough to turn this reversal to his own advantage. He rang up a few theatre critics, invited them to supper and revealed the true author. He had, he said, long been an admirer of Robert Browning and from earliest youth had intended to bring his works back on to the stage. The critics admitted that they had forgotten all about Browning and now hailed Gudgeon's 'triumphant risk' and 'fearless blow'. He rang up Mrs Grunt straight away and told her that he had known all the time that the play was by Browning. His point had been to show up pretentious critics: 'I think it disgusting the way these highbrows in the theatre always chase after the latest fashion.' He reassured an uncertain Mrs Grunt that his whole mission had been to show up these effete Londoners. She retired happily to her husband and the North East, cured of the fantasy of modernist plays in the metropolis.

'This Bloody Turf' takes a swipe at both West End commercial success and the theatre of the avant-garde. It shows how the patronage of fashionably idle rich women propelled the modernist movement in the theatre, just as it did in the world of poetry. The plays themselves are wilfully obscure to both the cast and the audience, encouraging people like Mrs Grunt to feel herself part of a small and superior group of those who 'Truly Perceive, Feel and Understand'. Squire noted the creation of a damaging schism between the minority theatre and the commercial one, between 'high brow, low brow, and no brow at all'. By contrast, how successful and inclusive the Victorian theatre was in producing *Charley's Aunt* and Browning's *Blot in the 'Scutcheon*!

Chapter 17

A Centipede with a Foot in a Hundred Camps

Squire decided to stand for Parliament again in November 1924, but this time as a Liberal, and fight his local constituency of Brentford and Chiswick. He stood against the Conservative candidate, Grant Morden. In his election address he attacked Labour whose constitution put the moderates in the power of the 'wild men' with their visionary Socialist theories involving state control and ownership. On a dinner programme honouring Ramsay MacDonald, he doodled 'The Red Flag': 'The people's flag is deepest red / And Ramsay Mac is off his head / And so are his supporters too / They are a most disgusting crew.' The Conservatives, he added, were just Liberals ten years out of date.

Only five years before he had stood before the electors of Cambridge, a paid-up Fabian, on a manifesto of state nationalisation. Old friends such as Edward Marsh were baffled by his change of heart. Beatrice Webb wrote to him of her surprise that he had deserted the Labour Party and thrown his lot in with the Liberals just at a time when their prospects were poor and Labour, at last, was the growing force. He replied he was standing as the Liberal candidate largely to oppose the sitting member, the Canadian industrialist Grant Morden. Had he been a Liberal, Squire said, he would probably have stood for some other party. 'My views are precisely the same mixture of Liberalism,

257

Labourism and Toryism as they always were.'[419] She cannot have been reassured.

This time he jettisoned the party line and wrote the manifesto himself: 'I think I may claim it is the result of my own honest thought and there is no vote-catching clap-trap in it.' It noted that the candidate captained a cricket side that had beaten the House of Commons eleven and assured the voters that he himself was a moderate drinker and would support any 'pub which is a club'. He added that he deplored the loss of the Burlington Arms, close to Chiswick Ferry (and Swan House), where, he promised the voters, he had himself enjoyed many a quiet drink.

The writer Rebecca West came to speak to women Liberals; G. K. Chesterton addressed a mass meeting at Chiswick Town Hall; additional support poured in from the most influential figures: Lloyd George, Herbert Asquith, Viscount Grey of Fallodon, Violet Bonham Carter, Arnold Bennett and even Evelyn Waugh. Both *The Times* and the *Daily Telegraph* editorials lent their support. Squire added his own touch to political debate by the innovation of a local song sheet. Schoolchildren were trained to sing choruses of 'Squire keeps on walking'. His ditty, to be sung at meetings to the tune of the recent hit, 'Yes! We Have No Bananas' was also popular:

Yes, we'll have no Grant Morden
We'll have no Grant Morden today
In Brentford
And Chiswick
We'll give him his physic,
Then we will send him away!
Back to the old firm in Canada
Though there they may also say:
O, yes, we'll have no Grant Morden
We'll have no Grant Morden today.

Eileen spoke at her husband's meetings and worked twelve hours a day for his campaign. In its editorial of 26 October, the local paper, the *Brentford and Chiswick Gazette*, urged its readers to vote for him. 'All one needs to win is the right wife, the right agent and the right opponent. I have all three,' declared Squire. Despite these advantages, his opponent polled 12,000 votes, and held the seat. He got only 2,540 votes and for the second time in his life lost his deposit – and with it any hope of a political career.

His focus turned from politics to architecture, the Cinderella of the arts, as he called it. If, as he thought, architecture was the best indication of a society's character, London was a test case. Always in his mind were dream Londons: the city of medieval times; the city of Edmund Spenser and Shakespeare; the city of elegant eighteenth-century houses and squares; the city imagined by William Morris in his prologue to *The Earthly Paradise*: 'small, and white, and clean/ The clear Thames bordered by its gardens green...' Like Morris, Squire saw how his dream London had become a dreadful wilderness of nineteenth century ugliness. 'London before the Great Fire was one of the loveliest cities in the world; in a few more years of subservience to the greed of soulless companies and it may become the ugliest. Once start reckoning everything in money and you are dead.'[420]

The Thames was an emblem of this widespread industrial pollution. Squire contrasted Tennyson's 'The Brook' with what it had become:

Another bend, another reach
(The fish are getting fewer)
And after that (forgive my speech)
I'm but a common sewer...

'Tis cellulose, 'tis cellulose
Within whose shrine there flickers,
The rainbow sheen of countless hose
And camisoles and knickers...[421]

Medieval London in the 1930s survived, he wrote, only in the romance of the names of its lanes and streets and in a few buildings that had escaped destruction. The city was being rebuilt under his eyes and nearly always, Squire felt, for the worse. 'Uglification' was his word for it. There were few buildings that had appeared between 1850 and 1900 that did not make him long for a second Great Fire. The period of London's greatest expansion was the period of its worst architecture. 'The Victorians with their mingled ignorance and misapplied book-learning had discovered architectural bad taste.'[422] Oxford Street was one of the dreariest arrays of paint and plaster in the world. You had only to stand in St Paul's Churchyard and compare Wren's cathedral with the tall offices and warehouses surrounding it to see the squalid mess that the City had become, in thrall to the greed of soulless companies. Nothing, he wrote, could be done to spoil the business quarters of the City, but there was much to fight for elsewhere in London and in high streets up and down the country.

Squire started a crusade to save London from developers and the demands of traffic. Again and again, he used his editorial columns in the *London Mercury* to draw public attention to the destruction of fine buildings.[423] Many of the great London houses of the nobility had been destroyed. Cassiobury, Devonshire, Lansdowne and Dorchester houses had all gone, but there was much that could be saved. One of his first campaigns was to preserve the medieval almshouses of Whitgift Hospital which were in the way of Croydon Council's road widening schemes. The case went right up to the House of Lords, who found against the council and turned down the scheme. His victory was the first of many.

The most important architectural issue of the time, Squire felt, was how to build a proper memorial for the war dead. When Sir Frank Baines, Chief Architect of the Board of Works, proposed an enormous rectilinear 'pylon' in the Ancient Egyptian style, flanked by two temples, there was an outcry in the press. Squire devoted his leading *Mercury* editorial to the issue.[424] He was appalled by the pylon, and felt that the scheme of inscribing the names of the fallen on the walls between two temples was inappropriate for an English war memorial. He echoed the public feeling against the design. 'We are delighted to find that a need of reverting to English and Western traditions of architecture – or in other words of rediscovering our own hearts and minds – was evident in many of the comments made on this revolting design. We do not want to make a cant of 'Englishness' in architecture or anything else. The point is that if we are true to ourselves, write and paint and build out of our natural loves instead of feverishly chasing after 'stunts' of design and theory from the four quarters of the globe we shall automatically find ourselves producing work which will be recognisably English as well as being better than we have recently done and more valuable to the rest of the world and to ourselves.' The plan was abandoned. Perhaps he would have approved of what we got – the National Arboretum…[425]

Squire therefore decided to form a club whose aim was 'to enlarge the public appreciation of good architecture and the allied arts, and especially the best work of today'. In July 1922 he was elected as the first Chairman of the Architecture Club and continued in the role for the next six years. Thomas Hardy, who had trained as an architect, was the inspired choice for its first president. Besides many of the well-known architects of the day, the club also recruited the great and the good: Hilaire Belloc, John Betjeman, Edward Marsh, Harold Nicolson, William Rothenstein, Lord Gerald Wellesley and Ambrose Heal all joined. At its first dinner meeting in October 1922 John Galsworthy proposed the toast to the new club and Gilbert Scott replied. The editor of *The Spectator,* St Loe Strachey, (who had long been forgiven for his Darwinian approach to war) made three proposals which instantly hit the headlines: plaques naming the architects on all buildings, houses on bridges, just like old London Bridge, and a return to grand entrance gates and approaches to public buildings. *The Spectator* gave the Architecture Club a rousing acknowledgement:

No one of any observation could possibly deny that for every decent building put up in England there is a disfiguring crop of calamitous erections to be numbered by the hundred. The voice of the Architecture Club will be loud in protest against what seems mean or unworthy in building, it may make suggestions and recommendations that will carry increasing weight as it becomes more and more recognized as the chief arbiter of taste in matters of architecture and tactile civic amenity... Those good citizens who hate and fear the ravages of the blind and idiot monster should welcome the young champion that was born at last week's dinner.[426]

The central originality of Squire's idea was to bring the arcane world of the architect into contact with leading political and artistic figures. He distrusted the kind of specialists who became so involved with their own world that they lost touch with the world outside. Membership should consist of a third architects, a third interested amateurs and a third the press, limited to a total of three hundred. What he suggested was for all those interested to form a pressure group to drive up standards. The press should review new buildings in the same way as they reviewed new artists in every other sphere. Just as he had tried to promote young poets he now wanted to encourage young architects.

The following year the club held an exhibition at old Grosvenor House, lent by the Duke of Westminster, with photographs and models illustrating the best architecture of the last twenty years. There was considerable press coverage. In February 1923 Squire wrote, of 'many signs of an awakening of interest in British Architecture'. Two years later a second exhibition was held, opened by G. K. Chesterton, at the Royal Institute of British Architects' Galleries. It showed, according to Squire, that 'we are putting up a few good buildings and that few people realise how many'. The club hit the headlines again with an attack on the villas and bungalows that were spreading like a rash along the newly built roads. In 1929 Ramsay MacDonald was the chief guest and Squire, from the chair, warned the prime minister against the threat of 'Ramsaygrad, huge public buildings, gaunt vulgar things built to impress for their immensity'. *The Times* wrote, 'The increasing interest in architecture in all journals is directly attributable to the pioneer efforts of Jack Squire.'[427]

In 1924 Squire went to the consecration of Giles Gilbert Scott's Liverpool Cathedral and thought it was one of the architectural glories of England. The Gothic Revival was 'a slavish mistake', but he felt Scott's work branched out creatively from it. Squire praised a very different building too – Wembley Stadium which he thought was 'really magnificent'. He heard the news that the Victorian Shakespeare Memorial Theatre at Stratford had been burnt down 'with unfeigned delight'.[428] Elisabeth Scott designed the new theatre in what was seen as a controversial modernist style. Outraged locals who wanted something half-timbered called it the Jam Factory; Sir Edward Elgar thought it 'unspeakably ugly and wrong' and J. B. Morton called it the new 'Soviet Barracks at Stratford'. Squire, on the other hand, admired a building which was solidly English and not 'a fake or an imitation of anything'. 'There is thought behind every curve, every relation of masses and the effect is not far short of majestic,' he wrote in the *Architectural Review*.[429]

Squire promoted and praised contemporary architecture that was sensitive to tradition. He felt that the achievement of a distinctive style for the age was often hampered by misapplied learning. This often led to terrible results. Greek temples did not suit chilly England and the dead details of the Gothic style did not suit railway stations. Too often mushroom developments aped foreign styles and thrived without any architects, designers or taste. It was useless, however, to go back and regret the passing of the Middle Ages. Architecture had to make terms with an industrial society and find a way forward. He praised those architects who designed cheap houses and made the industrial suburb a thing of beauty. One key principle was good manners. He noted, for example, that the old Grosvenor House was not especially beautiful but it did not 'boss' the park with its balconies and narrow bow-fronted houses and gave Park Lane its distinctive charm. 'Now the new Grosvenor House, a great barracks of flats in the modern American manner, is utterly discourteous to its neighbours'.[430] Squire pinned his hope on an educated lay public who would guide England from 'the vast mess into which we have strayed'.

Squire thought the leaders of the Church of England were often philistines. They were only interested in the kind of Gothic architecture associated with ivy, bats and owls. When the Archbishop of York wrote that the longer poems of Milton bored him, Squire was quick with a riposte, 'The Archbishop of York': 'Poetic Justice here we see, / Milton bores Ebor, / Ebor, e' bores me.' So, when the Bishop of London argued with 'the persistence of a termite ant' for the demolition of nineteen of Wren's City churches, Squire was not surprised. He was going to devote another editorial to campaign against the proposal but found his 'feelings were so powerful, that our customary prose would not content us and we were obliged to burst into song.' The result was a rollicking verse editorial: 'A New Song of the Bishop of London':

Sir Christopher came to the field of the fire,
And graced it with spire
And nave and choir,
Careful column and carven attire,
That the ships coming up from sea
Should hail where the Wards from Ludgate fall
A coronal cluster of steeples tall,
All Hallows, Barking, and by the Wall,
St Bride, St Swithin,
St Catherine Coleman,
St Margaret Pattens,
St Mary le Bow,
St Nicholas Cole Abbey,
St Alban, Wood Street,
St Magnus the Martyr,
St Edmund the King,
Whose names like a chime so sweetly call,
And high over all

The cross and the ball
On the riding redoubtable Dome of Paul.

After the list of churches doomed for destruction came the Grand Chorus:

Now let us sing
Hey-ding-a-ding-ding,
Long live the Bishop, Long live the King,
And long live Mammon and everything
Excepting our sires of old;
And let us pull all the churches down,
And the Abbey down,
And the Tower down,
And especially Fulham Palace down,
And sell the sites for gold.[431]

'Inspired propaganda,'[432] Edmund Gosse called it – and read the poem to everyone he could buttonhole. It was also a source of inspiration to the young John Betjeman who was to carry on its campaigning spirit. Evelyn Waugh, who detested Squire, was more critical. In *Decline and Fall* he wrote of Mr Jack Spire of the *London Hercules* who was busily saving St Sepulchre's, Egg Street, while he ignored the destruction of King's Thursday, the finest piece of domestic Tudor in England'. Squire's protest eventually won the day and the bishop's plan was abandoned – but German bombers succeeded where the Bishop of London had failed – and razed many of the churches to the ground.

After his successful campaign to save the City churches Squire turned his attention to Waterloo Bridge. For him Rennie's bridge with the swing and sweep of its arches and its fine columns was one of the most perfect buildings in the world; the best post-medieval bridge in London and the embodiment of William Morris's idea of the fusion of art and engineering. Built in 1817, it was, he wrote, just as much a war memorial as the Cenotaph, commanding the finest panorama of the capital, of the Embankment, Somerset House and St Paul's. It was a view that fascinated painters and gave London an architectural centre. The bridge was the subject of a ten-year-long controversy between the L.C.C. – who were concerned about traffic – and conservationists. Squire believed it should not be rebuilt or repaired in any way and once again used his editor's chair to give a blow-by-blow account of the wranglings. Cartoonist David Low of the *Evening Standard* pictured him along with J. L. Garvin, Viscount Lee and Lord Balfour on the bridge, surrounded by a steam of fury. A constable shouted at them, 'I must arsk you gents not to quiver with anger here. It ain't safe.' But it was one battle he could not win.

Squire applauded the effort of conservationists such as Viscount Rothermere who saved the Bethlehem Hospital and Staple Inn, whose black and white timbered front Squire thought was the best reminder of what Elizabethan architecture looked like. The preservation of Clifford's Inn, 'a picturesque survival' in whose garden he had often liked to eat his frugal wartime lunch, was another cause, as was opposing the plan to move Covent Garden to Bloomsbury. Later, Squire was to form a defence committee to save John Nash's Carlton House Terrace, where Palmerston and Balfour had lived, from a government plan to turn the site into offices. In two centuries half of the City churches had already gone. Regent Street had gone too and all Georgian Bloomsbury, he feared, with its squares and green spaces, would soon go with it.

Squire was not only concerned about buildings. The whole appearance of the streets showed poor design, from their lamp posts, letter boxes, sand bins, railings, and posters to the growing rash of advertisements and 'flashlight' hoardings. He warned how London's statues were disappearing fast – William IV and George III had already fallen to the demands of traffic. In 1925 he was pleased to be at the unveiling of a very different kind of sculpture by his friend Jacob Epstein in Hyde Park. The nude figure of Rima, the jungle girl heroine of W. H. Hudson's nature books, caused outrage. Squire defended the statue against a bevy of writers including Hilaire Belloc who declared it repellent and obscene and petitioned for it to be taken down. He suggested more statues of literary figures, following the example of the small town Hannibal Missouri who had just erected a statue to Mark Twain and Huckleberry Finn. What about Falstaff in Gadshill or East Cheap? Or Arnold Bennett in the Potteries – and who better than Mr Micawber for Downing Street?

Squire felt that design was an important part of the smaller things of everyday life. War medals showed lack of taste and skill: the lettering of the Mons Star, for example, lacked any kind of workmanship and half a million copies of the Victory Medal had had to be scrapped. The OBE medal looked to him as if it had come out of a Christmas cracker. Stamps too were poorly designed. Even the telephone book came in for abuse as badly put together and too fragile for use. 'Almost every object produced by the state from barracks to the insignia of the OBE has been repulsively ugly and shoddy.' What could be done? Squire was a believer in authority, whether of a literary, moral or political kind, and argued for a Minister of Fine Arts to take overall charge and clear up the chaos. He campaigned for this appointment for the next ten years, but acknowledged that the creation of such a post on its own would not solve the problem.[433]

In September 1925 Squire's financial position had improved and he moved both house and office. At Eileen's suggestion they moved from Chiswick to Frith Cottage, in the tiny hamlet of Bowlhead Green, Thursley. The village was hidden in deep lanes, surrounded by tall hedges in the Surrey countryside. It had three key requisites for Jack's quintessential English village: a church, a pub and a cricket side. The 'cottage' was in fact a substantial Tudor farmhouse, four miles out of the village, set high on a hill and surrounded by trees.

At Thursley Squire enjoyed the role of the country gentleman and, for a time, the family employed a nurse, two maids, two gardeners, a chauffeur and a cook. There was even talk of a servants' ball. They put on amateur theatrical shows for charity just as Eileen's family had done at Hintlesham. In January 1930 the performance of a satirical comedy, 'Three Uncles and an Aunt', written by Jack, directed by Eileen and featuring their three children, was performed at Thursley Village Hall – and was, somewhat astonishingly, reviewed at length in *The Times*. The family held musical parties where Jack reported the labourers came and 'sang like larks.' He drove a very fashionable and very large Buick and Eileen had a little Austin 7 which she crashed at regular intervals. Far away from the temptations of London, she hoped they could enjoy family life together in the country and shortly after the move their fourth child, Julia, was born. Squire's role as a family man was clear when he was invited by the young Stephen Spender to address the English Club at Oxford University:

> At the end of a rather convivial evening, he eyed me with a wavering severity to ask 'What you intend to do with your life, young man?' 'Write poetry.' 'Then you will be like me,' he sighed… 'You will write until you are twenty or twenty-one. Then you will fall in love with a fair young girl and you will write more poetry. Then you will marry the girl and you will write reviews and journalism. Then, when you are my age, you look back and think "Well, perhaps, after all to have married that girl and had those children is worth more than to have written four hundred sonnets."'[434]

Visitors to Bowlhead Green were concerned to note, however, that Squire was drinking whisky, and nothing but whisky, for breakfast.

The same year that the Squire family moved to Thursley the *London Mercury* moved from Poppins Court to 229 Strand, one of the very few surviving seventeenth-century houses within a four-mile radius. It was next to a bookshop and opposite the Law Courts close to the Temple Bar. It was a move full of confidence and put the magazine at the heart of London's journalism. There was a shop beneath but the rest of the overhanging building belonged to the *Mercury*. Squire had the front painted white with black window frames and hoped to add an orange and black sign outside bearing the emblem of the magazine, the head of Mercury. Inside the building was a warren of narrow cupboard-like rooms full of books. Squire's editorial room was reached by rickety steps and contained a kitchen range and a colossal dresser that was soon filled with papers. 'We were never more comfortable in our lives, and we now have a vested interest in preserving the ancient buildings of London,' he told his readers.[435] He knew that William Congreve had died in nearby Surrey Street and wondered if Burghley or Pope had lived there. He could almost hear the footsteps of Samuel Pepys, Mrs Thrale and Charles Lamb as they tramped by his windows towards the Cheshire Cheese where Dr Johnson had held court and declared that a tavern-chair was the throne of human felicity.

Hopeful contributors entered the offices of the *London Mercury* by a dark passage and went up the narrow staircase past the room where Mr Pink the accounts manager presided. A little further up was a small room with a large double desk where Squire and his co-editor Edward Shanks sat. Books and bulging files of papers were piled against the walls. To the young writer Geoffrey Grigson, looking for a job in publishing just as Squire himself had done twenty years earlier, it resembled a 'coprolite cave'. The editor himself was 'hunched and hutched and blunt among dead books as among the fossilized ordure of hyenas.' Squire's hardworking and tolerant secretary Grace Chapman occupied the top floor and kept some kind of order over the whole premises. There she supervised the eviction of bores, and the buying of buttonholes for the editor and gave advice 'straight from the shoulder'.[436] She was also in charge of a succession of red-haired young assistants who worked among a confusion of glue pots and files. Visitors of all kinds filled the building. Squire called it Bedlam. To Alan Pryce-Jones it seemed more like a house party than an office. When he had serious work to do he locked himself in the lavatory.

Squire was effectively a one-man band. He ran the whole operation from beginning to end: he wrote the editorials and most of the poetry reviews; he chose the outside contributors who wrote on their specialist subjects; he fixed the payments, read all the poems and short stories that came in and tried to reply to the senders.

Nearly always polite in his rejection, he wrote to an insistent Sylvia Pankhurst: 'Interested though we are in your proposal, I am afraid pressure on our space is too great to allow our publishing an article on a dead Roumanian writer.' He was encouraging to young writers such as Dorothy Sayers who sent him some short stories – 'The one about the man who electroplated his mistress sounds very attractive.' He often suggested other magazines that might take a rejected piece. When one young aspirant wrote to him saying that if he were not published in the *Mercury* he would commit suicide Squire had a week of sleepless nights.

The *London Mercury* was a complete and unpredictable mixture of material within a fixed template. Squire's editorials set the tone. Sometimes editorials were in verse; humorous or satirical comments went alongside angry denunciations and gossip. They were linked only by the editor's character, interests and sense of the absurd.

The main body of the magazine was a pot pourri of unpredictable material. In October 1928, for example, he celebrated nine years of publication. He began with an article on the shocking revelation of Dickens's affair with Maria Beadnell; there followed pieces on a malicious attack on Queen Victoria under the heading, 'No monopoly on Cads'; the preservation of London Squares; the censorship of *The Well of Loneliness*; the difficulties of librarians and a Chinese critic on Thomas Hardy. Where else could you find side by side the latest D.H. Lawrence short story, Ernest Bramah's 'Story of Chou the alluring', a learned article on ancient Japanese epics, Greek printing types, Arnold Lunn on mountaineering and a Russian émigré writing about medieval wandering scholars?[437]

There then followed a section of poetry which might last about twenty pages. The bulk of the magazine was made up with articles on the widest variety of topics. There were critical views of Victorian and modern writers, short stories, and detailed bibliographical studies. And there might be anything at all that caught the editor's eye – a piece on the silver collections at Oxford colleges, an account of Napoleon's exile on St Helena, the latest literature from South Africa, or a letter to Mussolini. The *Mercury*'s scope was not to be confined to literature. From its very first number there were articles about art, architecture and music. There was a correspondence section. Letters from America, France, Germany, China and Ireland became regular features along with accounts of the proceedings of learned societies such as the Society for the Protection of Ancient Buildings, the Folklore Society and the Royal Numismatic Society. Squire handed the next section of reviews to trusted sub-editors who wrote about the latest plays, exhibitions, books and concerts. The premise was that literature was central, but only a part of a general culture that readers of the *Mercury* shared.

Towards the back of the magazine was the review section. Squire had his regular reviewers whom he trusted to select their topics and buy their own books. He would then select six or so and choose the two best for more detailed treatment. There was a history reviewer; a biography and autobiography reviewer; a scientific reviewer; a theology and philosophy reviewer; a classics reviewer, and so on. They received between £3 and £5 for each article of between 2,000 and 3,000 words, but could keep the books. They were, or often became, trusted friends. The novelist and historian Maurice Hewlett covered biography. The Irish boxing writer Bohun Lynch covered sport. Squire found a Russian exile, the penniless Prince D. S. Mirsky, and put him in charge of foreign literature. Clennell Wilkinson looked after adventure and travel and Eileen reviewed children's books. Every month there was also a bibliographical section written by Iolo Williams. Squire himself often reviewed the latest poetry or otherwise handed it to Edward Shanks or later to his American sub-editor Milton Waldman.

The look of the *Mercury* reflected Squire's sense of the magazine's purpose. One advertiser, the type foundry Caslon, declared its typeface to be 'bold without coarseness, distinctive without eccentricity', the print expression of the *Mercury*'s own literary mission: 'to represent the newest and latest in literature without... giving in to seemingly ungrounded or unmoored experiment for its own sake.'[438] Squire believed that the steady decline in the quality of English books owed a great deal to the ugliness that was the legacy of Victorian capitalism. William Morris had shown at the Kelmscott Press how beauty and utility could be combined. The *Mercury* was an example of good book production in Morris's tradition. Its large format, antique wove paper, generous borders and heavily leaded type (Caslon Old Style) made it unfussy and attractive to read and set it apart from cheaper and flimsier publications. 'Small-format, half an inch thick, with squared spine and woven paper, the *Mercury* was consciously retrospective in its design, harking back to Victorian forebears like the *Edinburgh Quarterly*. In content, too, the journal was explicitly pitched at a readership for whom the physical object of the book held its own attraction, with sections devoted to "Book Production Notes" and "Bibliographical News and Notes."'[439]

Squire hired the scholar-printer B. H. Newdigate to be responsible for the design of the magazine and to write on all aspects of printing. His regular articles on book production brought the arcane world of printing, of typefaces and design, to wider attention. 'In a fit of madness', Squire devoted one number to a 'pied' printing made up of five articles in different typefaces.[440] The aim was to show the wealth and variety of type available to the printer. There were also pages of watercolour printing, facsimiles of printers' ornaments and a section on Monotype Rules, such as 'small spaces need stout borders'. This was followed by an all-black 'Book Printing Number' which showed the technological advances in printing techniques. The articles were printed in a variety of linotype varieties such as Baskerville and Venetia allowing 'the reader who shares the revived interest in printing to compare the practical and artistic impact of their different forms'.[441] 'These two numbers offer an unequalled look into the print practices of the early 1930s.'[442]

Increasingly, too, the *Mercury* used illustrations, line-drawn portraits of figures of the day, along with linocuts, and cartoons. Wood engravings by young artists such as Clare Leighton and Gwen Raverat often portrayed traditional rural scenes and country crafts and were more 'Georgian' than the rest of the magazine. The socialist Will Dyson's cartoons gave a caustic commentary on the literary world. The bloated figures of Belloc, Gosse and Arnold Bennett were gifts to a cartoonist and the snootiness of Bloomsbury and the highbrows was relentlessly mocked.

Thanks to Squire's enthusiasm his cricket side the Invalids expanded their fixture list and began to play regularly every weekend. He published a monograph on his eleven: 'Of this, we may take it the only, edition, 125 copies have been printed. Most of these have been given away to the scores of debilitated men, who at one time or another have tottered onto the field for the team.'[443] He dedicated it to Eileen, 'who usually kept the scorebook'.

For Squire, and for many bookmen, the appeal of cricket was inextricably involved with the English village and countryside. Bowlhead Green was an ideal place for the Invalids to hold their ten-day festival. Keeping cricket alive in its natural village setting became just as important to Squire as the preservation of England's architectural heritage. Cricket was essentially a community game. Cricket's true home, Squire thought, was not a test match at Lords or the Oval, but an English village green: 'the agrarian sides, though seldom the most efficient and never the richest, are usually the pleasantest to watch.'[444] Like his fellow Invalid Edmund Blunden Squire felt that 'The game is not terminated at the boundary, but is reflected beyond, is echoed and varied out there among the gardens and the barns, the dells and the thickets, and belongs to some wider field.'

The village cricket ground was a version of a better world where Squire thought 'the distinctions in life are temporarily forgotten; for the time being we live in an ideal republic where Jack is as good as his master and maybe a little better,'[445] bringing together the landed and the poor, the farmer and the postman. He recommended the journalist Neville Cardus to turn aside from reviewing the professional game and write more about country house and village cricket. 'He won't find the tedium and the too-perfect wickets, of which the popular

Press makes so great complaint, in the countryside.' He claimed that 'few men… would not rather play on a field surrounded by ancient elms and rabbit-haunted bracken than on a better field with fat black lands or gasworks around. There the national game is still the national game…'[446] No doubt he would have agreed with the historian G. M. Trevelyan's half-serious view that if the French nobility had played cricket with their villagers in 1789 their chateaux would not have been razed to the ground. Squire certainly suggested that after the war the Germans should be taught to play cricket to soften their character.

Nothing – the *Mercury*, the demands of family life, even poetry – could stand in cricket's way. Squire put up some of the cricketers in his house and found friends' houses for some to stay in. At weekends the Invalids toured Surrey and the Home Counties; an annual trip to the West Country also became a fixture. They also played against villages, minor public schools, the army. At the Oval in 1924 they played a combined House of Lords and Commons team. Squire said he never found it difficult to raise a team to play against village sides as it gave 'an excellent opportunity to raise a thirst'. The Invalids generally contained many more writers than war veterans. Hugh Walpole, Siegfried Sassoon, and A. P. Herbert were good cricketers, as was Alec Waugh, a talented all-rounder. The composer Arnold Bax and his brother Clifford were regulars. The Australian test wicketkeeper Bert Oldfield was an unlikely Invalid, as was a Polish airman, recruited by Squire, who had to be carefully placed at the crease by the umpire. The bulky G. K. Chesterton was asked to play. He declined, but said he could be the wicket.[447]

The role of captain was as congenial to Squire as that of editor. He imposed his own style and humour on his side just as he stamped his personality on the *London Mercury*. He organised the itinerary and, whatever his overdraft, paid all his side's expenses. A degree of chaos always surrounded the Invalids and each player had stories of his own to tell. Late arrivals, long lunches, plenty of alcohol and a mixture of locals and London 'swells' made for anecdote after anecdote, often centring on the captain himself. One village team, intimidated by the sight of seven 'blues in jackets and badges' descending from their coach, were amazed when they won an easy victory. None of the blues had been for cricket.

He was always modest about his ability: 'My main asset is that I keep cheerful when it rains,' he said. His fellow Invalids thought Squire, unschooled in cricketing tactics, relied on poetic intuition. His lack of tactics was shown in his field placings. Despite his short-sightedness he regularly chose to position himself at slip. Off a three-pace run-up, he launched very slow spinners. Batting, of course, was difficult: he always came in at number eleven. And yet, as Alec Waugh remarked, he had a mysterious capacity to get the best out of his side – and they sometimes chalked up surprising victories. The game was played seriously, but not solemnly. 'Beachcomber' recalled to his 1.6 million readers in the *Daily Express* an Invalids match when many of the batting side were passing the time in the village inn. 'A breathless spectator came rushing in saying, "The wickets are falling like rain!" He was dismissed with contumely.'

Squire was upset to see football being played in August and decided to organise a protest about this incursion into the cricket season. On a bright clear New Year's Day in 1929 the London Invalids gathered to play against the Hampshire Eskimos on Broadhalfpenny Down, Hambledon, where, according to tradition, cricket began. A bitter wind scythed across the down. Squire announced that the game would be played whatever the weather. White flannels were worn and gloves would only be allowed if the temperature fell below freezing. Two thousand spectators came to watch, including a lorry load of Invalids' supporters; the toss had to be repeated four times for the photographers. The local hunt rode by, pink coats on the skyline, as the Hambledon Brass Band played 'John Peel'. Tankards of hot ale were carried out at intervals. By midday 'The Bat and Ball' was drunk dry. The game made front-page news in the *Daily Mirror* with a photograph and the headline 'HOUNDS STOP PLAY AT THE BIRTHPLACE OF CRICKET'.[448] *The Times* sent its cricket correspondent, Dudley Carew, who felt he was watching an eighteenth-century sporting print come to life; it was not hard to imagine Squire Osbaldeston or Mr Jingle among the players. He reported the match as 'Pickwickian without descending into farce'.[449]

By four o'clock the light was fading; the Invalids had won by eleven runs. No one dared suggest a second innings. The two sides, umpires, bandsmen and supporters retired to the upper room of 'The George'. The fire blazed, clay pipes smoked and Peter Warlock composed a song for the event with a rollicking chorus which was sung over and over again. Finally, a cornet soloist gave a rendering of the 'Lost Chord'. There were clamours to repeat the match. Squire turned them down: 'It is always a mistake to endeavour to repeat perfection.' It was a glimpse of the Land of Lost Content.

The Invalids were much more than a cricket club. Non-cricketing friends such as J. B. Morton, Belloc and Chesterton often joined them at their regular dinners – bibulous affairs that went on long into the night – and Squire organised an annual celebration at the Cheshire Cheese. Morton remarked that no one would have guessed that cricket was the occasion for these goings-on.[450] Long clay pipes were smoked and apologies for absence in verse were read out. Singing played a large part in these evenings; Belloc's 'The Winged Horse' was always sung. Squire himself led the chorus of now-forgotten favourites such as 'The Jolly Little Ogo-Pogo,' 'The Man who Played the Oompah' and an interminable song about 'Little Billie'. Sea shanties were also very popular, as were French marching songs. Every Invalids' dinner broke up with a favourite number from the Edwardian music hall, *The Arcadians*:

It'll all be the same, all the same
A hundred years from now
No use in worrying, no use in hurrying,
No use in kicking up a row.

Chapter 18

Public Fame: Private Pain

The General Strike of 1926 polarised political opinion. Had it happened ten years earlier Squire would have supported the strikers. But now as a successful editor and Liberal his position was much more complicated. When a member of the Parliamentary Labour Party wrote to him asking for support to help miners' families, he replied that 'One is in a wretched dilemma.' He would have been only too glad to help and felt miserable not to: in his heart he supported them, but he thought he would only be adding to their strike pay and prolonging the wretched struggle which was bound to end, as it did, with the miners giving way. His main concern was getting the *Mercury* out and keeping up standards – but at the same time he managed to set up a Surrey local newspaper which was delivered by his chauffeur and, he boasted, included the lunchtime cricket scores.[451]

Literary feuds continued. While Jack and Eileen stayed for the weekend with Vita Sackville-West and her husband Harold Nicolson at Long Barn, their Kent home, Squire casually remarked how odd it was that poets did not write about people's work and their occupations. She seized on the idea and in 1926 published her long poem, 'The Land', given an adulatory review by Squire in his *Observer* column.[452] Virginia Woolf was now caught in an awkward situation. Welcome praise for her friend came from an unwelcome quarter. 'I think the better of him for it, though his manner is always that of a curate, a grocer, a churchwarden, someone sticky with jam and buns at a School treat, however, he admires you; and I'm jealous,' she wrote.[453] She had another reason to be jealous when the poem won the Hawthornden Prize, but she felt she had to attend the award.

The ceremony itself crystallised everything that she disliked about the literary establishment. Squire himself, John Drinkwater and Laurence Binyon were on the platform at the Aeolian Hall; Edward Marsh, Robert Lynd and Miss Warrender had been on the panel. John Buchan gave a long speech and was followed by a less-than-sober Squire who said he regretted that his friend Stanley Baldwin ('A man whom I loved, revered and respected') had been unable to give the Chairman's speech, as he was the first prime minister for half a century to love the English countryside. Virginia Woolf was struck by the ordinariness and the conventionality of the platform party: 'In truth it was the thick dull middle class that met, not the aristocracy.'[454] After the award 'Vita cried all night. The whole business of writing became infinitely distasteful,' Virginia Woolf wrote, as if her friend had been polluted by contact with the lower orders. (Vita Sackville-West was the only writer to receive the Hawthornden Prize twice when her *Collected Poems* won in 1933. Virginia Woolf never won it.)[455]

Virginia Woolf's attitude to journalism was snobbish and superior: 'I don't think I could go about scribbling in papers: that's all it amounts to: or admire the Squires and the Priestleys,' she wrote to Vita Sackville-West. She looked with disdain on them and on writers such as E. V. Lucas and Robert Lynd, 'men who write weekly, write daily, write shortly, write for busy people catching trains in the morning and for tired people coming home in the evening – one feels that a common greyness silvers all.'[456] They all belonged to the 'stinking underworld of hack writers'. She was outraged when Squire asked her for a story and promised 'to see if it will do'.[457] How demeaning it must have been for her to haggle with him over the fee for a piece she submitted to the *Mercury*. She had sent 'a memoir article' and asked the terms. He accepted the article and offered £13. '£15 or my ms back,' she replied:

it came back by return. She accepted £13. Virginia Woolf's bargaining highlighted the problem for many modernist writers. Although they looked down on 'middlebrow' publications like the *Mercury*, financially they needed them to survive. Even that most superior of journals, Eliot's *Criterion*, advertised regularly in Squire's *Mercury*.

If she drubbed him in print, he did the same to her. When her novel *Orlando* came out to some acclaim, Squire dismissed it as: 'a very pleasant trifle that will entertain the drawing-rooms for an hour: a suitable companion for the jade carving and the painted snuff-boxes.'[458] Orlando was not a believable character and the book was 'fatigued' and lacked 'gusto'. He thought even a trifle had to have some enthusiasm behind it. Arnold Bennett agreed and in his review in the *Evening Standard* called it 'a Woman's High-Brow Lark'. A very angry Sackville-West supported her friend and promised she would never speak to Squire again. Virginia Woolf, on the other hand, thought Squire's comments 'barking' and was delighted to have goaded the two of them. 'What a sting I am in the flanks of the Squires and Bennetts,' she boasted.[459]

Virginia Woolf met Squire for the last time at the farewell dinner to mark Edmund Blunden's appointment as Professor of English in Tokyo. It was held on 11 March 1924 at the Florence Restaurant in Rupert Street, Soho. Many of the senior staff of the *Nation & Athenaeum* (the re-formed *Athenaeum*) were there as well as other journalists and writers. She resented the presence of 'lustful and leering' Middleton Murry and the whole event ended, she wrote, with the 'fat and consequential Jack Squire' responding to the toast of Literature and leading the enthusiastic singing of 'For he's a jolly good fellow'. It was just the kind of roistering male literary gathering that Squire relished – and Virginia Woolf loathed.

Virginia Woolf's friend Katherine Mansfield was also full of scorn for the *Mercury* and echoed her disdain for Squire's 'tradesman' style: 'What a piece of *grocery prose* is his editorial. He's a rat. But the lack of style, poise, dignity – the boosting of his own shop, the crying down of the wares of the gentleman over the way – good God! his 'fungoid' writers and 'sterile' young men and so on – I take a deep malicious delight that his vulgar literary Harrods should be so bad. I had thought it would be a great deal better.'[460] The following year she wrote to Squire from France in very different terms: 'If you knew how much the *London Mercury* means to an exile! It is devoured even to the covers – and the last number always seems the best.'

When she submitted her story 'The Stranger' to Squire he wanted to alter the open ending, but she argued fiercely for it to remain – and it did. She also sent him 'The Daughters of the Late Colonel', for which he paid £20, and the longest piece he ever published, the semi-autobiographical 13,500 words that made up 'At the Bay' for which he paid five pounds more. Once again, he wanted to change the ending: short stories, he thought, ought to have a beginning, a middle and an end. She wrote 'under the influence of a theory that it is cheap and vulgar to let anything happen in a narrative.'[461] He praised her brilliant use of telling detail, but did not find her characters real enough and urged her to let herself go more. Despite his reservations, he admired Katherine Mansfield's talent and asked her to send anything else she had as soon as possible.

Squire was a pioneer broadcaster. He did not take the sneering view about the advent of radio common among intellectuals. In 1922 he had organised a programme to celebrate Hardy's life on the London station 2LO to a potential audience of 50,000. He sat with a water bottle and a little square microphone 'in a sort of artistic padded cell' in front of a strange-looking web of instruments. In one of the very first live sporting broadcasts Squire's was the voice of the radio commentary on the Boat Race on 2nd April 1927. In the little launch *Magician* he was joined by former Olympic rower and blue, Oliver Nickalls. A 100-watt transmitter sat behind them in coffin-like boxes to protect it from the rain. As they crouched in the bows they spoke into large microphones. Absolute stillness was required to avoid disturbing the transmission. It was feared that so much heavy equipment would sink *Magician* and its crew before the finish, but all went well. The broadcast was 'radiated' by aerials suspended between the masts – their height was limited as they had to go under Hammersmith Bridge. It was sent to two temporary receiving stations on the riverbank, and then relayed by telephone to a base at Savoy Hill. Listeners were amazed to hear, as the commentary went on, the sound of cheering crowds on the riverbank.

'How on earth you manage to keep talking the whole time, I can't think,' Raglan wrote to his father. At Blundell's Raglan basked in the popularity he got when he and his friends were excused lessons to listen to the race and its famous Old Blundellian commentator. His father's impromptu style and baritone voice suited radio well and he was asked to cover the next three Boat Races. Writing about the event on the 80th anniversary of the broadcast in 2007, the journalist Frank Keating quoted Nickalls's post-race account of commentating with Squire: 'We stood on each other's foot when it was our turn to interrupt and simply poured out words from start to finish, totally oblivious to being heard or not.' He did another outside broadcast in 1930, 'Exploring the Pool of London by Night'. Accompanied by Station Sergeant Emms of the Thames River Police, he took a boat from Tower Bridge to Limehouse Place and commentated as it wound its way through a mass of shipping. In the background listeners could hear 'actual noises from the riverside'. Three months later Squire commentated on Wimbledon, but he was never asked to broadcast on the sport that was closest to his heart.

The following year he gave a talk for the British Broadcasting Company about Robert Bridges and Walter de la Mare and chaired one of the first radio debates when H. G. Wells and Bernard Shaw discussed 'What is coming?' He read from Plato's account of the death of Socrates and gave a talk on 'Poet Adventurers' – Sir Philip Sidney, Lord Byron and Rupert Brooke. In January 1924 he organised and introduced another celebratory programme for Hardy which included the Victorian folk song 'The Death of Nelson', music from *The Dynasts* and Dorset songs arranged by Cecil Sharp. In the late afternoon he regularly broadcasted to schools for a quarter of an hour. On the day that the British Broadcasting Corporation took over from the Company and the idea of a national network finally became real, it was Squire's voice reading 'The Ancient Mariner' that reached the nation on Sunday 2 January 1927.

Squire thought that the wireless deserved as much critical interest as the theatre. In May the *London Mercury* began to run one of the first radio columns. He asked the critic Eric Gillett to write 2,000 words reviewing the last month's programmes. He could be as critical as he liked – but Squire reminded him that the BBC had been attacked by 'rogues and fatheads' who did not understand its constraints. Its one channel meant that it had to please all tastes.[462] In April 1924 in the new journal *Radio*, Squire called for state-subsidised broadcasting and was one of the first to propose broadcasting House of Commons debates. He also suggested to the BBC's Director Lord Reith a popular broadcasting magazine on the lines of *John O' London's* with excerpts from programmes, reviews and articles, but got no reply from 'Lord Wuthering Heights' (Winston Churchill's nickname) – and no credit when the *Listener* was finally launched in 1929 with its Reithian aim of education through broadcasting.

In 1930 and 1931 Squire gave a series of six talks on 'Words', followed by another six on 'Literary Forms'. As usual he spiced his arguments with humour and parody. Arguing that words had both a sound that could be musical or harsh, and that associations had a powerful positive or negative impact, he put the names of diseases in a pre-Raphaelite setting:

So forth then rode Sir Erisypelas
From good Lord Goitre's castle, with the steed
Loosed on the rein; and as he rode he mused
On knights and ladies dead: Sir Scrofula,
Sciatica, he of Glanders, and his friend,
Stout Colitis, out of Aquitaine,
And Impetigo, proudest of them all,
Who lived and die for blind Queen Cholera's sake,

Anthrax who dwelt in the enchanted wood
With those princesses three, tall, pale and dumb,
And beautiful, whose names were music's self,
Anaemia, Influenza, Eczema…[463]

Soon he broadened his scope with 'How to Appreciate Poetry', 'Saving the Countryside' and 'Things I Would Like to Hear on the Wireless'. 'Worse Verse' gave him the chance of reading some really inept poetry. 'Idle Thoughts' was the title of another series that particularly annoyed Virginia Woolf, who was infuriated by his chatty, informal style. He had become the voice of literature on the wireless.

When not at his editorial desk, Squire enjoyed sailing in the ketch *Nona*, owned and skippered by Hilaire Belloc. In fisherman's jersey and cap, Belloc sang French folk songs and sea shanties in his high tenor voice as he negotiated stormy seas from the helm. A. P. Herbert was on board when, avoiding the storm around the treacherous Portland Bill, they anchored at Bridport. Since they were in Wessex, Squire suggested a visit to see Thomas Hardy. They travelled the sixteen miles by taxi to find the eighty-year-old author resting upstairs after an exhausting bicycle ride. This was the first and only time that 'that Catholic journalist' (Hardy on Belloc) met 'that atheist novelist' (Belloc on Hardy). Both lovers of history, they got on surprisingly well and Squire, silenced for once, listened to their talk of a great legendary storm around the Bill.[464]

In late August 1927, Squire visited Hardy in Dorset again and found him still the best of company at eighty-seven. He brought with him the singer John Goss. From lunch till tea they sang old country songs and church melodies, and talked of fiddles, hautboys and serpents. Hardy joined in the choruses with his light but still vigorous voice, beating the time with his hand. In the evening, he dug out some scores from a chest upstairs that had been left untouched since the death of his first wife. Squire and he stood together behind Goss as he played the piano, his high tenor voice joining with Squire's baritone. They sang mid-Victorian folk songs, the sentimental ditty, 'The Mocking Bird' and 'The Cuckoo', a duet 'redolent of rosebuds and crinolines'. 'Dear, dear,' said the old man, smiling through tears as each old favourite appeared.

'I enjoyed my night with you as much as any night of my life,'[465] Squire wrote, thanking his hostess. Less than six months later he was at Hardy's grand funeral in Westminster Abbey where the Prime Minister Stanley Baldwin, Ramsay MacDonald, Kipling, Shaw, Housman, Galsworthy and Edmund Gosse were pall-bearers. Two months later Gosse too was dead.

A month after Hardy's funeral, in February 1928, the *London Mercury* reached its hundredth number. Squire announced the centenary with a brilliant red cover which showed his 'blush of pleasure at our survival, or perhaps a desire to paint the town red'. As the subject of its editorial notes, it took Hardy's death and funeral. Squire noted how the argument between the family and the poets' executors about the funeral and burial was straight out of one of *Life's Little Ironies* and *Satires of Circumstances*. (Hardy had wanted to be buried in Dorset alongside his first wife Emma: his executors thought otherwise.) Squire wrote that the shade of Hardy 'sighed for a village burial' such as William Morris's, carried in a farm-cart covered with flowers to the grave. Westminster was for politicians. 'Let the poets lie elsewhere or be scattered to the winds,' he urged. He was appalled by the hurried dissection which left Hardy's ashes in an urn in Poets' Corner of the Abbey and his heart in Stinsford churchyard.

Squire wrote 'Hardy in our Abbey' in which he enumerated 'the further distribution of parts'. It was a poem he thought 'a trifle too macabre' for publication and it survives only in one pencilled draft at St John's College, Cambridge.

Of all the tricks that are absurd
Preposterous and shabby
The worst occurred when they interred
Our Hardy in the Abbey.

Let statesmen lie there tête-à-tête
When they are taken from us.
They usually deserve their Fate
But not our Thomas.

When all was fixed for the cremating
The thought occurred to someone
That they were obviously frustrating
The wishes of the dear one
And someone said 'This will surprise
Provincial persons, so of course it
Would better be to compromise
And leave his heart in Dorset.'

Since part of him's in Westminster
And part is down in Wessex
Why could not others have their share,
Kent, Cumberland and Essex?
Why not more freely use the knife
Since it is now decided
That poets though united in life
In death may be divided.

When Kipling dies or Bernard Shaw
Let's broadcast well the bounty.
We almost might ordain by law
A piece for every county.
Let every place once known to him
When he has been disjointed
Receive a feature or a limb
And none be disappointed.

I'll end my song with just one plea
When I have finished smoking

Oh bury me by land or sea
In Winchester or Woking
Or in St. Michael's Limehouse Road
With coster, Chinaman and cabby,
Or any other low abode,
But not in our Abbey.

'The place that Sir Edmund Gosse filled in the literary and social life of London is one that no one can ever fill again, because it is, so to speak, an office that has been abolished', wrote T. S. Eliot.[466] The person who came nearest to inheriting Gosse's mantle was undoubtedly his friend Jack Squire, as Eliot recognised in a letter to Edith Sitwell: 'We shall be able to deal properly with JCS… when Sir Edmund is safely interred in the Abbey.'

The death of Hardy brought to mind all the deaths of his friends in the war. Squire felt that every outstanding piece of prose published in 1928 and 1929 bore some relation to it. As soon as war had ended there had been historical and military analysis galore, but very little of literary merit. Only now, ten years on, he noted in his *Observer* article, 'The War in Memory', could the voice of the ordinary soldier, or the ordinary junior officer, silent for many years and overwhelmed by the intensity of his experience of war, be properly heard. R. C. Sherriff's play *Journey's End*, Blunden's *Undertones of War* and Sassoon's *Memoirs of a Fox-Hunting Man* all came out in that year, followed in 1929 by *All Quiet on the Western Front*, Richard Aldington's *Death of a Hero* and Robert Graves's *Goodbye to All That*.

One less well-known voice was that of Henry Williamson. Squire was sent some linocuts of the Great War in black expressionist style by William Kermode, who had won the MC for gallantry. 'They are done by an Australian soldier who served, like yourself, on the Western Front', Jack Squire told Williamson when he introduced the two men. He suggested that Williamson might write some text to go along with Kermode's stark images. 'If you'd like to talk to him about it, we'll go into the pub next door.' Based on the pictures, Williamson wrote *The Patriot's Progress*, a bitterly scathing narrative of John Bullock's war. Bullock was an everyman figure whose 'progress' led to the amputation of his leg and a life of poverty and bitterness.[467] Williamson was never to forget Squire's kindness.

As Gosse had warned, Squire was spreading himself dangerously thinly. The most ubiquitous man of letters of his day, he found it hard to refuse any invitation. He was on the panel awarding three gold medals for 'the best eulogies of athleticism' for the 1924 Olympic Games; the founder and Chairman of the Architecture Club from 1922–28, a Governor of the Old Vic, Chairman of the Dr Johnson Society, Chairman of the National Book Council committee, Secretary of the Academic Committee of the Royal Society of Literature, on the committees of the Society for the Preservation of Ancient Buildings, the Elian Society and the Byron Centenary, honorary secretary of the Stonehenge Protection Committee, on the governing body of the Royal Victoria Hall, President of the Devonian Association, a member of the Arts Club, the Athenaeum, the Omar Khayyam Club, the Savile Club, the Saintsbury Club – and so on and so on…

So it was not surprising that after the death of the Poet Laureate Robert Bridges in 1930, Doll thought her brother should be the 'National Poet' – but if he had hopes of being Bridges' successor they were soon dashed. He was doubly disappointed when John Masefield was appointed. He said he knew of no poet who supported the choice, which had been made so quickly that the Savile Club had not even time to put up its sweepstake list. If the Poet Laureate was to set a standard for writers Squire told his readers there were many others who had a stronger case. He did not name them but among their names must have been Sassoon, Blunden – and perhaps, he may well have thought…[468]

Despite this disappointment Squire's reputation in London society had never been higher. He was at a celebration held at the Adelphi Hotel in July 1930 to mark Hilaire Belloc's sixtieth birthday.[469] In the chair G. K. Chesterton proclaimed it to be an 'immortal feast'. It had been agreed that there were to be no speeches. However, someone whispered that the organiser A. D. Peters ought to be thanked. Peters decided that the person sitting to his right, J. B. Morton, was the chief organiser and he too ought to be thanked. Morton passed the compliment on to his neighbour, Jack Squire, who said Belloc mixed the obstinacy of a John Bull with the pugnacity of an Irishman and the gay *panache* of a Gascon. He agreed with Belloc that the two things most worth having in life were laughter and the love of friends. In turn Squire denied responsibility and said that the true inspiration had come from the man sitting to his right – A. P. Herbert. And so it went on around the table with all the diners claiming it was the person to their right who really ought to be thanked. Maurice Baring recited an Horatian Ode to 'Hilario Belloc', balancing a glass of burgundy on his bald head as his fellow diners pelted him with pellets of bread rolls. The Conservative MP Duff Cooper made a speech pretending to be a Lloyd George Liberal; D. B. Wyndham Lewis, who thought he could avoid making a speech by hiding under the table, had to be dragged out. By the end of the evening all forty guests had spoken. It was just the kind of roaring, stamping, laughing event that Squire and his friends loved.

Drink, parties and celebrations like Hilaire Belloc's were central to the lives of Squire and his friends. Alcohol became totemic in the war of traditionalists and modernists. The English Inn, the pint of ale and the rollicking that went with them became badges of identity. Osbert and Sacheverell Sitwell recalled an incident at their first night at a hotel in Assisi which pointed the contrast between Squire's world and serious Bloomsbury. The dining room was 'full of mute aesthetes and pallid ascetics whispering over their meal and half a bottle of white wine, when suddenly no less a person than the late Sir John Squire… burst through the door, and shouted at them "Have you any whisky in your pub? Mine has completely run out," Whereat, we are told, guests at the other tables fell silent and then began to talk in ordinary tones.'[470]

Squire's social diary continued at a frenetic pace. In May 1931 he was staying at the Arundel Hotel in the Strand and described his day: 'I lunched with Maurice Baring, then went with him to the costumier Nathan's, (to get a Byron costume for the Waterloo Ball), then attended to Macmillan's, then went to Lady Dowd's cocktail party, then to Miss Douglas's, then to the Arundel to change, & then to Evan Morgan's where Lois in pyjamas and bare feet and 7 men played vingt-et-un till 3.30. I walked back to the Arundel...' (Evan Morgan was the homosexual Viscount Tredegar and his wife Lois a talented and outrageous Bright Young Person.)

The ball to mark the 116th anniversary of the Battle of Waterloo was held at Grosvenor House under the patronage of the Prince of Wales. The Duchess of Richmond's famous ball held the night before the battle was recreated; footmen were dressed in Regency livery and the stars of C. B. Cochran's latest West End revue glittered. At midnight it was Squire, in the costume he had just hired, as Lord Byron, who rose to his feet to declaim his account on the eve of the ball from *Childe Harold's Pilgrimage*:

Did ye not hear it? – No; 'twas but the wind,
Or the car rattling o'er the stony street;
On with the dance! Let joy be unconfined;
No sleep till morn, when youth and pleasure meet
To chase the glowing hours with flying feet.
But hark! – that heavy sound breaks in once more,
As if the clouds its echo would repeat;
And nearer, clearer, deadlier than before;
Arm! Arm! It is – it is – the cannon's opening roar!

There were countless invitations to lunches, dinners and to speaking engagements all over the country. He lectured to the English Association in Aberdeen, St Andrews, Devon, Cardiff and Nottingham; to the Library Association on reviewing and to the Royal Institution on the art of parody. He spoke on the opening to the public of Dickens's house in Doughty Street; on the centenary of his fellow Old Blundellian R. D. Blackmore in Tiverton, and at the memorial to Byron in Hucknall Torkard Church, Nottinghamshire. He chaired debates between Sheila Kaye-Smith and Rebecca West on the 'Future of the Sex Novel'. He read a selection of Dr Johnson's prayers from the pulpit of St Clement Dane's in the Strand where Johnson worshipped. His toast to the 'Immortal Memory' of Dr Johnson was broadcast live from the candlelit Guildhall in Lichfield, as was his toast to Drama as part of the annual Stratford Shakespeare festivities. He was the leading speaker at the opening ceremony of the Lewis Carroll Centenary Exhibition on 28 June 1932 where he met the original Alice. 'Well, Mr Chairman,' he began, 'since to-day, / I've nothing much to say / I thought it perhaps might be neater / To say that nothing much in metre'... and continued in verse for two hundred lines. No literary centenary, dinner or event seemed complete without him. He was everywhere.

When Queen Mary was given a miniature dolls' house designed by Lutyens for her birthday, Squire was sent a book of twenty tiny leaves to fill in; he contributed a perfect acrostic sonnet written in his most minute handwriting:

This is the house a thousand Artists made,
Honouring a lady with the things they wrought.
Each of his love and cunning craft has brought
Queen Mary tribute, in this house displayed.
Upon this house a thousand fancies strayed,
Ephemeral fancies, painting on a page
Eternal symbols of one dreaming age.
Numbering all the toys with which we played.
Suns rise and set, flowers fade and we:
Here will men find, when still are all the hands
Once busy in these rooms, in stranger days,
Us, and common habit of our ways,
Safer than Pharaohs buried in their sands,
Enshrined in open day, to all posterity.[471]

The high point of Squire's public success, however, came at the Dorchester Hotel in December 1932 when 500 guests celebrated his achievements and he was hailed by G. K. Chesterton, Duff Cooper and Sir William Rothenstein. But all was not as it seemed. Grand parties concealed the real crises in Squire's life. As the income from the *Mercury* dwindled, life at Thursley with its maids, chauffeur and horses was bankrupting him; he told a friend that his bank would not cash a cheque for £1 if he wrote it. The family had to move back to London and Jack promised he would start to economise. The stress of his commitments was beginning to tell. Pryce-Jones thought Jack must have become almost intolerable to his family at this time – 'grubby, insolvent, spendthrift, unreliable, tipsy...' He quarrelled with his ever-loyal sister Doll about money: she accused him of calling her *hard*. He apologised saying he could not accept that he had said that word to 'the most sensitive and self-sacrificing being who ever existed. I've never had a thought about you that was not loving, sympathetic and understanding.' He told her he was overwhelmed by the problems of the *Mercury*. The tax man was pursuing him relentlessly and he had nothing left he could mortgage; his books and pictures had all been sold. He promised her he was looking for another job.

Under the pressure of debts and work Squire's marriage was disintegrating. The tensions had been apparent for some time. In April 1931 he had published 'The Rebel Heart' in the *Mercury*. The poem begins with sleeplessness and the question, 'Heart, why dost thou ache?' to which the heart replies, 'Thou knowest why I ache / All the long dark and tired and turning night-time, / Trying, trying to break.' It ends on a note of defeat as the speaker pathetically concludes 'Why will these things not be as I would have them? / Others should fail not I.'[472]

Beginning with echoes of John Donne's 'The Ecstasie', 'Anarchy' got as close to a confessional poem as Squire ever wrote:

> In the dark, in bed, the brows of lovers will touch
> Closely, with nothing at all between bone and bone,
> Coffer against coffer of mind, and they will not move,
> Silent they'll be...

But this ecstasy is not a joining together, but a meeting of two distinct and enclosed beings ('coffer against coffer') even at this moment of intimacy. When day comes the bleak truth emerges:

Even those most pure and devoted must daily wage
The wars of love and the sweet diplomacies
Where self will plot for its ends in a fair disguise,
Or yield to love for the sake of love with seeming;
And coldness they sometimes know and even rage
Remorsefully checked, and days divorced when the dreaming
Of obscured and oblivious love is forgotten; and scheming
And striving in the world the ego fights for its own.
And neglect of love may bring of lovers the best
To a place where a careless petulant word expressed
May open before their feet a gulf of dread
In whose depths is the dreadful image of love lying dead,
And they shrink from a lonely life without ever a friend...[473]

The anarchy of feelings is mirrored by the anarchy of the verse form. It aspires to become rhyming couplets but the line lengths are irregular, the rhymes chaotic and the syntax of the long sentences congested and complicated: the language of a man torn by his feelings. This is certainly not, in any usual sense, 'Georgian' verse.

Squire's 'Anarchy' was a despairing, dark counterpoint to the 400 love letters he had written to Eileen almost twenty-five years before. The insecurity and secrecy that he hoped had been banished by love resurfaced. Now 'shame's most intimate secrets' could be revealed, as the 'thick wall of his defences' had been broached. If this nakedness can be revealed by a lover, then how much more so by 'the strangers we call our friends'.

Chapter 19

The Fight for England

'The Fight for England' was the title Squire gave to his review of *The Octopus*, a word coined by the architect and campaigner Clough Williams-Ellis.[474] The octopus was the spread of London and the big cities of the North, devouring rural England and destroying villages. Squire, a veteran of campaigns for socialism against capitalism and for literature against what he saw as spurious experiments, now fought a deadly threat to what he thought was once one of the most beautiful countries in the world. 'In many great cities including Manchester one is almost tempted to lose the great gift of sight.'

Conservation issues began to play a more important part in his life. He joined the ever-increasing number of societies which tried to protect the English countryside and its buildings. He became a member of the CPRE (The Council for the Protection of Rural England), SCAPA (The Society for Checking the Abuses of Public Advertising), the National Trust for Places of Historic Interest or Natural Beauty, the Royal Society for the Protection of Birds and the Pure Rivers Society. He gave the address at the Society for the Protection of Ancient Buildings annual meeting in 1923 and published articles in the *Mercury* on particular causes such as the 'Jeopardy of Oxford'. He asked his readers to support local pressure groups such as the Oxford Preservation Trust that were springing everywhere up to preserve buildings, flora and fauna and country crafts.

When he had been on his tramps through England before the war Squire had found the roads comparatively empty except for a few vagrants, often old soldiers. Cars, especially in the country, were a rarity. Now with the development of a network of arterial roads the number of tourists by car, charabanc and bicycle grew and grew. The car had changed everything. A new leisured class of people wanting to escape from towns threatened destruction to the countryside they had come to enjoy. Squire devoted many editorials in the *London Mercury* to the effects of the spread of roads. The garish colours and design of petrol pumps became something of an obsession for him. Pumps should, he argued, be designed and painted in colours to fit in with their surroundings. There was nothing to be said in favour of an outrage such as the startlingly red pump with a Union Jack suspended from it, set against the yellow Cotswold stone of medieval Broadway. He proposed that the Architecture Club should hold a competition for the best designs.

The roads might, in theory, be fine – but the ribbon development that went with them was not. Half-timbered villas and hideous bungalows began to straggle along the new roads. The mushrooming rise in 'filthy speculative building' was a feature of the twenties and thirties that Squire and the Architecture Club deplored. Poplars could be planted at road junctions and each new road could be an avenue behind which properly planned houses could be built. Instead of this the Kingston bypass, for example, and the Great West Road sprawled through virgin countryside. You only had to drive down one of the new arterial roads to see new squalors leaping up. The day after King George V opened the Great West Road in 1925, Squire, with A. P. Herbert as his passenger, drove down it. 'Here and there were urban patches; in between were fields, orchards and copses. Within a few years, although it will be both inconvenient to the dwellers and unpleasant to the travellers, this will be a hideous double-row of houses and factories with fields behind, instead of a country road with little planned towns like knots on a string.'[475] Squire urged his readers 'to leave no stone unturned which is available for flinging at slack local bodies, arrogant local surveyors or greedy speculative builders.'

Squire suggested that a draughtsman could publish a series of drawings to illustrate the development of the modern beauty spot:

There is a village with a row of thatched cottages, three or four fine old houses, a Tudor Inn, an ancient elm and a church tower brooding over all. A motorist arrives and is enthusiastic. Then (he tells his friends) two motorists arrive. Then four. Then a dozen. The blacksmith sees his chance and supersedes his forge by a garage and a petrol station, suitably decorated. The brewers, finding that the business of the Fox and Grapes is going up, pull it down and erect a larger building in Ye Olde Tea Shoppe style with 'Dated 1500' written above the door, and built 1927 evident everywhere. A mart for china dogs, pot lids and fake chairs is opened. One by one the cottages are provided with shop windows or converted into Private Hotels. The accession of bungalows inhabited by peace-seekers increases trade to such a point that Liptons, the International Tea Stores and such like macro-organisms arrive. Signs for 'Teas, TEAS, TeAS, and even tEAS' are everywhere. Ultimately nothing is left of what was there before save the poor old church peeping over the new roofs. And one fine day perhaps the charabancers awake to the fact that what they came for is no longer there; and the village, deserted but defiled, resumes its ancient obscurity.[476]

Despite poor eyesight, Squire himself was a keen motorist. He enjoyed trips through the Devon countryside in his Buick with his fellow Devonian John Lane. He was a realist about roads and cars: 'It is no good merely revolting against present day civilization; retreating into a tapestried room as the Pre-Raphaelites did. We may regret the whole thing but a reasonable and responsible person will come to terms with it.' Perhaps surprisingly, he thought a very large petrol station on the Kingston bypass as beautiful as any thatched cottage church. With the growing number of cars, he imagined garages might become centres of communal life like modern cathedrals. But control was needed.

The changes in the countryside raised questions about what sort of nation England was, or wanted to become. Squire's answer was that its backbone was still to be found in the country, not the towns; in agriculture, not industry. Georgian poetry (although not Squire's) often reflected this ruralism, but it was not just in poetry that attitudes to town and country were being examined. The English landscape, its villages and cottages became the staple diet of British publishing in the 1920s and 1930s. According to the historian and journalist Simon Heffer, 'The twenties and thirties represented a Golden Age for British topographical writing.'[477]

Examinations of the nature of England and Englishness often took the form of the journey. Travel guides were much in vogue: Arthur Mee's *The King's England* ran to forty volumes. H. V. Morton's *In Search of England*, a quest for the village that best symbolised the country, was a bestseller in 1929; Henry Williamson's *The Village Book* came out in 1930 and the *Shell Guides to Britain* started under the editorship of John Betjeman in 1934 with his own *Cornwall*. The critic Valentine Cunningham wrote that they were all rewritings of *The Wind in the Willows*, but 'Mr Toad, that car-mad Ur-Futurist looked set now really to rule the roads.'[478]

'Nothing is more characteristic of England's countryside than the cottage homes which, for century after century, have sheltered her sturdy sons of toil,' wrote Stanley Baldwin. In 1927 he launched the Fund for the Preservation of Ancient Cottages. Squire became an enthusiastic supporter. In the *Mercury* under the title 'Folk Architecture' he urged his readers to support the fund, especially as it was headed by the Thomas Hardy as well as the prime minister. But not only cottages were under threat – whole villages and counties were menaced by the 'octopus'. With ribbon development went the growth of something else Squire and SCAPA hated: advertising. Along the new roads were enamelled hoardings advertising bicycles, detergents, cigarettes and bootmakers. Squire noted that a famous soap firm had applied to Dover Council for permission to put up a large hoarding, 'These Cliffs were Washed by --- Soap. Why not try it?' The signs were as ugly as they were redundant: 'Do not miss on any account these noble cliffs, one of which was mentioned by Shakespeare.' The blight of advertisements was everywhere and becoming more obtrusive: 'Even in the heart of the capital the once beautiful night spectacle of the Thames Embankment is ruined by tall blazing night-signs, all the worse because the lights of them jump in and out or incessantly change colour.'

Signage 'spread like eczema' across cities and the countryside. Squire believed that it was a trend from America where he had seen signs such as 'WELCOME TO TROY: Pop 1914: 3,000. Pop 1920: 10,000. The Chamber of Commerce Greets You.' The 'maddeningly monotonous' red and gold fascia of Woolworth's stores were distinctively hideous, but everywhere companies plastered their names over Tudor or Georgian frontages. The RAC and the AA were as guilty as the commercial advertisers: they insisted on putting the names of rivers on bridges on hideous yellow signs. When, he asked his readers, would it ever stop? He imagined the country littered with signs such as, 'This is a very old oak tree' or 'A spotted fritillary was found here'. On the way to Tintagel, thinking of Malory, and tales of Tristram and Iseult, he found old shacks and sheds emblazoned 'Ye old Queen Guinevere Tea House' and the 'Sir Lancelot Petrol Station'. In his 'Ballade of the Poetic Life' Squire mocked the degrading and trivialising effects of advertisers using great poets to sell their products.

Shelley's a trademark used on sheets
Aloft the sky in words of flame
We read 'What porridge had John Keats?
Why, Brown's! A hundred years the same!'
Arcadia's an umbrella frame
Milton's a toothpaste; from the tide
Sappho's been dredged to rouge my Dame –
For this the poets lived and died.[479]

Plymouth, Squire's home town, was an emblem of what had gone wrong. When he became president of the Devonshire Association Squire gave an impromptu address on how much of the old town had suffered from civic destruction and how badly built was the new: 'It is deplorable to think how much Plymouth, in common with almost every other town in the country, has lost in the last century and how much it has created which could have been created better.' He warned against the threat of Devon becoming like the Home Counties. As yet there was not so much ribbon development, but the number of cars needed to be controlled before they took over. He then made a radical proposal that was to become national policy. He suggested that the Association and other like-minded bodies should draw up lists of buildings and sites that should be preserved and defended.

'Town Planning' was a product of the trip, jotted down in 'a wayside hotel after a tour through long-remembered and much-changed places', recalling the Plymouth of his boyhood:

> Still the little harbour fronts are there, at any rate, in part
> And each country town has beauty at its heart,
> But beyond these fronts and centres where the roads relentless march
> There's neither curve nor crescent, there's neither square nor arch.
> The man who looks for Church or Inn his throat and soul must parch
> For he'll only see
> Miles of red-brick coops (the reddest)
> Miles of lead-slate roofs (the leadest).

By January 1932 there were more societies and groups concerned about the countryside, the purity of rivers, advertisements, jerry-building and ribbon development than ever before. Why then, Squire asked, did the government and the authorities not act to regulate as they had power to do?[480] The answer he thought was simple: 'Mammon was King.'[481] Yet he was no Jeremiah. He saw signs of hope in the growing influence of the Architecture Club, the Garden

City movement and in the way that the press had begun to report issues of conservation. He suggested that newspapers should use his own favourite method: ridicule. They might subtitle, for example, a photograph: 'Repellent New Cottages at Cobham'. Popular campaigns would shame developers and vandals.

Squire himself wrote the foreword to Edmund Blunden's *The Face of England*[482] in the 'English Heritage Series' he edited. No poet, he wrote, had so extensively described English ways, English scenes and English characters. In poem after poem he had captured the variety and gentleness of the English countryside. Most poets and writers of the natural scene set their scenes in dramatic weather or lighting: Blunden was a poet of the ordinary and everyday. He had also captured the vividness of childhood experience, just as Squire had tried to do. 'There never was snow like the snow of infancy nor cider like the first cider taken under the hedgerows with the harvesters…' All in all, the book might have been dedicated to the Society for the Protection of Rural England. Squire ended with a warning that summed up the whole series: 'It will be the business of our age to decide whether it will be a record of abiding things or a beautiful epitaph.'[483]

The cause for which Squire became best known, the preserving of the site of Stonehenge, came about by accident. The story goes that he was bet half a crown by a lady he met casually at a party that he could not save it from the invasion of the modern world – just the kind of challenge he could not resist. He devoted himself to the task, co-founding the Stonehenge Preservation Society, of which, naturally, he became secretary, to look after the whole site for the nation. 'Saving Stonehenge' became a rallying call for conservationists:

> Observatory, altar, temple, tomb,
> Erected none knows when by none knows whom,
> To serve strange gods or watch familiar stars,
> We drive to see you in our motor cars
> And carry picture postcards back to town
> While still the unsleeping stars look coldly down.[484]

The stones fascinated him. He had first seen them as an undergraduate in 1904 when he walked from Cambridge home to Plymouth and on the way stayed at Amesbury, where Guinevere, he remarked, had last seen Arthur. He had risen at seven o'clock, walked westward a couple of miles along an undulating road and then onto a plain littered with British antiquities. He climbed a crest and then, suddenly against the horizon, were 'the great slabs, as it were gates, set upon other gates, the group of stones which had been engraved upon our memory in our infancy, coeval with the alphabet.'[485] He insisted that they had to be seen against an empty sky. Stonehenge could only speak in its solitude and silence Restoring Stonehenge was restoring something of his younger self.

The 'awe and amazement' that he had felt when he first saw Stonehenge were now no longer possible. The stones themselves had been given to the nation, but there was nothing to stop commercial development all round them. The site had suffered in the war from being next to an aerodrome; disused old huts surrounded it; a wire fence, a turnstile, and a caretaker's box added to the mess. Now pressures of post-war tourism were beginning to add a new kind of threat. The nearby café set up in 1927 in a little bungalow was, he feared, just the beginning. He imagined a future dance hall, hotel, and even a Stonehenge Golf Course with artificial bunkers round the stones and bright red petrol pumps...

The government refused to help and earned Squire's rebuke in the *London Mercury*: 'Where the chief blame lies we neither know nor care: the Government will probably maintain it has *no* powers, but it is much to blame for not getting them.' He followed the precedent that had saved the City churches: organise a dinner; set up a club; appeal to the public. So, after a good lunch, the Stonehenge Protection Society was formed and found a base in the offices of the National Trust. This appeal was followed by a letter to *The Times* signed by the Prime Minister, Stanley Baldwin, the leader of the opposition, Ramsay MacDonald, Viscount Grey of Fallodon and Squire himself, appealing for £35,000. King George V contributed twenty guineas and the fund reached £13,000 in a month. Three hundred acres were bought, but it was not enough and, despite the support of the prime minister, the government still refused to act. By December £16,000 was still needed. Another lunch was held, hosted by the Lord Mayor of London, and another letter written to *The Times*, signed once more by the prime minister. The campaign reached people who had little idea of what the ancient monument was. 'Now Squire, what about this Henge of yours?' asked a rich potential donor.

The letters finally did the trick. By March 1929 the battle was won. An area of two square miles around the stones had been saved. Under the headline 'Victory', in his *Mercury* editorial, Squire announced the success, but by the time of the final appeal he had lost interest and did not sign the public letter. His was a startling achievement (and one which many felt earned him his knighthood) but it also summed up his character: an imaginative, energetic start, followed by boredom with methodical progress. Nevertheless, he told his readers: 'It seemed at the beginning a pretty uphill job. But optimism and persistence have triumphed and the land around Stonehenge is saved.'[486]

Literature was centrally important in the debate about the nature of England. Squire's response was to look to the reassurance of the traditional canon of English writers. From 1926 to 1930 he was General Editor of the third 'English Men of Letters' series for Macmillan's. The first two books to emerge were on Herman Melville and Swinburne. Other titles included Blake, Meredith, Pepys, Peacock, Christina Rossetti, Trollope, Horace Walpole and Walt Whitman. No doubt both Melville and Whitman – not to mention Christina Rossetti, given the series' title – would have been surprised to see their names included. The selection reflected Squire's sense of the tradition of English literature – and lack of confidence in the writers of his own time.

With Lord Lee of Fareham, Squire edited a parallel selection, the 'English Heritage Series', from 1929 to 1936. Stanley Baldwin, a 'thoroughly representative Englishman', according to Squire, wrote the general introduction. 'These books are the more needed because much of what they treat is changing. Children need to know the rock from which they are hewed,' wrote Baldwin. The first volumes appeared in 1929: *Shakespeare*, *Wild Life in England*, *English Humour* and *The Public School*. The titles Squire chose and the writers he asked to edit them were an attempt to 'capture the "Spirit of England".' *The Monarchy* and *The Constitution* appeared next. Other volumes planned were on the Sea, English Liberty, the County Spirit, the English Road, and Fox Hunting. Squire himself wrote the prefaces to Neville Cardus's *Cricket* and I. A. Williams's *Folk Song and Dance*. Hilaire Belloc volunteered to do *The English Inn* and G. K. Chesterton *The Road*. Rudyard Kipling was to cover *The County Spirit*, and Ramsay MacDonald *The Bible*.

The England that the series addressed was Squire's England, securely based on the monarchy, the constitution and the law. Shakespeare and the Bible were the cornerstones of its literature and belief. Its centre was the South of England; it contained villages and county towns, but not the towns of the industrial North or Midlands; it had public schools, but no state schools; its people hunted foxes and played cricket, but not football. It was a rural England, with a rich vein of humour, at whose heart were the inn and the parish church; a seagoing nation singing and dancing to shanties and folk songs, listening to English music. It had little interest in politics and economics. Not all the editors completed their tasks but sixteen books finally appeared. Viscount Lee congratulated Squire on his choices of writers and themes. Taken together, they represented a view of a country that had largely disappeared after the Great War; an elegy to a vanished, or fast vanishing Albion.

All was not well with the *Mercury* or with its editor. An August heatwave made London and Squire's tiny office stifling. He launched a long chatty verse editorial which expressed his frustrations, asking his Muse:

Can it be wondered at that we
Should wander off in lunacy,
When week by week, in one small room,

Too small for an Egyptian's tomb,
The hottest, most enclosed of crypts,
We have to drudge through manuscripts,
Write cordial letters, pay off bills... [487]

The heaps of unanswered correspondence were beginning to cause problems with writers and friends. The translator of Proust, Charles Scott Moncrieff, was furious. His work had been proofread inaccurately: he told Squire that no one with any taste could possibly have passed *mutatis mutander* when everyone knew the tag *mutatis mutandis* – and then launched into poisonous criticism of the *Mercury* before cancelling his subscription. What really hurt Squire was the accusation that he was losing interest in the *Mercury*. He replied 'Nothing goes in I have not myself taken. I read all the proofs... I am in the office virtually every day. I am directly and personally responsible for every single thing that has ever appeared in the paper. When you say "I know your editorship is purely nominal" I cannot... conceive how you can write such a thing to me without realising it is an insult.'[488] In 1928 Squire invited Robert Graves to contribute to the ten-year celebration number of the *Mercury*, just as ten years earlier Graves had asked him to support *The Owl*. The reply was harsh: by now Graves had had enough. Squire kept manuscripts for too long; his payment was often late or did not appear at all. The fee was parsimonious. Graves reminded Squire that he was a professional writer and had a large family to feed. (Squire would have noted the irony of that remark.) He had therefore decided not to submit anything.

Chapter 20

The Thirties: *Entre Deux Guerres*

A young American journalist Louise Morgan was looking down from the window of the *Everyman* magazine in Great Queen Street when the hatless Squire strolled by, head flung back, hands in pockets, pink carnation in buttonhole. 'There goes a man I would die for,' she said.[489] In the early 1930s Squire was a public figure apparently at the height of his career. He certainly also looked the part to the writer A. G. Macdonell when they first met. He called him by the name of the archetypal countryman:

> Mr Hodge was a man of about forty. He was of medium height, squarely built, rather stout, a little bald, and he had a pair of brown eyes behind enormous horn-rimmed, thick-lensed glasses. He was clean-shaven, or rather the last time he had shaved he had been clean-shaven. He was wearing patent-leather shoes, striped trousers a morning coat, a grey waistcoat, a grey bow-tie, a huge pink carnation, and a grey bowler hat.[490]

Jack Squire, now the epitome of the well-dressed, successful editor, was very different from the rustic Fabian drawn by Tom Tit when he first arrived in London twenty years earlier.

In October 1930 Squire's sister Doll received a letter from W. W. Matthews and Pearce, Tavistock solicitors. It informed her that her father Jonas, whom she had not seen for more than forty years, had died in a friend's house in the town. He had no regular income and appeared to have been supported only through the generosity of a Mr Field who was paid sixty pounds a year interest from the War Stock Jonas owned. The solicitors wrote that 'Had Mr Field not allowed your father to remain in his house during his illness the only place he could have been sent was the Poor Law Institution, with the attendant responsibilities on the members of the family, as no hospital or home would have taken the case' – one of those institutions Jack had stayed in and written about twenty years before. His father had died a lonely pauper's death. Doll and her mother shed no tears.

Jack's money had run out too. He, Eileen and their young daughter Julia had to abandon Thursley and move to a modern house at 18 Rosslyn Hill in Hampstead. It was Eileen's choice. From the start Jack hated it. The ever-hostile Virginia Woolf reported Maire Lynd's view that Squire 'runs about, won't do anything, drinks and has deposited Mrs Squire in a small ugly house in Hampstead. No longer the old country gentleman, he is, as he always was, a scallywag'.[491] His marriage was falling apart; there was no money and he was drinking heavily.

Friends tried to advise Squire about managing his overdraft; Alec Waugh felt that all he needed at this stage was an organised budget – but that was not in his nature. He did make a determined effort to control his life. 'What I wouldn't give to play one more game of rugger,' he remarked to his friend from the Savile Club, Hugh Mackintosh. As Squire was then forty-four years old Mackintosh suggested that before he did so he needed fitness training. He persuaded Squire to join the Rosslyn Park Rugby Club and the two of them ran up and down Mackintosh's lawn passing the ball to each other, Squire sporting his new red and white Rosslyn Park jersey. Mackintosh kept up the strict regime, gradually increasing the practice time. Rugby meant giving up cigarettes and alcohol, and for ten weeks Squire kept going. Soon, Mackintosh promised, he would be fit enough to play for the club. At this point Mackintosh had to go to hospital. When he returned, he found his protégé in a post-prandial stupor at the Savile Club. 'No good, Hugh old boy,' he muttered, 'too old for football, have to stick to cricket.'

Squire no longer saw history as determined by economic forces or the inevitable progress towards the socialist dream. It now seemed to him the result of many unpredictable contingencies, of chance and powerful individuals. His own life, he felt, was shaped by meetings with an assortment of very different powerful characters who fired his imagination: Thomas Hardy, G. K. Chesterton, Hilaire Belloc, Rupert Brooke, Rudyard Kipling, Mussolini, and Winston Churchill. Three 'heroes' whom he said he had never met were Gabriele D'Annunzio, Lenin and King George V: certainly, an odd list. He edited *If it Had Happened Otherwise,*[492] a series of essays on imaginary or counterfactual history inspired by G. M. Trevelyan's essay on 'What would have happened if Napoleon had won the Battle of Waterloo?' Winston Churchill imagined General Lee's victory at Gettysburg, G. K. Chesterton considered the marriage of Don John of Austria to Mary, Queen of Scots. Milton Waldman, Squire's American assistant editor, wondered what would have happened if Booth's shot had missed Lincoln, and Squire pondered the consequences of a professor proving that Bacon did write Shakespeare.

Italy was the country Squire said he loved most after England. In Florence on a visit in late 1930 he had dinner with a senator who asked him if there was anyone he would like to meet: 'I'd rather like to meet Mussolini,' he replied jocularly. Squire returned to Rome and took a cab along the old Appian Way to Lake Nemi, now partially drained to reveal the state barge of Caligula. He was enormously impressed by the hundreds of thousands of pounds the work had cost and by the restoration of Herculaneum, ordered by Il Duce himself. After Howard Carter's spectacular discoveries in Egypt the romance of archaeology gripped Squire. He hoped that not only would the excavation reveal richer decorations on the barge than any American millionaire had ever dreamt of, but also a library which might contain lost works of Greek tragedy, possibly even a play by Aeschylus...[493] When he returned to his hotel he found a telegram: 'Kindly tell Squire immediately that interview is arranged on Friday. Have telegraphed Hotel de la Ville.'

The two men met in the long many-windowed gallery of the Palazzo Veneziana, from which Mussolini addressed the assembled Romans. Squire stepped along the shiny marble floor, past walls undecorated by pictures, listening to his heels clicking in the echoing chamber, hoping that he would not slip. Why hadn't anyone told him to put chalk on his shoes, he wondered, as he slithered along. At the far end of the room was a small dark figure in his morning coat, hunched over a large desk. Mussolini was intently reading his papers. Unlike 'that fanatic and conceited ignoramus Hitler', as Squire called him, Mussolini was an educated man, learning English. They agreed to speak in French.

Squire found Il Duce natural, 'gay, agreeable and humane' and noted that there was 'a lot of humour and poetry about him'... 'Do you English consider we are a living people or a museum?' he asked. 'Both,' Squire replied and then they discussed politics. Mussolini summed up his role with a grin: '*Moi, je suis democrate, comme Jules César.*' He asked Squire what English people thought about him. Squire replied that on the one hand people felt he was, like Garibaldi, building a nation, but they were worried too about violence and the murder of his prominent opponent Matteotti in 1924. Mussolini replied that it had disgraced his cause. The conversation turned to what really interested Squire – the archaeological finds in Herculaneum, Ostia and Rome, where a statue of one of the Vestal Virgins had been unearthed cradling the wooden model of a baby she could not have. 'Isn't this pathetic?' Mussolini kept on repeating, insisting that Squire should show some feeling and abandon his English reserve. He told Squire that he had every hope that new plays by Greek tragedians or Sophocles might be found at Herculaneum. After an hour they walked back together the length of the gallery. As they shook hands Mussolini said, 'Send me your collected poems.'[494]

The long conflict between the world of the *London Mercury* and the modernists began to be seen as the conflict between *middlebrow* and *highbrow*. The keyword *highbrow*, a recent import from the United States, replaced the Russian *intelligentsia*. Its opposite *lowbrow*, according to the *OED*, had first appeared in 1923. No one really wanted to be called *middlebrow*, first recorded two years later: "'Middlebrow' has always been a dirty word, used disparagingly since its coinage for the sort of literature thought to be too easy, insular and smug.'[495]

Such was the interest in the topic that in 1932 the BBC invited J. B. Priestley to give a talk 'To a Highbrow' and Harold Nicolson to reply with 'To a Lowbrow.' The reading public was becoming self-consciously aware of its place in a divided society. D. S. Mirsky, Squire's foreign literature editor, now back in Russia and a Marxist intellectual, saw the 'Battle of the Brows' (Virginia Woolf's phrase) as more a matter of class and status than literary taste. Highbrows, he wrote, made frequent trips to Paris and recognised the superiority of French cuisine over a pudding diet; they had abolished the distinction in sexual matters between what was permissible and what was not; they read Freud and bowed to the cult of Proust. Opposed to these intellectuals were the *mezzo brows* or, as they were increasingly called, *middlebrows*, the motley crowd round the petty middle-class *London Mercury*, 'people far removed from any kind of aesthetic extreme, and eminently suspicious of all foreigners...'[496] This was ungracious to Squire who had employed Mirsky for many years on the *Mercury* when he was a penniless exile in London. It was true, however, that discussions of the various 'brows' were just as much about class as they were about literature.

These divisions were nowhere more apparent than in the contrasting ways the *Mercury* and the modernists dealt with the growing popularity of the mass media of cinema, television and wireless. The mandarin critic and friend of Eliot, John Hayward, pointed out that he was the only person he knew who listened to the wireless. Evelyn Waugh kept his in the servants' quarters. It was left to *middlebrows* and *lowbrows* to enjoy the variety of talks, classical music and variety shows that made up the programmes. It is no accident that the first recorded English use of *middlebrow* came in an account of the BBC in *Punch* on 23 December 1925: 'The B.B.C. claim to have discovered a new type, the "middlebrow". It consists of people who are hoping that some day they will get used to the stuff they ought to like.'[497]

Virginia Woolf thought the BBC itself was the epitome of the middlebrow. She christened it the 'Betwixt and Between Company'. In a letter to the *New Statesman*, which she did not send, but was published posthumously in her collection *The Death of the Moth and Other Essays*, she wrote that she was proud to be highbrow, intellectual, and aristocratic. She declared a natural sympathy with lowbrows: 'I love them; I study them; I always sit next to the conductor on an omnibus and try to get him to tell me what it is like.' But for the middlebrow's 'poor middle state' and for his spiritual home the *London Mercury*, she had no sympathy at all – 'the bloodless and pernicious pest which is the bane of all speaking and living'.[498] To focus more sharply she chose an image of a batsman poking and prodding at the ball, the feeble efforts of a man afraid to hit out – or a writer afraid to take a stance. Her target is clearly Squire, batting at number eleven for the Invalids, seen over the hedge from Monk's House. She wrote that the true home of the middlebrow was suburbia – neither highbrow Bloomsbury where she lived, nor Chelsea, but South Kensington – just where he happened to live at the time.

Squire watched closely as his readers' tastes developed and noted how the fiction of 'the common reader' was being replaced by discrete readerships. He saw that there was, as never before, a large and literate readership ready to read more widely. 'The suburban housewife shops in Kensington High Street, her evenings are spent darning socks and reading cheap novels, leaving highbrow books to the highbrows.'[499] She might never have seen a copy of the *Criterion* but wanted more than *Tit-Bits* could give her. It was exactly that kind of reader whom he hoped to attract to make the *London Mercury* a financial and literary success. And they, unlike Virginia Woolf, listened to the wireless. As Squire pointed out, in words from a music hall song, 'Everyone's a high-brow to someone.'[500]

Just as Virginia Woolf, Joyce, Eliot and Pound were narrowing writing's audience to the highbrows Squire was beginning to broaden its appeal. The wireless was as welcome to him as it was disdained by 'high-brows'. *The Listener*, which published the best of the week's programmes, soon gathered a readership of 50,000. His talks, often republished in the magazine, were given with an eye to this new and more widely educated public. He chose a plain-speaking almost conversational style, just as he had urged on Pryce-Jones. 'Alan, dear, do learn to write prose as you write letters. Just be yourself. It took Priestley and Macdonell about fifteen years to learn that. It applies to everybody. Be yourself with the public as you write to your friends.'[501] (Priestley certainly learned the lesson and outdid his mentor when he became one of the best-known voices on the radio for his wartime broadcasts.)

Squire reassured *Listener* readers they did not have to read and admire everything in the whole canon of English Literature – 'Just follow your preferences.' 'Classics I Can't Read' encouraged those who might not be confident enough to follow their own tastes. He encouraged them to enjoy his own favourite essayist, Charles Lamb, as a model of humour and readability. He wrote of 'the honesty and whimsicality and confidential buttonholing that make people love Charles Lamb.' It is a very accurate account of his own essays. He told listeners: 'The word essay is an intimidating one, but really the genre is the equivalent of the conversation at an ideal dinner-table, only slightly polished.'[502] To Squire writing was a social contract, a contract that modernists ignored or despised at their peril.

One of Squire's virtues, according to Pryce-Jones, was that he paid no attention whatsoever to the fashionable. Unlike the modernists he was never afraid to praise popular writer. He was one of the few serious critics who respected the enormous success of the Victorian novelist Marie Corelli, 'read in her hey-day by the entire middle class', and enjoyed the 'master' Edgar Wallace – one of every seven books read in the British Empire was by him, estimated Squire. He enjoyed *Bulldog Drummond* and devoured the crime stories of Ernest Bramah and Sax Rohmer's 'shockers' such as *Three-Fingered Mike* and *A Bucket of Blood*. He read too the best-selling women novelists of the day such as Helen Rose Hull and Ethel M. Dell ('Dull as Hell'). He wrote of the enjoyment of literature at a time when the word *enjoyment* had been long banished from serious literary discussions.

Squire now welcomed the other growing mass media of the twenties and thirties: films and television. Unlike Virginia Woolf or the conservative T. S. Eliot, who wrote in April 1932, 'I am, unfortunately, incapable of being convinced by the arts of the cinema,' Squire felt that films deserved the kind of attention that was given to other arts. He decided to run a regular feature in the *Mercury* on the latest releases. Reluctant to call them 'talkies' or 'speakies' he, rather surprisingly, opted for the American 'movies'. A poet and pioneer of film criticism, Robert Herring, was appointed to write a monthly column – Charlie Chaplin's *The Gold Rush* was the first film he reviewed. At first Herring was sceptical about the future for the talkies. Was not, he asked, seeing and hearing at the same time ducks quacking, a tautology? The first talkie reviewed was Al Jolson's *The Jazz Singer*; Herring thought the songs sentimental and not nearly as good as the music hall, but his column continued as the talkies quickly began to fill the fast-growing number of Odeons and Regals across the country.[503]

The *London Mercury* began to publish articles on the newest invention of all – television. Herring had been to a demonstration and seen a picture so small that two people squeezed in front of the tiny screen was the maximum possible audience. Later in July 1930 he saw another demonstration of the new medium on a much bigger screen at the London Coliseum. At first, he was unimpressed and predicted that people would not want to see newsreels or whatever might be broadcast. 'We saw what TV is and what it does; frankly the latter was uninteresting.' Herring's view changed when the Baird TV Company gave him a 'televisor' to try in his own home. With a mere twiddle of a knob the grey chaos of the screen could become a clear image: 'It is very remarkable. It is absolutely magical.' By 1931 his review in the *London Mercury* was enthusiastic. It was now possible to see the complete figure of a person, not just head and shoulders. It was true that the programmes so far could be dull: neither Oswald Mosley saying good day to Logie Baird, nor Betty Bolton's display of national headdresses with appropriate music, thrilled. But there was, he saw, tremendous scope – he himself suggested, cautiously, a programme on the different breeds of dogs. Looking at the rise of radio from its beginnings in 1922 with half an hour's broadcasting a day to its position ten years later, he could now predict a remarkable future for televisors too. Colour, he was sure, would come; and perhaps the 'feelies' and the 'smellies' were just round the corner.

The young aesthete Alan Pryce-Jones, one of the bright young people of the post-war generation, had been sent down from Magdalen College, Oxford, in his first term without attending a lecture or a tutorial.[504] In disgrace with his publisher father, who cut off his allowance, at twenty years old he was jobless and penniless. Walking the London streets, he ran into an old friend in Trafalgar Square. 'You have only one thing to do,' he was told, 'J. C. Squire, the editor of the *London Mercury*, wants an assistant. He is at this moment having his hair cut at the National Liberal Club.'[505] In a flash Pryce-Jones was there and found 'a benevolent, mildly intoxicated old – at forty-five he seemed old to me – gentleman sitting in a barber's chair.' Squire had somehow heard of Pryce-Jones and by Monday he was employed as his unpaid assistant editor, hoping to make his way in Fleet Street. It was a reprise of Squire's own apprenticeship in Plymouth. Pryce-Jones's account of his four years at the *London Mercury* gives a vivid picture of the editor and of his magazine in the last days of his pomp.

He knew how unfashionable a figure Squire was becoming and how the Bloomsberries looked down on him as a slightly absurd, badly shaven, confused-looking West countryman. He knew too that the chorus of critical opinion, led by Eliot, Middleton Murry and Leavis, was increasingly hostile. Yet Pryce-Jones, to his own surprise, began to be impressed: 'You could not watch Squire in his daily operation without forming a deep and grateful affection. His enemies and his family did not see a man of great tenderness and generosity, and an exemplary friend.' Pryce-Jones admired Squire as a poet 'whose successes, which came into being like impromptus, still give pleasure, often witty, often touching.' He was in all things deeply innocent. He had a sense of his mission which verged on – and beyond – the absurd: 'You have no idea, my dear fellow, what it is to carry the whole weight of English poetry on one's shoulders,' he once told his young protégé. He noticed how Squire charmed women who often tried to rescue him. The devoted Alice Warrender tried to reform him by taking him away from clubs and public houses into a more sober and feminine atmosphere. The society beauty Vittoria Colonna, Duchess of Simonetta, invited him to stay with her in her villa on Lake Como. Hilaire Belloc's sister, the novelist Marie Belloc-Lowndes, said she enjoyed with him the greatest friendship she had ever known.

A look through Squire's letters shows a man at full throttle. There was never enough time. He was juggling the roles of editor, poet, and playwright with an all-consuming literary and social life. In the background there was constant anxiety about money and the strain of a marriage that was near to breakdown. A growing reliance on alcohol was pushing him very near to the edge. Pryce-Jones respected him as an editor. 'He was amazingly fluent. Always late, he could write admirable prose sense at the printer's last minute, propped against a bar counter and dispatching his copy page by page. He corrected proofs with lightning speed and total accuracy.' He seemed to work best to a deadline with the aid of 'strong waters'. Priestley was his complete opposite, the careful professional writer who delivered his work on time with the exact number of words as specified, but he too was impressed by the way Squire wrote reviews, poems and articles with the same speed as it took others to read through what they had written: 'Squire had astonishing mental gifts as a writer. He was far more richly endowed than the people who soon began to sneer at him,' wrote Priestley in the *Observer*. But he also saw Squire's weakness: 'through some flaw of his character he did not put his gifts to their best use... everything he did was done at the last moment, rushed to the printer with the ink still wet. Given the circumstances, he performed some astounding feats of composition.'

Pryce-Jones began to accompany his boss to literary parties, readings, and talks and the two very dissimilar characters became great friends. There were always lighter moments; Squire was prone to absurd accidents. In front of Godalming station, a lady managed to get the point of her umbrella stuck under Squire's nose, neatly dislodging his spectacles. Pryce-Jones then had to face a journey in Squire's Buick knowing that the driver could not see to the end of the bonnet. Cricket balls knocked him prostrate when fielding; his balding head was attacked by two ravens at the Tower of London. On a shooting weekend Squire, whose aim was notoriously bad, succeeded in shooting a pheasant. It landed on his head and knocked him out. More ominous was the time when Squire was due to address the Johnson Society at the Cheshire Cheese. Shortly before dinner he fell on the floor. Pryce-Jones thwacked him and set him upright, but Squire entered the room covered in sawdust. He took a couple of drinks but was silent during the meal. After coffee he gave a coherent, witty twenty-minute speech before relapsing again into total silence.

There were discoveries to be made in the heaps of manuscripts and letters in the *Mercury*'s office. There was always a great pile of correspondence and invitations to which Pryce-Jones had to reply on the editor's behalf. He remembered particularly Sybil Colefax's almost unreadable handwriting: 'Do dine on Tuesday. Just ourselves and Pirandello.' In a cupboard behind his desk he came across an unbound proof copy of *Ulysses* which Squire had requested from Paris from the bookseller and publisher Sylvia Beach. 'Burn it at once!' came the order. (Grace Chapman had been commanded to do the same thing but had been unable to set it alight because she could not get enough flame from her tiny Victorian iron range.) Naturally enough, Pryce-Jones put the copy in his bag and took it home. Squire had now savaged in print two key works of modernism: *The Rainbow* and *The Waste Land*, and tried to consign his copy of another one to the fire.

Almost every lunchtime contributors and friends met in the

Temple Bar below the *Mercury*'s offices; Among the smoke and potted palm trees, Squire held the ring between the young Oxford aesthetes, led by Pryce-Jones, John Betjeman and James Stern, and the seasoned writers: Arnold Bennett, J. B. Morton, D. B. Wyndham Lewis and Hilaire Belloc – in flowing cape. Edward Shanks was often there; sometimes Edmund Blunden dropped in and there were rare glimpses of Stephen Spender or perhaps Robert Frost on a visit from America. In the club-like atmosphere there was laughter, banality and 'occasional verbal violence'. Wyndham Lewis called it the Mermaid Tavern of modern London. Priestley said it was there that he heard the liveliest talk among a gathering of wits he ever remembered. If one wanted to find the epicentre of the Squirearchy, the Temple Bar for two hours at lunchtime might have been the best place to go.

When Squire's friends were not carousing in London pubs and clubs, at summer weekends they gathered together as cricketers to play for or support the Invalids. Squire had long wanted to meet the music critic Neville Cardus whom he had signed up to write the cricket volume in the 'English Heritage Series'. They met by accident on the top floor of the Lyons Corner House at Piccadilly Circus for a cricket club's annual dinner. Cardus was impressed straightaway. 'Only to look at him is satisfying and strengthening: a triumphantly ravaged face, quizzical yet kindly, with an air of nobility running to seed, to flower again immediately, worldliness and unworldliness in splendid contention – but all ready to cope with the best and the worst... after some hard peering at things through and over his spectacles.' 'I count him amongst the few who have reconciled me to life in my worst moments.'[506]

His account of what followed stood for many of Squire's evenings. In the room at the Corner House was a long table covered with gin-and-Italian cocktails with cherries sticking up 'like a field of poppies'. The two men went through them 'as with a scythe'. At the dinner Squire made a speech which soon digressed from cricket into a full-scale attack on jerry builders and despoilers of the English countryside. Afterwards he led Cardus back to the Savile Club where they argued about Shakespearean sonnets till dawn broke. Squire asked his friend why he did not belong to the club. Cardus asked which club he was in. 'Why the Savshe of course,' said Squire and repeated the same sound. The next day, Cardus wrote, 'I applied for membership of the Savage Club.'

Neville Cardus was duly invited to play for the Invalids. His account captures as nearly as possible Squire's schoolboy-like enthusiasm and gossipy conversational style, moving restlessly from one subject to another:

One day in August, Sir John Squire came to me and said: 'I want you to play for me next Saturday at Taunton… it's going to be a very serious affair. I want to win. We are playing the Somerset Stragglers – or some such name – I forget which at the moment – but it's a team that lives in Somersetshire somewhere. And I want you to bowl for me. You can bowl, can't you?' I told him I hadn't bowled for three or four years. 'Still,' he said you *have* bowled some time or other in your life, haven't you? Well, that will be a useful help in my team. I've got a good lot of players – listen.' He pulled a piece of notepaper from his pocket (with a heap of other scraps, probably the beginnings of poems or book-reviews). 'I'll read you my team – very strong all round. First there's Arnold Bax; now, as you know he's a pretty good composer and I believe has just finished another symphony. Then there's his brother Clifford – a first-rate man. Did you see his play *The Rose and the Thorn* or whatever he called it? And Alec Waugh's coming with us; I believe he is working on another novel. Old Hugh Walpole is in my team also… C. R. W. Nevinson has promised to play for me too and, as you know, he's one of our most promising painters… Then I've asked William Murdoch – have you heard him play Brahms? – but of course you have; isn't it splendid? Well, there you are – there's the nucleus for a strongish team. We meet at Paddington, 4.30 Friday; and we're staying at the Old Castle Hotel…'[507]

The Invalids provided Cardus with some of his best stories and anecdotes, including his favourite cricket story. One of the opposition's batsmen skied a catch very high to mid-wicket. Five or six fieldsmen advanced, hands outstretched to take the catch. 'With rare presence of mind and true leadership, Sir John cried out, "Thompson's catch! Leave it to Thompson!" Each of the fieldsmen retreated obediently – and the ball fell harmlessly to earth. Thompson was not playing that week. 'Of no other man except Sir John – could I – or would I tell this, the best of my cricket stories.'[508]

The Invalids were immortalised in Archie Macdonell's *England, their England* (1933). Macdonell wrote drama criticism for the *Mercury* and played for Squire's side. The book was a Scotsman's quest to understand the essence of the country south of the Border. It is often remembered for one chapter only, the cricket match. The captain, Mr Hodge, is a thinly disguised portrait of Squire. It ends with a dream vision looking down on King Alfred's city of Winchester. Crowds of soldiers appear in a mist, carrying weapons, some archaic and some modern. They are a laughing band of men who are all poets. Gradually they disappear into the mist, leaving only a thin one and a fat one. 'Shall we shog off?' Jack Falstaff asks. As Shakespeare and Fat Jack link arms and vanish into the mist they seem to merge into one person: 'Both looked a little like Mr. Hodge.' Macdonell's search for England ends with a vision of a pastoral landscape and a cheerful warrior race led by its poets and its cricketers. Its embodiment is Jack Squire. Macdonell dedicated *England, their England* to 'J. C. Squire: The English Poet', as if he were the only one worth speaking about. Squire thoroughly disliked the novel, perhaps because cricket was too important a subject to be treated so lightly, and advised Macmillan's against its publication. He was overruled: it became a bestseller.

As the coterie wars of the twenties simmered down the small London literary world met at parties, clubs and dinners. At the large evening parties in the early thirties that were the forerunner of later more exclusive cocktail parties there was a wide mingling of all opinions. Friendships too crossed boundaries – Siegfried Sassoon, friendly with both the Sitwells and Squire, was upset they did not like each other. The Georgian poet John Freeman was adopted by Edith Sitwell. Some writers like Aldous Huxley and Stephen Spender flitted from group to group. There was, however, one clearly divisive feature: the war. Those who had fought, and those who had lived through the war, felt very differently from those for whom war was only a childhood memory. Alan Pryce-Jones knew that he was at the end of the 'soaring, stamping, period', and belonged to a new generation at Oxford 'who brushed their hair carefully, drank cocktails, liked lifts in cars, read German, smoked Russian cigarettes rolled in black paper. By contrast, Squire's generation looked considerably blown about by the wind; they drank beer, they hated Germans, and their curtains reeked of pipe smoke... Squire, therefore, although he was still a youngish man, seemed to me to possess a dinosaur quality: a dinosaur of rare tact, discrimination and bounty.'[509]

Pryce-Jones tried to introduce the editor to some of his contemporaries. He succeeded with one Oxford friend, John Betjeman, who contributed a short story, 'Lord Mount Prospect', to the *London Mercury* while still an undergraduate. He was always grateful to his first publisher. The writer of short stories, James Stern, was another discovery. But as the thirties progressed, the younger politically and socially minded poets of the 'MacSpaunday group' – (MacNeice, Spender, Auden, C. Day Lewis) – began to hold sway and take over from the coteries of the 1920s and write poetry as different from modernism as it was from the Georgians. All the squabbles about free verse and imagism began to recede into the past.

In November 1931 Squire was sacked from the job of chief literary reviewer at the *Observer*. The editor, J. L. Garvin, often had to send a messenger boy to Squire's home to wait for him to finish his latest dispatch or scour the pubs around South Kensington and Fleet Street. A series of taxis then rushed his weekly piece page by page to the printer's. Garvin finally lost patience. Squire maintained to his brother-in-law that he was a megalomaniac who felt overshadowed by his literary editor. He had threatened to take over Jack's role in choosing the popular 'Book of the Week' and then decided who should write the review. Squire now regretted his loyalty to the paper – he said he had turned down £3,000 a year from another Sunday and had been asked to name his fee at the *Sunday Times* when Edmund Gosse died. His brother-in-law loyally felt that the *Observer* would lose thousands of readers. Many of them, he felt, took the paper only to read Jack.

The poetry had dried up too: Squire had published almost nothing between 1925 and 1930. Inspiration was capricious and unreliable for him, closely related to the world of childhood imagination. The adult learned to analyse, to compare and to criticise; rationality cut him off from the experience itself. Some writers came to realise that 'the truest aesthete is the child'; others forgot, or blocked out the child's vision. He could easily apply to himself the 'lovely and concise' lines of his friend the nature poet W. H. Davies:

I saw this day sweet flowers grow thick –
But not one like the child did pick…
A hundred butterflies saw I
But not one like the child saw fly…

'That is not sentimentality: it is truth,' he wrote.[510] But he was not a mystic like Blake, nor did he claim to be; he was more like Tennyson pursuing a gleam, or Thomas Hardy seeing 'moments of vision'. He thought that his friend Walter de la Mare's most dominant theme was his 'sense of the mystery beyond all the superficial beauty and dreadfulness of existence.' That sense of the numinous is deeply embedded in Squire's own poetry. Like Wordsworth, however, he felt that 'the things which I have seen I now can see no more'. Moments of vision in his poetry are cloaked in negatives. From earliest childhood he had felt a sense of unattainment, of failure to penetrate the mystery. Hence the elegiac note is always there. Paradise existed; Eden existed – but both were unknowable and unreachable. The idea of life as a mysterious journey from the unknown to the unknown was a constant theme. From his earliest days the voyage of Coleridge's Ancient Mariner had haunted his imagination. The traveller, be it a walker, a tramp, a gipsy or a sailor, became a common figure of his poetry and prose. In the epigram 'The Epitaph' he was the 'poor wanderer freed at last from seas you could not sail, / A wreck upon the shores of Paradise.'

One of his rare nature poems, 'Paradise Lost', expressed both the enchantment and the alienation.

What hues the sunlight had, how rich the shadows were,
The blue and tangled shadows dropped from the crusted branches
Of the warped apple-trees upon the orchard grass.

How heavenly pure the blue of two smooth eggs that lay
Light on the rounded mud that lined the thrush's nest:
And what a deep delight the spots that speckled them.

And that small stream that ran from hedge to hedge,
Shadowed over by the trees, and glinting in the sunbeams,
How clear the water was, how flat the beds of sand
With travelling bubbles mirrored, each one a golden world
To my enchanted eyes. Then earth was new to me.

But now I walk this earth as it were a lumber room,
And sometimes live a week seeing nothing but mere herbs,
Mere stones; mere passing birds: not look at anything
Long enough to feel its conscious calm assault:
The strength of it, the word, the royal heart of it.

Childhood will not return; but have I not the will
To strain my turbid mind that soils all outer things
And, open again to all the miracles of light,
To see the world with the eyes of a blind man gaining sight?[511]

His childhood delight in the clear streams of the Devon countryside is caught by the fast-tripping exclamations, only to come to a dead stop in the disappointment of the heavily stressed half line: 'Then earth was new to me.'

In 'The Muse Absent' the overworked editor again lamented the way in which 'Duty, routine and common sense'…

> Have beaten me and taken me…
> Necessity that knows no law,
> With iron rule oppresses me;
> Sealed are the ancient founts of awe,
> No stranger wind caresses me.
> But when this rigid road is past,
> Aeolian airs may breathe for me
> With that old tenderness at last,
> And autumn laurels wreathe for me:
> The clarions of a final dawn
> May challenge me and waken me,
> When all that hate, or love, or fawn,
> Forgetting, have forsaken me.[512]

John Betjeman wrote, 'Oh! I do sympathise there. I know that feeling and have never seen it so well expressed.'[513] Despite the suggestion he was awaiting 'the clarions of a final dawn', Squire was only forty-eight years old.

Chapter 21

Faces in Candlelight

Margaret Lucy Mayne, born in 1900 in India, was a child of the Indian Civil Service. Under the name Henrie Mayne she wrote the story of her parents' unhappy marriage and her own in her autobiographical novel *An Unreasonable Man*.[514] Adventurous and independent-minded, at the age of eighteen she had joined the British Red Cross in Switzerland where she earned a medal for working with German prisoners of war. In her novel the heroine 'Lucy' is transformed from gangly teenager into attractive young woman. 'She wore a rather low summer frock, very high heels, a lavish amount of lipstick and her conspicuous red hair was coiled beneath a floppy transparent hat, better suited for Ascot or Henley.' Her mother, shocked by the amount of rouge on her lips, and the length of her skirt, thought her daughter looked far from respectable. This was the young woman whom Squire had first met in Soho at the end of the war when she was only seventeen. She told him how much she admired his poetry...

It was not till more than ten years later that they met again. By then she had become a lecturer on the history of architecture and a translator of Pirandello, mixing with theatre directors and artists. She had married 'perversely, odiously, in secret',[515] but that had not lasted, and now she was nearly thirty. Squire was lonely. He wooed her with almost daily poems, nearly all of which are lost. The relationship was bound to be complicated. He was completely taken by the beauty, sexual attractiveness and experience of his younger and more worldly mistress. She was clever, witty and sophisticated; he was middle-aged, broke, and married with four children. The affair was as brief as it was passionate and painful.

'To an Inscrutable Mistress' reveals the conflict:

Proud alien eyes, command me, body and mind,
If my surrenders can but make you kind.
Do with me as you will, be eloquent
Of all you want from me, only relent.
In vain I plead. O pitiless lovely eyes,
The more I yield, the more you tyrannise.[516]

An early unpublished draft of the much more conventional poem he later published as 'They Learn in Suffering' also reveals the tensions of the love affair as clearly as the later version tidies them up. It has an agonised rawness of sexual feeling that Squire normally shaped and distanced himself from:

Beloved, do not fret or knit your brow,
Never be feared for me,
You have forced my heart to red eruption now:
I am full of fire and free.

It hurt me in that shaded room, you were
So logical and blind,
It hurt me in the autumn woods, you were
So lovely and so kind.

Whatever I see of you hurts me, visions come
Of you, chameleon-wise,
Surprising, expected, voluble and dumb –
Oh, **enigmatic** eyes!

Go on as you've begun
With voice and form and face,
Do what you will with me, for at their height,
Great joy, great pain embrace.

Hurt me, oh, hurt me, press the ichor out,
Torture the thing that's I,
Let me but bear my destined fruit, I'll shout
With joy, and happy die.

There was a time when you, with eyes averse,
Said that I was a fool:
I was hurt and glad: you'll never hear me curse,
Flogged in Apollo's school!

I cannot any longer separate
One prompting from another,
Or yet distinguish mate from inspiring mate,
Joy sister, and pain brother.

Everything pains, and everything exalts,
The world's ablaze with light,
I do not think of merits or of faults,
Even of wrong or right –

Only I live for Poetry, only I long
To fructify; only I cling
To this conviction, now so sure and strong,
That I was born to sing.[517]

In the later, published version the poem omits the second, third and the final four stanzas, simplifies the complex relationship and makes the conclusion much blander. Here the combination of love and pain has a strong sexual and masochistic element, but the triumphant conclusion suggests that out of the fire of violently conflicting feelings poetry is forged.

According to Squire's first biographer Patrick Howarth, the affair ended when, back from a holiday in Switzerland, Squire's eye fell on the engagements column in *The Times* where he came across Henrie Mayne's name. It was a bitter shock. Not only had she been unfaithful to him, but her fiancé was his own literary agent, A. D. Peters. The poetry dried up once more and alcohol took its place... Letters recently deposited at St John's College, Cambridge, however, reveal a different story and a different love affair. The first volume of poetry Squire published for seven years was a collection of love poems. *A Face in Candlelight and Other Poems* emerged in 1932 and was misleadingly dedicated 'To HM'. But it was not she who inspired most of the poems; he was not broken up by news of the engagement and he did not turn to drink. He was in fact at his happiest in 1930 – he had fallen in love, but not with Henrie Mayne.

Under the strapline of 'The Chatelaine of Thenford House, Banbury', in 1921 the *Tatler* devoted a full-page picture to Cecily Severne and her daughters, with the lake behind her and two swans in the background. She sits between two pretty young girls in party frocks. The family Alsatian stands guard over the family group. Six years earlier Cecily Mary Burdon-Muller had married Edmund Severne, an aristocrat and landowner. Later, a full page of *The Sketch* was given up to pictures of the three young children of the Severne family and their parents, but in 1929 she and her husband divorced. In June the following year Squire first met Cecily through his fellow editor Lord Lee of Fareham. She was four years younger than him, a rich and sophisticated divorcée now living in Eaton Terrace in Mayfair with her children, her maidservant and her cook.

The story of their affair is told elliptically in *A Face in Candlelight and Other Poems*.[518] Squire dedicated his final volume of poetry to Cecily Severne. In autumn 1930 they had been together on a shooting party. 'The Woods in November' is about the instant when he knew he had fallen in love. He relished the fact that his feelings were entirely private and marked him out from his fellow shooters – and from Cecily herself.

> Fragile and clean and virginal,
> Still as a startled doe,
> You looked as from a place apart
> On me who passed below:
> Your haloed hair was fiery
> As autumn's cohorts are,
> Your scarlet lips were parted...[519]

'Dining Out' was a poem he did not dare to show her till much later.

> The gilt, the glass, the plate, the wine,
> The chatter of the London Zoo:
> Oh what a privilege is mine,
> Amid a crowd, alone with you!

> So undeservedly preferred,
> Divinely licensed for an hour,
> Disdaining all the luckless herd,
> To wear your beauty like a flower.[520]

Invitations to lunch and dinner followed; they went together to theatres, restaurants and the ultrafashionable nightclub the Café de Paris and enjoyed exhibitions of Swedish, Byzantine, and Persian art at Burlington House. Still he concealed his deeper feelings with badinage and wit. He teased her about her handwriting as he had teased Eileen, but with a lighter touch: 'Perfect your face, ineffable your wit / Your voice is music and your form divine: / A paragon: but still, you must admit, / Your handwriting is even worse than mine.' He was a courtly lover, a worshipper: she a dryad. 'Poets like statesmen or soldiers serve queens best,' he wrote, 'they like carrying a glove and bringing back trophies.' He was attracted by her gamine figure, pale face, high cheekbones, long eyelashes, and pre-Raphaelite red hair. Perhaps he recalled how, in a poem he had translated at school, Baudelaire had been enraptured by 'La Chevelure'.

It was not until six months after they first met, in January 1931, that he wrote to her as 'Dear Cecily' for the first time, adding, 'if I may', in brackets. He signed himself, 'Ever, Jack.' In March he suggested they might have dinner and afterwards see the revue *Chelsea Follies*, or perhaps just talk. Falling in love with Cecily and poetic inspiration were indissolubly linked for him: 'Poetry gets penned in so long that at last it bursts like an abscess.' *A Face in Candlelight* is about the almost miraculous ability to write poetry again: 'Suddenly I had a burst last winter at a pheasant shoot... while waiting for the beaters I dashed down a lot of stuff on the backs of envelopes... During some months in 1930 and 1931 I not only wrote many new poems, but found myself able to finish poems, lines of which had been lying about for years.'[521]

The central image of *A Face Seen in Candlelight* is the flower coming into bud. It is the leitmotif of Squire's poetry – new life suddenly, amazingly, bursting out after apparent death: the lily breaking its sheath in 'In My First Flower-time', the poem he chose to open his *Collected Poems* with; the acacia tree budding in his garden at Swan House, and the mysterious lily of Malud itself. 'The Seldom Flowering Tree' appeared in the *Mercury* in May 1931 just as his romance with Cecily also blossomed. 'After long, parched years / The wilderness has blossomed as the rose.' The trunk may be old and hidden but that made the flowering all the more miraculous. Squire devoted the sonnet's octave to the fragile beauty of summer garden flowers but the sestet points the contrast between them and the strength of the ancient tree's more powerful and lasting blooms. Squire was fond of noting how his poetry seemed to emerge in seven year 'bursts' after long silence.

I envy not these flowers so often seen,
For I am of those trees, coiling and dark,

Which year-long stand in shrouded sombre green,
But sprouting from whose patient iron bark
A few large, shapely, glimmering blooms appear,
Burning in darkness, every seventh year.

After Cecily returned from a skiing holiday in Switzerland their relationship deepened. By June he had become much bolder; the shooting party in the autumn had become his romantic myth; he told her he felt he had suddenly strayed into an enchanted wood and her phantom stayed with him everywhere. He recommended what she should read – some love poetry, the essays of Charles Lamb, the short stories of Henry James, and promised that he would come round and read her some of his own favourites – but he still had not revealed to her that he had fallen hopelessly in love. By July he could control his feelings no longer. He summoned up his courage and visited Cecily at Eaton Terrace at night, 'knowing instinctively it was the crisis.' The following day he wrote to her to say how glad he was that 'Archbishop Galahad' had managed to break down the barriers. If she didn't know that now, 'she damned well ought to.' The letter ended with a kiss for each eyelid: 'Good night, Botticelli Venus.'

Cecily was puzzled by this sudden passion. How was it that all the badinage, the trips to the theatre and galleries, had become something completely different? How had her witty companion turned into an ardent lover? Why had he not been more open with her about his feelings? Why had he shown no guts? She called him enigmatic, and asked him to tell her about previous love affairs. When he next saw her Squire promised he would conceal nothing except the names – and they were very few. Cecily herself had a generosity and openness that made him feel he could finally unburden his inner self. 'You have unsealed fountains long frozen and made a man speak after a long habit of reticence… a life of repression has bottled me up inside, layer on layer of crust, and I've defended my over-sensitiveness from the world (and propose to go on doing so) by assuming brusqueness, harshness, easy cynicism and all kinds of armour that the silly world can't see as armour... I wish I could pour out my heart to you. I shall manage it sometime but I have been reticent all my life and only allowed my real me to peep out in the poems.'

In November 1931 Louise Morgan interviewed Squire for the magazine *Everyman*: 'At the moment he is in an intense state of excitement because he is having a burst of poetry writing. His inside coat pocket is crammed with papers – envelopes, bills, post cards – and nearly every one is scribbled over with poetry, much of it about the joy of beginning again.' He pulled out a bill from the costumiers Nathan's for the Byron costume he had worn at the Waterloo Ball; on the back he had written:

> Songless for years, with Custom's other slaves,
> I sing again, and, counting well the cost,
> Have joined the Muse's legion of the lost
> Who die that flowers may grow upon their graves.[522]

On a grubby sheet of brown paper he had jotted down the beginnings of four more poems. 'These I wrote yesterday in a cab. Some of the best poems I've written lately I began twenty years ago.' In one morning he finished a long poem and claimed to have written more than a hundred poems in the last winter. He promised that the same thing was going to happen this winter. 'I'm having another burst. I'm absolutely choc-a-bloc full of it. I'm writing every day...'

He took to heart Cecily's criticism and tried to show he was not passionless nor cold. He implored her to read the end of his Keatsian 'Anarchy' in order to show that however cynical he might appear, he 'hankered after a Utopia where love is freely given and taken, and there is no jealousy, and fidelity may, perhaps, flourish all the better because of the absence of restraint':

> Yet sighs the absurd unreasoning voice of our blood
> For a world, alas! – and there is no bitter cold there,

Nor scorching heat, nor blossom with worm in the bud,
And babes do not die, nor blindness comes to the old there,
But the sun shines fair, and the rain falls soft, and the clime
Conspires with the seed for the loveliest fruits of time,
And the young are strong, and the old go green to the grave
Without pain, and none is master and none is slave,
And music sounds from the boats, and garlands are woven
By maids at noon, and great calm statues are cloven
Out of the cliffs, by the shrines of sunnier gods.[523]

In a sequence of poems, Squire used pastoral images both to express his powerful feelings for Cecily and to distance himself from them. In the 'Surrendered Shepherd to the Enigmatic Shepherdess' he tells her: 'Take me, and make me, break me if you will.' In 'The Cruel Nymph to the Dejected Shepherd', the suggestion is that Cecily might have understood how passionate he was if he had made more physical advances. Perhaps he had been too shy, too gentlemanly? In the final couplet Squire took on his mistress's teasing voice: "T'was not I that was colder, but you that were blinder, / And if boys were but bolder, girls would be kinder.' Cecily's criticism that he had shown no guts in their courtship had hit home, but he denied it was that that made him hide his feelings. He blamed it on his puritanical upbringing in Plymouth which meant that if he did not do what he wanted to do 'the Eternities would approve'.

Letters to 'dearest Cecily' and 'My sweet' followed, along with poems and cards. 'The Surprise Visit' is one of the few survivors of the kind of billet-doux that he produced apparently effortlessly:

A step
On the stair:
'Who is it?'
You came,
The daintiest portrait,
The door for a frame.

Laughing eyes,
Tilted chin,
Budded lips…
You were drest –
Well, a hat, a fur coat
And a rose at your breast.

'I dropped in,
Just one second, one second,
No more,
As you might like a kiss.
I've a cab at the door.
There you are…

Now, goodbye.'
'You've an ear
Like a shell.'
'What another? Oh no!
Not another…
Oh well!'[524]

Once again, he poured out his love and devotion in more than
500 letters. Sometimes he wrote three times a day; sometimes he
wrote half an hour after he had left her. He loved romantic images
of Cecily: singing Schumann in the soft lamplight of her room; her
face in candlelight framed by dark cushions; a walk through spring
woods, suddenly coming on constellations of anemones. She was the
secret hidden name in 'Anonyma': 'O Eve, O Lilith, Helen, O virgin
Cecily, / O Magdalen, O Ruth…' In this springtime he was sure he had
now thrown off the burden of past unhappiness: 'I, who was once a
woman's slave / Will never be again.' Years of struggle and failure lay
behind these bitter complaints, but Squire still felt that somewhere
there was a hidden genius that might emerge. Even when proclaiming
this new openness, he still wanted to keep his love a secret, 'a jewelled

casket'. Emotionally, however, it was a new life, a turning back of years. 'I'm blissfully happy… happier than I've ever been… How wonderful that this should have come now when one thought one would never know that kind of youth or love for the rest of one's drudging days.'[525]

Love poem after love poem flowed from him, rather like Thomas Hardy's late lyrics. Some he included in *A Face in Candlelight*; many he never published:

> Love always passes, so the sceptics say,
> Well, let them say, and, haply let it pass,
> And should there ever come our parting day,
> It shall not wring from me one faint 'Alas':
> I shall not curse the Heavens for love that died,
> But let it waft away on soundless wings,
> Like sunset, or the ebbing of the tide,
> Or any other end of natural things.[526]

But the exact opposite proved to be the case.

A letter of 3 July to his mother showed a sad state of affairs: 'Raggie' had been greeted at the beginning of his second year at his father's old college by the bursar, account book in hand. His fees had not been paid and he was sent away.

> I haven't written lately because I've been much under the weather – leaving the house, having to take Raggie down from Cambridge & having no money. BUT at last the musical comedy I wrote with Dennis Arundell [*Robin Hood*] has been taken for production in October, &, if it comes off (which I think it will) the whole lot of us will be in clover. October: the odds are on: tell Doll and Paul. The longer I live the more miraculous I think the way you have raised your children… and if this comes off we are commissioned to do a series and I shall be the first poet since Shakespeare who has raised a family respectably having no means.
>
> Your loving son
> Jack.

The letter is typical. The hope was that just around the corner was a scheme, or a play, or a publishing venture that would make his fortune. Jack would be generous in sharing the profits and then the whole family could all live in clover. But despite all the projects and all the work and the loans from his mother and his wife's family, his money had now run out completely.

After a holiday to Norway Bessie had lunch with her son at Romano's plush Edwardian restaurant in the Strand. She seemed in high spirits and full of energy. But in the spring of 1932, she fell ill. Jack began to write her almost daily letters. He did not go to see her in Plymouth but promised he would take the night train if necessary; he was only a telephone call away and would drop everything; she only had to write... His sister was bitterly angry with him and his aunt wrote, infuriated by his behaviour, 'I cannot understand Jack. I am glad I have no son if that is how they treat their mothers.'

Instead, he continued with his plans for a fortnight's holiday in Switzerland with Cecily. On 9 April 1932, after a journey of nineteen hours, the lovers arrived in Lucerne in late snow; the Jungfrau, fifty miles away, stood out in the brilliant sunshine. 'My room had a little balcony, trellised and twined with roses, over the blue lake. I stood in it and watched the approach of evening. As the sun sank over the waters a wide ray crept along the mountains above the southern shore, a faint golden veil which as it moved, turned the dark blue to purple...' It was a rare moment of complete happiness. In the mornings Cecily, an experienced skier, swished by him elegantly as he struggled on Wengen's nursery slopes. He finished his preface to *A Face in Candlelight* and gave the place and the date: Lucerne, 1932. It was a secret love token. In a postcard to his mother, he told her that he had played golf, visited the casino and heard *Die Fledermaus* at the opera house. 'Better already,' he ended.

When he returned to England letters from Doll awaited him. She insisted that he should come to Devon immediately to see his mother who was now dangerously ill. On 10 May he replied that he did not need to be told his mother was 'magnificently plucky' as she was 'the bravest person I have ever known'. He promised to come at a moment's notice, a promise Doll must have called in, because five days later he finally took the train westwards. On his return he wrote to Bessie from the Savile Club:

All my life, at crises, I have thought I have a brave mother & I mustn't be unworthy of her. For the rest of my life I shall think I had the bravest of mothers and can I ever live up to her? I might have said it long ago but I think you have always known it – what I felt.

Good night darling mother.
Jack.

On the 30 May he ended his letter: 'God bless you for your whole devoted life.' In June Bessie fell unconscious and died. Squire had just gone to the Savile Club to change for dinner when he got the news through a message from Eileen. He immediately wrote to Cecily and described his mother rather distantly as a 'noble, witty, & domineering woman.' To Doll he wrote, 'I am glad she's gone. It was ghastly to think of her lingering on & on unconscious.'[527] He told his sister that in her will she had left a letter for him containing 'things beautiful and sacred'. Doll, still angry, accused him of having forgotten them all. In a letter which combined defensiveness and self-pity he replied that there was a bond between them that could never be broken and that they were as close as humans could ever be:

Don't think, my dearest sister that I've changed. I've only appeared to change as a man must who desperately struggles to bring up a large family and still not entirely to lose contact with his art, and seldom gets a proper holiday in the country. I never feel less close to you merely because I don't see you. I am a foul correspondent as anyone writing all day articles and business letters must be. One

III. Incorruptibly unpopular novelists exhibiting a proper austerity towards a less fortunate brother whose new book has run into its three thousands

Will Dyson's cartoon – from the left, Virginia Woolf, unknown, Osbert Sitwell and E. M. Forster.

THE
LONDON
MERCURY

EDITED BY J. C. SQUIRE   MONTHLY

A Selected List of CONTRIBUTORS to The London Mercury 1919–1932

J. R. ACKERLEY
CONRAD AIKEN
RICHARD ALDINGTON
SHERWOOD ANDERSON
MARTIN ARMSTRONG

KENNETH ASHLEY
STACY AUMONIER
HERMAN BAHR
MAURICE BARING
H. E. BATES

CLIFFORD BAX
MAX BEERBOHM
HILAIRE BELLOC
ARNOLD BENNETT
STELLA BENSON

REGINALD BERKELEY
LAURENCE BINYON
AUGUSTINE BIRRELL
EDMUND BLUNDEN
ERNEST BRAMAH

FRANCIS BRETT-YOUNG
ROBERT BRIDGES
GERALD BULLETT
OSBERT BURDETT
KAREL CAPEK

G. K. CHESTERTON
JOHN COLLIER
JOSEPH CONRAD
A. E. COPPARD
O. G. S. CRAWFORD

W. H. DAVIES
GEOFFREY DEARMER
THOMAS DERRICK
AUSTIN DOBSON
LORD ALFRED DOUGLAS

JOHN DRINKWATER
JOHN VAN DRUTEN
LORD DUNSANY
WILL DYSON
HAVELOCK ELLIS

POWYS EVANS
DARRELL FIGGIS
SIR J. FORBES ROBERTSON
E. M. FORSTER
ROBERT FROST

ERIC GILL
LOUIS GOLDING
LORD GORELL
SIR EDMUND GOSSE
ROBERT GRAVES

PHILIP GUEDALLA
THOMAS HARDY
A. P. HERBERT
JOS. HERGESHEIMER
MAURICE HEWLETT

ALFRED ALOYSIUS HORN
ALDOUS HUXLEY
E. V. KNOX
D. H. LAWRENCE
SIR SIDNEY LEE

NOW
ON SALE
AT
ONE
SHILLING

[Previously 3 /-]

Its appearance and size and nature of contents will remain unchanged

Order the *London Mercury* for monthly delivery. You will enjoy its poetry, short stories, cartoons, articles, woodcuts, critical studies and reviews. It deals with *all* phases of literature. It will keep you in touch with the best work being done to-day and with the work of the great writers of the past. Its contributors include new writers of promise and the acknowledged masters of contemporary literature.

The Leading Review of English Literature

SUBSCRIPTION FORM

To THE LONDON MERCURY, 229 STRAND, W.C.2

Please send me THE LONDON MERCURY until countermanded, commencing with the October, 1932, issue. I enclose 15/- for one year's subscription, including postage.

Name ....

Address...

....

And of all Newsagents, Booksellers, and Libraries

No other paper in the world can command such talent

CLARE LEIGHTON
SHANE LESLIE
VACHEL LINDSAY
G. LOCKER-LAMPSON
E. V. LUCAS

ROBERT LYND
ROSE MACAULAY
KATHERINE MANSFIELD
WALTER DE LA MARE
ALICE MEYNELL

HAMISH MILES
A. A. MILNE
PRINCE D. S. MIRSKY
C. K. SCOTT MONCRIEFF
C. E. MONTAGUE

GEORGE MOORE
T. STURGE MOORE
ELINOR MORDAUNT
J. B. MORTON
R. H. MOTTRAM

GWENDOLINE MURPHY
J. MIDDLETON MURRY
ABU NADAAR
JOHN NASH
SIR H. NEWBOLT

B. H. NEWDIGATE
ROBERT NICHOLS
FREDERICK NIVEN
GILBERT NORWOOD
ALFRED NOYES

LIAM O'FLAHERTY
W. J. TURNER
A. R. POWYS
J. B. PRIESTLEY
G. RAVERAT

E. T. RAYMOND
ERNEST RHYS
EDGELL RICKWORD
V. SACKVILLE-WEST
MICHAEL SADLEIR

GEORGE SAINTSBURY
GEORGE SANTAYANA
SIEGFRIED SASSOON
DOROTHY SAYERS
R. G. MCNAIR SCOTT

EDWARD SHANKS
G. BERNARD SHAW
DAME ETHEL SMYTH
E. Œ. SOMERVILLE
J. C. SQUIRE

J. ST. LOE STRACHEY
FRANK SWINNERTON
EDWARD THOMAS
LOUIS UNTERMEYER
ALEC WAUGH

ERNEST WEEKLEY
I. A. WILLIAMS
HENRY WILLIAMSON
VIRGINIA WOOLF
W. B. YEATS

The Shilling Mercury

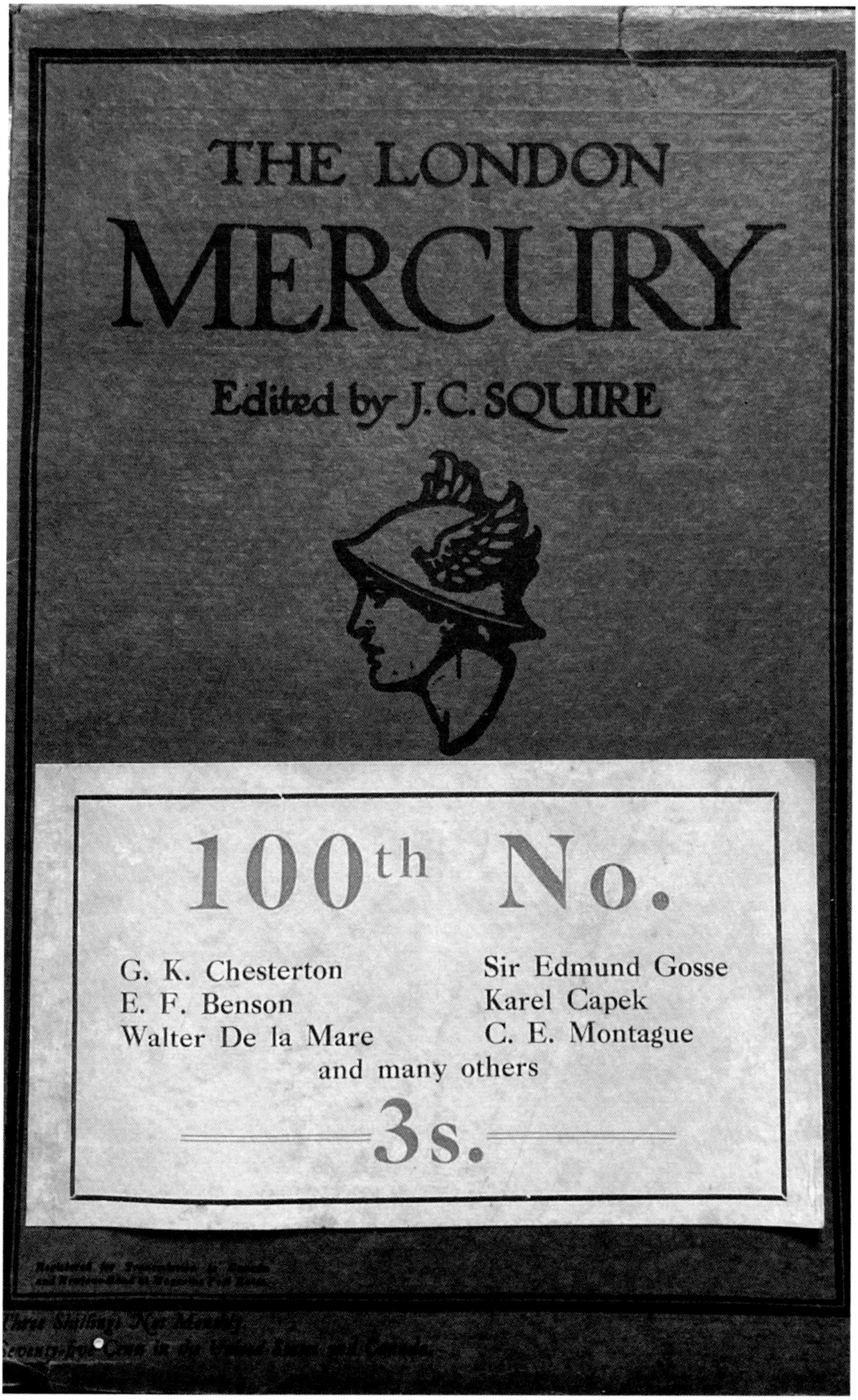

THE LONDON

MERCURY

Edited by J. C. SQUIRE

100th No.

G. K. Chesterton

E. F. Benson

Walter De la Mare

Sir Edmund Gosse

Karel Capek

C. E. Montague

and many others

3s.

Celebratory hundredth edition of the London Mercury.

Cecily Severne.
Dolly and her mother, Bessie.

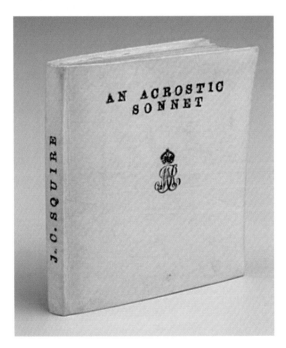

Jack's miniature book for Queen Mary's Dolls' House.

PICK-ME-UP.

My heart leaps up when I behold
    A broker in the sky,
With wings and halo all of
        gold
    And eyeglass in his eye,
A-leering at his brimming cup—
    And what does that contain?—
It is, it is, a Pick-me-Up—
    (Observe his watch and chain):
One third of Brandy (viz. Martell),
    One third of Dubonnet,
A trace of gin, Ojen is well,
    White egg — then shake — O.K.
                        J.C.S.

Pick-Me-Up: cocktail menus in verse.

Had his meal of bread
and cheese and good
beer . . . . under the
hedge

Sir John Squire has collected a galaxy of talent to make
this one of the most delightful and entertaining gift books
that have ever been published. Other books have sung the
praises of our English gardens and woodlands, or of our
farmer's year, but the literature of cheese, which is the

Cheddar Gorge: Illustration by E. H. Shepard.

THE SYMBOL

(On the statue of Cœur de Lion outside Westminster Hall, bombed and his sword bent.)

By heaps of shattered glass and stone
The horseman waits, erect, alone,
And, in his glove, still brandished high,
Challenging the invaded sky,
Bent, but not broken, is the sword
Which led the armies of the Lord.

J. C. SQUIRE.

October 1940. *Blitzkrieg.*

The Symbol: Squire's 1940 Christmas card.

BALLADE OF A FAVOURITE NAZI

Hitler has points ; speaking, he's quite a lark
  A lunatic haranguing in a zoo ;
He murdered half his cronies in the dark
  And yet can talk of morals till he's blue ;
  He chucks his arms around the Moscow crew,
Having accused them all of every crime ;
  He has his points, I say, and not a few
But give me Dr Goebbels every time.

Fat Goering, as voracious as a shark,
  No-one can tell me how his medals grew ;
Joachim Ribbentrop's another spark ;
  He said he knew his England through and
    through ;
  I have a friend who was a German Jew.
He thinks that Streicher touches the sublime ;
  Poor chap, he is entitled to his view ;
But give me Dr Goebbels every time

Lord, what a boy ! Just listen to him ! Hark !
  He's never at a loss for something new.
'Twas Churchill sank the inconvenient bark
  Telling the passengers his name was U.
  'Twas Churchill killed the King of Timbuctoo,
And told the world it was Von Pappenheim
  Himmler's a tryer, Hess knows what to do ;
But give me Dr Goebbels every time.

Envoi
Prince, as you say (and I agree with you)
They all can do a pretty bit of slime.
  Baron Munchausen knew a thing or two—
But give me Dr Goebbels every time.
                                    J. C. SQUIRE.
(Reprinted by kind permission of the author
and of the Editor of the " Weekly Review ")

From Punch.

Sons in uniform. From left, Julia, Raglan, Eileen, Jack, Anthony and Maurice.

Maurice Squire.

Portrait: Jack at 70.

Family cricketers. Jack, Raglan, Roger and Michael. Rodmell, 1955.

*The last match at Rodmell. From left, Jack, Bertha Usborne,
Raglan, Michael, unknown, Roger and Eileen.*

Jack with Clement Attlee, 1955.

(III) FOR OVER TWENTY YEARS THE CONTRIBUTOR OF OUR PRINCIPAL WEEKLY BOOK PAGE : SIR JOHN SQUIRE AT THE GATE OF HIS SUSSEX COTTAGE.

Jack's farewell photo, from The Illustrated London News, Diamond Cottage, 1956.

The church of St Nicholas, Broadwoodwidger.

John Squire's headstone, Broadwoodwidger.

loathes pen & ink. I'm very glad to have had your letter.

Mother was never out of my thoughts: I've always desperately longed to pull off something big in order to make her and you comfortable. She, poor gallant soul, is beyond it now: but don't think you'll ever be less close to me in spirit than we were when we were schoolchildren together.'[528]

His grief was compounded by guilt. The neglect of his mother and the failure to see his sister in Devon are hard to understand. The journey from London to Plymouth was certainly tiresome; it took the best part of a day. His excuse of an extremely demanding business life was also true – but he did find time in London for cricket, for drinking and for a highly complicated social life. The affair with Cecily was a compelling distraction.

There was something else deeply embedded in his character that kept him away. It was a refusal to face the obvious truth. A romantic at heart, he hated the mundane and the drably realistic and saw life through the prism of art and imagination. He needed to shut out the difficult, the humdrum and the painful and live a life of myth and hope. He was reluctant to visit his mother because her dying was terrible to him and could not be faced.

Chapter 22

They Learn in Suffering

When it emerged in 1932 the reviews of *A Face in Candlelight* were disappointing. Squire and the Georgians were looking like relics of a distant past. *The Times* was respectful, but the *Spectator* put the state of affairs baldly: 'About Mr. Squire's position in English Literature it is becoming increasingly difficult to be frank. There was a time, not so very long ago, when the name of the editor of the *London Mercury* was something to be conjured with. Can anyone, honestly, still find the heart to persuade themselves that Mr. Squire is a literary portent, a light in the surrounding darkness?' If they still felt convinced, the *Spectator* reviewer argued, then his latest volume of old-fashioned poetry would be a grave disappointment. 'But of course, the truth is that for Mr. Squire nothing has happened to English poetry since Mr. Belloc and Mr. Chesterton, or for that matter since Tennyson. So far as he is concerned, Mr. Eliot might never have lived nor Owen died. This much is plain as soon as one turns to the poems themselves... It is all very wistful, very beautiful, very "poetic". But to suppose that it has any connexion with poetry is to be too ingenuous.'[529]

Squire's last, misleadingly titled, anthology *Younger Poets of Today* was also published in 1932 and met the same damning response. After Middleton Murry's hostility it is a surprise to find that Squire included two (woodenly conventional) poems by him. He also included one poem by Edith Sitwell and five by Roy Campbell –

certainly not members of a coterie of friends. But the excitement and the challenge of Georgian anthologies had long gone stale. There was too much 'dull stuff'. The anthology attracted the condemnation of F. R. Leavis in *New Bearings in English Poetry*. The kind of poetry Squire's anthologies stood for was, he argued, a Victorian hangover, as dead as Robert Bridges' *Testament of Beauty* – and it had been dying since the 1890s. A fresh start was needed and the poets who were to supply it were T. S. Eliot and Ezra Pound. It was the last straw for Squire and the Georgians. They had been mocked by the Sitwells, attacked by Eliot and finally despatched by Leavis.

The *London Mercury* was in trouble too. With a circulation of 20,000 it could, and did for a while, make money, but it was proving hard to maintain this figure. After 1930 it seldom reached 10,000. (Its highbrow rival the *Criterion* very rarely got into four figures.) The sorry state of the magazine went on public show on 23 November in the Westminster County Court. Miss Agnes Mure Mackenzie had been asked by Squire to write an article on Sir Walter Scott. She was paid £9 which she felt was not enough, as she received two or three guineas per thousand words from other publications. She claimed that Squire owed her £6 15s for the article. She stated that she never bargained; it was clear that the fee was not agreed before publication and therefore she decided to sue.

Squire gathered an impressive army of supporters to speak on his behalf including his old friend from St John's, Raglan Somerset, now a barrister, A. P. Herbert and the historian Philip Guedalla. The editor of the *Church Times* and the assistant editors of *The Times* and the *English Review* also came to support him. Squire appeared before the judge and argued that the *Mercury* could not afford to pay more. He said that he himself had started with a salary of £1,500 which had been cut to £1,200, then to £750, and then to £500. Now he got nothing. His 5,000 shares in the company were now worthless. The company had never paid a dividend and never would. The standard rate of pay for articles had gone down from £3 10s per thousand words to £1 10s, which loyal contributors such as Hilaire Belloc, G. K. Chesterton and

A. P. Herbert were happy to accept. The judge, pointing out that *The Times* paid three guineas, split the difference between Miss Mackenzie and the *Mercury* and awarded her £2 10s. Squire felt wronged by the compromise. Clearly, however, he had taken his eye off the ball; he had not negotiated the rate for the article and he had not replied to any of Miss Mackenzie's letters. The case revealed the disorganisation of the *Mercury* and the parlous state of its finances. Things could not continue for long like this.[530]

The crisis deepened in 1932 when the world slump meant that subscribers could not afford the *Mercury* and advertisers had vanished with them. Squire thought of his readers, contributors and advertisers as a club of friends. In August he wrote his most personal and direct appeal to them: 'It would not be a good idea to let this paper die. It was started in 1919 with two main objects: to talk sense, in a bewildered world, about literature and the arts and to help young authors who could not get a hearing elsewhere.'[531] He boasted that almost every young author now flourishing had made their first or early appearance in the *Mercury*. Let those who doubted this achievement look at the index, he asked. There they would find great names of an older generation – Hardy, Gosse, Conrad, and Alice Meynell. There too they would find young writers such as Aldous Huxley, D. H. Lawrence, Siegfried Sassoon, Graham Greene, Katherine Mansfield and Robert Graves. Had the *Mercury* gone in for Bolshevism or Neo-Toryism or any kind of new religion he was sure it would have attracted sponsorship. But as it had only stood for 'good sense, exact scholarship, a recognition of the links between past and present', it was now in danger of going under.

Floods of correspondence continued to pile up, demanding the editor's replies. There was nothing too small for him to deal with. If a subscriber had a complaint, he replied: if the magazine had not been sent on time, he apologised. When a reader from Tottenham wrote cancelling his subscription because he was hard up, Squire promised that he would send him a year's magazines as a personal present. Under no circumstances should he think of repayment. It is not surprising that things often went out of control. Squire's own energy and interest began to flag. More and more complaints and confusions appeared. The magazine was losing its gloss; many contributors no longer wrote for it and the quality dipped. Manuscripts were lost or, as was the case with Max Beerbohm's short story, lay for eight years forgotten in Squire's desk drawers. Squire wrote to him congratulating himself for keeping it safely for such a long time: 'I am returning your manuscript. It is rather a triumph of orderliness to have retained it in the same desk drawer for eight years.'

The files kept by Grace Chapman reveal persistent complaints from contributors to whom he had to apologise and make excuses:

All right, we will return the 15/- to her… we have not lost the poems… the reason for my continual lateness was the fact that I always approached the job with an empty mind… the charwoman must have tidied it up from my table as there is not a trace of it… unfortunately the address is out of date and it never reached me… the manuscript blew out of the taxi window as I was bringing it to you… I am sorry you haven't heard about the article but I have just taken a month's holiday for the first time in my life and am in hideous arrears… very many thanks for your letter, that was a dreadful misprint to have let past… the strike has held up everything… I am so angry about your March cheque… I am sorry we only returned half your manuscript… I have just found this letter was not posted… It may be they rung me about it; these things are always happening… I made every effort but the horse would not go… you sent it to my house, and when manuscripts come to me there I always bung them into my pocket to take to the office. By some error this one stayed in the pocket…

He urged his readers to find other subscribers amongst the kind of people whom he thought were his chief customers all over the country: parsons, schoolmasters, schoolmistresses, retired soldiers and civil servants – emphatically not highbrows – and not the metropolitan elite. 'I know the readers better than anyone else,' he told Cecily. He included a form for them to recommend their friends. After all, he pointed out, the sub was only the price of a repainted golf ball or a small whisky. He had a plan which might put an end to the awful difficulties the magazine faced...

After discussions with the printers Squire decided that the choice was stark: either slow death or the drama of 'Death or Victory'. 'On September the First the *LONDON MERCURY* will appear at the price of one shilling. In appearance, size and the nature of its contents it will be unchanged.' This would slash the cost by two shillings. The magazine would cost more than a shilling to produce but he hoped the increased circulation and the advertising that would come with it would return the magazine to profit. It was his last gamble: 'If we die, we die.' 'So much for the sob-stuff,' he concluded. 'But will all those who wish the paper to survive induce as many as possible of their friends to take out annual subscriptions? It sounds like company-promoting; but, my goodness, it certainly isn't!'

When the 'Shilling Mercury' duly emerged in a celebratory red cover in October 1932 booksellers were enthusiastic; the newsagent W. H. Smith's put in an order for more than 3,000 additional copies. Every post brought in appreciative letters. Jack told Cecily that the past three months had been a terrific nerve strain but if he could put all his vigour into the *Mercury* for the next weeks he might 'pull off the miracle, for the whole world seems friendly disposed.'[532] He concluded his editorial notes: 'We live in a despondent world: we appeal to the non-despondent.' In October he wrote that the last number had been 'a magnificent success'. More than 20,000 copies had been printed and it looked as if they would sell out; forty pages of advertising flooded in.

Squire was in high spirits. He claimed to have received from an enterprising firm in Birmingham the gift of a mouse-trap to review. He printed a letter that had been sent to the 'Editress of our Women's page' (there was of course no such person or page), enclosing a picture of a new improved mouse-trap. He reprinted the sketch and promised that he would order a gross of them or more 'if ever the mice, hearing of our increased prosperity, desert the sinking churches and return to us'. He guaranteed to review in his columns in the future any of the following items:

Steam Yachts
Rolls-Royces
Mortgages
Cases of Champagne
Sweepstake Tickets
Old Masters
Guns
Cricket Bats.

In December he thanked those who had sent him lists of possible subscribers. Hundreds of them had already taken out their subscriptions. With his usual optimism he promised his old friends that with a little more help the magazine would not only survive but enter 'an unexampled era of prosperity and usefulness'. These were very difficult times but there was no choice. 'Defeatism is a poltroonish attitude and everyone should rally round.'[533]

In February 1933 Cecily and he returned to Switzerland. They stayed in the Victorian splendour of the Regina Hotel, Wengen. Something happened there that completely changed her feelings for him. Whatever it was, it was connected with his drinking. She kept all his letters and carefully numbered them in pencil on the envelopes. During the time in Switzerland, he wrote her three letters. She carefully numbered the envelopes 229, 230 and 231. Letter 230 is missing, destroyed or lost. Curiously, she moved from room 5 to room 8 at some time between the letters, perhaps moving from adjoining rooms.[534] What she did preserve is a long list in pencil of complaints about his behaviour which she may or may not have sent. In it she told him that he was ruining his life, losing old friends and not making any new ones. She lamented his terrible weakness for alcohol. Cutting down on his drinking was the one thing she had asked him to do – and he had not done it. He became a different man drunk: opinionated and boastful; a social embarrassment.

When they returned to London, without cutting him out of her life so surgically, she became unavailable. She did not answer his telephone calls, she went away for long periods without letting him know, and she did not answer the invitations he showered upon her. Jack knew how angry she was, but told her that if she left him he would still love her devotedly. The prospect of parting from her had been in the back of his mind from the start, but now it became real. He promised that he was now a reformed character; he told her he had given up drinking and vowed not to visit the Savile Club where temptation lay. He kept on writing love letters, signing them, 'Your own, even when you don't want him, Jack.' And, 'Forgive, Forgive, Forgive.' He compared their lives: 'Your life, if a little cramped, is settled. Mine is lonely and passionate and a gamble. If I am not adequate discard me.' He reminded her of happier times: dinner at the swankiest restaurant in London, the Blue Train; Lake Lucerne with the Jungfrau in the distance; walking from Macmillan's along Jermyn Street to the Ritz for dinner and pinning a bunch of violets to her furs. He sent her lilies for her birthday. He bought a new suit and had his hair cut. He was getting up at six in the morning and working all day. 'For months,' he wrote, 'I've thought of nothing but winning back your respect.' He dedicated *Outside Eden*, a collection of his short stories, to Cecily Severne. But for her the affair was over.

A series of poems in his final volume of poetry chart the loss. In 'Winter Midnight' the rhyming participles and repetitions drag out the nagging pain:

> The wind in the woods is moaning to-night,
> The boughs of the pine-trees are groaning to-night,
> The creaks of the hollies
> Rebuke all our follies,
> The skies a long dirge are intoning to-night.

Oh, I would I were dreamlessly sleeping to-night,
Where Death all our dreams would be keeping to-night,
Not regretfully longing
Over mutual wronging,
Awake lying, hopelessly weeping to-night.[535]

In 'Change' he wonders: 'Why should she be so changeable, what sin / Have I committed that she frowns on me / Who am innocent of change?' 'A Love Returned' is a poem with a sad ironical twist. It begins, 'Oh, once I had a love, / She left me long ago, / She flew to Heaven away / While I stood dumb below.' The final stanza apparently brings a happy reunion 'But now, by blissful chance, / She is in my arms again, / Hugged to my heart most desperately...' But the final line springs a terrible surprise: 'And her sweetest name is Pain!'

'Long Ago' is the epitaph for their love affair. In the first stanza Squire writes of Cecily's beauty; her ravishing voice, her small shoulders and slender form – but most of all, 'How strangely am I haunted by your hair!' The poem ends:

I see it everywhere: in every street
It flames across the faces of the crowd,
Streaming and challenging, as odorous sweet
As was the Queen of Love's ambrosial cloud:
And billowing wide, the glory of it lights
The darkness of my solitary nights.

On King George's birthday, 3 June 1933, Squire was knighted for services to literature. He was '<u>deluged</u>' with congratulations. He got letters from friends of thirty years back: 'I didn't know until this event... how much unreleased and unsuspected love there was lying about in the world,' he told his friend the art dealer and historian Yvonne ffrench. 'Bless thee, Bottom, thou art translated,' wrote the *Westminster Gazette*. Eileen did not hear the news till the night before and fled the storm of publicity. She told the Telephone Exchange to put the line out of service and retired to an unknown address in the country to enjoy the June heat, lazing in the garden with no telephone, no news, no letters – and no husband. She told a friend she felt 'a bit overloaded by such a ridiculous title' and a bit silly, but had no doubt that Jack would be able to live up to the title of 'Sir John' easily. He had deserved it for his various works, including saving Stonehenge, she thought.

Perhaps Jack recalled his earlier comment, 'The knighted litterateur, as a rule, is either a second-rate man or a man long past his prime.'[536] Perhaps he remembered too that he had written that he did not know why a distinguished writer wanted a knighthood 'unless he is poor, and thinks that a title would add a guinea or two per thousand to the price of his work.' That was what was on his mind when he told his sister that the title was bound to make a 'practical difference.'[537] He went to the College of Arms to sign the Roll of Knights Bachelor. There they suggested that, punning on his surname, he should 'revive' the family arms of a squirrel sejant. He was interested and discussed details. Finally, they told him the cost would be £76 10s. 'My Christ,' he said, 'do you suppose I've got £76 10s? If I ever have, we'll do it.'[538]

By June 1933 Squire's literary fortunes had sunk as low as his financial ones. The combined attacks on him, the Georgians and the *Mercury* led even that mildest of men, Edmund Blunden, to attack the modernists: 'I have long detested the self-seeking detractors of *Georgian Poetry* and E. M. [Marsh] – indeed their noise has proceeded from a want of personal acquaintance with the books and their editor. Still, they should have an occasional correction...'[539] Like Squire, Sassoon felt out of touch with the poetry of his time. He wrote to Edmund Blunden complaining that he was discouraged 'by the autocracy of Eliot under which we exist and are ignored.' He added that he was now seen 'as an ex-war poet, leaving the fashionable world to re-Joyce with Joyce, compound with Pound, cavort with Quartets, make dates with Yeats and roister with Morgan Forster.'[540] The whirligig of time had brought in its revenges.

At last Squire was beginning to accept that he had taken on too much. His paid work of reviewing, newspaper articles and numerous forewords and introductions meant that he had not time for the *London Mercury* ménage. As ever the basket was full of unanswered correspondence. Growing heaps of manuscripts lay unread on his desk. The year ended with Cecily and her brother enjoying a Christmas skiing holiday without him in Switzerland in the luxury of the Bellevue Hotel, Kleine Scheidegg. Thinking back to the two holidays he had spent in Switzerland with her he wrote:

> Yet though the spring be sunless,
> And void of swish of ski,
> For Bear in Bear-pit sunless
> He'll drink in memory
> Of days when Cecily left him
> To sail the wastes of snow,
> And she, when she'd bereft him
> Would hang around below,
> Still nursing his preposterous hopes
> Upon the Wengen nursery slopes.

'Bear' was a reminder of how he had signed his love letters.

He spent his own holiday with his family in 'that wretched house' in Hampstead. On Christmas Day Eileen was in a state of fury, suffering from a '*crise de nerfs*' that sent her to bed in tears. Boxing Day was a gloomy trip to *Iolanthe* at Golders Green Hippodrome. The following day Jack returned to a bitter cold, foggy, half-empty London. Then he caught the flu.

Chapter 23

Weepings and Wailings

The New Year of 1934 began badly. Priestley wrote that Squire no longer lived with his family who were terribly hard up and was becoming a 'mysterious and pathetic figure.'[541] Squire was suffering from insomnia. Reading small print had left his eyes like two blazing fires – his oculist told him that for the last year he had been using a totally wrong prescription. As a heavy smoker he suffered badly from catarrh; the doctor advised him to give up Player's cigarettes and take to the much duller ones that had 'wool stuffed down the near end of the orifice'. His appearance was showing the strain. 'He peered at you through heavy lenses. He was untidy and usually looked as if he had shaved himself with a blunt razor eighteen hours before,' wrote Alec Waugh.

As the slump of the thirties deepened, both communism on the Russian model and Mosley's brand of English fascism were gaining adherents. Squire began to think that democracy was failing. 'The British democracy, all my life, has been living in a Fool's Paradise. It did not listen to Lord Roberts' call for Universal Service or Admiral Jackie Fisher: Ypres and Passchendaele followed. Churchill also preached in the wilderness. The Fool's Paradise leads to a Hell on Earth.'[542] He felt that politicians had betrayed the soldiers who had died in the war. In 'Armistice Eve 1932' he had written of his own survivor guilt and shame:

Silence across the earth creeps with the sun;
Traffic will end, the crowds stand voiceless still,
Bugles will wail a dirge for things fordone,
And echoes of old death the air fulfil.
And we all standing, for two minutes thinking,
Left for two minutes with ourselves alone,
Must face our lives full of remorse and shrinking,
Comparing their endeavour and our own.[543]

So began Squire's flirtation with right-wing politics. He was never an admirer of Hitler, but like many of his generation, including Hilaire Belloc and Winston Churchill he did admire Mussolini's leadership. Like Bernard Shaw he thought that the Italian version of fascism was better than the capitalism that had brought poverty, unemployment and financial chaos. The journalist and Catholic politician Douglas Jerrold was advocating strong leadership and also looked to Mussolini's Italy as an example of the modern state. He hated the greed and materialism of mainstream conservatism. Squire joined him to write a two-page pamphlet asking Conservative members of the House of Commons to organise propaganda in the country on behalf of true 'Conservative Principles'. He wrote to Hugh Walpole to suggest that he might sign an 'Appeal' to help. Walpole replied he could no longer think on the old party lines. 'This is an experience that many people are having. I wish I were sure of my views – but there it is – I am at present a wretched parti-coloured creature!'[544] T. S. Eliot was also asked to sign the appeal but replied he could not because the main opponent of conservatism was the Conservative party – and also because he could not support Jack Squire.

Squire did not see fascism and socialism as polar opposites: both promised to share the rewards of labour more fairly. He liked to quote Dr Johnson's dictum that the only test of a government was the provision it made for the poor. The common enemy, as always, was the rich capitalist, as he had been back in Squire's Fabian days. 'What I *really* think', he wrote to Cecily, 'is that capitalism – a monstrous ugly growth anyhow – has broken down; the system simply does not work. The problem is whether something can be devised which will be an alternative to State Socialism, which would be equally inefficient and drab to a degree. Some organization on a world-basis – world-currency, world regulation of staple production, guaranteeing a living to producers etc. etc. – must come unless all is to go to ruin.'[545]

Squire became one of the founder members of the January Club and was soon elected its Chairman. The Club was set up on New Year's Day 1934 by Oswald Mosley, another ex-Fabian, whom the *Daily Mail* called 'the paramount political personality in Britain.'[546] To Squire it was a discussion group made up of independent thinkers who confronted the problems of the times, more like a Cambridge debating society than a mouthpiece for fascism and Mosley. He did not think that his position committed him to any kind of fascism, and always called members of the Club 'enquirers'. In a letter to *The Times* on 22 March 1934 he stated that the Constitution's aims were to bring together men interested in 'modern methods of government', to offer a platform for 'the leaders of Fascist and Corporate State thinking', and to learn the views of non-fascists. The membership at this time covered a wide spectrum of views: aristocratic Tories, Labour supporters, Jews, admirers of Germany and Italy, and indeed fascists of both the Italian and German kind. The only common ground was a general concern about the state of the nation and a distrust of democracy.

Squire had no sympathy for Russian communism, but he had no sympathy for Germany and Hitler either. He sympathised with the exasperated Hilaire Belloc who always talked of 'Prussians and Germans', but he did not always make the distinction himself. For four years of the war his friends had agreed with him about the Prussian threat but they had forgotten the lesson. Now many of them had become shocked back into sense. He was horrified by Nazi barbarism which he (wrongly) conflated with Prussian militarism: 'the Prussians are killing Jew shopkeepers and keeping unconvicted prisoners in <u>chains</u>.'[547] He told Cecily that 'Prussians had the sentimentality of the Teuton and the savagery of the Slav.' One 'fact' that had become obvious to him during the First World War was the nature of the Prussian character. Cecily and her friends called him prejudiced, but he insisted in private that the Prussian 'worshipped Odin and Thor and the Sword'. His ideas of race, he said, were the result of scientific observation and not, he insisted to her, prejudice. 'Politicians and revolutions come and go; alliances are formed and cease; marks and francs go through their strange and unintelligible performances; but the races of men retain their characteristics like the races of dogs. To realize this is the beginning of international wisdom.'

The January Club was soon riven with its own disputes. Squire was chairman for one of the first meetings in January 1934. After the Labour MP Kenneth Lindsay had given 'a superb and critical speech' an official from the British Union of Fascists gave an hour-long tub-thumping harangue. He was offensive about ghettos and insulted Squire's guest, Geoffrey de Freitas, President of the Cambridge Union, on account of his foreign name. Some Jewish members, including the biographer Philip Magnus, resigned on the spot and stalked out. Squire was disgusted. He felt that only his diplomacy managed to keep the warring parties apart and that 'this most interesting club' might have to be dissolved if BUF speakers continued to be invited and behaved in this way. In May the Club held a 'Black Shirt Dinner' at the Savoy. Squire was photographed in white tie and carnation. William Joyce (later Lord Haw Haw) was the only man wearing the blackshirt uniform to be seen. The *Tatler* reported 'a very serious argument between the two main speakers, Oswald Mosley and the radical Tory historian Sir Charles Petrie.'

'The Fascist thing grows and grows,' he told Cecily in May. At its peak the British Union of Fascists could claim more than 34,000 supporters: Mosley had spoken to a crowd of 7,000 in Birmingham. Squire felt he would lose all the support he had if he continued 'flag-wagging and did not discipline his followers and prevent them from wicked appeals to crude hate and suspicion of the foreigner. Their slogan was Britain first, the Dominions second and the foreigner nowhere. Squire called the first two obvious, but the last had 'a beastly spirit' behind it. He was sure great changes were afoot, but if he himself had been in charge 'we should not in England beat Jews, placard girls or give people castor oil, but it is the way the world is going.'

After violent scenes in June at Oswald Mosley's rally at Olympia events came to a head. At a dinner held by the Monday Club at the Cavalry Club the secretary of the British Union of Fascists gave a violent hate-filled speech. In Piccadilly afterwards he met the novelist Cecil Roberts who asked what he thought about the meeting. 'I'd sooner take rat poison than join up with a fellow like that... Who the Hell is the reptile anyway?' Squire replied.[548] The scales began to fall from Squire's eyes. He was still trying to see the January Club as a civilised debating society. Characteristically, he set about organising a Ladies' Night. Not surprisingly, his membership did not outlast the year. Squire 'found the atmosphere uncongenial before long.'[549] According to Charles Petrie, who also resigned in 1934, Squire found it intolerable once it finally became clear the club had become the voice of Oswald Mosley and the British Fascist Party.[550]

To Squire there was no longer any clear ideology that offered hope. He told Cecily, 'I have seen too much of practical life to think Utopians much good who get notions out of books and dreams, unless they are saints and the books inspired.' His generation talked about Utopias but bequeathed posterity nothing but slums and a ruined countryside, he told her. Other Fabians who had looked to the state for social reform were also looking in different directions: eugenics was the fashionable pseudoscience, fascism and Stalinism were both tempting logical extensions of the strong state. H. G. Wells went to Russia to meet Stalin: 'I never met a man more candid, fair and honest.' Bernard Shaw, who had admired Mussolini's achievements, had Stalin's photograph on his bedside table till he died... Squire, by contrast, began to toy with the idea of the return to some kind of aristocratic government. He thought the peerage was essentially comic make-believe, but that it had its uses. In a time of revolutionary ideas it was a good thing that 'the mob through the magic of names should believe that it is being governed by superior beings out of fairy-tales.' He was appalled at the parliamentary debate in 1934 where the Tory 'goats' led by Lord Salisbury compromised with the democrats over the hereditary principle. 'Silly modern democratic views' were peddled by aristocrats who should have been defending an older principle. They tried to deal with revolution without any conviction: the only proper way to fight it was with a counter-revolution. He was quite sure he could make a better defence of tradition than the one offered in the House of Commons. As it was, the best brains trained for the professions and let England be governed by 'the vast remnant of brainless tradesmen.' In a complete volte-face, he told Cecily, 'Kipling was <u>always</u> right.'

How did the Fabian radical thinker of his *New Age* and *New Statesman* days come, twenty years later, to become an admirer of Mussolini and Chairman of the January Club? One answer is that Squire was never a coherent political thinker. Unlike the Webbs, he had no political theory. He had strong emotions that were stirred by radical causes: his socialism was of the heart not the head. Unfair treatment of women, hypocritical millionaires, bloated capitalists, Big Business, cruelty to animals and jingoism all angered him. The events of the thirties did not change his basic ideas: he simply swapped from the radicalism of the left to a flirtation with the radicalism of the right.

Just as his affair with Cecily was coming to an end, so was his editorship of the *London Mercury*. Squire's high hopes for the 'Shilling Mercury' were dashed when even with a rise in circulation to 20,000 copies the crucial advertising revenue did not materialise. Then the circulation dropped steadily to 4,000. The receivers were called in. They made an inventory and asked him which items belonged to the magazine and which to him. On their list was: 'No. 26. Stuffed Bird in glass case, badly broken.' It was, he told Cecily, 'The Mercury Totem, the Goose!' He offered it to Cecily but she turned it down. She was not interested in the Victorian case of stuffed hummingbirds either...

Two of the *Mercury*'s leading backers, Owen Hugh Smith, a governor of the Bank of England, and Squire's old friend Iolo Williams, began to separate him from his magazine. In December he was moved out of the office to two small rooms in the top of an evacuated vicarage in Burleigh Street, Covent Garden, with no telephone and no office boys. He said to his accounts manager Edgar Pink that the thought of moving to another building made him feel miserable. 'Don't you worry about that, Sir John. We shall none of us ever lose touch with you.' 'Bless him,' wrote Squire.

Enormously relieved to be free from all responsibilities for the financial state of the company, he was full of hope. 'I may find a peace I haven't known for several years... I shall <u>never</u> have to worry about the business side of the Mercury any more... No more balance sheets! What bliss! No more board meetings! How lovely!' If he felt he was still going to be in charge of the magazine, he was wrong. In September 1934 his name disappeared from the masthead. There was no mention of his leaving but the principal backer had had enough. He had lost confidence in his editor – as well as a great deal of money. On 4 September *The Times* announced: 'Sir John Squire has resigned the editorship of the *London Mercury*, which he founded in 1919 and has edited ever since. Sir John Squire is retiring in order to devote himself to creative work.' In October he was replaced by R. A. Scott-James who immediately announced a change of course by printing articles by Wyndham Lewis and E. M. Forster.

Squire told Cecily he was 'keeping his pecker up', but he knew he had suffered a humiliating defeat. He wrote to Priestley lamenting the 'excruciating anguish and the ruined lives' that the loss of the *Mercury* had caused. He was 'touched to the heart' by a commiserating letter from Edward Davison in America and replied:

> I <u>loathed</u> letting the *Mercury* go – but it had ruined me financially –
> I hadn't taken a penny for many years, and with my eyes troubling
> me as well as my creditors I *had* to fade out. I'm sorry that I wasn't
> given by the chief debenture holder a chance of passing it on to
> Shanks or somebody else who would have continued my tradition.
> The *Mercury* is dead and something else is bearing its name. I didn't

mind writing my books and poems by proxy. I never wanted fame and was content if I could but leave (as I shall) a few good poems behind me. But bankruptcy would ruin my family.'[551]

Squire's role as the editor of the *London Mercury* has been neglected until recently.[552] In its heyday, the monthly sold up to 20,000 copies and had an international following. His reputation was not confined to England. It spawned a sister magazine, the *American Mercury*, edited by H. L. Mencken. The *Chicago Tribune* wrote, 'Mr. Squire is unquestionably the most read of the younger English literary critics.'[553] In Mysore the young writer R. K. Narayan got his bright orange copy every month and thought of J. C. Squire as his neighbour.[554] According to a Canadian critic, 'No living poet has a wider influence on the views and tendencies of his age.'[555] Looking back on Squire's life, an 'Old Friend', Iolo Williams, wrote in *The Times*, 'Both as editor and publisher's reader (he was a reader of genius, who must have recommended an immense number of manuscripts for publication) he exercised great power in the literary world. Indeed, in the 1920s he was – as reviewer, essayist and editor – the outstanding literary journalist, with the ball at his feet.'[556] But if the *Mercury* made Squire's reputation, it also exhausted and bankrupted him.

Squire was thinking of starting again with a new magazine to be called the 'London Phoenix'. This time it would not be exclusively literary and would be run on commercial lines – but the phoenix never rose from the flames. He decided to leave London and retire to the country. As usual, he was optimistic. He told his sister, 'It's like getting out of prison & I may even become rich through doing what I want to after 30 years' servitude.'[557] He added that he hoped to 'get through the tunnel and write a few final masterpieces.' Frank Swinnerton thought that Squire was at last free to devote his time to poetry, and writing the work for which he would probably be best remembered – his autobiography.[558] When he reached fifty, he had begun to write it. But in the end the chronological account never came about: it was not his style. 'I found that I simply could not do it, beginning at the Year One, and flogging through elections, dinner parties, and important people.' Another problem was the sheer amount of material he had hoarded over the years – fifty great boxes of letters and diaries, enough for twenty volumes, he promised.

The Silver Jubilee in May 1935 was a time of great national celebration. London was decorated with flags and ceremonial arches; huge crowds saw King George and Queen Mary wave from the balcony of Buckingham Palace and roared their approval. Squire was a great admirer of the King and loved all the pageantry. Still haunted by the first war, he feared a second might be on the way, but history gave him hope that all would be well in the end. The nation had faced crises and calamities before. Above all, he had a patriotic sense that England would put aside divisions and face the enemy as a united nation under King George. His poem 'The Sailor King' was published in the *Sunday Times*. As he wrote in 'After the Jubilee: 1935': 'And still whatever the chemists may brew, and the men who add the sums, / Though the mean malign, and the pampered pine, there are flags in the heart of the slums.'

Five months after the Jubilee celebrations Mussolini invaded Abyssinia. As one of the original members of the League of Nations Society, founded in 1914 by his friend Aneurin Williams, Squire was surprisingly unconcerned. On his wandering journey round England in 1936 he described how he had met a major in a Salisbury hotel who took a grimly prophetic view of the future: 'It seemed to be getting brighter before this chap Musso began breathing fire and slaughter against those damned Abyssinians… But damn it all, they're in the League, and if people start breaking treaties at this hour of the day what the devil is the good of making them. Pity! A year ago Musso seemed the soundest of the lot. Now they're only waiting for the rains to stop and hell will be let loose. Another wretched European war I suppose.'[559] Squire dismissed the major's views and simply told him how his meeting with Mussolini had shown him as sympathetic and human. Anyway, he thought that English people did not care about the invasion, but were frightened that if the Italians suffered a setback Hitler would become more aggressive in Europe.

In early January 1936 Squire wrote to Eileen that he had, in just the last week lost the three people he most admired: his brother-in-law Clennell, Rudyard Kipling and King George V. Squire's elegy appeared in *The Times*:

Another pageant must thread the streets and the flags are half-mast
>   high;
And all the way the folk will be mute as the Dead King goes
>   thereby,
Who served and suffered and seldom spoke, and then spoke better
>   than all,
Whose voice was heard but a bare month hence, and is now
>   beyond reach,
Like all the voices of all the dead, that deep rich voice is gone,
And the father's wrinkled smile, and sailor's eyes that kindly shone
The steadfast heart forever is still, and there is no other thing
Empire and people can say today but these: God Save the King.[560]

After living for six years without a salary Squire was being pursued by debt. 'I am up to my neck in worries,' he confided to Cecily. His main income now came from being senior publisher's reader for Macmillan where he had a small office. With a nose for a successful book, he could still turn over manuscripts and proofs with speed and insight. He picked out Thornton Wilder's *The Bridge over San Luis Rey* when all British publishers had rejected it. It won Wilder a Pulitzer Prize and began his career. His biggest scoop, however, was *Gone with the Wind*. He loathed reading galley proofs, cumbersome long slips that covered two and a half pages, but when he saw Margaret Mitchell's novel he was sure that Macmillan's had to take it. He carried an armful of galleys down to Daniel Macmillan's office saying, 'You have a best-seller here. Don't hesitate. Print it, and your fortunes will be made.'[561] He wrote, 'This novel is about 420,000 words long – equal in length to six ordinary novels – and it is about the American Civil War & the background of it in the South. Could anything sound more unpromising? But, although the author's style is no more than good and efficient, and although her central character, Scarlett O'Hara, is a selfish &, to the reader, unattractive, girl, there isn't a line that isn't interesting... when one finishes one feels that one has left a circle of people whom one has known all one's life.' He went on to say that this book just might have a success in America 'comparable to that of *Anthony Adverse* (a popular novel of 1933) and that it ought to sell in Britain if the reviewers could be persuaded to read it.'[562] Macmillan duly published *Gone with the Wind* and it became a worldwide bestseller.

Squire supplemented his income by becoming a literary Jack-of-all-trades, editing, rehashing anthologies and publishing his own essays and broadcasts. He edited the poems of Flecker and the letters of John Freeman. He wrote the introduction to the catalogue of the library of Wadham College, Oxford compiled by his old bibliophile friend Henry Wheeler. There were numerous introductions to all kinds of books from the architecture of golf courses to the history of billiards. He wrote a detailed description of the Hall of the Institute of Chartered Accountants, edited a collection of *Times* leaders and an anthology of poetry for schools. Sometimes out of the blue a chance to make money turned up, as when the BBC asked him to do a poem for the first page of the Christmas number of the *Radio Times* on the theme of 'King and Christmas.' They wanted seven stanzas and paid £200. He thought the invitation vulgar – 'like ordering a cut off the joint' – but agreed. He even appeared in an advert in the *Daily Herald* for 'Fifty Shilling Suits' from the 'Rational Tailor'. Members of the Savile and the Athenaeum Clubs went up to him and started pinching the cloth of his jacket asking if it was real and where he had got it from. But despite advertisements, regular journalism and countless book introductions many bills remained unpaid.

One more substantial venture sprang from Squire's love of cheese. Squire's championship of English cheese reflected his love of all things rural and traditional. A Frenchman wrote to *The Times* complaining that he could not find any Stilton in England and bemoaned the lack of interest or knowledge that the English had about their native cheese. As a habitual letter writer to *The Times*, Squire suggested that the inventor of Stilton, 'this noble fragrant cheese, the cheese of poets,' should have a statue erected to her. T. S. Eliot replied, praising Squire for his 'manly and spirited defence' of the cheese, but contesting Stilton's claims. Wensleydale was the 'Mozart of cheeses'. In any case, a statue was not a good idea: 'A Society for the Preservation of Ancient Cheeses' was the way forward. (Squire was of course a keen supporter of the Society for the Protection of Ancient Buildings.) 'But this is no time for disputes between eaters of English cheese: the situation is precarious and we must stick together.' The appreciation of cheese was perhaps the only thing the two men could agree upon.

Cheddar Gorge, a Book of English Cheeses[563] emerged in 1937 for ten shillings and sixpence. The editor, Squire himself, wrote on Stilton and asked Vyvyan Holland, Oscar Wilde's son, to write on Cheshire, André Simon on Blue Vinny, and Ambrose Heath on Wensleydale. Each contributor was sent off to tour the region of their cheese, visit farmers and dairies and talk to the cheesemakers. The book becomes a series of journeys through England from Devon to Yorkshire, celebrating the countryside and its traditional crafts. The 'quite lovely' illustrations of rural life were by E. H. Shepard. Squire thought them 'the most English things of our generation,' far superior to his 'Christopher Robin stuff'.

Betty Wilson, a young journalist with a rather breathless style, was sent from the *Western Morning News and Daily Gazette* to write a homes and gardens piece about a famous Devonian.[564] She was greeted by Lady Squire and shown round 18 Rosslyn Hill. Both the house 'in the peacefulness of old Hampstead' and her hostess charmed her. Eileen was now the chatelaine. There was so much for Betty Wilson to admire: solid oak furniture, red oilskin curtains in the sitting room, a light fawn carpet and a little gem of a corner cupboard which housed a collection of floral liqueur glasses. The dining room had whale-backed chairs, a gate-legged table and an oak sideboard covered with brass and silver.

It all reminded Betty of an old country house. Jack's presence was, she thought, everywhere, from the book-lined walls, to the English watercolours, and the china spirit barrels. Upstairs in the main bedroom she noted Eileen's influence in the primrose walls, green curtains and ultra-fashionable twin beds. In Jack's 'den' were a signed portrait of Hilaire Belloc by James Gunn and photos of Jack's friends and heroes: Edmund Gosse, Maurice Hewlett, and Professor George Saintsbury. In the middle stood a photo of the Invalids surrounding a spectacularly overdressed G. K. Chesterton in black cloak and hat. Lady Squire assured the journalist that what she saw was only a fragment of the family's furniture and furnishings; the rest was in storage. Betty Wilson could only wonder about the house they had left in the Home Counties and the magnificent country mansion that Eileen would fill with all her lovely things when they came out of the store. She took one more peep at the 'Christmas-card' dining room and left.

Of course, it was all a fiction. There was no mansion and very little money. They had been tenants, not owners of the house in Surrey, and they were still tenants. The furniture in storage did not exist. Jack hated the modern pokiness of the red-brick villa. '*Per ardua ad aspidistra*,' he commented. It was a little box, surrounded by pleasant hills, 'but Lord give me the country or Mayfair.' He never wrote a word in the writing room Eileen had set up for him. 'History repeats itself,' she wrote sadly.

In November 1938, after thirty years of marriage, they finally split up. They divided the furniture and their pictures. 'Take anything you like,' he said. 'You are the soul of generosity,' she replied. He decided he had to stay on until his rental agreement ran out. Eileen rented a flat in Chelsea. He hated being alone in the half-stripped, echoing house and began to look for a studio where he could entertain his friends. He finally found a fourth-floor flat in Earl's Court where he had no pictures, photographs or books. In summer it was like an oven. Just as his father had done almost fifty years before, he had deserted his wife and the family home.

Squire now began to live a drifting semi-vagrant life in London at the Savile Club, with friends and in the country and with Miss Warrender. There, in her large Victorian house, 'ugly but full of flowers', attended to by a cook and several maids, he could escape at the weekends to write and read undisturbed. She set aside a bedroom and a room for him to write in. By December he was regaining his confidence and then, in the spring, he took the longest holiday of his life, to Lake Como. He went alone.

On New Year's Eve he had dinner with his artistic friends Anne and Christopher Fremantle who drove him back to the Savile Club, deserted except for the travel writer Robert Byron. It seemed to him a desolate place. As the midnight chimes struck they raised glasses to each other. The toast was: 'Better luck next year.'

Chapter 24

Winter Nightfall

1939 began with a series of misadventures and sometimes farcical disappointments. Out of the blue Squire received some poems from a prisoner serving time in Dartmoor for house-breaking, Frank Arthur Stanley. Squire, convinced by Stanley's claims that his mental illness had been ignored and that he had been victimised by prison officers, began a correspondence with him. He wrote detailed criticisms of the penal system and the injustice of Stanley's treatment. Released from Dartmoor, Stanley very soon got into trouble again and appeared before a judge at the Old Bailey. In court Squire pleaded for leniency. Sir Holman Gregory, the Recorder of London, ruled that probation was better than prison and talked of the extraordinary kindnesses that Stanley had been shown by his supporters. Squire waited outside the courtroom and told a journalist, 'There is every reason to believe he will write a good book.' Stanley was installed in the basement of Squire's home and began work as his manservant.

The arrangement worked well until Squire sent Stanley to the bank to cash a cheque for £12. He cashed it – and disappeared. Squire reluctantly called the police and Stanley appeared on 19 September 1939 before the magistrate Sir Gervais Rentoul, who read his sixteen previous convictions and noted 'one of the worst records I have ever had before me'. Squire told the magistrate that Stanley had been working hard for him and had published a book before he committed the crime: 'If you will deal leniently with him, I am prepared to take charge of him and see that he is medically treated.' Sir Gervais remarked that Squire's offer was extremely generous. He told the accused that if it had not been for his offer, he would have received the maximum sentence.

Immediately, Squire sent one of the 'Convict Poet's' poems to the *Daily Sketch*. 'Fancy' was published on the Saturday following the hearing. Over the weekend several readers wrote in to say that they thought they had read the poem before. It was an almost exact copy of 'Daisies', written by an American poet in *A Treasury of Verse for Little Children*. 'I cannot believe I have been hoaxed,' said Sir John. 'I cannot say anything until I have seen my secretary tomorrow morning. The poems that I gave out were among other matter. It may be that I have got this one mixed up with something else.' After this, Stanley disappeared from his employment and the next record of him is an attempt to defraud the Post Office by forging his bank book. At his trial the author proudly produced a book of his own poems dedicated to Sir Holman Gregory, the Recorder of London, prefaced by a laudatory essay by Sir John Squire. He was sent down for six months.

Squire still had grand, even grandiose, literary ambitions. He started work on his magnum opus on Shakespeare, which he thought might be half a million words long, some short stories and the first volume of his autobiography, which he promised to deliver by Christmas. Another poetic burst was, he hoped, about to come. Perhaps it was all to the good that he had left his major works till now – pain and rejection would enrich them. No more hack work and an author's life at last! He could do 1,000 words of autobiography a day. All the books would be finished and 'goodness knows what else will spring forth from the unsealed wells.' No typist would be able to keep up with his pace. He told Cecily she was responsible for the success. No poet before had managed without money to keep surface respectability, bring up a family and give his children old school ties. At the age of fifty the said poet, he promised her, had now given up being middle class, which poets, great soldiers, great sailors and women never were, and was retiring into the country to write. After thirty years he felt that he was like a dog let off his chain. His head was full of lovely and profound things and he promised he was about to find again the sheer joy of writing.

Raglan urged his father to write a book of advice to his own children, Cecily's children and the youth of all nations telling them about religion, politics, war, peace and sex. Jack agreed that he simply must write something for all the young, 'chucked into this bewildering world'. He was a most unlikely Agony Uncle, but it was the kind of challenge that he was bound to like – and equally bound never to finish – or, in this case, start. There could be no doubt, however, about his energy and productivity: in one month alone, September 1935, he published three substantial books: *Shakespeare as a Dramatist, Reflections and Memories* and a collection of literary essays, *Flowers of Speech*.

Shakespeare as a Dramatist was the first of three planned volumes, which Squire hoped would become the great work of Shakespearean criticism. He relied on the advice of the dramatist and critic Harley Granville Barker. The *Times Literary Supplement* review was kind, but the critic and director George Rylands in *The Spectator* did not spare him in a woundingly sad review:

> Dr. Johnson or Lord Macaulay would have found words in which to dismiss this disastrous and unashamed publication... Without going so far as to ask where the great Achilles whom we knew is, we mourn the eclipse of the poet of talent, the parodist of genius, the journalist of long, too long experience. In the words of the immortal Sir John: Am I not fallen away vilely? Do I not bate? Do I not dwindle? I am withered like an old apple-john.'[565]

Squire's publisher, Hodder's, offered him £200 to cancel the contract for two more books. He accepted immediately and told his agent to contact Heinemann, but no more was heard of the half-million words.

The knighthood and retirement of Edward Marsh from politics formally marked the end of the Georgian movement. On 17 March 1937, 140 guests attended a Presentation Dinner at the Mayfair Hotel to celebrate. Four of the leading Georgians headed the writers' tables: Lascelles Abercrombie, Laurence Binyon, John Drinkwater and Jack Squire.[566] Winston Churchill, the main speaker from the top table, proposed the toast, 'Eddie Marsh, the man', and declared to laughter and applause that if there were a Ministry of All the Talents those present would be the cabinet and Marsh the prime minister. It was jolly enough. But for the poets it was more of a delayed funeral than a party.

In May 1938 Squire stepped off the pavement in Regent Street straight into the path of a police car. After an argument he started to tell the police how he had been wrongfully arrested twice as a young man. He became belligerent, was arrested for being drunk and disorderly and spent the night in a cell. Once released, he went home and read 'a shocker', thinking that the whole incident was over. Two days later he received a letter telling him that he had failed to surrender to his bail. He had no recollection of bail being asked for or even mentioned but to avoid publicity he pleaded guilty, as his solicitor advised, to the charge of being drunk. He was fined a shilling for the offence (the least possible amount, he said, just like a farthing damages) and ten and sixpence for doctor's expenses. This was not a story he could easily tell Cecily. He told her his behaviour made the police think he was mad and so they had to take him to the station. The incident of course only confirmed what she already knew – in a word Squire thought she could only have learnt from the American writer Damon Runyon, she accused him of being 'bottled'. He continued to write her love letters, to send poems and remind her of the past. The letters gradually became less frequent as she did not answer the telephone or accept any of his invitations despite his promises that he had become a reformed character: 'I've gone through Hell these last few years,' he pleaded.

Squire described *The Honeysuckle and the Bee*, the first volume of his memoirs, as 'a prelude to a more chronological set of recollections'. It was the first book that he had deliberately addressed to a large public, written in the style of a man talking to a casual stranger. 'It is the best thing I have done,' he confided to Cecily. He was appalled when the newspaper he hated most, the *Daily Mail*, made it the 'Book of the Month'. The title came from a moment when, as a schoolboy, sitting in a mustard-yellow field on a summer afternoon, he heard the sound of the Tiverton town brass band drifting on the breeze. They were playing one of the hits from 1901, a popular Victorian music hall song: 'You are my honey, honeysuckle, / I am the bee...' The image was still clearly in his mind when he reviewed Osbert Sitwell's autobiography: 'He travels across countries or in libraries and then like a bee returns to his writing desk and distils his honey.'[567]

The framework of Squire's story was an eleven-day trip on horseback and foot from London to Devon, retracing many of the steps he had taken thirty years before as an undergraduate looking for work. Squire had certainly established his credentials as a serious walker – the 'Jorrocks of Fleet Street', if not a Super-Tramp. Sandwiched into his narrative were memories, anecdotes and poems as they came to mind, prompted by the events of the walk. It was a stream-of-consciousness travelogue. Spontaneous thoughts and memories were, he argued, the truest and most accurate way of recording a life and a personality. The final scene of his journey back into the past took him to Blundell's and School House as the present melted away. Once more he is in the sixth form:

A mist came in front of me and I saw forms long dead or strayed. Boys swarmed up the drive in strange bowler hats. Boys ran out at the news of motor-cars. Boys sat late in their studies drinking coffee. Boys told stories to each other in dark dormitories, creepy stories which made them spring up with stopped hearts when strange wailings came from gas-meter or radiator. Fags came from farms loaded with eggs, cream and flowers. People over beyond the Tower played fives. Others were in the tuck-shop. And Willy was there.[568]

Squire dedicated 'The Passion of Man: 1918–1937'[569] to the British Legion. It was a poem he dismissed as journalistic, but told Cecily was absolutely sincere. The savagery of the Sino-Japanese conflict and the Spanish Civil War – 'I bomb the babes in China, I rack them all in Spain' – could only lead to despair or laughter. In Squire's nightmare the tempter says, 'You only have to face / With a little cynic merriment the monstrous human face.' But Squire could recall the voice of a friend from the trenches with a quite different message:

We died, unhating, killed and died, that wars at last should cease,
And man, to fuller structure, grown, honour us Dead with Peace.

He was still hoping for peace when in January 1938 Hitler's 'hopefullest speech' was reported in *The Times*. He noted all the positive signs: roads were built, unemployment was low and the country was much more prosperous. A strong government certainly would not have allowed ribbon development, Squire added. Perhaps Hitler could lead his country into a growing European community... On the other hand, he seemed to want to revive the old Germany with its belief in the army, the state and the creed that Germany was God. The persecution of the Jews was an appalling sign. Only time would tell.[570] By July he had made up his mind. He was sure the Prussians were on the warpath again, as in Belgium in 1914. It was a pity, he wrote, that Bavaria could not split off from Germany and join Austria. At last the pro-Germans in England were coming round to a belief in 'Belgian atrocities'. Squire quoted Rudolf Hess that in a time of crisis, killing one out of ten was a good thing. He met the politician and diplomat Sir John Wheeler-Bennett who had dined with two men on the staff of Hitler's Vice-Chancellor von Papen who had drafted his speeches. Two days later they had been shot in their rooms in the Night of the Long Knives. Nobody knows, Squire added, whether Hitler signed the order to murder them.

Squire's second autobiographical work, *Water-Music, or a Fortnight of Bliss*, was published on the eve of the Second World War. A cross between the comedy of *Three Men in A Boat* and the Edwardian romance of the riverbank, *The Wind in the Willows*, it recounts another journey, this time by canoe, in the cold May of 1938. He and his seventy-three-year-old companion William Bliss travelled by canal from Oxford via the Cherwell, the Oxford canal, the river Avon and the upper reaches of the Thames – and then back to Oxford. It is a day-by-day story of how these two managed to get a canoe through broken locks and overgrown canals. Often they had to carry the canoe to the next stretch of navigable water.

Water-Music is a journey through a pastoral England, through Oxfordshire and Warwickshire. Squire always wanted to stop to view a country house, a church, or a public house that caught his fancy. The narrative mirrors the vagrant nature of the canals, rivers and streams, echoing a writer Squire admired, Lawrence Sterne, who said he 'wrote down one sentence and trusted God for the next'. Interspersed in the account of the journey are all kinds of material; the flora and fauna of the canal; scraps of an autobiography; reminiscences of childhood and his mother, of Cambridge and friends and places visited. The narrative constantly drifts from one form into another. Meeting a local in a pub is bound to produce a conversation… which leads on to a memory… which might lead on to a dialogue between Squire and his Devil… which leads on to… something else. The journey ended on the Thames near the Windrush and the Evenlode. At Bablock Hythe Squire thought of Matthew Arnold and 'The Scholar Gypsy', the wanderer who had been at the back of his mind throughout the trip.

Perhaps it was modesty about his own importance, or perhaps the dullness of a chronological format to a poet who thought in terms of images and memorable scenes, or perhaps it was the chaos of his life and papers that led Squire to this approach to autobiography. Finding and unearthing materials would certainly have been hard even for a highly organised man – and for Jack it was impossible. The elegiac tone reflects the fact that that canals themselves belonged to a more unhurried time, overtaken at first by the railway, and then the arterial road. They were survivors of a nearly lost world.

And as if this was not enough to sadden or disturb, Adolf Hitler cast his shadow over the whole trip. There were moments when he wondered whether it was worthwhile going on. 'I am writing this by a lock in a canal in Warwickshire. From the bottom of the lock I had a shouting conversation with the lockkeeper. I yelled, "Have you got your gas-mask?" He replied, "No, guv'nor. I 'ad a spot of that in the last war. Nowadays, if it isn't the weather it's another war… if there's goin' to be two or three more wars in my lifetime, I'd rather pass out quiet." There spoke the kindly, romantic Englishman… a man who would rather die on a mountain than kill another man.'[571] Squire compared Hitler with Stalin who 'butchers and robs thousands.' When he had retired to an inn and begun to read the cricket reports in the *Daily Mail,* a lorry driver came to the bar and started chatting. "'Ole Hitler, I reckon he's got to keep shouting to make 'em think he's doin' something." As Herr Hitler had just walked into Austria, I wondered what the speaker's notion of a deed was…' Squire's mind went back to the trip he had paid to Berlin and Germany just before the first war and his sense then that war was on the horizon. The chapter ends: 'There were line after line of dark crags and castles by the Rhine. It was 1914 and the kings were on their thrones.'[572]

In the book's final scene Squire returns home tired and happy. He is sitting on a veranda in the high Chilterns as the sun goes down and the moon rises in the approaching dusk. 'The end of the day was always the same as it was always different and little did it bother about us and all our self-torment and all our torment of others. Here was our mood,' says Squire, and ends with his sombre and Hardyesque poem, 'Crepuscular':

Pale in the east the moon wafts high,
By branches carven, black, at ease;
Southward a greying evening sky
Behind a row of poplar trees.

And in the west a bar of gold,
A burning rim that soon must wane,

While banks of lilac cloud enfold
A formless, sinking, ruby stain…

Yes, all this evening's vivid gold
Faded as now to even grey,
The wide unwitting waters rolled
Beneath the unchanging end of day.

And stars gleamed through the darkening air
Before there was a human heart
To solace, but they did not care
And will not care when men depart.[573]

Water-Music did not sell. In July Squire remarked bitterly to Alan Pryce-Jones that despite a grand press it was killed by 'the present state of paralysis agitans and the Mikado' (Hitler) as surely as his last one had been by the coronation. It was to be his last original book. The vogue for 'current and recent books' meant that, according to him, any book was dead in two months, unless it was a bestseller that went like a prairie fire. He did embark on a third volume of memories, a much more conventional and consecutive account. He first decided to call it 'The Flowers of the Forest' and then, to maintain the pattern of musical titles, 'Overture to the Valkyries'. Its theme was to be his Cambridge days. 'The older I get the less difficult I find retrospect to be,'[574] he wrote. However, when war broke out the project, like so many other things, had to be abandoned.

On the wireless he listened sceptically to Prime Minister Neville Chamberlain, 'too much like the Chairman of an Insurance Company', declare that he was going to meet Hitler the following day. He failed to announce any support for the Czechs, that 'small forsaken folk', and accepted the partition of their country. In a precisely timed poem: 'Eight o' Clock (1938 – Before Munich)' Squire, was full of foreboding:

Their thunder waits beyond the hills,
Nor yet their ravening fires they light:
Now, should it come that one man wills
The murder of the heavens to-night,
Shall it be ours to droop our hands
In shame, resigned once more to see
A small forsaken folk which stands
Awaiting its Thermopylae?[575]

There was popular relief and jubilation in England as war seemed averted. Winston Churchill, however, denounced the agreement and in early October Duff Cooper resigned as First Lord of the Admiralty. Squire shared their fears. He had no confidence in Chamberlain and thought that the government had the courage of mice. In October he flew to Prague for a fortnight. The city, he thought, was one of the most beautiful in the world and the people plucky and friendly, but, surrounded by Germany, they were besieged in their own capital. Only aeroplanes offered a way out. He found the overall situation fascinating, but ominous.

Finally convinced that war was inevitable, he told Cecily that everyone was fed up with the Germans. 'Men are too little for events when the wheels have started to rumble.' Everyone's mood was that life was not worth living in the shadow of Hitler's Berlin: 'For God's sake let's have a war now and get it over.'[576]

Chapter 25

Winter Midnight

On 1 September 1939 Hitler invaded Poland and two days later, on Maurice Squire's twenty-first birthday, war was declared. After the years of drifting *entre deux guerres* the British declaration of war stirred Squire to respond in *The Times* with a scathing attack on the BBC for its war coverage. As theatres and cinemas shut he feared that the BBC's obsession with the war and its 'mournful and moaning tones' would depress everyone in the war of nerves. News bulletins, he wrote, should be restricted to six and nine o'clock. In October he wrote to *The Times* again. He noted that, in sharp contrast to 1914, there was no enthusiasm for the war – but instead there was a steely resolution. He asked why they had published no war poetry. Robert Barrington-Ward, the deputy editor, replied that none had been published as none had been received. Squire determined to put that right. Asked by a journalist why there were no war poets – a common refrain – he replied: 'Because today they have no Jack Squire to shepherd them.[577] In a burst of poetic energy he broadcast on the wireless, and continued to write serious public poetry in *The Times* and topical satire in *Punch* for 'quick money'.

Frustrated once again from playing an active part in the war effort, Squire began training as a parashot in the Bucks Local Defence Force, later renamed the Home Guard. (After the successful parachute raids ahead of the main advance in France and Belgium it was feared that the same thing would happen in England. The parashots' role was to stand behind hedges and shoot down any invaders.) He felt part of a tradition that stretched back to train bands and local militia – volunteers who rose up in an emergency to defend their country. He regretted he had no uniform as yet and no arms, but he brought his own shotgun. As he had not been able to shoot pheasants that season, he said a German parachutist would be better than nothing.

He was proud that all three of his sons, Raglan, Anthony and Maurice, were joining up to do what their father had been unable to do in 1914. They were eager to get into uniform and fight in Finland against the Nazi-Soviet Pact Russians. 'To the Dead: November 11, 1918–1939' appeared on Armistice Day in *The Times*.

> Your Peace, she never came of age,
> That Peace you bought with bitter price;
> Nor now survives in this dull rage
> One sign of all your sacrifice.
>
> Your sons must arm again to do
> What all you, dying, thought you'd done...[578]

Squire wrote to Alan Pryce-Jones to say how frustrated he was not to have a part in what the government insisted on calling the war against the Nazis, which he thought should be called the war against the Germans. To lighten spirits he composed 'a very nice war song' for Hitler, with a refrain of 'Pack up your Goebbels in your old Kit-Bag / Heil, Heil, Heil' and 'What's the use of Goering?' The month after war was declared he wrote in *Punch*:

> The smoke rolls over Warsaw,
> In Prague they walk in fear,
> A thudding swarm of aeroplanes
> May shortly greet us here,

Athenia's hundred passengers
Lie quiet in the sea
But the gentle German people
Are just like you and me.

Now when our sons go overseas,
Remember this is true,
The Germans aren't responsible
For what the Nazis do
Those interfering Nazis love
To murder, steal and lie
But the nice kind German people
They would not hurt a fly.

But it will not be the Germans,
The Germans never arm,
They're fond of beer and Beethoven,
(Wherein resides their charm);
Some other bully will arise
And drive them on once more,
But it will not be the Germans' fault –
They loathe the thought of war.[579]

In a letter to *The Times* he celebrated the Finns' courage standing against the might of the Soviet Union: 'The defence of Finland has been the most heartening thing in modern history,' he wrote, quoting Tennyson: 'The glory or grief of a battle won or lost / Solders a race together...'[580] Poland's response was heroic too. They were the first nation to face the 'foul black tide' of German invaders:

When others wavered, hesitated,
About the price of being free
Shone in its glory unabated
The pride of your old chivalry.

By contrast he deplored the neutrals of Sweden, Belgium and Holland who were hanging on in the vain hope of peace and had no doubt that the 'Hounds of Hell' in the shape of the Hun and Adolf Hitler would destroy them. Thinking of the slow response of his own country to the war, he wrote: 'O Democracy, how many crimes are committed in thy name.' 'Oh this dear but slow England,' he complained to his sister, 'we could have had the Italians on our side long ago.'

Squire had hoped to spend the first Christmas of the war in Lincolnshire at a shooting party but he smashed up his knee in the blackout and had to spend the holiday in Chesham with Alice Warrender and some young German refugees. Maurice, on leave, looked desperately for his father all over London but could not find him. He left a note: 'Your minstrel boy is gone.' During the week Squire lived in a one-room flat at Palace Gate, Kensington and spent long weekends with Miss Warrender. Meanwhile, as his world collapsed around him, he was putting his poems together for his collected edition and, in one of his grander moments, assured his sister that 'If Christian civilization survives, my poems will.'[581]

In *The Times* Squire continued to write a stream of poems about the war as a heroic cause with clear heroes and clear villains; King Leopold of the Belgians was denounced as a coward. (A year later he came to regret these words and apologised in his column in the *Illustrated London News*.)

Squire saw France as a nation paralysed by political divisions, unable to meet the challenge of 'hordes from the East Lands'. But he looked back for reassurance to the heroism of Joan of Arc and a tradition of Western Christianity defended by:

Your old Kings,
Crusaders, dreamers, watching from the shades,
An endless pageant since your race began,
Now stand with England at the barricades
Shielding the Soul of Man.

The conflict was, he thought, as old as Europe itself: West against East; freedom against slavery; Christian against pagan; civilisation against barbarism.

'Sick at heart because of the thought of those savages who invented indiscriminate bombing, the machine-gunning of shopping women and the murder of drowning soldiers',[582] he continued to use his wartime journalism to boost morale, especially when he became aware that not everyone shared his views. 'I was walking home at midnight in the black-out, and heard at the corner of Park Lane and Piccadilly thin young men whispering to every passing soldier: "All wars are made by capitalists" – the said young men probably believing what they said (though they may have changed their tune after Russia was attacked), while every boy one knew was donning uniform to do, and perhaps to die, not for dividends, but for decency.'

French and British troops in Calais halted the German advance in May and held on for four days allowing British forces to escape from Dunkirk. It was the kind of heroic resistance that made Squire recall Rupert Brooke leading his troops from the flames of Antwerp. He immediately penned 'To the Calais Garrison: May 1940', which he wrote in the Athenaeum as air-raid shelters were being built under the window. It was published in *The Times* as 'A Silence Reigned over Calais':

Dim was the memory of that ancient pain:
But now you have played this most heroic part,
We may tell all France with pride that once again
England has Calais written on her heart.[583]

Edward Marsh congratulated him for an idea that was 'remarkable and felicitous'. Squire told Edward Davison that he had full confidence in Churchill and his crew. Everything, happily, was done by order now – 'the Government puts you where they want you.'[584] Unfortunately, they did not want him. He wrote that they did not seem to want anyone 'who was not, a) a mechanic aged 21/2, or b) Sir John Simon.'

Squire had been critical of the politicians who he thought had taken so long to negotiate an alliance with Italy. And then on 10 June he heard that Mussolini had made a pact with Germany. It was a shocking blow, not least because he had been so sure after meeting him that Mussolini was a fellow poet. Italy, he felt, was the fount of Western civilisation and would never betray it. He turned to his pen once again and wrote 'To Italy: 1940', adding underneath the title the epigraph, 'Every poet's second country':

Fairest of lands, most dear to fame,
Mother of learning, arts and laws,
Now in the nightfall of your shame
Abandoned to the basest cause.

Your children stand aghast to see,
Deriding their august estate,
Rome kissing Hell, and Italy
With the Barbarian at the gate.[585]

Throughout the war Squire used his weekly book review in the *Illustrated London News* on behalf of the war effort. His piece on 14 June 1940 read more like a war report:

Events are moving rapidly; as I write this, there are reports that the Vichy Government has given the Germans the *entrée* to Syria, certain ports, including Dakar, and that the Germans have kindly given the French Fleet the right to fight against England. Anything may have happened between the writing of this and its appearance. The Germans may have been able to blackmail the French, by threats of torture and starvation of prisoners and women at home, into war with England.

Squire ended on a rousing note. The country was stiffening its defences and recovering from years of sloth. Millions of British people were prepared to fight to the last. French women were listening surreptitiously to BBC radio in the evenings and praying for General de Gaulle and the RAF. Less than a fortnight later news came of the surrender of France. By chance he met Hilaire Belloc outside South Kensington Station. Half French, Belloc seemed to have aged twenty years in a week. Together they went into an inn and drained a bottle of burgundy. Belloc told Squire he felt ashamed of his nation and the cowardice of French politicians.[586]

Television shut down so as not to help enemy planes navigate by using the signal. Everyone listened to the Home Service. Nine million radio licences meant that the BBC had an audience of about 34 million at home, and more in pubs and clubs. When the BBC felt that a patriotic voice was called for to counter the propaganda from Lord Haw-Haw (William Joyce), they called on Squire to broadcast on English history and poetry. On 28 July 1940, a month after Churchill's Dunkirk speech ('We shall fight on the beaches') the *Radio Times* announced the programme. After the Sunday evening service and the National Anthems of the Allies the main feature was 'The English Heritage', a selection of verse and prose compiled and spoken by Squire and a group of actors. Squire, who was seen as unreliable because of his alcoholism, was succeeded in the role by his protégé J. B. Priestley whose reassuringly warm Yorkshire tones helped to make him the voice of wartime broadcasting.

In August he warned his readers in the *Illustrated London News* not to expect a speedy victory. Under the headline 'Heil Hunger' he told them not to believe the reports of German famine or weakness. The phrase 'Over by Christmas' brought back the dangerous delusions of the first war. Now he did not avoid the word 'Hun' and his reports are full of the word 'fanatical'. His attitude was a total contrast to his feelings in 1914. No longer was he concerned about the abuses and hypocrisy of the Home Front. No longer did he feel for the common humanity of the soldier. In review after review in the first years of the war his was the voice that stiffened resistance.

Under the strapline 'The Spirit of London', he corrected a gloomy

American journalist's view of the devastation of the capital by German bombs. The Blitz had certainly not destroyed Georgian London. He granted that 'many of the City churches that some of us saved from demolition by British vandals have been burnt out and there were a few unsightly holes, but St Paul's still towered over the city.' In fact, he told his readers, the destruction was not nearly on the same scale as that caused by the Great Fire. Another Christopher Wren, he promised, would rise to the challenge when the city was rebuilt. The confused and confusing politics of the 1930s had resolved themselves for him into a simple all-embracing struggle to defeat Germany.[587]

Squire was staying at the Savile Club on 14 August 1940 when he was woken by the sound of an enormous explosion. Early the next morning he left to inspect the cause. In the middle of Pall Mall he found great mounds of rubble. High explosive had destroyed the roof and masonry of the Carlton Club, although miraculously no one had been killed. Climbing over the rubble 'like a chamois in the Alps', wearing a squashy hat, was the prime minister, Winston Churchill, cigar in mouth. Back in Devon, Doll feared for her brother's safety. She listened to his broadcast and was worried enough to try to call him on the telephone. He replied in khaki-coloured light from the Athenaeum where the windows had all been blown out. The club played host to refugees from other clubs that had been bombed or burned. He told her he had just seen Winston Churchill inspecting the smoking ruins of the Carlton.

Two months later Squire was walking through Blitz-torn Westminster past the statue of Richard Coeur de Lion outside the House of Lords. This too had been bombed and uprooted from its pedestal, but suffered only a bending of the sword. He immediately wrote 'The Symbol', a six-line poem for *The Times*:

By heaps of broken glass and stone
The horseman waits, direct, alone,
And in his glove, still brandished high,
Challenging the invaded sky,

Bent, but not broken, is the sword
That led the armies of the Lord.

October 1940 Blitzkrieg

They telephoned to say they had set it in type for instant publication. However, the Office of Works had been in touch with them and reported that the sword had now been straightened – and so the poem was invalidated. 'That's the spirit that has got us into the last two wars,' he wrote.[588] He had fifty copies printed and sent it as his Christmas card. He began to work on a selection of Tennyson's verse including *Idylls of the King*. Reviewing a collection of Anglo-Saxon poetry, he quoted the heroic words of the Anglo-Saxon leader at the Battle of Maldon facing the Viking invaders 'which have a renewed meaning in these days when the fight of Arthur against the consuming heathen is waged again.'[589] He was now writing the kind of heroic patriotic verse he had pilloried for its abstractions and clichés in the first war. He had finally become a Victorian.

With his usual speed Squire brought out his final anthology: *Poems of Two Wars*.[590] 'This book is dedicated, without bothering so busy a man for his permission, to the Rt. Hon. Winston Churchill, Prime Minister of Britain, who in his greatness has roused all the poetry in our race…' Unsurprisingly, most of the poems in fact dated from the first war, but Squire also included some he had written for *The Times* and *Punch*. *Poems of Two Wars* was greeted by great praise. The *TLS* said it exactly hit the mood of the moment. Under the heading 'The Heroic Theme', the reviewer commented again on the wartime silence of the poets in sharp contrast to 1914. It seemed as if all the poets, he wrote, apart from Squire and Siegfried Sassoon, had been struck dumb by the bestiality of the German war machine. Now, at last, as the reviewer gazed into the skies watching the Battle of Britain above him, 'a stirring fills the air. This is the time for epic… this is the time for songs of defiance, hymns of deliverance.'[591]

For the first years of the war Squire maintained his reassuring stream of topical light verse in *Punch* and showed the kind of humour that wartime Londoners prided themselves on. Even Hitler could be dismissed as ridiculous. Squire remembered how in 1914 Ernst Lissauer (he of '*Gott strafe England*') had composed a poem that he said for a few months was on every German's lips, '*Hassgesang gegen England*', a 'Hymn of Hate', with each verse ending 'ENGLAND!' The idea for Squire's version came when he overheard 'a small grey Londoner, who looked like a sub-inspector of water mains, wish that 'ole 'itler 'ad caught a touch of flu.' He developed the character of the innocence of the little man who could wish Hitler no worse harm than a series of minor ailments:

> Grrr! Hitler! Yes, a touch of flu:
> When my monkey's up and my bloods aglow.
> HITLER!
> May you have a corn on your little toe
> Or a chilblain perhaps, or in your eye,
> A rather, but not too painful stye,
> Or else again may you martyred be
> By a moderate touch of Housemaid's knee.
> HITLER![592]

And so on…

His 'Ballad of Non-Rationed Food' was dedicated to Lord Woolton, then Minister of Food, who introduced rationing and his notorious vegetarian 'Woolton pie':

> Time was I called for moutong Mantenong
> When superciliously I used to say:
> 'I want – be quick about it too, Garsong! –
> Oon ontray, oon sooflay, oon canapay,
> All done in butter, and oon consommay
> Of pray salay' et cet. – but now Lor' strike

Me pink! I want no truck with such as they:
At last I've found the food I really like....

October 1940 was one of the worst months for daily air raids on London. Squire's secretary Mrs Crick could not stand them and abandoned him and the capital. He evacuated his old house when he found the ceiling down, the windows smashed and telephone out of action. As he was crossing the road, he had another close shave when a bomb burst destroying nearby houses. He walked to Macmillan's and found it had been bombed and was deserted. He went to visit his agent A. D. Peters but the office was locked up and the windows broken there too. Three thousand émigrés from other clubs filled the Athenaeum. He put all his furniture in store and slept at his flat at Palace Gate. By November he had moved back to his old house in South Kensington, alone with two cats, fallen ceilings and burst pipes. Finland was still on his mind. 'I wish I could go,' he wrote, but he could not, as he had a wife and child to support. It did not occur to him to wonder whether a fifty-six-year-old untrained Home Guard member would be of much military use to the Finns. He was in Chesham on all-night guard duty with an old sergeant in the hut when he heard the thunder of incessant bombers going overhead. 'They're heading for Coventry,' the sergeant said. 'They were,' he wrote to Cecily. Someone brought in a wireless set and in the December night they listened together to Winston Churchill. It was bitter cold and the trees, Squire wrote, were coming out in sheer exasperation.

Squire wrote a Christmas letter to his sister telling her he was busy helping to provide comforts for the Home Guard and for troops abroad, trying to supply them with dart boards and billiard tables. Before long he had obtained 150 tables, including one from Lord Baldwin, and money to transport them. He carried on with, as he put it, a small job for the Red Cross. He was sent an expensively bound album and began to fill it. He watched for a couple of hours as Augustus John drew for him a beautiful sketch of a girl's head. There were contributions from Rex Whistler, Ralph Vaughan Williams, Lord

Reith and the Prince Consort of Luxembourg and even, he hoped, one from the Queen. At auction at Sotheby's, he told Cecily, it could well bring in £10,000. He became a familiar figure walking through London carrying the album at the bottom of his green fishing bag.[593]

The following year continued the story of mishaps and disasters. Squire tore his Achilles tendon when doing a Church Parade with the Home Guard and then developed 'housemaid's knee on his elbow' and intercostal neuralgia. He told his sister that the Queen of Sheba (Eileen) had become matron of an evacuee children's home in Berkshire, abandoning her title and calling herself, quite unnecessarily, Mrs Squire. In the postscript he added casually, 'Everything I possessed has been bombed – I don't mind.'[594] In a poor state himself, he lived 'sans a secretary, sans a house in London, sans everything except Miss Warrender and sanity'.

In March 1941 Squire reviewed *When Hell came to London*, an American journalist's account of the destruction of the Blitz. Squire wrote that he thought half of his readers, including himself, had lost most of their possessions, but insisted that Londoners were not dispirited. 'We do not take bombing very seriously… England is now in the front-line trenches and it is as nothing compared with the Somme and Passchendaele. We have no desire to be called heroes. We are merely hanging on in the sure knowledge that the vast majority of us, fighting in a just cause, will see certain victory.' The Polish spirit was still there and the Dutch continued to resist the 'stupid square heads tramping through their country'. The Free French were rousing themselves under General de Gaulle and American help was on the way.[595] 'We are recovering from years of sloth,' he wrote. The Army, Navy and the RAF were all strong and one and a half million had joined the Home Guard, lining every hedge and making it difficult for the Germans to mount a surprise attack. It was an upbeat and reassuring message from a soldier who had finally found his way into the trenches.

April brought the biggest Blitz ever. Poppins Court was destroyed. Squire, as usual, had stayed up all night with the Home Guard in

Chesham and returned to London to sleep. Two cats snuggled up to him in bed. He was woken up when houses at the back of his crashed down and his windows were again blown in. At the Savile Club he reported the devastation: 'Parts of the West End look like the ruins of Ypres.' Ragged children charged a penny to show him around the devastation of the previous night just as they had done in 1917. After the bombing of Sloane Square tube with seventy civilian casualties, Jack suggested to Cecily that now was the time for her to escape from London into the country. When she followed his advice in May, she needed a caretaker to look after her house and asked him to live in and do the job. He had a small bedroom on the top floor and brought in his own writing table and chair. He did his imaginative work at Chesham. Eaton Terrace was for journalism.

Now once again, he wrote, young men were fighting and dying for the very soil of England. The real England, Squire believed, survived in the countryside. He reviewed Henry Williamson's *The Story of a Norfolk Farm* and commented, 'It is always worthwhile to write about the country.' Love of the country, he thought, united the lover of landscape, the lover of tradition, the lover of sensible, simple people and the naturalist and antiquary. In January 1941 he wrote the foreword to *The English Scene*, a series of illustrated essays on country sports and pastimes, tithe barns, moot halls, pounds and roundhouses, clocks and sundials.[596] His heart went out to a compiler of a book about the English countryside when half the world seemed to threaten it and blackout curtains blocked the view of 'the endlessly living England, obstinate under all superficial change, persisting from the Roman day until our own. Here are the immemorial life of the village, the fights of our country life for survival as well as "the loveliest village of the plain", and alders drooping over the stream, and the hounds pouring over hedges, and the sound of ball against bat on the green and Stoke Poges and the holly and the mistletoe...'[597] This vision of the country, Squire believed, was shared by all classes in villages and towns across the country. He saw evidence of it every day as he walked past by all the bright window boxes full of flowers in the bombed East End. It would take more than Hitler to shake it. 'What we must all do to keep going the civilisation which a few struggling souls kept going in the Dark Ages is to preserve what bits we can during the turmoil and pick up what bits we can – from personal freedom to the Derby – afterwards.'[598]

After fourteen months of parades and sentry-go with the Home Guard Squire applied to join a mobile squad with cars and tommy guns which could rush off at once to any scene of danger. He was proud that his three sons were now all in uniform and he kept on reassuring his sister that they were 'intact'. Anthony was piloting 'colossal' Coastal Command Bombers, and Maurice was in Canada training to be a pilot in the Fleet Air Arm. Raglan was in the army acting as liaison between the government and architects about the rebuilding and reconstruction that would follow the war. Although Squire bore all the dangers and hardships stoically, the war was taking its toll. In July 1942 a taxi drew up outside Rose Macaulay's flat and, to her surprise, Jack Squire stumbled up the stairs to her flat. He asked her about her cousin, Donald, his old friend from St John's. She told him that Donald had died some months before. At this he broke down and began to weep inconsolably. She managed to calm him and helped him downstairs to the waiting taxi.[599]

On a financial level the war came as a great relief. The tax inspector had better things to do than to pursue one of its smaller debtors and the Governors of Blundell's decided that it was the wrong time to prosecute Squire for non-payment of historic school fees. Squire now had a settled and almost comfortable routine: weekends in Chesham and midweek trips to London to deliver his articles to Macmillan's and pick up books for reviewing, drilling with the Home Guard, writing articles, even playing an occasional game of golf.

But there was terrible news ahead. When Maurice was on leave his father had asked him what it was like on naval patrol in the Far North and admired the reply, 'It gets rather cold in the evenings on deck.' In April 1943 he replied to Yvonne ffrench: 'I got your letter on my birthday, and the same day a letter and a jolly grinning photograph from my Maurice. The next day – he had transferred from the Navy to the Fleet Air Arm in Ontario – he went off for a final night bombing exercise before he went on leave again. Within three days Eileen got an Admiralty telegram saying "Missing, believed killed" – they went out over the dark sea and never came back.'[600] It had been a moonless night and Maurice did not see the light of the target bobbing about in the water, misjudged the height and, along with his observer, plunged straight into the sea.

It was this image of darkness that came to Squire in 'The Comforter', the last of the elegies that he wrote for those lost in two wars. He dedicated it to 'M. W. H. S., Pilot, Fleet Air Arm: Killed April 3, 1943'. The poem was completed with his usual speed and the following day he submitted it to *The Times*:

The budding hedges take the warmth
Of the soft April rain:
But Maurice will not see this Spring
Nor any Spring again.

Here, by our milder southern ways
The chestnut buds are breaking;
The cherry's white, the apple trees
Are flushed with their awaking;

The thronging multitudes of birds
Shout from the dusk of morn,
Greeting their mates in reckless joy
For they have children born;

But Maurice will not hear such birds,
Nor see such blooms begin:
He has returned to mysteries
That he was nurtured in.

....

Spring had not touched those northern hills,
Nor yet had soared their lark,
When he took flight, and suddenly
Descended in the dark.

All in a moment: gone his Spring
Ere flower had grown to fruit:
His smile effaced, his muscles slack,
His mortal music mute.

Deep in the ooze: no lettered tomb,
No wooden cross, no grave
For love to strew a flower on:
Just cold and wandering wave.

Squire's pastoral elegy echoes another poem about a young man lost at sea – Milton mourning the loss of Edward King in 'Lycidas'. 'The Comforter' ends, as does 'Lycidas', on a note of consolation:

Yet dawning on this bitter night
Two smiling eyes I see,
A voice I hear: 'Tell those I loved
Things have gone well with me.'[601]

In the *Illustrated London News* Squire wrote of 'this most devilish, murderous and ruinous of wars'.

*

It became a commonplace among Squire's friends, when his name was mentioned, to speak of the tragedy of his life. Led by Speedwell, the socialist wife of H. J. Massingham, they tried to raise a fund to support him. Squire himself did not see his life as tragic; he felt no self-pity and carried on drilling with the Home Guard, writing and broadcasting. In May 1943 he signed a contract with Heinemann's for another volume of memoirs to be called 'After the Ball' – but nothing came of it. 'God willing, I shall make a new start after the war. These turmoils are inhospitable to artists,' he wrote to Doll. Still a member of the Athenaeum and the Savile Clubs where he spent much of his time when he was in London, his appearance told the story of his wartime life. He appeared in the Athenaeum wearing 'white flannels, black evening slippers, a badly moth-eaten blue high-necked pullover, a winged collar and an Old Blundellian tie.'[602] On another occasion tottered in walking on the sides of his heelless shoes. But whatever the hardships, as war went on, he became more and more confident of an Allied victory. He found time to play some cricket and was pleased to be put in charge of Home Guard cricket for the whole south-eastern district. The clearest sign that the war was near its end for him was that by May 1944 cricket had resumed at Lords and soldiers were oiling their bats ready for the following summer.

Squire's movements become hard to trace. For a while he moved to a small cottage in Elystan Place, Chelsea. In August 1944, as he was at his desk writing his piece for the *Illustrated London News*, a 'doodle' (V-1 rocket or 'doodlebug') blew in the door, smashing the bow window and filling his lap with a snowstorm of blasted glass. Ironically, he was in the middle of his piece on Hitler's end: 'It is highly unlikely that we shall capture him at all. Millions are after his blood, and he is likely to commit suicide in order to have an effective fifth act to his glorious tragedy.'[603] Squire himself suffered no worse than a badly cut arm and hand: a larger fragment might have cut his throat – it had happened to a friend, he remarked. The cottage was, however, uninhabitable. He had to move to the last of his wartime homes, a tiny room at 4 Ranelagh Grove, Pimlico. His landlady there was Nina Weld. She had endured a terrible childhood, deserted by her mother soon after her birth and looked after by a foster mother. Married three times, semi-literate, nearly penniless, she depended on alcohol just as much as he did. Nina was a complete contrast to the educated and aristocratic ladies who had helped him in the past, but she too was charmed and became dependent on job references and his affection. For some years they became regular drinking companions in dingy London clubs and pubs.

In December 1944 he met his old friend 'Bob' Nichols at a bus top in Piccadilly just before his sudden death. He said, 'Look, let's come and talk for half an hour.' Bob Nichols replied, 'Sorry, old boy, I'm in a frightful hurry.' 'There was no next week,' wrote Squire. News came in April 1945 that 'shocked me to sickness': the death of Mussolini. Squire's mind went back fifteen years to their meeting at the Palazzo Veneziana and his memories of a likeable romantic figure, the heir of Garibaldi, a lover of architecture and history, an excavator of the glory of Rome, 'a nice Napoleon, with less education, an equally strong historical sense and more compassion'.[604] Mussolini and his mistress had been captured and executed trying to escape to Switzerland. Their bodies were taken to Milan and dumped with other corpses in a marketplace near the station. They were shot at, spat at and urinated upon by an angry mob and then hoisted upside down on meat hooks. Squire thought Mussolini's appalling death was the story of a good man gone wrong, unlike Hitler's – who was an evil man gone worse. In the same month came more shocking news from Buchenwald and Auschwitz prison camps.

Squire had always admired great leaders and the character of Hitler also held an appalled fascination for him. As early as 1940 he had predicted Hitler's Wagnerian end in a Berlin bunker:

Self-centred, half-baked, moody, he lives in cloudy and incoherent dreams admired, sometimes as spectator, sometimes as actor in vast Wagnerian dramas. At one moment... he dreams of a vast European confederation under German hegemony. At another, prompted by Nietzsche, his aim is to breed the Superman; and it doesn't matter to him, in his unbridled mania for using humanity as paint for his pictures, that when he saw the Superman [Winston Churchill] he shrank from him. He toys in turn with every sort of grandiose vision; alternately he is half-mad with excitement at the revivalist emotion of a mass-meeting, at another he flies to his mountain tops and stalks and broods like lonely Manfred; at one moment he is at a pitch of exaltation as he sees his millions of Germans marching in a blaze of sunlight to a vague Utopia and sometimes, when the black cloud of coming failure shadows him, his fists fly into the air in wild rage—and he is Samson in the house of the Philistines, who, if he falls, will bring half a world down in ruin with him… The one thing certain is that his mind and temper are those of an undisciplined artist. He, the frustrated architect, has a passion for building… The one thing certain is that when his Twilight of the Gods comes, he will go down muttering, like Nero, 'Qualis artifex pereo.'[605]

Chapter 26

Crepuscular

After war in Europe ended in May 1945 Squire wrote his despatch for the *Illustrated London News* in a room that had been partially wrecked by one of the last V-2 rockets. He feared that unless some peace proposals were accepted a third world war would bring a 'Deep Shelter Age'.[606] He imagined subterranean bunkers, floodlit by artificial sunlight and air-conditioned by all sorts of novel fanning apparatus and chemical filters – and predicted the nuclear shelters that were soon to be built at the time of the Cold War. He would have no truck with the argument that war had become so terrible that it could never happen again. He thought back to 1914, the war to end all wars, and remembered how the 'the German indiscriminate bombing of civilians, shooting at swimming sailors in the sea, use of poison-gas, started another degringolade.' There were however no aerial reprisals in the First World War; the motto was, we shall not sink to their level. In the Second World War Squire knew that the Germans were not the only guilty party; the English had destroyed Dresden and bombed other cities with huge numbers of civilian casualties. This did not make him a pacifist; he wrote that civilisation rested on the existence of weapons and power. 'The chivalry of the Middle Ages knew it, and Sir Thomas Malory knew it; there were good knights and evil knights, and if the good knights, believing that some Great Dawn had come, disarmed themselves, so much the worse for the good knights.'[607]

The Americans, Squire thought, had launched new levels of atrocity with the bombing of Hiroshima. Then came the second atom bomb at Nagasaki: 'I have never heard explanation of that; perhaps somebody in America could not bear from experimenting with a second test of a new and beautiful toy. But as for the human race being shocked into decency, I can only say that, the morning after Hiroshima, I met a man in the street who said to me, "The Japs seem to have had a bit of a pasting."' Squire was appalled.[608] He had hoped for a League of Nations or a Kellogg Pact to outlaw war. But he feared it was all too late. The atomic bombs of the second war disproved the idea that war had become too terrible for any nation to contemplate: 'We have become sceptical and hardened... inured to the most indiscriminate of attacks.' His hopes for peace were replaced by nightmare visions of what kind of war would come next.

> We don't know what is going to happen in the next war. My own opinion, for what it is worth, is that the Atom Bomb is going to dominate everything, and that even airborne troops, novelties though they so recently were, will become as old fashioned as cavalry. About twenty of these bombs (and they may be making bigger and better ones) would suffice to obliterate London, leaving behind them millions of corpses and multitudes of men, women and children withering away to death.[609]

The Labour victory in the general election two months after war ended came as a complete and unwelcome surprise to Squire. He had offered Patrick Howarth, later to be his biographer, odds of ten to one against the result. Squire felt the country's rejection of Churchill was a betrayal. It was not just the defeat of a man whom he had come to admire so much. He told his readers in the *Illustrated London News* that the history of the country had always been achieved by exceptional individuals. He loathed the victory chorus of the *Red Flag* – 'that dismal, crawling anthem which the Labour Party sang in 1945, when in mass they triumphantly invaded the House of Commons.'

Now the outlook was gloomy: exceptional individuals were punished by ever higher taxes and a 'pagan and ungrammatical system of education' was set up. Squire thought the country was governed by socialists to whom 'Christian Europe means nothing. Doctrinaires were in the chair.'[610]

The socialists, Squire thought, were not even true socialists: it was 'Nominal Socialism, which is actually State Capitalism, with highly paid managers.' Intellectual and artistic socialists did not understand the British working class. The urban trades unionists under the influence of the Industrial Revolution had become rich and had little to do with the body of rural blacksmiths, woodworkers, thatchers and even lace-makers, who were content, like sailors and fishermen and ploughmen and cowmen, to do their job and let the world go by.[611]

The war had not restored his faith in democracy. Democracy had not prevented Hitler from taking power. Even the Kremlin talked about 'people's democracies', but in practice 'it means government by a small gang in the Kremlin in the name of a proletariat which is a small minority of workers.' In England democracy meant government by one or two parties who obtained a majority of votes cast. Squire's epigram 'On a General Election' made his point: "The battle's set 'twixt Envy, Greed, and Pride:/ Come conscience, do your duty: choose your side.' The Greeks, Squire, wrote, would have thought this version of democracy was lunacy. 'And if there is one thing dead certain, it is that the democracies must segregate foreign affairs and defence measures from the control of electorate which is voting about coalminers' wages, widows' pensions, or whatever, at the moment, may be pinching the shoe. Over and over again, in the last hundred years, the franchise has been extended. Every time there has been domestic justification... but every time (and when the women, interested in husbands, children, cooking and hats, came in, this was truer than ever) the electoral roll has been diluted.'[612]

Degraded by greed and consumerism, the electorate had turned its back on Churchill and the sacrifices that had been made for them. 'The Century of the Common Man drifted towards common architecture, common music, common books and bread and circuses in the form of tinned salmon and professional football.'[613] Now Squire had rejected socialism and the women's cause, the heroes of his youth were discarded with them. He called Wells a less romantic Rousseau and Shaw a less logical Voltaire, 'carrying on the doctrines of the French Revolution into an age which has discovered their inadequacy and is weltering in murder and groping towards the recovery of God'.[614]

The war had at least, for a while, sheltered Squire from the demands of the Inland Revenue. Now their inspectors started to get to grips with his back taxes. He tried to argue that the loss of his property destroyed in the war should be set against the money he owed. It was the kind of desperate bargaining that had become all too familiar to them. This time it did not work and in January 1947 he was declared bankrupt. Friends, including Miss Warrender, immediately rallied round and he was quickly able to pay his creditors twenty shillings in the pound. Her death later in the same year, aged ninety, came as a great blow. Squire had lost his most loyal friend and supporter. When his *Selected Poems* came out in 1948 he prefaced it with his tribute: 'This volume was to have been dedicated to Alice Warrender but is now inscribed to her memory.' It emerged to a largely silent press. *The Sphere* saw him as a relic: 'A few of the poems deal with the late war, but somehow they do not breathe quite the spirit of 1939–45. There is a Chestertonian touch about them, healthy and robust enough, but not of this realistic day and age.'

After this, he too fell silent.

Miss Warrender's death posed the familiar problem of where to live. He began to look for a small house to rent. Absolutely tired of London, which he told his sister he had always detested, he dreamed of going back to Devon. He was an exile, and like all exiles felt that 'there was no spot as pleasant as that from which they came... he could ask for no greater boon in the evening of his days than to live on such a beautiful spot as Drake's Island, just off the Devon Coast.'[615] He asked Doll to rent as many rooms as she could spare him and promised to work in the garden and do his own cooking. He was in arrears for the contracts for books and found working in London impossible: 'I have never been able to work in this pandemonium of a town.'[616] Then he found a semi-derelict thatched cottage in the tiny village of Campsea Ashe in Suffolk, close to where he and Willy Smith had enjoyed the last summer of their Cambridge days. Water had to be pumped from a well and there was no electricity or gas. At last, in the quiet and isolation of Ashe Green Cottage he felt he could settle down to write. Three months later, when he was away in London, the thatch caught fire and his cottage burnt down. He lost his books, diaries, a vast number of hoarded papers and correspondence and nearly all his possessions. 'At the age of sixty-six he found himself once again homeless and destitute.'[617]

Still a reader for Macmillan, twice a month he visited their office to collect his salary in cash and get next month's selection of books and manuscripts. Quite often he tried to negotiate an advance from the cashier. Quite often he got one. He also maintained his weekly column in the *Illustrated London News*, dutifully arriving at the office every week wearing an old Home Guard great coat, turtleneck sweater and antique trousers. He carried a large green fishing basket and bag in which to file his piece and collect next week's book. His choice of subjects was based on historical memoirs and diaries. His love of exploration and exotic places, his appreciation of architecture and art, and thoughts on the war as it developed, are all common topics. He covered every kind of subject. He was at home with Balinese dances, Chinese ceramics, Trollope, the Esquimaux of King William Island, mountaineering, Pushkin, a Maori chieftainess, Edwardian ballet, Nepal, and the largest telescope in the world. Literary reviews included Pliny, Mrs Thrale, Thackeray and his old enemies Sacheverell and Osbert Sitwell, whom he now praised generously. He did not extend the same generosity and tolerance to Paul Klee's work which 'might have come out of an asylum', or to Chagall's, 'just a fad', or to Joyce's *Ulysses*, 'that mound of incomprehensible muck'. All of them, he was sure, would pass quickly into oblivion. 'Where are the Dadaists of yester-year?' he asked.

The humour and wit that had first marked the *New Age* and the *New Statesman* remained to the last. His columns and editorials were studded with anecdotes, asides and jokes. He had always loved the quirky, the bizarre and the debunking English sense of humour. He remembered speaking at a political meeting with a Mr Salmon who developed his points at some length. 'Get back into your tin,' came a shout from the back of the hall – and he was finished. He collected snippets from newspapers such this from the *Daily Telegraph*: 'An applicant named Ephraim Very Ott told the Kent tribunal that he was employed in the frozen meat trade.' A lady in California, on hearing about the stars through the latest telescope, asked him: 'They are millions of miles away, how did you ever get to find out their names?' From a serious naval history, he picked out the most crackpot schemes proposed, including freezing a cloud to put a machine gun on top to shoot down passing Zeppelins, a pneumatic gun firing poisonous snakes into the enemy trenches and training cormorants to eat the masonry from the cement of the arms manufacturer Krupps's chimneys.

On 10 October 1949 came news of the death of one of his closest friends and collaborators, Robert Lynd. He wrote to Lynd's widow Sylvia:

> I loved and admired Bob without reservation. He was too modest to dream that anybody could have those sorts of feelings about him: but I know that, in a jam, I should have called him to my rescue, and that, had he been in a jam, I should have flown to his. Long ago, as you know, we saw each other constantly: and he was my only daughter's Godfather. When I saw about his death in *The Times* it was like a straight blow on the heart. I had easily assumed that he would always be here, and that I could, at any moment, take a taxi to Hampstead to see you both. I should be only too glad to come and remember the sweetest, loveingest, kindest husband that ever woman had.

'POLICEMAN MAKES A LIFE CATCH' reads a headline from the

Daily Herald on 6 February 1950. PC Bell broke both his arms as he caught a woman who fell from a first-floor window in Ranelagh Grove, saving her from being impaled on the spiked railings outside her home. After what looked like a suicide attempt Nina Weld was admitted to Westminster Hospital with a broken skull. She was still dependent on Squire when she became a patient at Spelthorne St Mary, a refuge for women alcoholics run by Anglican nuns. She had nothing and had to accept vest and knickers from 'Superior', as she called the Sister in charge. Squire sent Nina some money and cigarettes and wrote job references. She wrote desperate letters asking for more, to her 'Dearest Idiot'. Finally released from the convent, she fell into the road and was hit by a bus. Once again, she thanked Jack for his kindness coming to her rescue 'from deep down in that great heart of yours'. 'I cannot feel she is capable of standing on her own two feet. You are the only friend she has,' wrote the Sister. This time he could not help; he too had no money. Nina was again released from the convent. Her final scribbled card was dated 29 September 1952. It read: 'Try to meet me at Sloane Square Stn. Tomorrow Tuesday. But the situation is <u>very</u> <u>seriouse</u> (*sic*). I have a bed for the night.' Then she disappeared into the darkness from which no biographer can rescue her.

Despite the loss of his papers, Squire offered his agent, Peter Lewin, the promise of another volume of his memoirs. Through him Squire was introduced to George Greenfield, a young man at the beginning of a successful career as publisher of Enid Blyton, Jilly Cooper and David Niven. The thought of tales from someone who had known the great names of the twenties and the captain of a famous cricket side was attractive. Greenfield offered the considerable sum of £200 as an advance. He described their meeting for lunch at Kempinski's, a rather smart restaurant in Swallow Street off Piccadilly.

> I arrived early and sat nervously fingering a small glass of dry sherry when my special guest turned up. He could have stepped out of the pages of the *Pickwick Papers*. He was wearing a black coat, green with age when the sun's rays caught it, and formal pinstripe trousers. He

had a cataract of white hair and small round spectacles far down on a red nose. He greeted me with considerable courtesy. I offered him a pre-lunch drink. He asked for a large scotch, no water. We chatted briefly and then I asked if he would like another drink before we went into lunch. He had another large scotch. When we reached the dining table he confessed that he never ate lunch. 'In you go ahead, my boy, and order yourself some food. If I may, I will have another large scotch.' It is unnerving in any event for an inexperienced publisher to take lunch with a distinguished guest more than twice one's age; doubly so when the guest just drinks his scotch and watches each mouthful on its way from the plate to the host's mouth. So that he would not feel out of things, I ordered him another large scotch and yet another. And, alas, somewhere between the fourth and sixth large scotch, his eyelids dropped as his voice became slurred. By the end of my solitary meal, he could still stand up and with a little elbow gripping made his stately, if erratic, progress out of the restaurant.[618]

Squire, naturally, accepted the money, but the volume of memoirs was never delivered. The publisher was consoled by the thought that £200 meant 'at least 2,000 large scotches to lend a rosy glow to Squire's last years.' Peter Lewin's other gift was more lasting. He introduced Jack to his aunt, Dr Berry, a generous philanthropist. Through her he got to know Bertha Seton Usborne, the daughter of a Canadian sculptor. Dr Berry loaned Bertha the £1,300 necessary to pay off his debts, without any security, or indeed much hope, of getting her money back. Bertha, twenty years younger than Jack, was clever, literary and artistic. Both of them had led wandering, unsettled lives during the war. She began to untangle the chaos of his finances and, as she did so, began to fall in love with him. He could now establish himself, as he had so long wanted to do, away from London. For two years they lived together at the Sutherland Hotel, Surbiton, and then at 25 Grove Road – alien suburban territory for him. He grew a white beard that gave him the look of an ancient prophet and began to call himself 'the Sage of Surbiton'.

Bertha Usborne and Jack moved to the hamlet of Chiddingstone Hoath in Kent, and then to Churches Green, Dallington before finally settling nearby in Diamond Cottage, Rushlake Green, East Sussex, a tiny village in the middle of Invalids territory, not far from Rodmell. A diamond-shaped green, which stood well above the road, gave the cottage its name. A cricket square stood in the middle. The buildings clustered round the green: the half-timbered Horse and Groom, the village stores and a group of thatched cottages were about the whole of it. Diamond Cottage itself was larger than it sounded, a red-brick seventeenth-century building with mullioned windows overlooking the green and only a few yards from the Horse and Groom. Jack paid for three steps to be installed which allowed him to avoid the road and get home safely. Somehow, he had also acquired a large mongrel, Bingo, which had been found as a stowaway on a plane and attached himself to him. It barked furiously at the gate at any passer-by. Squire was pictured by the photographer of the *Illustrated London News* in the front room of Diamond Cottage sitting comfortably in an armchair, cigarette in hand, books neatly shelved behind him, flowers in a vase, a picture of Poppins Court on the wall, with Bertha's spinning wheel beside him. It is a picture of the kind of domestic order, and perhaps even contentment, which he had not enjoyed since before the war.

As the Cold War deepened Squire's hatred and fear of Russia grew. 'That brigand' Stalin replaced Hitler as the chief enemy. On one side Squire saw a Christian Europe based on Athens, Rome and Jerusalem and on the other the 'atheist gang' in control of Russia. After what he thought was the humiliation of the Berlin airlift, he felt it was time to stand up to 'Stalin and his gang' so the countries that had fallen under the Soviet Empire could be liberated. The lesson of history was that 'appeasement' did not work. It had not worked with Hitler – and it certainly would not work with Stalin. Resistance was needed, but Squire saw the public were more interested in football, strikes and shopping. 'It's a Woolworth world, my masters. It may be that we are living in a decaying, even collapsing civilization.'[619] The news of Stalin's death in March 1953 was welcome. 'Stalin has died at last, after as treacherous, pitiless and bloody career as any tyrant whom history records,' he wrote in the *Illustrated London News*.

The threat of war was once again on his mind after the Iron Curtain, or 'Iron Cage' as he called it, had descended over Europe. In Korea and in the Malayan jungle, British soldiers faced another savage enemy: 'utterly unscrupulous and relentless cut-throats inspired from the same source as the warriors in North Korea. They cut men to pieces; they burn women alive; and then they go back to fleeting jungle camps to eat their rice, listen to lectures from their Kremlin-instructed instructors.'[620] And now in December 1953 he wrote: 'The Atom bomb is here; and the Hydrogen bomb; the Cobalt bomb apparently is coming.' The threat of all the great cities being turned to dust and ultimate destruction was real. The expansion of Russia meant that once again Europe was threatened from the East. The only way to stop conflict was, he thought, not the recently founded U. N. O. but a second League of Nations to set up an International Control of Atomic Weapons including the Kremlin. 'Let us hope that the mental iron curtain be penetrated.' Emile Zola had envisaged a tremendous explosive so terrible that it persuaded people that war was no use to anybody but Squire did not believe it: 'Things don't work that way: an atom bomb being invented, people begin to think (once released from the restraint of religious, or even sporting or gentlemanly, rules) of bigger, better and more numerous atom bombs. *Facilis descensus Averno*.'[621] He concluded: 'Why on earth cannot people agree to grow their crops in peace and live in peace? To that question I have never had an answer.'[622]

Despite his concerns about nuclear war, Squire was thrilled by the accession of Queen Elizabeth in 1953 and hailed Winston Churchill's return as her prime minister. The 'wrong 'un' had a become a hero:

Once more we have a young Queen, with a worthy Consort. She has come to the Throne in one of the most perilous and tumultuous times since the Dark Ages, with the whole world in a ferment, and swords ready to leap from their scabbards in every quarter of the earth, and in some quarters unsheathed. On the other hand, she has, as her first Prime Minister, the most buoyant and versatile man, old in years, unquenchably young in spirit, soldier, historian, orator, artist, enthusiast and sage, who has ever served a Sovereign of England. Let us hope that fifty years hence another Cecil (and I cannot believe that the brains of that tribe will run out) will be able to write a book (her Majesty still being alive) called *Elizabeth II and Her Prime Ministers*, recording an illustrious reign, a succession of outstanding statesmen, and a recovery of this country's status in the eyes of the world, and in her own eyes.[623]

In March he was surprised to get a letter from J. B. Priestley telling him that thirty old friends and colleagues wanted to organise a dinner to be held in a private room at the Garrick Club to celebrate his seventieth birthday. The invitation list included John Betjeman, Siegfried Sassoon, Sir Alan Herbert, Clifford Bax, Dudley Carew, Milton Waldman, Ivor Brown, Daniel Macmillan, Sir Francis Meynell, Alan Pryce-Jones and J. B. Morton. Priestley had never been a close friend and Squire feared he might not even know some of the guests he had invited. He wrote to his old secretary Grace Chapman: 'I have to go to London tomorrow, for the first time for months, because a small stag party is being got up for me... I haven't a notion as to what stags will be assembled – but I imagine they will all be good fellows.' But he did have a long list of absentees: 'Belloc, Shanks, Chesterton, Reggie Berkeley, Bohun Lynch, John Freeman, W. J. Turner, E. Gosse, T. Hardy, R. Bridges, M. Hewlett, B. H. Newdigate, R. Lynd etc. won't be there. I shall feel lost.'[624]

Priestley took the chair. There were dozens of letters from 'stags' such as Walter de la Mare and the historian Arthur Bryant. Telegrams came from friends in Dublin, Alec Waugh in California, and Edmund Blunden in Hong Kong. The one from New York was signed by seven friends including his old protégé Edward Davison, Ralph Hodgson and, surprisingly, W. H. Auden. Priestley presented Squire with a huge inscribed silver cigarette box, but absent friends were more on his mind. Squire was disappointed that the guests represented only one of his centipede's feet – the literary. Hugh Mackintosh wrote a ballade for the occasion which Squire was too shy to look at in public. He left it behind – and so never had a chance to read it. The last of the ceremonial dinners that he had relished so much turned out to be a sad affair. He was lost among the living and at home among the dead: in his memory at least the sodality he had talked about losing was reunited.

At midnight 'April 1–2 1954', as he carefully dated his letter to Cecily, he turned seventy. Surrounded by country darkness and silence, as Bertha and Bingo slept in their separate quarters, he wrote to the woman from whom he had parted twenty years before. It was the moment when he was trying to clear up all the arrears of conscience, but he admitted, 'I shall never catch up'. He asked for another meeting and ended, 'But, Cec, for what I'm worth I'm always yours'.

Chapter 27

Testament

In the incessant snowfalls of the winter of 1956 the pipes froze in Diamond Cottage and Jack Squire began to take to his bed. News of the death of Dolly's son Michael, killed in an accident, saddened him so much that he could not write to his 'beloved sister' the stock phrases that he said he could normally find. In fact, he had become invisible. 'Your friends are worried about you. They never see you. No one <u>ever sees you</u>,' she wrote. For news about her brother she had to make do with his column in the *Illustrated London News*. She tried to communicate via his publisher, Macmillan, and called herself 'a voice from the dead through space to the dead'. 'I write now and again and tried to contact him through the Athenaeum but his letters were returned, address unknown.' One correspondent did manage to find him. John Warrender (Alice's great nephew) was becoming more and more angry that the only surviving member of the selection committee of the Hawthornden Prize had not organised a meeting or awarded the prize since 1944. Squire had accepted £50 from him to reform the committee, but still had done nothing and he never replied to his letters. Questions were being asked in *The Times* and he feared that when the whole history of the prize emerged Squire would face severe criticism. (The prize was next awarded in 1958 after Jack's death.)

He did write to his niece Bridget that he had had a good deal of illness and was sorry that he was unable to visit her and his sister in Devon: he had had a fall and it was impossible to get new tyres to fit his ancient car. An immense distance now seemed to separate them, but ever Micawberish, he added that he hoped to see them both in the spring. He told her that he was delighted that she had visited his grandson Roger twice. He was delighted too that Roger was following in the family footsteps to Blundell's, but disappointed that he was not in School House where he, Raglan and Maurice had all been. 'I almost feel as though a member of the family has been naturalised in a foreign country.'

On his bed in the isolation of his cottage, Squire cared nothing of how the literary world had moved on. Magazine wars and quarrels about modernism were over and long forgotten. Eliot, 'a grunt would serve,' had become the dominating figure. At Faber's he enjoyed the kind of controlling influence on publishing that had not been seen since Squire's own time and that of Edward Marsh. The audience for poetry had shrunk since then. The political poetry of the 'MacSpaunday' group of the 1930s had given way to a more disparate audience for post-war poetry. Another kind of avant-garde theatre had begun with Samuel Beckett's *Waiting for Godot* in 1955. Harold Pinter's *The Caretaker* brought to the stage the kind of dramatic language that Squire had imagined – and thought absurd. John Osborne's *Look Back in Anger* exploded on to the stage of the Royal Court where another angry young man had seen Shaw, Ibsen and the theatre of the suffragettes fifty years earlier. In television, films and novels the focus moved north, away from London to the industrial cities of Leeds, Manchester, Nottingham and Liverpool. The 'slice of life' realism that Squire had disliked so much had taken over the popular imagination. Squire mused, 'I think I shall have to go back and refresh myself with Housman or Chesterton or Belloc or Conrad, or de la Mare, even Beatrix Potter.'[625]

Many of Squire's friends were enjoying the kind of success that had always eluded him. The once disreputable Alan Pryce-Jones was now the editor of the *TLS*. The all-but-forgotten Ivor Gurney was beginning to gain the posthumous reputation as a musician and one of the leading poets of the Great War that Squire always thought he deserved. J. B. Priestley had outdone his mentor as a wartime broadcaster and become a highly successful and rich novelist and playwright. John Betjeman was a 'national treasure', to be appointed Poet Laureate in 1972. He played the part that Squire had done forty years earlier as the nation's favourite man of letters, an architectural campaigner and the highbrows' bête noire.

Whatever personal disasters occurred, there was still cricket. In September 1950 Squire had challenged John Wisden and Co. to a match to celebrate their centenary. The match was duly played on the Dripping Pan cricket ground in Sussex, the county of Wisden's birth. Two original Invalids, Squire and Blunden, played and at lunch Squire told his audience that he did not mind admitting that he only knew the Bible before he knew Wisden. He still kept up to date with every fixture. At the age of seventy-one he turned out for the Invalids for the last time. The match was played at Rodmell. 'I hope to take wickets,' he promised. He did not field but bowled and batted. He made nought not out, as, he observed, he had done for the last four years. After the match, as President of the club, he donned his Invalids blazer and entertained both teams at Diamond Cottage.

In British politics Squire was resolutely anti-Labour. Reviewing the life of an Elizabethan general in the *Illustrated London News*, he commented on how small the circle of influential people was then, but it embraced politicians, warriors and poets just as Athens in its heyday had done. 'It isn't like that now. I, a man of letters, will probably sink into the grave before I have had the honour of meeting Mr. Aneurin Bevan or Mr. Gaitskell. So, evidently, I shall be unhappy.' In 1957 Squire wrote to Harold Macmillan congratulating him on becoming prime minister and was delighted by a personal reply which began 'Dear Jack'.[626] Macmillan wrote that the job he had taken on was not easy, but thanked him for his good wishes, 'which as you know I appreciate most deeply', and ended 'Yours, Harold.'

Out of the blue in spring 1958 came a letter from Henry

Williamson, whom he had not met since the war.[627] He had settled in Devon; in a fragment of a letter to him Squire mentioned his love for 'my Devon'. Perhaps he recalled a poem he had written forty years earlier about the rivers and streams that criss-crossed the county. After a long catalogue of the great waterways of the world, whatever exotic foreign river he dreamed of…

There is something still in the back of my mind
From very far away;
There is something I saw and see not,
A country full of rivers
That stirs in my heart and speaks to me
More sure, more dear than they…

No, even were they Ganges and Amazon…
I would lose them all, and more,
For a light chiming of small bells,
A twisting flash in the granite,
The tiny thread of a pixie waterfall
That lives by Vixen Tor.

Those rivers in that lost country,
They were brown as a clear brown bead is,
Or red with the earth that rain washed down,
Or white with china-clay…

Okement and Erme and Avon,
Exe and his ruffled shallows,
I could cry as I think of those rivers
That knew my morning dreams;
The weir by Tavistock at evening
When the circling woods were purple,
And the Lowman in Spring with the lent-lilies
And the little moorland streams.

For many a hillside streamlet
There falls with a broken tinkle,
Falling and dying, falling and dying,
In little cascades and pools,
Where the world is furze and heather
And flashing plovers and fixed larks
And an empty sky, whitish blue,
That small world rules.

There, there, where the high waste bog-lands
And the drooping slopes and the spreading valleys,
The orchards and the cattle-sprinkled pastures
Those travelling musics fill,
There is my lost Abana,
And there is my nameless Pharpar
That mixed with my heart when I was a boy,
And time stood still.

The poem fades out on an unresolved, sadly prophetic note:

And I say I will go there and die there:
But I do not go there and sometimes
I think that the train could not carry me there,
And it's possible, maybe,
That it's farther than Asia or Africa,
Or any voyager's harbour,
Farther, farther, beyond recall...
O even in memory![628]

Williamson knew how ill Squire was and wrote: 'But before the schnorrer, this totter [rag and bone man], this ragman pushes his barrow round the corner, let him say the principal thing that is on his mind: Deep and abiding affection for Jack Squire, with crystal-clear memories of the *London Mercury* office, the visits there, the encouragement, the help given, the spreading of the fame which came to a head with the Prize for *Tarka*… That is why I have an abiding affection for Jack Squire.' He asked if he could dedicate his latest work to him. Squire replied that he would be 'entranced', adding that he hoped sometime to meet Williamson's two Blundellian sons. The wheel had come full circle. Book Seven of Williamson's magnum opus, *Chronicles of Ancient Sunlight*, was dedicated to the trinity of Sir John Squire, John Collings Squire and Jack Squire 'in ever grateful memory of Past and Present help and Kindness'.

Another voice from the past was John Betjeman's. Squire had sent him a signed copy of his *Selected Poems*. He immediately put it in his cabinet of favourite books. Betjeman must have been surprised to hear from a man who had disappeared for so long from the literary scene, but replied to him: 'Dear old friend, dear publisher of my first writings… I owe you more than I can repay. You gave me encouragement as you did for hundreds of others.' He went on to list the poems that were his favourites and praised Squire for being 'MUSICAL, MEMORABLE, CLEAR.' All these qualities, Betjeman felt, were now coming back after so much neglect. 'It is a treat,' he wrote, 'to find a book of poems so full of lovely things of yours in the tradition which I am sure is the lasting tradition of English poetry.' Jack was a great poet as well as a great editor, and he would charter aeroplanes to see him. In default of that, Betjeman put him on his list to be prayed for and promised his name would come round every Saturday for the rest of his praying days. 'Don't bother to answer this. It is only to tell you how much I admire you.'[629]

In April 1958 a birthday letter from Doll reached Diamond Cottage. It was, Jack said, a tremendous consolation, and, at last, she received a reply. Typed for him by Bertha, it said how sorry he was that he had not been able all those years ago to take over 'beautiful Whitehall' which would have saved him from spending 'outrageous sums on furnishing cottages, with no amenities or services and rapacious landlords. As usual he made a series of brave promises that he would not be able to keep: 'I hope that Raggie will take me down to Blundell's to see an inter-school cricket match and then take me on to see you; I wish I had been able to settle in our ancestral county.' He ended, 'All love my darling and I hope to see you in the summer.'

What upset Jack most was that he was so unwell that he had to fall down on his *Illustrated London News* article. For the past three months he had had to dictate everything he wrote. On 2 July 1958 he posted his farewell to the editor: 'During 25 years I have felt myself a member of an ancient team, with you as Captain; and nothing but desperate circumstances would have induced me to resign from the Club. But desperate my situation has become... I never said goodbye to anybody or anything with greater grief... I have never enjoyed a job so much as I have mine with you.' It was severance from the last of that long list of clubs, formal and informal, to which he had belonged all his life. Photographs in the *Illustrated London News* show him as a white-bearded Tolstoyan figure looking over his dilapidated garden gate. His eyes look sad and weary.

On 2 August Sir Charles Petrie wrote, as his successor in the *Illustrated London News*:

> It will be a cause of real regret to the readers of this page to learn that it will be no longer contributed by Sir John Squire. Ill-health has compelled him to lay down his pen after more than twenty years' service, but few will deny that during this time he has made his weekly article one of the leading features of literary criticism and entertainment in the English-speaking world. How often has one heard in places where authors and publishers meet the remark, 'A review by Jack Squire sells a book,' and this is, indeed, nothing but the sober truth. His articles were a source not only of enlightenment but also of very real pleasure to an ever-widening circle of readers.

One of the last visitors was an old colleague from Macmillan's, Lovat Dickson, who, in the summer of 1958 found his way to the cottage in spite of Squire's detailed directions. He knew he had found the right place as the grass had been unscythed all the year and the gate hung lopsidedly from one hinge. A large yellow dog bounded towards him. 'Shut up! Lie Down! Come here Sir,' came its owner's stentorian tones through the door. Jack was in bed. With the windows open and the smell of flowers and tar from the road drifting in, the two men finished off a bottle of scotch as they reminisced throughout the long summer afternoon. They discussed the preface that Jack was never going to write to his *Collected Poems*.

Lovat Dickson sent Squire the manuscript of his own autobiography, *The Ante-Room*, which he later dedicated to him as 'Poet, man of letters and unforgettable friend.' He continued his visits into autumn and then winter. The situation was entirely different; the cottage was icy; there was a damp smell of heaps of decaying books and papers; a log fire burned ineffectually at one end of the room. Jack himself was bundled up with sweaters and a mountain of blankets. Dickson sat by the bed as a wintry blast came from under the front door. Only Jack's company and the whisky made his discomfort bearable. 'It was plain to see that he was dying and with him a whole world. He was nearly the last of the brave, bright hard-living, hard-drinking band of Georgians,' Lovat Dickson thought. 'What giants, what tremendous fellows they had appeared to be! – G. K. Chesterton, Hilaire Belloc, Desmond MacCarthy, Tom Welby, Robert Lynd, Archie Macdonell, Dick Shanks, Jack Squire: all gone, every one of them, except Jack here, this bearded man who cried when he thought of death, like a little child afraid of going into the dark.'[630] Despite the discomfort of the cold cottage and the sense of waste that surrounded Squire's end, Lovat Dickson remembered him with admiration:

Throughout a long life never to have betrayed a friend or compromised with the truth for personal advantage or for the sake of comfort and security: that seemed to me really admirable. It did not matter if you drank a little too much, or were extravagant, if you borrowed money and forgot to pay it back, if sometimes you did silly things, if at the end of your life you had not a penny left and had to die in someone else's cottage at someone else's expense, if all your life you had maintained these other virtues.[631]

Bedridden for a year and a half, he was cared for with great kindness by Bertha who found him 'perpetually uncomplaining'. Unable to eat solid food, he was still mentally alert, supposedly preparing his long-delayed edition of his *Collected Poems* for publication. In September Alastair Boyd, the captain of the Invalids, was almost his final correspondent. He sent him a detailed account of their season. Jack Squire did not outlast the winter of 1958. Whether Jack ever saw the dedicatory words of Henry Williamson when they finally emerged in November is not known, for he died peacefully at Diamond Cottage a month later on 20 December. He was seventy-four.

He had already written his own 'Testament':

All things go and come never again;
Life is parting and parting pain.
I lived, I suffered, I loved, I died,
Lust I knew and remorse and pride,
Hope that comes with a morning's rose,
And sadness that falls at a twilight's close,
The daily token of all things' ends:
Beauty and bravery, pity and friends;
And loved the earth and her blossom shed
And thought upon death and shrank in dread.
Yet not to earth should I turn when dead...

Think this: 'He is gone. He will not return,
Though rains may chill us and suns may burn,
Though love is lovely and beauty bright
And the moon still shines in earth's velvet night,
He has gone, he has done with us all at last,
And only to us remains the past.'
And it may be, then, so far away

That I shall be riding the Milky Way
On a strong-winged horse with a heart like fire
In a new-born youth, with the old desire,
Ranging the ranks of a host of stars
For stranger glories and stranger wars,
Prouder devils and sterner worth
Or a peace that never was found on earth.[632]

Jack Squire had always talked about returning to the county of his birth but his will revealed to his family's surprise that he wanted to be buried in the tiny Devon village of Broadwood Widger that he had once, one hot July afternoon long ago, tried to find. It seemed a very peculiar choice to Doll. 'I don't even know where it is,' she wrote. But in his mind's eye Jack knew very well where it was. Just like Thomas Hardy and John Freeman he wanted to be alongside his forebears in a country churchyard. 'In the high, remote churchyard of Broadwood Widger, in Devon, not far from the Cornish border, there is a simple tombstone to my great-grandfather, with cherubs carved on the upper corners. The tors of Dartmoor, holier and nobler to me than all the Alps and all the Andes, can be seen in the distance. The inscription, with dates, runs "John Squire, Yeoman." He owned, as his son owned, and his eldest (alas!) grandson owned, broad acres.'[633] The graveyard of St Nicholas's church is on a hill with wide views over Dartmoor and the winding river Wolf. At a high point is Jack Squire's grave. Under his name is carved one word: 'Poet'.

Afterwords

In his will Squire named two main creditors. He gave generous (and impossible) instructions that the money he owed to the Horse and Groom should be paid before the Inland Revenue took their share. Raglan duly paid them £21. John Betjeman looked after the preparation of his Collected Poems *for publication; they were published a year after Squire's death by the firm he had worked with for nearly thirty years, Macmillan. The dedication was to Bertha Seton Usborne. She wrote to Raglan, 'One wouldn't want him back to suffer. But for me, life is meaningless without him.'*

Fifteen years after Squire's death, the Cornish poet Charles Causley came across a review of the Oxford Book of Twentieth Century English Verse, *which referred casually to 'the unspeakable Squire'. In response he wrote 'A Visit to J. C. Squire (1884–1958)'.*[634]

> High in the church yard, even higher
> Than the church tower, the poet Squire
> Lies in the fist of Devonshire.
>
> Crumpled grasses grow aslant
> His tall grave. At his hand, spent
> Daffodils, and the wild mint.
> Never a note I hear, nor cry,
> But an aircraft hurling by
> Hidden in the whining sky.

As I read the standing slate
Warming in the Maytime heat
His heart moves. I hear it beat.
And his voice is speaking still.
When the sear days come to kill,
And the year begin to fail;
And the stony tors unfold
Certainties of winter cold.

Broadwood Widger, August, 1973

Eileen enjoyed good health until she had a stroke in April 1970, and died two weeks later surrounded by her family. She was buried in the graveyard of Hintlesham church with her mother and father. Cecily did not remarry and died in 1981. Bertha stayed on at Diamond Cottage until her death. Anthony became a film director. Julia pursued a career in theatrical and costume design and married the actor George Baker. Raglan became a very successful architect. The Architecture Club still thrives, as do the Invalids.

Alan Pryce-Jones edited his pocket anthology Georgian Poets *in 1959. The* Georgian Poetic *by Myron Simon helped to rehabilitate the movement; James Reeves's anthology,* Georgian Poetry,[635] *(1962) was apologetic. The* Georgian Revolt: Rise and Fall of a Poetic Ideal, 1910–1922, *by Robert H. Ross (1967)[636] began a reassessment. Ross developed the idea that a group under Squire of 'Neo-Georgians' were responsible for watering down the poetic quality of the first two Georgian anthologies. Merryn Williams's excellent anthology* The Georgians 1901–1930 *(2009)[637] demonstrated the variety of Georgian poetry and is a sign of a changing climate of opinion, as are essays on Georgian verse and Rupert Brooke in* British Poetry 1900–1950 *(Macmillan 1995).[638] Peter Howarth's* The Art of Modernism, Cambridge, 1925 *is a sympathetic critical account. Tim Kendall's anthology* Poetry of the First World War *(OUP 2013) reclaims Georgian poetry as the voice of the First World War.*

D. J. Taylor has written on Squire incisively in The Prose Factory. John Betjeman edited the Collected Poems in 1959 and in 1963 Squire's friend and fellow cricketer Patrick Howarth published Squire: Most Generous of Men. Squire's own poetry has not enjoyed the beginnings of the general reassessment of Georgian poetry. Since the 1930s there has been almost nothing written about it. The selections of parodies in Mock Modernism,[639] and the account of Squire's reaction to Pound and Eliot in The Difficulties of Modernism by Leonard Diepeveen[640] are signs that Squire has not been completely forgotten, but he remains, as Alan Pryce-Jones wrote eighty years ago, 'an unkindly neglected voice'.[641]

Acknowledgements

D. J. Taylor has been an inspiration: *The Prose Factory* (Chatto and Windus, 2016) started my interest in Squire and this book is indebted to his ideas and scholarship. Michael Daly's careful reading helped a great deal. Alan Midgley saved me from many historical and geographical errors. I have relied on his insights. David Sharp gave me a historical and military perspective. Adrian Barlow gave me copies of the *London Mercury* and, as always, much encouragement and advice. Ewen Gilmour and Richard Butler (President and Captain of the Invalids) gave me the benefit of their knowledge of the club's history. William Thomas read and improved the manuscript at a late stage. Ken Jones has been a patient advisor on the internet and rescued me from computer illiteracy. Tony Leech has managed the photographs with his usual generosity and skill. Roger Squire, a grandson of Sir John, has been generous with his time, his advice, his archive and his hospitality. No biographer could have been luckier.

My wife, Sue, has lived with every moment of the writing. Without her deciphering skills, advice, encouragement and patience I could not have written this book.

My thanks also to:

Jonathan Ballakian
Margi Blunden
Richard Bradford
Stephen Clarke

Celia Clear
T. M. Farmiloe
The late John Harrison
Louis Jebb
Christopher Matheson
Richard Peaver
Frederic Raphael
Sylvia Reynolds
Professor Martin Ferguson Smith
The late Bernard Waites
Ann Watanabe-Rocco
Michael Wace

John Smart
Thornage, Norfolk

Source References

Abbreviations used:

Beinecke: Beinecke Rare Book and Manuscript Library, Yale University

Berg: Berg Library New York. Letters to and from Edward Marsh.

CA: Chiswick Archive of Roger Squire. Letters to his sister Doll and his mother et al.

CP: *Collected Poems of Sir John Squire*, ed. John Betjeman, Macmillan, 1959.

Gosse: *The Life and Letters of Edmund Gosse*, Evan Charteris, Heinemann, 1931.

H and B: *The Honeysuckle and the Bee,* Heinemann 1937

Howarth: *Squire: Most Generous of Men*, Patrick Howarth, Hutchinson, 1963

Huculak: *The Oxford Critical and Cultural History of Modernist Magazines*, 'The London Mercury and other Moderns', J. Matthew Huculak, Oxford University Press, 2009.

ILN: *Illustrated London News.*

LM: *London Mercury.*

LW: *Land and Water*

NS: *New Statesman.*

R and M: *Reflections and Memories*, William Heinemann, 1935.

St J: St John's Archive Cambridge. By permission of the

	Master and Fellows of St John's College, Cambridge
Texas:	Harry Ransom Center, University of Texas at Austin.
TLS:	*Times Literary Supplement.*
UCLA:	Department of Special Collections, Young Research Library at the University of California, Los Angeles.

Endnotes

Prelude

1   *The Rise and Fall of the Man of Letters*, John Gross, Macmillan 1969.

2   *TLS*, 18 January 2002, 17.

3   *Guardian*, 2 August 2002.

4   F. R. Leavis thought Squire 'the epitome of what men mean by the word philistine'. The poet Thom Gunn, reviewing Squire's *Collected Poems* in 1961, is a very good example of a still-prevailing literary consensus. 'Squire is now so forgotten that it is surprising to note that he that he died only two years ago.' There was no point, he felt, in attacking a man nobody read, and yet he did so. 'His style is painfully dated, and appears transparently bad today resembling a schoolboy who has just discovered the work of Sir Henry Newbolt.'

5   *Collected Letters*, ed. R. K. R. Thornton, Carcanet, 1991, 31 December, 521.

6   *Ibid*, 12.

7   Peter Howarth in *The Art of Modernism*, Cambridge, 2005, noted four distinct strands: those included in *Georgian Poetry*; precursors such as W. H. Davies and Walter de la Mare; sympathisers such as Owen and Frost; a post-war coterie led by JCS. Divisions between modernists and traditionalists have taken various forms: traditional vs avant garde; rootedly natural vs exiled international; unified vs fragmented; formal vs free. None of the above divisions applied in 1912. These are hints not categories.

8   *CP*, viii.

9   12 December 1922.

10   *Required Writing: Miscellaneous Pieces,* Philip Larkin, Faber and Faber, 1983, 216-7.

11   Peter Howarth in *The Art of Modernism*.

12   *The Times*, 24 December 1958. There has been almost no comment on Squire's short stories and essays. In a world of quiet neglect, D. J. Taylor's account of

his work in *The Prose Factory* and Richard Bradford's essay in *Literary Rivals* are notable exceptions.

13   22 December 1958.

14   Huculak, 240.

15   *The Sphere*, 31 December 1932.

16   *The Times*, 16 December 1932.

Chapter 1: The Honeysuckle and the Bee

17   *CP*, 1.

18   *CP*, 9.

19   This is now Broadwoodwidger but was then written as two words.

20   *Reflections and Memories*, Heinemann, 1935, 23.

21   *Ibid*, 53.

22   UCLA, Letter to Eileen, July 1906.

23   *Sunday Mornings*, Heinemann, 1930, 186.

24   A Polyphloisboisterous Critic,' *Books in General*, Heinemann, 101.

25   *Little Innocents*, Cobden Sanderson, 1934, 124.

26   *Water-Music*, 110-111.

27   *WM*, 112.

28   *Ibid*, 307.

29   *CA*, Letter to Doll, 22 December 1933.

30   *ILN*, 3 April 1954.

31   *Water-Music,* Heinemann, 1939, 59.

32   *CP,* 'A Dedication', 37.

33   'Letters to Posterity', unpublished MS, Box 1 UCLA.

34   *Poems and Baudelaire Flowers*, New Age Press, 116

35   *CA*, 'To Doll', 22 December 1933.

36   *Ibid*, 40.

37   *History of Blundell's School*, Mike Sampson, Blundell's School, 2011.

38   *Life at the Mermaid*, Collins, 1927, 9.

39   *H and B*, 209.

40   *H and B*, 198

Chapter 2: Cambridge: The Rebel Heart

41   *Squire: Most Generous of Men*, Patrick Howarth, Hutchinson, 1961, 24.

42   This account of Squire's Cambridge days is based on 'Reminiscences of Sir John Squire,' published in World Review August 1950 as an extract for a forthcoming autobiography. St J.

43   *R and M*, 'The Gold Tree', 57-62.
44   *H and B*, 155-7.
45   This account of Keeling is based on Rupert Brooke, Christopher Hassall, Faber, 1964, 117-9.
46   *Ibid*, 22 December 1933.
47   *Diary of Beatrice Webb*, Norman and Jeanne Mackenzie, LSE, 1984, 98.
48   *Ibid*, 98.
49   *CP*, 'An Impression Received from a Symphony', 56.

Chapter 3: You are my Sky

50   UCLA.
51   St J, 24 September 1905.
52   *Poems and Baudelaire Flowers*, 33.
53   UCLA, Letter to Eileen, 1 May 1906.
54   *Ibid*, 20 March 1906.
55   *Ibid*, 16 May.
56   *CP*, 28.

Chapter 4: Journalism

57   *R and M*, 'A London Reverie', 33.
58   *Ibid*, 35.
59   UCLA, Letter to Eileen, Sunday 23 September 1906.
60   *CP*, 42.
61   *R and M*, 'A London Reverie', Heinemann, 1935, 37.
62   UCLA, Letter to Eileen, November 1906.
63   *Art and Socialism*, 15.
64   New Age, vol. 2, no. 1, 31 October 1907, 17.
65   UCLA, Letter to Eileen, 3 February 1907.
66   *Rupert Brooke: Life, Death and Myth*, Nigel Jones, Richard Cohen, 2001.
67   UCLA, Letter to Eileen, nd.
68   UCLA, Letter to Eileen, 4 February 1907.
69   *R and M*, 'A London Reverie', 28.
70   *Ibid*, 29.
71   *Ibid*, 30-31.
72   *Ibid*, 41.
73   *Life at the Mermaid*, Collins, 1927, 111.

Chapter 5: Marriage and the New Age

74   *The Times*, 24 December 1958.

75   *R and M*, 7-12.

76   *Ibid*, 40-41.

77   *Ibid*, 38-41.

78   *H and B*, 213.

79   *WM*, 226-8.

80   *H and B*, 215.

81   Huculak, 246ff.

82   *Ibid*, 213.

83   *ILN*, 21 December 1940.

84   *Ezra Pound: A Portrait of the Man and his Work*, vol. 1, 'The Young Genius,
      A. David Moody, OUP.

85   This account is based on *The New Age under Orage*, Wallace Martin,
      Manchester University Press, 1967.

86   *Poems and Baudelaire Flowers,* New Age Press, 1909, 16.

87   *Ibid*, 18.

88   *New Age,* 6 Jan 1910, 234.

89   *Ibid*, 28.

90   Howarth, 74.

91   *Ibid*, 73.

92   UCLA, 1 April 1913.

93   *WM*, 239-40.

94   *The Gold Tree*, 'A Summer's Day', 31-5.

95   *The Times,* 8 February 1912.

96   'Scrapbook', February 1919, UCLA.

97   *Collected Parodies,* 160-61

98   *The New Poetic,* C. K. Stead, Continuum, 2005, 41.

99   *Harold Monro and the Poetry Bookshop*, Joy Grant, Routledge and Kegan
      Paul, 1967, 28.

100   *Literary Taste: How to Form it,* Harmsworth-Penguin, 1938, 101.

101   *The Observer,* February 26 1921

102   *ILN*, 26 February 1949.

103   *H and B*, 211.

104   *Sunday Mornings,* Heinemann, 1930, 330-337.

105   *R and M*, 41.

106   *Strange Meetings: The Poets of the Great War*, Harry Ricketts, Chatto and
      Windus, 2010, 5-7.

107   *Collected Parodies*, Heinemann, 1920, 51-2.

108   *Ibid*, 56.

109   *The Georgian Literary Scene*, Frank Swinnerton, Dent, 1938, 197.

110 This account is taken from *Rupert Brooke: A Memoir, Edward Marsh*, John Lane, 1918, 189-191.

111 Stead, 44.

112 *A Number of People*, Edward Marsh, Heinemann,1939, 321.

113 Dominic Hibbert dates the earliest use of Georgian as a term of abuse to January 1920 in a letter of Monro's to Bax. *Harold Monro: Poet of the New Age*, Palgrave, 2002, 208 n.

114 *Georgian Poetry*, 1911-12.

115 *Edward Marsh: Patron of the Arts,* Christopher Hassall, Longmans 1959, 190.

116 *Selected Literary Criticism*, ed. Antony Beal, Heinemann, 1956, 75

117 *Poetry and Drama*, ed. Harold Monro,1 March 1913, 51.

Chapter 6: New Statesman

118 *Coming to London*, Rose Macaulay, ed. John Lehmann, Phoenix House, 1957, 165.

119 The account of Squire is based on *The New Statesman: The History of the First Fifty Years*, Edward Hyams, Longmans, 1963, passim, and the *New Statesman: Portrait of a Political Weekly*, Adrian Smith, Frank Cass, 1996.

120 *Diary of Beatrice Webb, 1905-24*, vol.3, ed. Norman and Jeanne Mackenzie, Virago, 1984, 288.

121 *Ibid*, 287.

122 *Ibid*, 288.

123 *NS*, 3 May 1913.

124 *NS*, 26 April, 1913.

125 *Collected Parodies*, Heinemann, 1921, 31.

126 *NS*, 14 January 1915.

127 *Collected Parodies*, 81-2.

128 *Ibid*, 38.

129 *TLS*, 8 March 1918.

130 *More Books on the Table,* Scribners, New York, 1921, 147.

131 *Tricks of the Trade*, Martin Secker, 1917, 28-9.

132 *Ibid*, 33.

133 JCS to Marsh, 29 December 1913, Berg.

134 26 August 1920, Berg.

135 *CP*, 58.

136 *CP*, 55-6.

137 *By-Ways Round Helicon*, Iolo Williams, Heinemann, 1922.

138 *CP*, 'On a Friend Recently Dead,' 138.

139 'Fragments of a Memorial Ode,' *Form*, vol. 1, no.1 ,1916.

140 *CA*, JCS 'To Mater', Christmas Day 1913.

141   *The Three Hills and Other Poems*, Howard Latimer, 1913, 73.
142   *Ibid*,24.
143   *Ibid*,51.
144   *Ibid*, 51.
145   *Ibid*, 80.
146   *Ibid*, 81-2.
147   'A Reasonable Protestation,' *The Three Hills and Other Poems*, 83.
148   7 August 1913.
149   20 August 1913.
150   20 December 1913.
151   *WM*, 93-103.
152   *ILN*, 15 January 1938.
153   I am indebted to Adrian Barlow's essay, 'If Armageddon's On', in *'Archiv fur das Studium der neueren Sprachen und Literatauren'*, 2015, 252: 2.
154   *ILN*, 5 April 1952.
155   *ILN*, 26 February 1949.
156   *Life for Life's Sake*, Richard Aldington, New York, 1941, 148.
157   *NS*, 4 July 1914.
158   *Collected Parodies*, 90.
159   'Books in General', *New Statesman*, 4 July 1914, 406.
160   *NS*, 11 July 1914.
161   *NS*, 11 July 1914.

Chapter 7: The Great War: The March

162   *NS*, 5 December 1914.
163   *Books in General*, 'August 1914', Heinemann, 1918, 75.
164   *Rupert Brooke: a biography*, Christopher Hassall, Faber, 1964, 459.
165   *NS*, 29 August 1914.
166   *Ibid*, 75-79.
167   *The Survival of the Fittest and Other Poems*, George Allen and Unwin, 1916, 57.
168   *NS*, 29 August 1914.
169   *Ibid*, 4 November 1914.
170   *Books in General*, First Series, William Heinemann, 80.
171   *NS*, 21 November 1914.
172   *Ibid*.
173   *Books in General*, First Series, 199.
174   *Poems of the Great War and Songs and Sonnets for England in Wartime*, reviewed NS, 26 September 1914.
175   *NS*, 25 September 1915.

176   *Keeling: Letters and Reflections,* ed E.T. George, Allen and Unwin, 1918, 238-241.

177   Baring to JCS, 21 August, UCLA.

178   This account is based on *Books in General,* Second Series, 'Songs of the Trenches', Alfred A. Knopf, 1920, 212-216.

179   *Letters of Virginia Woolf,* Nigel Nicolson, The Hogarth Press, vol. 2, 23 January 1915.

180   *Virginia Woolf,* Hermione Lee, Chatto and Windus, 1996, 378-79.

181   *Diary of Virginia Woolf,* Anne Olivier Bell, Hogarth Press, 1976, 133.

182   *Ibid,* vol. V, 62.

183   *Western Mail,* 5 February 1925.

184   *LW,* 17 September 1917.

185   Marsh to Squire, 25 April 1915, Berg.

186   Squire to Marsh 27 April 1915, Berg.

187   *Ibid,* 1 May 1915.

188   *H and B,* 152.

189   Cadbury Research Library, Birmingham, JS 42.g

190   'Overture to the Valkyries,' Miscellaneous Papers, UCLA.

191   *Form: A Quarterly,* vol. 1, John Lane, 44.

192   *NS,* 1 May 1915.

193   *NS,* 22 May 1915.

194   *NS,* 5 June 1915.

195   *NS,* 18 April 1914.

196   *NS,* 26 July 1913.

197   *NS,* 14 August 1915.

198   *NS,* 20 November 1915.

199   Squire to Marsh, 13 January 1916, Berg.

Chapter 8: They Thought War was an Evil Thing

200   29 December 1915, Berg.

201   *NS,* 8 December 1914.

202   Allen and Unwin, 191.

203   *CP,* 193.

204   Appended to letter to EM, 16 April 1915, Berg.

205   *Figures in Modern Literature,* Heinemann, 1924.

206   *Forward,* 27 May 1916.

207   *R and M,* 40-41.

208   *NS,* 'In Kitchener's Army,' 12 December 1914.

209   *CP,* 'An Epilogue,' 26.

210   *Ibid,* 25-7.

211   *Ibid*, 30-32.

212   *Collected Poems of Roy Campbell*, 'The Georgiad', Bodley Head, 1949.

Chapter 9: Wars and Rumours

213   *NS*, 25 March 1916.

214   The first section of *Tricks of the Trade* was called 'How they do it'. The second imagined how various writers might have tackled other poets' themes and titles, for example, 'If a very new poet had written Tennyson's *The Lotos-Eaters*.' The best known was a double parody, 'If Gray had written his elegy in the Cemetery of Spoon River instead of in that of Stoke Poges.' Edgar Lee Master's series of verse poems was a catalogue of the crimes of small-town Illinois.

> The curfew tolls the knell of parting day,
> The whippoorwill salutes the rising moon,
> And wanly glimmer in her gentle ray,
> The sinuous windings of the turbid Spoon.
>
> Here where the flattering and mendacious swarm
> Of lying epitaphs their secrets keep,
> At last incapable of further harm
> The lewd forefathers of the village sleep…
>
> Full many a vice is born to thrive unseen,
> Full many a crime the world does not discuss,
> Full many a pervert lives to reach a green
> Replete old age, and so it was with us…

The effect is not so much parody as surprise in joining together the poise of eighteenth-century English couplets and the tabloid excesses of Illinois – the comedy of the incongruous.

215   JCS to Marsh, 11 August 1917, Berg.

216   *The Soul of Wit*, George Rostrevor Hamilton, Heinemann, 1923, xxii.

217   *CP*, 21-2.

218   *CP*, 39

219   *Ibid*, 23.

220   *Figures in Modern Literature*, 180.

221   *CP*, 28.

222   *Ibid*, 363-4.

223   *LM*, vol. xxi, no.121, 1929, 1-2.

224 *LW*, 27 September 1917.

225 *The Observer*, 14 May 1922.

226 *Life and Letters*, Hodder and Stoughton, 1920, 35.

227 *NS*, 28 April 1917.

228 *NS*, 16 November 1918.

229 'J. C. Squire v. Modernism', in *Literary Rivals*, Richard Bradford, Robson Press, 2014, 253.

230 This paragraph is based on Squire's review of *Marching on Tanga*, *Life and Letters*, 27 September 1917.

231 Oxford, 1936, xxxiv.

Chapter 10: Georgian Poetry

232 *CP*, 'The Moon', 158.

233 *LM*, December 1919.

234 *CP*, 159.

235 JCS to Edward Marsh, Berg, 26 August 1919.

236 *Aberdeen Press and Journal*, 26 August 1920.

237 In Harold Monro's Chapbook, vol 2, No. 9 March 1920. See *Oxford Critical and Cultural History of Modernist Magazines*, 'The Cause of Poetry', Mark S. Morrison, 421-22.

238 *Western Mail*, 5 February 1925.

239 'The Verse of G K Chesterton', *The Living Age*, 1 August 1928.

240 *CP*, 114.

241 *Ibid*, 117-8.

242 *Tatler*, 4 July 1917.

243 4 July 1917.

244 *Letters of Virginia Woolf*, vol.4, Hogarth Press, 1976, Nigel Nicolson, 188

245 *Egoist*, 'Verse Pleasant and Unpleasant', T. S. Eliot, March 1918, 43ff.

246 *Edward Marsh, Patron of the Arts*, 420.

247 *LW*, 73ff.

248 The figures are given in *Georgian Poetry, The Critical Heritage*, ed. Timothy Rogers, Routledge, 1977, p.17

249 Leonard Parsons, 1920.

250 *Ibid*, 149-151.

251 According to the American critic Robert Ross, 'Neo-Georgianism' was beginning to replace Georgianism as Squire's influence grew over the last three numbers. When the term Georgian is so slippery, *Neo-Georgian* merely adds to the confusion. Joy Grant defined its characteristic features as 'a vacuous nature worship, a false naiveté and the resurgence of a romantic vocabulary'. It is ironic that Monro's own sonnet sequence 'Week-end' gave its name to

the vices of the later Georgianism he so much disliked: it was pounced upon by critics such as F. R. Leavis who dubbed all of them – Georgians and Neo-Georgians – 'Week-end poets'. Neo-Georgian has become part of the literary currency, but there is much more continuity and variety in *Georgian Poetry* than Monro and Joy Grant suggest: it is a distinction without a difference. For the second decade of the twentieth century and afterwards the Georgian tradition was the mainstream of English poetry.

252   Cadbury, Research Library, University of Birmingham, JS32.
253   *Letters of Lytton Strachey,* ed. Paul Levy, May 1917, Viking, 2000.
254   26 August 1917, Berg.
255   *Arnold Bennett: A Biography*, Reginald Pound, Heinemann, 1952, 252.
256   Howarth, 114.
257   Published later in the *New York Times*, 12 December 1914.
258   *LW*, 9 October 1919.
259   *Lytton Strachey*, Michael Holroyd, Heinemann 1973, 756.
260   *NS*, 19 October 1918.
261   *CP*, 16.
262   *Old and New Masters*, Robert Lynd, Scribner's, 1919, 211.
263   *Tradition and Change*, Arthur Waugh, Chapman and Hall, 1919, 138-145.
264   Howarth, 113.
265   Edmund Gosse to Squire, 25 May 1918, UCLA.
266   Prospero in *The Tempest* Act I Scene 2.
267   *CP*, 155.
268   *Ibid*, 156.
269   Edmund Gosse to Squire, 3 August 1918.
270   *CP*, 2-4.
271   *CP*, 72.
272   *ILN*, 9 July 1949.
273   *NS*, 19 October 1918.

Chapter 11: Peace

274   *Letters of Virginia Woolf,* Nicolson, vol. 2, 361.
275   *NS*, 31 January 1920 and LW, 17 July 1919.
276   *Ibid*, 26 June 1921.
277   *NS*, 19 April 1919.
278   *Ibid*, 29 May 1915.
279   *Books in General,* First Series, William Heinemann, 230.
280   *NS*, 28 June 1919.
281   *LM*, January 1920, 260.
282   *Selections from Modern Poets*, Martin Secker, 1921, vi-vii.

283   *NS*, 31 January 1920.

284   Squire to Marsh, 2 September 1918, Berg.

285   *Edward Marsh*, 448.

286   *Diary of Virginia Woolf*, vol 1, 143.

287   *Essays on Poetry*, 'Subject in Poetry', George H. Doran, 1923,12.

288   *Coterie*, Spring 1920.

289   *NS*, 18 August 1917.

290   *Life for Life's Sake*, Richard Aldington, Viking Press, 1941, 218.

291   *Letters of T. S. Eliot*, ed. Valerie Eliot and Hugh Haughton, Yale, 2009, 416.

292   *The Complete Prose of T. S. Eliot: The Critical Edition: The Perfect Critic 1919-26*, ed. Anthony Cuda and Ronald Schuchard, Baltimore, 2013.

293   *Letters of T.S. Eliot, vol.1 1898-1922*, Faber and Faber, 2009, 10 November 1919, 415-6.

294   *Letters of John Middleton Murry to Katherine Mansfield*, New York, Franklin Watts, 1983, 199.

295   *Letters of JM to KM*, 26 Nov 1919, 232.

296   *Ibid*, 227.

Chapter 12: 'The London Murkury'

297   *The Oxford Critical and Cultural History of Modernist Magazines*, 'The *London Mercury* and other Moderns', J Matthew Huculak, Oxford University Press, 2009. Ezra Pound: The Critical Heritage, ed. Eric Homberger, Routledge and Kegan Paul, 1972, 83.

298   Robert Graves to JCS, 24 September 1916, UCLA.

299   *CP*, 13.

300   It came to an end in 1919 after only three numbers.

301   *Western Mercury Morning News and Daily Gazette*, October 1935.

302   Squire to Marsh, 26 August 1919, Berg.

303   *LM*, November 1919, 1-6.

304   *Ibid*, 4.

305   Gosse to Squire, 31 October 1919, UCLA.

306   *Letters of John Middleton Murry to Katherine Mansfield*, C. A. Hankin, Constable, 1983, 185.

307   *Diary of Virginia Woolf*, vol. 2, 16.

308   *Observer*, 12 March 1920.

309   *Ibid*, 19 March 1920.

310   The Royal Society of Literature had awarded the Edmund de Polignac Prize for the three years before the war to Walter de la Mare, John Masefield and James Stephens.

311   Edward Marsh to Alice Warrender, 16 January 1920, Berg.

312 A. D. Peters in *Evelyn Waugh*, Selina Hastings, Minerva, 1995, 349.

313 *Wheels*, Sixth Cycle, C. W. Daniel, 1921, 57-8.

314 *Edward Marsh, Patron of the Arts,* 483.

315 *Athenaeum*, 5 December, 1284-5.

316 *Edward Marsh, Patron of the Arts,* 474.

317 *Ibid*, 29 November, 235.

318 *CP*, 35-36.

319 *H and B*, 155

320 *Figures in the Foreground*, Frank Swinnerton, Hutchinson, 1963, 70.

321 Squire: Miscellaneous Papers, UCLA.

322 *The Georgian Revolt, Rise and Fall of a Poetic Ideal, 1910-1922*, Robert H. Ross, 1967, 221.

323 15 November 1924.

324 *The Art of Letters,* 'The Group', Robert Lynd, New York, 1921.

325 T. S. Eliot, 'London Letter,' *Dial*, New York, vol. LXX, no. 4, (April 1921) 448-453.

326 *Letters of T. S. Eliot,* vol. 1, 29 April 1922, 663.

327 Huculak, 240 ff.

328 *T. S. Eliot: Inventions of the March Hare*, ed. Christopher Ricks, Faber and Faber, 1996, 284.

329 'To John Quinn', *Letters of T. S. Eliot*, Faber and Faber, 2009, 435.

330 *New Age*, 21 December 1911

331 *Ezra Pound: The Critical Heritage,* ed. Eric Homberger, Routledge and Kegan Paul, 1972, 83.

332 *Letters of T.S. Eliot,* 'To John Quinn', vol. 1, 435.

333 *LM*, March 1921, 467.

Chapter 13: Approaching America

334 This account based on Howarth, 150-53 and Broker and Thacker, 248-249.

335 *The Outlook*, 6 November 1920.

336 T. S. Eliot, 'London Letter,' *The Dial*, New York, vol. LXX, no. 4, (April 1921) 448-453.

337 'Sketch Book of Miscellaneous Notes,' Box 2, UCLA.

338 *CP*, 36.

339 *CP*, 75-6.

340 *Daily Northwestern*, 23 November 1921.

341 20 March 1926.

342 T. S. Eliot, 'To John Quinn', *Letters of T. S. Eliot,* vol. 1: 1898-1922, 378.

343 JCS to P. B. Clayton, 3 November 1922, UCLA.

344 *Portrait of Logan Pearsall Smith*, John Russell, Dropmore Press, 1950, 101ff.

345   *CP*, 77.

346   *CP*, 76.

347   *Ibid*, 78.

348   *Ibid*, 178-87.

349   *CP*, 187.

350   This account of the American trip is based on *Punch, A. P. Herbert*, Reginald Pound, Michael Joseph, 1976, 68-74, and 'Sketch Book' passim.

351   Gosse to Squire, 2 January 1922, Texas.

352   *The Spectator*, 18 December 1959.

353   *Chicago Tribune*, 24 September 1922.

354   *Radio Times*, 12 July 1923.

Chapter 14: Best of Editors

355   *Diary of Virginia Woolf*, 127.

356   *Ibid*, 62.

357   *Ibid*, 127.

358   *LM*, May 1921, 19.

359   *Sunday Mornings*, 289.

360   Thomas Hardy to JCS, 3 June 1924, Texas.

361   This account is based on *WM*, 222-26.

362   *ILN*, 15 July 1939.

363   Thomas Hardy to JCS, 16 June 1923, Texas.

364   *Gosse*, 446.

365   *Ibid*, 31 October 1919.

366   22 April 1920, UCLA.

367   Gosse to Squire, 9 October 1919.

368   *Ibid*, 26 November 1919.

369   *LM*, December 1919, 206-7.

370   *Selected Letters of Edith Sitwell*, Richard Greene, Virago, 1997, 235.

370   *Edward Marsh, Patron of the Arts*, 1959.

370   *Selected Letters of Edith Sitwell*, 158.

371   LM, January 1920, 335.

372   *Wheels*, (Sixth Cycle) 1921, C.W. Daniel, 62.

373   *The Collected Satires and Poetry of Osbert Sitwell*, London 1931, 92-103.

374   *Facades: Edith, Osbert and Sacheverell Sitwell*, John Pearson, Macmillan, 1978, 151-2.

375   *Who Killed Cock Robin, Osbert Sitwell*, C. W. Daniel, 1921.

376   *Collected Poems and Satires of Osbert Sitwell*, Duckworth, 1931.

377   JCS to H. E. Palmer, 13 December 1938.

378   *Tatler*, 'The Bystander', 19 April 1939.

379   Prefatory Note, *Georgian Poetry 1920-22*, The Poetry Bookshop, 1922.

380   *LM*, vol. VI, 1922.

381   *Letters of T. S. Eliot,* vol. 2, 2 May 1924, 393.

382   *Ibid*, 14 February 1920.

383   *Threnos for T. E. Lawrence and Other Writings of Henry Williamson*, John Gregory, Henry Williamson Society, 1994.

384   Private correspondence with the author.

385   Arnold Bennett to JCS, 10 July 1917, Berg.

386   *TLS*, 26 June 1948, 362.

387   *Background with Chorus,* Frank Swinnerton, Hutchinson, 1956.

388   Letter to Squire, Berg, November 1913.

389   Quoted by J. C. Trewin, *Birmingham Post,* 31 December 1958.

390   *Some Contemporary Poets*, Harold Monro, Leonard Parsons, 1920, 149.

391   *CP*, 33.

Chapter 15: London: Back to Work

392   Gloucester Archives, D10500/1/P/3/127.

393   'Dwelling in the Shadows: Writing the Biography of Ivor Gurney,' Kate Kennedy, *The Use of English*, Summer 2014, 85.

394   Gloucester Archives, D10500/1/P/325.

395   JCS to Walter de la Mare, 25 June 1923, UCLA.

396   *WM*, 226-8.

397   *LM*, 'Poetry,' October 1923, 655-6.

398   JCS to Elizabeth Belloc, 17 March 1923, UCLA.

399   *LM*, 'The Man Who Wrote Free Verse,' August 1928, 337-346. I am indebted to 'J. C. Squire v. Modernism' in *Literary Rivals*, Richard Bradford, Robson Press, 2014.

400   'Evening,' Richard Aldington.

401   *The Sphere*, 15 November 1924.

402   *NS*, Feb 1920, 387.

403   *Georgian Poetry, 1911-1922: The Critical Heritage,* Timothy Rogers, Routledge, 1977, 17.

404   *The Group: The Art of Letters,* Robert Lynd, New York, 1921.

405   *LM*, vol. vii, 1923, 432.

406   Gosse to Squire, 26 October, 1923, UCLA.

407   *LM*, 14 November 1928.

408   'Journal 1924-1930,' Cambridge University Library, CMS Add9852//1/20 124-5.

409   *LM*, March 1926, 547-8.

410   *LM*, 27 June 1926, 117.

411   *LM*, March 1926, 548.

412   *LM*, August 1928.

413   *Glimpses of the Wonderful: The Life of Philip Henry Gosse,* Ann Thwaite, Faber, 2002, 506.

Chapter 16: Hassan and the Theatre

414   *LM*, October 1923, 363.

415   *LM*, December 1925, 260-261.

416   *Copper Gypsy,* unpublished MS, UCLA.

417   *Outside Eden,* 'This Bloody Turf,' William Heinemann, 1933, 3-24.

418   The first three are genuine German dramatists.

Chapter 17: A Centipede with a Foot in a Hundred Camps

419   JCS to Mrs Sidney Webb, 23 November 1922, UCLA.

420   *LM*, vol. viii, no.3, May 1923.

421   *Face in Candlelight,* William Heinemann, 1932, 51.

422   *The Hall of the Chartered Accountants of England and Wales,* Morgate Place, 1937.

423   Huculak, 252.

424   *LM*, August 1920.

425   I owe this thought to Roger Squire.

426   *The Spectator,* 29 July 1922.

427   *The Times,* 29 December 1922.

428   Later he was to admire Liverpool Cathedral and became a keen supporter of the Shakespeare Memorial Theatre and its architect Elisabeth Scott. He wrote an appreciation of the building in the *Architectural Review* in 1932.

429   *Portrait of an Architect,* Raglan Squire, Colin Smythe, 1984.

430   *LM*, March 1928, 503.

431   *LM*, December 1923, 113-16.

432   Edmund Gosse to Squire, 7 September 1926, UCLA.

433   *LM*, vol. 3, 15.

434   *World within World,* Hamish Hamilton, 1951, 98.

435   *LM*, vol. xii, no. 72, October 1925.

436   *Coming to London,* Alan Pryce-Jones, Phoenix House, 1957, 119ff.

437   *LM*, August 1927

438   *Modern Print Artefacts,* Patrick Collier, Edinburgh University Press, 2017, 164.

439   *Modernism/modernity,* vol. 24, no. 3, September 2017, Dennis Duncan, John Hopkins University Press..

440   *LM*, March 1931.

441   *The Times,* 13 November 1931.

442   Huculak, 252.

Chapter 18: Public Fame and Private Pain

443   *The Invalids,* J. C. Squire, Westminster Press, 1923.

444   *Cricket*, Neville Cardus, 1930, viii.

445   *Quill on Willow,* Eric Midwinter, Aeneas Press, 2001, 135.

446   *ILN*, 10 May 1952.

447   *Sing Willow*, Jeremy Paul, The Book Guild, 2002, 22-23.

448   *Daily Mirror,* 2 January 1929.

449   *The Times,* 2 January 1929

450   *Hilaire Belloc: A Memoir,* J. B. Morton, The Garden City Press, 1955, 73.

451   Howarth, 194-5.

452   *Observer*, 10 October 1926.

453   *Letters of Virginia Woolf,* Nicolson, vol. 3, 297.

454   *Diary of Virginia Woolf,* vol. 3, 146.

455   This account is based on *Harold Nicolson: a Biography 1886-1929*, Chatto and Windus, 1980, 305-6.

456   *Critical Times*, Derwent May, Harper Collins, 2001, 135.

457   *Harold Nicolson*, 239.

458   *Observer*, 21 October 1928.

459   *Diary of Virginia Woolf,* vol. 3, 206.

460   *Katherine Mansfield and the Modernist Marketplace: At the Mercy of the Public,* J. Mc Donnell, 148.

461   *Observer*, 9 January 1921.

462   JCS to Eric Gillett, UCLA, 5 March 1927.

463   *Flowers of Speech*, George Allen and Unwin, 1935, 33.

464   *A. P. Herbert,* Reginald Pound, Michael Joseph, 1976, 77-78.

465   JCS to Hardy, 25 September 1927, UCLA.

466   *Glimpses of the Wonderful: The Life of Philip Henry Gosse*, Ann Thwaite, Faber, 2002, 506.

467   *Henry Williamson: Tarka and the Last Romantic*, Anne Williamson, Alan Smith, 1995, 113-4.

468   *LM*, June 1930, 100.

469   *Autobiography*, G. K. Chesterton, Hutchinson, 1933, 304-6.

470   *Tales My Father Taught Me,* Osbert Sitwell, Hutchinson, 1962, 112, in ILN, 24 February 1962.

471   https://www.nytimes.com/1924/08/24/archives/an-acrostic-sonnet.html Accessed 8 January 2021.

472   *LM*, April 1925.

473   *CP*, 124-6.

Chapter 19: The Fight for England

474   *Observer*, 15 July 1928.

475   *ILN*, 21 April 1945.

476   *LM*, vol. XVI, no. 95, 1927, 451.

477   *Daily Telegraph*, 27 January 2018, 13.

478   *British Writers of the Thirties*, Valentine Cunningham, OUP, 1988, 229.

479   *CP*, 109-10.

480   Cadbury Centre, University of Birmingham, Squire Papers, JS40.

481   *LM*, January 32.

482   Longmans, 1932.

483   *Face of England*, Longman, Green and Co, vii.

484   *CP*, 'Stonehenge', 209.

485   *LM*, April 1929, 564.

486   *Ibid*, 564.

487   *LM*, August 1928, 337-346.

488   JCS to Scott Moncrieff, 6 April 1927, UCLA.

Chapter 20: The Thirties: Entre Deux Guerres

489   *Everyman*, 19 November 1931.

490   *England, their England*, Macmillan, 1933.

491   *Diary of Virginia Woolf*, vol. 4, 30 October 1935, 349.

492   *If it had Happened Otherwise: Lapses into Imaginary History*, Longman, Green and Co., 1931.

493   *Listener*, 'The Romance of Excavation', 25 September 1929.

494   *H and B*, 124-30

495   *The Feminine Highbrow Novel*, Nicola Humble, OUP, 1991, 22.

496   *D. S. Mirsky: A Russian English Life*, Gerald Stanton Smith, Oxford, 2000, 91.

497   First used in 1923 in the *Daily Chronicle*. 'The BBC claim to have discovered a new type, "the middle brow". It consists of people who are hoping that some day they will get used to the stuff they ought to like.' *Punch*, 23 December 1925, 673.

498   See '"The Appreciative Understanding of Good Books": *The Listener*, literary advice and the 1930s reader', *Edinburgh Research Literature and History*, vol. 24, no. 2, Alexandra Lawrie, 38-52 for a full discussion. Accessed 8/10/2020.

499   *LM*, March 1929, 227.

500　*Masculine Middlebrow: What Mr.Mr Miniver Read 1880-1950*, Kate Macdonald, Palgrave Macmillan, 2011, 128.

501　JCS to Alan Pryce-Jones, nd., Beinecke.

502　*The Listener*, 14 January 1931.

503　*LM*, 25 November 1927.

504　*The Bonus of Laughter*, Alan Pryce-Jones, Hamish Hamilton, 1987.

505　*Spectator*, 15 April 2000, 46.

506　*Autobiography*, Neville Cardus, Collins, 1947, 192-4.

507　*Ibid*, 193.

508　*Ibid*, 195.

509　Coming to London, 120.

510　*R and M*, 24.

511　*CP*, 38-9

512　*CP*, 83.

513　JB to JCS, UCLA, 14 May 1958.

Chapter 21: Faces in Candlelight

514　*An Unreasonable Man,* Quartet Books, 1946.

515　*Ibid*, 178.

516　*CP*, 209.

517　'Miscellaneous Papers,' UCLA, Box 5. https://clarespark.com/2009/09/21/managerial-psychiatry-jung-henry-a-murray-and-sadomasochism-1/ Accessed 21 June 2020.

518　*A Face in Candlelight,* Heinemann, 1932.

519　*CP*, 85.

520　*CP*, 98.

521　*Ibid*, vii.

522　*CP*, 216.

523　*Ibid*, 125-6.

524　Howarth, 237-39. Henrie is almost certainly not the subject of the poem. The playfulness of the tone and the society background point to Cecily. Howarth either did not know of Squire's affair with Cecily or tried to cover it up.

525　St. J, 12 August 1931.

526　St. J, nd.

527　*CA*, 7 June 1932.

528　*CA*, 20 June 1932.

Chapter 22: They Learn in Suffering

529　*Spectator*, 16 November 1932.

530 *The Times,* 22 November 1932.

531 *LM,* August 1932.

532 St. J, September 15, 1932.

533 *LM,* December 1932.

534 I am indebted to Kathryn McKee, Sub-Librarian and Special Collections Librarian, St John's College, Cambridge, for this piece of sleuthing.

535 *CP,* 92.

536 *Books in General,* Series I, 'Sir William Walton and Mr Lloyd George', 233.

537 *Ibid,* 233.

538 Howarth, 223ff.

539 *John O' London's Magazine,* 2 May 1935.

540 *Selected Letters of Siegfried Sassoon and Edmund Blunden,* Carol Z Rothkopf, Routledge 2020, vol 3, 3.

Chapter 23: Weepings and Wailings

541 *J. B. Priestley,* Vincent Brome, Hamish Hamilton 1988, 142.

542 'My Autobiography', unpublished, unpaginated, UCLA.

543 *Poems of Two Wars,* Hutchinson, 1940.

544 Hugh Walpole to Squire, 13 February 1932, Berg.

545 St J, September 1931.

546 *Fellow Travellers of the Right,* Richard Griffiths, Constable, 1980.

547 St J, 12 December 1933.

548 *Sunshine and Shadow,* Cecil Roberts, Hodder and Stoughton, 1972, 112.

549 *A Historian Looks at His World,* 1972, 115.

550 *Fellow Travellers of the Right,* 49.

551 Squire to Edward Davison, 29 November 1934, Berg.

552 There have been the beginnings of a reappraisal of his editorship of the London Mercury by, for example, J. Matthew Huculak, in his article in the *Oxford Critical and Cultural History of Modernist Magazines,* 'The London Mercury and other Moderns.'

553 17 December 1922.

554 *Guardian,* 29 June 2001.

555 *Later English Poems 1901-1921,* ed. J. E. Wetherell, Mc Clelland and Stewart, Toronto, 1922.

556 'An Old Friend', *The Times,* 24 December 1958.

557 Letter to Doll, 8 September 1933.

558 *Chicago Tribune,* 26 January 1935.

559 *H and B,* 122.

560 *Poems of Two Wars,* 34.

561 *House of Words,* Lovat Dickson, Athenaeum, 1964, 213.

562 Helen Taylor, 'Transatlantic Afterword: The British Gone with the Wind,' in *New Approaches to Gone with the Wind*, ed. James A. Crank, Louisiana State University Press, 2015.

563 Collins, 1937

564 2 February 1937.

Chapter 24: Winter Nightfall

565 *The Spectator,* 27 September 1935, 26.

566 *Edward Marsh: Patron of the Arts,* 599.

567 *ILN*, May 14, 1942.

568 *H and B*, 265-6.

569 *CP*, 204-5.

570 *ILN*, 15 January 1938.

571 *ILN*, 4 June 1938.

572 *WM*, 103.

573 *Ibid*, 278-79.

574 'Autobiography', Box 9, vol. 3, UCLA.

575 *CP*, 205.

576 St J. JCS to Cecily, 28 August 1939.

577 *Daily Telegraph*, 29 December 1958.

578 *CP*, 206.

579 *Punch*, 5 November 1939.

580 13 March 1940.

581 *CA*, Letter to Dorothy, 22 Dec 1939.

582 *ILN*, 15 August 1942.

583 *CP*, 208.

584 JCS to Edward Davison, 31 May 1940, Beinecke.

585 *Punch*, 25 October 1939.

586 *Britain Today,* no. 210, October 1953.

587 *ILN*, 15 August 1942.

588 *CA*, 17 Oct 1940.

589 *TLS*, 3 May 1941, 209.

590 Hutchinson, 1940.

591 *TLS*, 7 September 1940, 447 ff.

592 'Hymn of Hate', March 1940, Birmingham, JS4.

593 In 1944 the 'Tribute to the Red Cross' was sold at Sotheby's for £300.

594 *CA*, 31 January 1941.

595 *ILN*, 30 August 1941.

596 Batsford, 1941

597 *ILN*, 12 July 1941.

598   *ILN*, 16 May 1942.
599   *Rose Macaulay*, Sarah le Fanu, Virago, 2003, 238.
600   Howarth, 266.
601   *CP*, 223-4
602   Howarth, 278.
603   *ILN*, 12 August 1944.
604   'Here and There', *Everyman*, 27 October 1933.
605   *ILN*, 27 Jan 1940.

Chapter 26: Crepuscular

606   *ILN*, 23 June 1945.
607   *Ibid*, 14 August 1943.
608   *ILN*, 2 April 1955.
609   *Ibid*, 2 April 1955.
610   *Ibid*, 5 November 1949.
611   *Ibid*, 8 January 1949.
612   *Ibid*, 9 February 1952.
613   *Ibid*, 23 June 1945.
614   *ILN*, 14 May 1944.
615   *Western Morning News and Daily Gazette*, 4 July 1934.
616   *CA*, 1 July 1949.
617   Howarth, 276.
618   This account is based on *A Smattering of Monsters: A Kind of Memoir*, George Greenfield, Camden House, 1995.
619   *ILN*, September 1948.
620   *ILN*, 22 August 1953.
621   *Ibid*, 10 June 1950.
622   *Ibid*, 1 November 1947.
623   *Ibid*, 24 January 1953.
624   Howarth, 280.

Chapter 27: Testament

625   *ILN*, 26 February 1949.
626   JCS to Harold Macmillan, St. J. Archive, 21 January 1957.
627   https://www.henrywilliamson.co.uk/a-lifes-work. Accessed 20 November 2020.
628   *CP*, 136-8.
629   Betjeman to Squire, 14 May 1958, UCLA.

630   *House of Words,* Lovat Dickson, Athenaeum, 1964, 298.

631   *Ibid,* 296.

632   *CP,* 118.

633   *ILN,* 8 November 1955.

Afterwords

634   *Sunday Telegraph,* 26 August 1973.

635   Penguin, 1962.

636   *The Georgian Revolt: The Rise and Fall of a Poetic Ideal,* Robert H. Ross, Faber and Faber, 1967.

637   Shoestring Press, 2009.

638   *British Poetry 1900-1950,* eds. Gary Day and Brian Docherty, Macmillan, 1995.

639   *Mock Modernism: An Anthology of Parodies, Travesties and Frauds,* University of Toronto, 2014.

640   *Difficulties of Modernism,* Leonard Diepeveen, Routledge, 2003.

Index

Key to abbreviations:

GP	*Georgian Poetry Anthologies*
LM	*London Mercury*
NS	*New Statesman*
TLS	*Times Literary Supplement*

Abercrombie, Lascelles, xv, 102, 187, 230, 363

Aldington, Richard 102, 114, 115, 119, 187, 198-9, 240, 242, 286

Allan, Maud 158

Allison, J. M. 221

American Mercury 212, 214, 219, 353

Andersen, Hans 6

Architecture Club xii, 261, 262, 287, 294, 299, 414

Asquith, Herbert 34, 165, 258

Athenaeum 191, 197, 198, 201, 204, 205, 207, 208, 279

Auden, W. H. xi, 318, 399

Austin, Alfred 46, 87, 101

Balderston, John 253

Baldwin, Stanley 278, 284, 296, 301, 302, 380

Barclay, Mrs 136, 180

Bard, Wilkie 133, 210

Baring, Maurice 126, 288

Barrie, J. M. 178, 223, 226, 254

Barrington-Ward, Robert 370

Bartók, Béla 77

Baudelaire, Charles 14-15, 34, 54, 81, 82-3, 111, 206, 248, 327

Bax, Arnold 274, 316

Bax, Clifford 274, 316, 399

Beardsley, Aubrey 87-8, 91, 254

Beckett, Samuel 402

Beerbohm, Max 339

Bell, Clive 37, 237, 243

Belloc, Hilaire xi, 22, 98

Belloc-Lowndes, Marie 313

Bennett, Arnold 77, 79, 87, 154, 167, 192, 193, 234, 258, 267, 273, 279, 315

Benson, A.C. 23, 115

Bergson, Henri 24, 78

Betjeman, John xi, xii, xiii, xv, 174, 261, 265, 296, 315, 318, 321, 403, 406

Billing, Pemberton 158

Binyon, Laurence xv, 187, 195, 199, 200, 278, 363

BLAST 115-17, 131, 137, 191

Bliss, William 205-6, 366

Blitz 377-8, 381

Blundell's School 13-16, 19, 26, 110, 281, 364, 383, 402, 407

Blunden, Edmund in *Georgian Poetry*, x;

 Matador

For exclusive discounts on Matador titles,
sign up to our occasional newsletter at
troubador.co.uk/bookshop

1. mild
217: empty
364: yellow